Conviction
of the
Innocent

Conviction of the Innocent

Lessons From Psychological Research

EDITED BY
Brian L. Cutler

AMERICAN PSYCHOLOGICAL ASSOCIATION
WASHINGTON, DC

Published by
American Psychological Association
750 First Street, NE
Washington, DC 20002
www.apa.org

To order
APA Order Department
P.O. Box 92984
Washington, DC 20090-2984
Tel: (800) 374-2721; Direct: (202) 336-5510
Fax: (202) 336-5502; TDD/TTY: (202) 336-6123
Online: www.apa.org/pubs/books
E-mail: order@apa.org

In the U.K., Europe, Africa, and the Middle East, copies may be ordered from
American Psychological Association
3 Henrietta Street
Covent Garden, London
WC2E 8LU England

Typeset in Goudy by Circle Graphics, Inc., Columbia, MD

Printer: Edwards Brothers, Inc., Ann Arbor, MI
Cover Designer: Berg Design, Albany, NY

The opinions and statements published are the responsibility of the authors, and such opinions and statements do not necessarily represent the policies of the American Psychological Association.

Library of Congress Cataloging-in-Publication Data

Conviction of the innocent: lessons from psychological research / edited by Brian L. Cutler. — 1st ed.
     p. cm.
   Includes index.
   ISBN-13: 978-1-4338-1021-3
   ISBN-10: 1-4338-1021-2
1. Criminal justice, Administration of—Psychological aspects. 2. Criminal investigation—Psychological aspects. I. Cutler, Brian L.
   HV7419.C692 2012
   364.3—dc23
                                        2011021401

British Library Cataloguing-in-Publication Data

A CIP record is available from the British Library.

Printed in the United States of America
First Edition

DOI: 10.1037/13085-000

CONTENTS

CONTRIBUTORS

Jacqueline L. Austin, BA, John Jay College of Criminal Justice, City University of New York, New York

Neil Brewer, PhD, School of Psychology, Flinders University, Adelaide, South Australia

Rebecca Bucht, PhD, John Jay College of Criminal Justice, City University of New York, New York

Donald Bucolo, PhD, Department of Psychology, University of New Hampshire, Durham

Tara M. Burke, PhD, Department of Psychology, Ryerson University, Toronto, Ontario, Canada

Kimberley A. Clow, PhD, Faculty of Social Science and Humanities, University of Ontario Institute of Technology, Oshawa, Ontario, Canada

Ellen S. Cohn, PhD, Department of Psychology, University of New Hampshire, Durham

Brian L. Cutler, PhD, Faculty of Social Science and Humanities, Justice, and Policy Studies, University of Ontario Institute of Technology, Oshawa, Ontario, Canada

Amy Bradfield Douglass, PhD, Department of Psychology, Bates College, Lewiston, ME

Itiel E. Dror, PhD, Institute of Cognitive Neuroscience, University College London, United Kingdom; and Cognitive Consultants International

Keith A. Findley, JD, University of Wisconsin Law School, Madison

Sarah M. Greathouse, PhD, Department of Psychology, Iowa State University, Ames

Lisa E. Hasel, PhD, Department of Sociology and Criminology & Law, University of Florida, Gainesville

Larry Heuer, PhD, Department of Psychology, Barnard College, Columbia University, New York, NY

Nicholaos Jones, PhD, Department of Philosophy, University of Alabama in Huntsville, Huntsville

Saul M. Kassin, PhD, Distinguished Professor, Department of Psychology, John Jay College of Criminal Justice, City University of New York, New York

Margaret Bull Kovera, PhD, John Jay College of Criminal Justice, City University of New York, New York

Amy-May Leach, PhD, Faculty of Social Science & Humanities, University of Ontario Institute of Technology, Oshawa, Ontario, Canada

Stéphanie B. Marion, MA, Department of Psychology, Ryerson University, Toronto, Ontario, Canada

Joy McClung, MA, Department of Psychology, University of Alabama in Huntsville, Huntsville

Jeffrey S. Neuschatz, PhD, Department of Psychology, University of Alabama in Huntsville, Huntsville

Robert J. Norris, MA, School of Criminal Justice, University at Albany, State University of New York, Albany

Afton Pavletic, BA, Department of Psychology, Bates College, Lewiston, Maine

Kathy Pezdek, PhD, Department of Psychology, Claremont Graduate University, Claremont, CA

Allison D. Redlich, PhD, School of Criminal Justice, University at Albany, State University of New York, Albany

Rosemary Ricciardelli, PhD, Faculty of Liberal Arts & Professional Studies, Department of Sociology, York University, Toronto, Ontario, Canada

Carolyn Semmler, PhD, School of Psychology, University of Adelaide, South Australia

Diane Sivasubramaniam, PhD, Faculty of Social Science and Humanities, University of Ontario Institute of Technology, Oshawa, Ontario, Canada

Laura Smalarz, PhD, Department of Psychology, Iowa State University, Ames

Samuel R. Sommers, PhD, Department of Psychology, Tufts University, Boston, MA

Gary L. Wells, PhD, Department of Psychology, Iowa State University, Ames

Stacy A. Wetmore, MA, Department of Psychology, University of Alabama in Huntsville, Huntsville

David M. Zimmerman, MA, John Jay College of Criminal Justice, City University of New York, New York

ACKNOWLEDGMENTS

First and foremost, I thank the authors who contributed the chapters for this volume. These authors include established scholars and the next generation of scholars. Your efforts are deeply appreciated. Several of the authors went above and beyond contributing chapters by providing encouragement, advice, and social support for this project. Thanks to Kimberley A. Clow, Margaret Bull Kovera, Amy-May Leach, Jeffrey S. Neuschatz, and Diane Sivasubramaniam for these contributions as well. I am also grateful for the encouragement and assistance of Maureen Adams, Tyler Aune, and Kerri Tolan from the American Psychological Association, who provided expert assistance with review, editing, and production, respectively. Your efforts are admired and appreciated.

Conviction
of the
Innocent

INTRODUCTION: THE PROBLEM OF CONVICTION OF THE INNOCENT

BRIAN L. CUTLER

Modern criminal justice systems in democratic countries acknowledge the detrimental consequences to societies and individuals when citizens who are actually innocent are convicted of crimes. These justice systems have procedural safeguards designed to minimize the risk of such unfortunate occurrences. The modern criminal trial is, broadly speaking, such a safeguard. Citizens are not pronounced guilty until they have been given a trial by judge or jury and have had the opportunity to confront their accusers and challenge their accusations. Although these criminal justice systems may minimize the risk of convicting innocent citizens, miscarriages of justice nevertheless occur. Police, prosecutors, and court systems continue to modify their procedures to further reduce the risk of such miscarriages, yet such miscarriages persist.

Scholarly attention to the problem of conviction of the innocent can be traced back to, at least, the work of law professor Edwin Borchard (1932), who assembled a set of 65 cases of miscarriages of justice and described each in detail. As noted by Leo (2005), about every 20 years since Borchard (1932), another such collection of cases of miscarriages of justice has been brought to our attention through the publication of books and articles. I have more to say about the scholarly literature later.

The investigation of cases of conviction of the innocent experienced a breakthrough with the work of the Innocence Project. Attorneys Barry Scheck and Peter Neufeld founded the Innocence Project at the Benjamin N. Cardozo Law School at Yeshiva University in 1992. The mission of the Innocence Project is to use groundbreaking DNA technology to exonerate actually innocent citizens who have been wrongly convicted of crimes and sentenced to prison terms. To date, the work of the Innocence Project has led to the exoneration of more than 250 innocent-but-convicted citizens, many of whom spent significant portions of their lives behind bars. The Innocence Project is now an independent not-for-profit organization closely affiliated with Cardozo Law School. Their efforts led to the development of affiliated innocence projects in most U.S. states. Innocence projects are typically staffed by some combination of law professors; law students; and practicing attorneys, investigators, and other professionals who have relevant motivations and skills. Similar organizations exist in Canada, the United Kingdom, Australia, and New Zealand.

The work of the Innocence Project extends well beyond the exoneration of wrongfully convicted citizens. Innocence Project staff analyze their cases for underlying causes and contributing factors to wrongful conviction, publish their findings in reports and articles, and act as vigorous advocates for justice reform aimed toward minimizing the risk of miscarriages of justice.

BRIEF HISTORY OF SCHOLARSHIP
ON MISCARRIAGES OF JUSTICE

As noted above, scholarship on miscarriages of justice has been around since the work of Borchard (1932). In his excellent review of this scholarship, Richard Leo (2005) divided the scholarly landscape into three categories of scholarship: big-picture books, the true-crime genre, and specialized literatures. The work of Borchard (1932), Brandon and Davies (1973), and Frank and Frank (1957) are examples of big-picture books, which Leo (2005) characterized as follows:

> First, they announced that the United States legal system had an ideology that it was better that some number (typically 100, sometimes as low as 10 or as high as 1,000) of guilty men went free than for one innocent one to be wrongfully convicted; then they pointed out the myriad procedural and legal protections seemingly designed to ensure this result; and then they argued that the wrongful conviction of the innocent problem had occurred regularly and was largely unnoticed, despite our vaunted democratic ideals. These works then discussed a number of wrong-man cases (often a parade of "horribles"), the seeming causes of wrongful conviction

(from eyewitness misidentification to police and prosecutorial misconduct to ineffective assistance of counsel), and the reforms that should be implemented to lessen or eliminate the problem of wrongful conviction in American society. Although they followed a similar plot line, these diagnostic and reform-minded books were motivated by moral outrage about one of the most fundamentally important, yet one of the most scholarly and publicly neglected, aspects of American criminal justice. (p. 203)

Leo further characterized the extant literature on miscarriages of justice as adopting a familiar plot:

The familiar plot of wrongful conviction scholarship usually begins with a harrowing, if unlikely, story of an innocent man (and it almost always is a man) who was unjustly accused and arrested for a heinous, high-profile crime he almost certainly did not commit. The arrested innocent was then prosecuted by a hard-charging district attorney and eventually convicted by jury trial, only later to be exonerated—typically as a result of the sustained, at times heroic, efforts of someone or some group outside the criminal justice system—and eventually released from prison, sometimes even from death row. The exoneration and release often occurred only after many years of incarceration and unjust suffering. The causes of wrongful arrest, prosecution, conviction, and incarceration appear to be well known: mistaken eyewitness identification (either as a result of memory errors and police suggestion and overreaching); false confession (almost always brought on by police suggestion, if not psychological coercion); the perjured and concocted testimony of jailhouse snitches (typically motivated by the institutional rewards the system holds out for them when they offer false testimony that supports the state's theory); police and prosecutorial misconduct (often in the form of the withholding of exculpatory information and the knowledgeable or willful mischaracterization of case facts at pretrial proceedings and at trial); forensic and scientific fraud (seemingly brought on by a law enforcement bias, not an intentional desire to frame innocent suspects, once a suspect is presumed guilty and a case is being built to support that bias); ineffective assistance of counsel; and so the list goes. Once the causes have been identified, a number of familiar policy solutions are advocated, ranging from restricting the use of particular types of evidence (e.g., snitch testimony) to improving methods of collecting and analyzing particular types of evidence (e.g., videotaping interrogations) to altogether abolishing certain practices disfavored by the author (e.g., the death penalty). (p. 207)

Although this literature is important and interesting, Leo (2005) criticized the big-picture, familiar theme approach as an "intellectual dead end" because the big-picture sources are repetitive and have not advanced our understanding of the phenomena of miscarriages of justice beyond the points raised in the earliest publications in the genre of scholarship.

The true-crime genre refers to books that present detailed accounts of individual cases of extreme miscarriages of justice. These books, Leo (2005) noted, are typically written by journalists (e.g., Olsen, 2000; Taylor, 2002) and tend to reach broad audiences, document historically important cases, and bring sorely needed attention to the problem of miscarriages of justice. Nevertheless, these books are of limited scholarly value. According to Leo, they do not contribute to theory or even offer penetrating explanations for the miscarriages of justice and rarely play a role in the scholarly literature.

Third, Leo (2005) described the development of a more specialized literature on miscarriages of justice. Here Leo referred to the research conducted by cognitive and social psychologists on factors that have been identified as causes of miscarriages of justice, for example, mistaken eyewitness identification and false confessions. The current volume fits squarely into Leo's category of the development of more specialized literature—specifically—psychological research on the causes and consequences of conviction of the innocent. Leo described research on mistaken eyewitness identification, suggestibility of child witnesses, and false confessions as successful programs of research and the work of some criminologists whose theoretical work shows promise for the development of theories of miscarriages of justice. Leo ultimately concluded that the scholarly understanding of miscarriages of justice is nascent and in need of more theory and high-quality research.

GROUNDWORK OF THIS VOLUME

I took a keen interest in psychology and law, in general, and eyewitness memory, in particular, while I was a master's student (State University of New York, College at Geneseo) around 1983.[1] I began conducting research on eyewitness memory with cognitive psychologist Ken Kallio. I continued to conduct research on eyewitness memory as a doctoral student under the mentorship of Steve Penrod and continue to conduct eyewitness research with colleagues and students to this day.

Psychology and law research on topics associated with conviction of the innocent—mistaken eyewitness identification, false confession, racial discrimination, and others—has largely developed as independent research programs. Leo's (2005) article was the first that I had encountered that drew some of these research areas under a larger umbrella of miscarriages of justice. His article stimulated me to think about the commonalities and parallels between

---

[1]Shortly after I graduated from this program with a master's degree in experimental psychology, the college closed the program. I like to think that I was not the cause of the program's closing, but I cannot be sure of this.

research on the seemingly independent topics of mistaken identification, false confession, and other causes. Are there common social and cognitive psychological phenomena that underlie these seemingly independent causes of wrongful conviction? How similar are the research methods used to study the independent causes? Are there parallels in the reforms that emerge from this research? Do some of the same factors that cause conviction of the innocent contribute to the stigmatization and mistreatment of exonerated citizens?

My first attempt to explore these questions was to assemble a symposium on this topic at the 2009 American Psychology-Law Society Conference. Discussions with colleagues at and after the meeting led to a proposal for this book.

GOALS FOR THIS VOLUME

I had several goals for this volume, as I summarize in this section. I am confident that thanks to the high-quality work of my chapter authors these goals have been met, and I hope readers will agree.

Advance the Literature on Conviction of the Innocent

I hope to advance the literature on conviction of the innocent by providing contemporary reviews of the relevant psychological research and to provide direction for future research on this compelling social problem. By advancing the literature, we will be better positioned to recommend and implement effective policy and procedural changes for reducing the risk of conviction of the innocent. Such work is already well underway, as explained in the chapters in this volume.

Integrate the Research

I strive toward an integration of the psychological research on conviction of the innocent. The research on the various causes of conviction of the innocent has developed largely in isolation. In other words, eyewitness researchers focus on eyewitness memory exclusively, false confession researchers focus on false confession research exclusively, and so on. By drawing together research on these various topics, I hope to facilitate integrative research that will eventually lead to more comprehensive theories of the causes and consequences of conviction of the innocent. Toward this end, I asked authors to adopt a common structure for all but one of the chapters. The structure consists of the following sections: (a) relevance of the subtopic (e.g., at-risk defendants, false confession, alibi witnesses) to conviction of the innocent, (b) scientific psychological foundations underlying the subtopic, (c) scientific methods used in research on the subtopic, (d) relevant research, (e) application of the research, and (f) conclusions. The authors kindly granted this request, although there is some variation in the ordering of sections and much variation in the size of the sections owing to nature of the individual research literatures. The use of this structure should facilitate comparison of underlying theory, methods, and applications across research topics, contribute to a more comprehensive understanding of the interconnected causes, and motivate research on these interconnections.

Chapter 8 differs in both content and organization from the others. Whereas the other 14 chapters cover broad causes or consequences, Chapter 8 narrowly focuses on a single cause: the ineffectiveness of the motion-to-suppress safeguard designed to protect defendants from wrongful conviction, following mistaken identification. In essence, Chapter 8 is a model for how to integrate research (such as that summarized in Chapters 5, 6, 7, and 9) to address a pressing legal issue pertaining to conviction of the innocent. The predetermined chapter structure was less effective for this chapter than for the others, so I relaxed the structure for Chapter 8.

Encourage Research

Psychology and law, in general, and conviction of the innocent, in particular, provide fertile grounds for psychological research and the foundation of a productive and satisfying research career. In the same way that earlier research collections (e.g., Kerr & Bray, 1982) greatly inspired me and guided my research interests and career directions, I hope that this volume will draw new and established scholars alike to this stimulating and rewarding area of research.

PRIMARY AUDIENCES FOR THIS BOOK

This volume is geared toward several audiences. Beginning and seasoned researchers with interests in conviction of the innocent or interests in any of the specific causes and consequences of conviction of the innocent should find these chapters to be up-to-date summaries of the literature, scientific methods, practical implications of the findings, and further research ideas. Practitioners (lawyers, judges, Innocence Project staff, expert witnesses) and policy makers should find in these chapters useful summaries of the recommendations for reform and the underlying scientific research that establishes the need for such reforms.

OVERVIEW OF THIS VOLUME

This volume is composed of 15 chapters and divided into seven parts associated with the various roles that laypeople and professionals occupy (e.g., investigators, witnesses) in the process of convicting the innocent. The size of the sections denotes, in part, the relative attention given to the various roles in the psychological research. Part I focuses on the suspect and contains only one chapter concerning risk factors associated with conviction of the innocent. Part II focuses on the investigators and presents chapters that concern investigators' abilities to detect deception among suspects, their methods of interrogation and how these methods can lead to false confessions, and their perceptions of the fairness of these interrogation methods that presumably contribute to their use. Part III examines various facets of eyewitness identification. This is the largest section of the book, reflecting the relatively large amount of psychological research devoted to this topic. This section includes chapters that examine the fallibility of eyewitness memory, the contribution of suggestive identification procedures to false identifications, the confidence of the eyewitness, and how jurors are influenced by eyewitness testimony. Part IV examines other, less well-understood trial witnesses: informants who often provide secondhand confessions, the influence (or lack thereof) of alibis for the defendant, and the forensic science expert. Part V examines the pervasive issues of tunnel vision and racism, phenomena that contribute to conviction of the innocent at virtually all stages of the investigation and adjudication. Part VI contains a single chapter on the consequences of conviction of the innocent with particular reference to stigmatization, again reflecting the dearth of psychological knowledge on this topic.

Collectively, this volume draws on the various traditional subdisciplines of psychology, including cognitive, developmental, social, clinical, and biological, although the social and cognitive psychological are the predominant approaches. The research described in the chapter draws heavily on experimentation but includes other methods as well (quasi-experimental methods, surveys, and field studies).

REFERENCES

Borchard, E. (1932). *Convicting the innocent: Sixty five actual errors of criminal justice*. New York, NY: Garden City.

Brandon, R., & Davies, C. (1973). *Wrongful imprisonment: Mistaken convictions and their consequences*. London, England: Archon Books.

Bright, S. B. (1999). Neither equal nor just: The rationing and denial of legal services to the poor when life and liberty are at stake. *Annual Survey of American Law, 1997,* 783–836.

Findley, K. A., & Scott, M. S. (2006). The multiple dimensions of tunnel vision in criminal cases. *Wisconsin Law Review, 2006,* 291–397.

Frank, J., & Frank, B. (1957). *Not guilty.* New York, NY: Da Capo.

Innocent Project. (2010). *250 Exonerated: Too many wrongfully convicted.* New York, NY: Benjamin N. Cardozo School of Law, Yeshiva University.

Kerr, N., & Bray, R. (1982). *The psychology of the courtroom.* New York, NY: Academic Press.

Leo, R. A. (2005). Rethinking the study of miscarriages of justice: Developing a criminology of wrongful conviction. *Journal of Contemporary Criminal Justice, 21,* 201–223. doi:10.1177/1043986205277477.

Olsen, J. (2000). *Last man standing: The tragedy and triumph of Geronimo Pratt.* New York, NY: Doubleday.

Taylor, J. (2002). *The count and the confession.* New York, NY: Random House.

I

THE SUSPECTS

1

AT-RISK POPULATIONS UNDER INVESTIGATION AND AT TRIAL

ROBERT J. NORRIS AND ALLISON D. REDLICH

It has been well established that persons with vulnerabilities come into frequent contact with the criminal justice system as suspects of crimes. It has also been well established that persons with vulnerabilities are overrepresented among proven wrongful conviction cases (see Innocence Project Report, 2007). Vulnerability can come in many shapes and sizes, but typically the immaturity of youth and cognitive impairments (both mental illness and intellectual disabilities) are cited and researched as dispositional factors that can impede due process, lead to the wrongful conviction of the innocent, or both. Every year, law enforcement arrests approximately 2.2 million juveniles, approximately 1 million adults with serious mental illness, and approximately 700,000 plus adults with developmental disabilities (FBI, 2008; National GAINS Center, 2006; U.S. Office of Juvenile Justice and Delinquency Prevention, 2007). Given the large volume and high frequency of criminal justice contact with vulnerable suspects, do contemporary investigation and adjudicative procedures sufficiently account for these vulnerabilities? More important, do contemporary investigation and adjudicative procedures recognize that persons with vulnerabilities have an increased risk of falsely implicating themselves? In addition, if recognition is present, are practices altered accordingly?

In this chapter, we discuss how three vulnerability factors—youthful status, mental illness, and developmental disability—contribute to the conviction of the innocent. We focus on interrogation-induced false confessions and the adjudicative competence of these groups. Although there are numerous contributing factors to wrongful convictions, to our knowledge the majority of research relevant to at-risk populations and wrongful convictions has stemmed from the study of false confessions. However, research that investigates at-risk populations and the propensity for eyewitness misidentification,[1] ineffective assistance of counsel, governmental misconduct, and so forth, is notably missing from the burgeoning literature on wrongful convictions.

RELEVANCE OF VULNERABILITIES TO CONVICTION OF THE INNOCENT

To date, the Innocence Project has exonerated more than 250 wrongfully convicted individuals through DNA exoneration. After the 200th person was exonerated, the Innocence Project (2007) issued a report that highlighted characteristics of the individuals (e.g., race) and their cases (e.g., crimes, number of years imprisoned). Of the approximately 50 cases of false confessions or admissions, 35% were juveniles, had mental impairments, or both. Other analyses that involve DNA and non-DNA exoneration cases have painted a similar picture of the risk of juveniles and persons with mental impairment falsely confessing (Drizin & Leo, 2004; Gross, Jacoby, Matheson, Montgomery, & Patil, 2005). Although there are dozens of case examples of juveniles and persons with mental impairment we could use to illustrate this risk, we describe the case of Eddie Joe Lloyd, who was exonerated and released from prison after serving 17 years for a rape–murder he did not commit.

In 1984, Eddie Joe Lloyd, a Detroit, Michigan, man diagnosed with bipolar disorder, was committed to a state psychiatric facility. Earlier that year and the year before, Detroit had experienced a spate of sexual assaults on young girls, the most heinous of which was the rape and murder of 16-year-old Michelle Jackson. Lloyd was fascinated by Michelle's case, and while in the hospital he contacted the investigating police officer. Lloyd was interrogated four times in the hospital and eventually confessed to Michelle's murder and rape. Reportedly, he was duped into believing that his confession would help "smoke out" the true perpetrator. His confession was recorded (though the interrogations were not) and was rich with details, including motives for the killing and for the confession. Lloyd was not Michelle's killer, but his

---

[1]Two exceptions are the small literatures on the own-age effect in facial recognition (see Perfect & Moon, 2005) and eyewitness identification and intellectual disability (Ternes & Yuille, 2008).

confession was sufficient to convince the prosecutor, the judge, jury, and even his own lawyer of his guilt.

In large part because of his actual innocence, Lloyd refused to allow an affirmative defense and plead not guilty by reason of insanity. The jury deliberated for 30 min, convicting Lloyd of first-degree felony murder. He spent 17 years incarcerated for this crime before DNA analyses definitively excluded him as the perpetrator. As a result of this case, Michigan now requires that interrogations be videotaped in their entirety. Lloyd was awarded $4 million in a civil suit, though he passed away only 2 years after his release. Today, his case highlights the need for appropriate interrogation techniques for suspects with mental illness (Redlich, 2004).

Eddie Joe Lloyd's case and numerous others also highlight how confession evidence—regardless of its veracity—can be quite damning in the courtroom. Jurors are known to value direct evidence (Heller, 2006), most particularly confession evidence (Kassin & Neumann, 1997). Mock-jury studies have demonstrated how confessions, even those recognized as coerced and inadmissible, spike conviction rates (Kassin & Wrightsman, 1980). Confessions can also effectively leverage guilty pleas, even when they are false (Redlich, 2010). Unrecognized false confessions almost assuredly lead to false convictions, particularly when competence deficits present in vulnerable defendants are considered.

The link between competence and wrongful convictions is sorely in need of investigation. To our knowledge, a relationship between the two constructs has yet to be empirically established. However, an underlying reason behind competence as a constitutional safeguard is to prevent miscarriages of justice, including the conviction of innocents. Moreover, when innocent suspects are wrongly targeted, having a rational as well as factual understanding and appreciation of the situations becomes all the more important. Recently, Ken Murray, Chairman of the National Association of Criminal Defense Lawyers, was quoted as saying that "competency claims are gaining acceptance among judges, prosecutors, and defense lawyers in part because of the growing efforts to identify the wrongfully convicted. Some of these people who made false confessions had competence problems to start with" (Johnson & Seaman, 2008).

SCIENTIFIC PSYCHOLOGICAL FOUNDATIONS OF THE VULNERABILITY–WRONGFUL CONVICTION RELATION

The participation of juveniles and persons with mental illness and developmental disabilities in the criminal justice system has been of great interest to psycholegal researchers. There is a large psychological base from

Juveniles' immaturity, including limitations in their cognitive abilities and psychosocial skills, leads to impulsiveness in their ability to make decisions and an inability to consider long-term repercussions. This impulsivity affects juveniles' ability to fully comprehend the situation before them, which may lead to decisions not in their best interests (Owen-Kostelnik, Reppucci, & Meyer, 2006). Additionally, children and adolescents can be emotionally volatile and susceptible to outside pressures or influences. Juveniles are more likely than adults to display restless energy and boredom, which can have severe consequences in the isolation of the interrogation room and in the court-room. For example, juveniles' increased suggestibility and diminished ability to maintain focus can impede their abilities to truly assist their attorneys in preparing a defense (Grisso et al., 2003).

Similarly, individuals with mental illness can have varied symptoms that influence their abilities to fully understand their rights in the interrogation room and at the adjudication phase (see Appelbaum & Appelbaum, 1994; Rogers, Harrison, Hazelwood, & Sewell, 2007). Depending on the mental illness, possible symptoms can include rash and impulsive behavior, delusional and disorganized thought patterns, and feelings of hopelessness and despair. These characteristics are important to consider in the context of interrogations and courtrooms. Additionally, defendants with mental illness may be more suggestible and less assertive (Redlich, 2004).

Persons with developmental disabilities are also disadvantaged as criminal defendants, often displaying impaired communication and social skills, as well as a lack of self-direction. As with other vulnerable defendants, those with developmental disabilities show a diminished ability to understand and appreciate their rights as suspects and defendants, including *Miranda*. They are also more likely to adapt to societal norms. This is strongly related to the psychological nature of interrogations, as the increased suggestibility of this group leads some to falsely confess. Individuals with developmental disabilities often look to figures of authority to solve problems and show a desire to please these figures (Perske, 2004). They may actively seek out friends, a characteristic that is typically exploited by the interrogating officer. Other traits of defendants with developmental disabilities, such as a lack of control over impulses, gaps in memory, and a willingness to accept blame, may also increase the likelihood of false admissions (Kassin et al., 2010). In addition, because of difficulties in recalling facts and maintaining focus and attention, the ability of the defense attorney to build an adequate case can be obstructed. These defendants may also have difficulty understanding legal decisions to be made and be unable to carefully weigh available options. At trial, a defendant with developmental disabilities may have difficulty under-standing not only his role but also the roles of other legal actors as well (Appelbaum & Appelbaum, 1994).

In summary, basic science on adolescent development, psychopathology, and intellectual disabilities supports the conclusion that vulnerable individuals (as defined here) are at increased risk of false confessions in the interrogation room, increased risk of having deficits in legal understanding, and thus at increased risk of wrongful conviction. On the basis of basic science, psycholegal researchers have theorized and subsequently tested different reasons for and consequences of these increased risks.

RESEARCH METHODS USED IN THE STUDY OF THE VULNERABILITY–WRONGFUL CONVICTION RELATION

The methods used to study relations between vulnerable populations and wrongful convictions have varied from the laboratory to the field, from the use of deception to self-report interviews and from suspect to interrogator to juror. In this section, we describe methods used to study interrogations and competence.

Methods Used to Study Police Interrogation

Police interrogations and confessions, particularly false confessions from vulnerable populations, have been difficult to study for several reasons. First, police interrogations are notoriously secret endeavors, and typically researchers have been allowed only minimal access. With increased efforts to make electronic recordings of interrogation institutional policy (along with increased awareness that false confessions do indeed occur; Sullivan, 2010), researchers have begun to access videotaped interrogations, though these studies are still in their early stages (i.e., not published). Second, because of ethical concerns, laboratory studies in which juveniles or persons with mental impairments are accused truly or falsely of committing mock crimes, are lacking. Third, although there is no one perfect methodology, research on interrogation and confessions can suffer from external validity (in that actual crimes cannot ethically be studied in the lab) and internal validity problems (in that the veracity of observed or self-reported confessions cannot easily be determined).

Nevertheless, numerous studies have been conducted on the actual and perceived capabilities of vulnerable populations and police interrogation. In part, the methodologies can be grouped by the actor under study, which have included the suspects themselves, police interrogators, and triers of fact. For youthful suspects, those with mental impairments, or both, although sparse there have been lab-based studies (e.g., Billings et al., 2007; Redlich & Goodman, 2003). In these studies, the vulnerable suspects have either witnessed or took part in a mock crime, or they were asked to imagine themselves as defendants in hypothetical scenarios (Grisso et al., 2003). In addition, several studies relevant to Miranda comprehension have been conducted. These studies include the testing of vulnerable individuals' knowledge and appreciation (those charged with crimes and those not; see Everington & Fulero, 1999; Redlich, Silverman, & Steiner, 2003), as well as analyses aimed at the comprehensibility and comprehensiveness of warnings used in practice (Rogers, Harrison, Hazelwood, & Sewell, 2007).

Police interrogators have been surveyed regarding their perceptions of standard police tactics used with vulnerable suspects. For example, Meyer and Reppucci (2007) surveyed police officers about their perceptions of young suspects, their knowledge of child development, and the type of interrogation techniques used with minors. For triers of fact, most often mock jurors, researchers have presented case scenarios to respondents asking for their perceptions of the interrogation, the suspect–defendant, the coerciveness of the interrogation, guilt, and so forth. Within the scenarios, dispositional (e.g., age, disability status) and situational factors (e.g., use of interrogator threats) have been manipulated (e.g., Najdowski, Bottoms, & Vargas, 2009).

Methods Used to Study Adjudicative Competence

In examining the actual capabilities of defendants, researchers typically have used standardized instruments, examined clinical judgments, or both. Standardized instruments to measure competence to stand trial include, for example, the MacArthur Competence Assessment Tool for Criminal Adjudication (MacCAT-CA) and the Fitness Interview Test—Revised (FIT–R; Roesch, Zapf, & Eaves, 2006). In these studies, persons with and without vulnerability factors are interviewed by using the normed measure (e.g., Hoge, Poythress, Bonnie, Monahan, Eisenberg, & Feucht-Haviar, 1997). In studies that involve clinical judgments, closed cases in which defendants' competence was raised and assessed may be aggregated and analyzed (e.g., V. G. Cooper & Zapf, 2003).

In examining the perceived capabilities of defendants, again most often researchers use mock jury paradigms. More specifically, case scenarios (written, videotaped, or even live) are presented to individuals and perceptions captured. The case scenario may vary on characteristics of the defendants (e.g., whether the accused is a juvenile or an adult), the crime (sexual abuse vs. murder), or the presence of certain evidence (confession or no confession). Perceptions that may be measured include intelligence, suggestibility, legal knowledge, and other aspects relevant to competence (e.g., Ghetti & Redlich, 2001).

RELEVANT RESEARCH ON THE VULNERABILITY–WRONGFUL CONVICTION RELATION

The knowledge base on the risk of juveniles and persons with impairments falsely confessing and not being considered competent continues to grow. In this section, we describe research findings for our three populations of interest, separated by interrogation and competence research, and separated by studies of actual and perceived capabilities.

Vulnerable Populations and Police Interrogation: Actual and Perceived Capabilities

A variety of methods have been used to study the actual capabilities of suspects being interrogated. Though few in number, several laboratory-based studies support the notion that vulnerable suspects are at a disadvantage in the interrogation room. Redlich and Goodman (2003), using the ALT key experiment (Kassin & Kiechel, 1996), demonstrated that younger and more suggestible participants were more likely to sign a statement that claims responsibility for a mock crime not committed. Clare and Gudjonsson (1995) examined the understanding of a hypothetical interrogation situation and of the decision-making process among individuals with intellectual disabilities. Forty-one participants (21 who suffered from a mental handicap and 20 with average intellectual abilities) were shown a video of a staged interrogation. The case involved a suspect who had committed a burglary but was wrongfully suspected of murdering the homeowner, but who nevertheless confessed to both crimes. Though almost all participants understood that the suspect had not killed the man but had committed the burglary, subjects with intellectual disabilities were more likely to believe the suspect would not be sent to prison and believe that he would be allowed to go home between the interrogation and trial. These participants were also more likely to believe that the court would acquit the suspect of the murder, even with the false confession evidence. Of importance, only about half of the disadvantaged group believed that legal advice was necessary at the beginning of a police interview, even if no crime had been committed.

Researchers have also examined knowledge of police practices and Miranda rights (e.g., Grisso, 1981). Generally, the research shows that all three vulnerable populations have deficient understanding. Woolard, Clearly, Harvell, and Chen (2008) tested Miranda knowledge as well as knowledge of police practices and parental protection among juveniles in three different age groups (11–13, 14–15, and 16–17) and their parents–guardians. Consistent with past research, Woolard et al. (2008) found that understanding of Miranda warnings increased with age (e.g., Grisso, 1981; Redlich et al., 2003). However, both juveniles and their parents were lacking in their knowledge about police interrogation procedures. For instance, about half of the participants believed that the police must tell the truth during an interrogation, and over half of them believed that investigators must wait for the parents before questioning a juvenile.

Others have focused on Miranda understanding and reasoning among defendants with mental illness. Rogers, Harrison, Hazelwood, and Sewell (2007) studied 107 individuals to examine their understanding of their rights as well as their reasoning for exercising or not exercising those rights. Using standardized measures for different aspects of intelligence and Miranda comprehension, Rogers, Harrison, Hazelwood, and Sewell (2007) found that Miranda warnings administered at or above a sixth-grade level were only well understood by approximately 10% of defendants with mental illness. It should also be noted that in earlier research, Rogers, Harrison, Shuman, Sewell, and Hazelwood (2007) found that most warnings are written at grade levels higher than sixth. Studies of individuals with developmental disabilities paint similar pictures. Everington and Fulero (1999), for example, compared probationers with and without developmental disabilities on their comprehension of Miranda rights and suggestibility. They found that those who did suffer scored significantly lower on standardized measures of Miranda understanding, with about two thirds receiving a score of zero on at least one of the four comprehension statements.

In a legal sense, the perceived capabilities of suspects and defendants can be almost as important as the actual capabilities. For example, if police do not perceive a juvenile suspect to be vulnerable to suggestion or deception, they would be unlikely to alter interrogation techniques. Similarly, if jurors and judges do not view persons with cognitive impairment as vulnerable to false confession, they will be unlikely to discount confession evidence.

Researchers have begun to inquire about the perceptions police hold of juvenile suspects under interrogation. (To our knowledge, police surveys relating to offenders with mental illness and developmental disability have not been undertaken. However, there is evidence indicating that John Reid and Associates[2] acknowledged that these offenders, as well as juveniles, are at risk of false confessions; see http://www.reid.com.) For instance, Meyer and Reppucci (2007) surveyed 332 Baltimore law enforcement officials about police interrogation practices and their knowledge about developmental issues in youth and adults. In general, although officers displayed knowledge of developmental differences and understanding that juveniles' behavior may

---

[2]The Reid technique is the best-known set of criminal interview and interrogation techniques. The technique comprises nine steps, which arose "as a result of many years of experience" (Inbau et al., 2001, p. 212) and are based on the principles discussed above (see Kassin et al., 2010; Chapter 3, this volume).

differ from than that of adults (making less eye contact, slouching), they reported using the same techniques to analyze suspects' behaviors. In addition, police agreed that juveniles were more immature in judgment and more malleable than adults in general, but they remained neutral when asked about juvenile suspects' suggestibility in the interrogation room. Using the same measure of police interrogation practices, Kostelnik and Reppucci (2009) compared Reid-trained and non-Reid-trained officers' perceptions of and practices with adolescent suspects, finding that Reid-trained officers were less sensitive to the developmental maturity of adolescents (less likely to believe that adolescents are suggestible and more likely to believe that they comprehend their rights and the purpose of an interrogation). Additionally, Reid-trained officers were more likely to endorse the use of false evidence and deceit with adolescents and adults and minimization tactics in interrogations with adults, adolescents, and children.

Jurors' perceptions of vulnerable suspects in criminal cases are also vital, as they are commonly required to assess the reliability and voluntariness of confession evidence. Several studies have attempted to examine jurors' perceptions of young suspects. Redlich, Ghetti, and Quas (2008) compared perceptions of juvenile suspects with those of juvenile victims. With suspects, they found that age influenced perceptions of credibility. It is interesting to note that inconsistencies (admitting guilt and then recanting) did not influence the perceived credibility of child suspects, but they did greatly increase belief in the child suspect's guilt. Recently, Najdowski, Bottoms, and Vargas (2009) simultaneously examined two risk factors: mock jurors' perceptions of confessions from juveniles with and without intellectual disabilities. Among developmentally challenged juveniles, jurors completely discounted coerced confessions and were more likely to discount voluntary confessions in comparison to voluntary confessions provided by nonchallenged juveniles. Additionally, when the defendant was intellectually disadvantaged, jurors perceived the police as less fair and more coercive than when the juvenile was not. However, dichotomous guilt judgments were not directly affected by disability or confession status, though they did affect more sensitive degree-of-guilt judgments (on a 20-point scale).

To summarize, across a variety of methodologies, interrogation and confession research on the actual and perceived capabilities of juveniles and persons with cognitive impairments has supported the trends identified by wrongful conviction cases. That is, compared with their counterparts, these three populations are at increased risk of not understanding and appreciating their rights and of false confessions. Confession evidence, even when false (albeit unrecognized as such), dramatically increases the risk of prosecution and conviction (Drizin & Leo, 2004). As such, the suspect's adjudicative competence becomes a particularly pertinent consideration.

Vulnerable Populations and Adjudicative Competence: Actual and Perceived Capabilities

Adjudicative competence has been the focus of much research. A consistent picture has emerged for all three types of vulnerable person studied here. Juveniles and persons with mental health problems, intellectual impairments, or both, demonstrate deficits in adjudicative competence (e.g., Ericson & Perlman, 2001; Hoge et al., 1997). For example, Grisso et al. (2003) determined that juveniles (regardless of involvement in the justice system) age 15 and younger were more likely than older youth and young adults to have impaired abilities relating to legal competence. In fact, one third of the 11- to 13-year-olds and one fifth of the 14- to 15-year-olds were as equally impaired as adults with serious mental illness. In attempting to determine the reasons underlying competence deficits, Nestor, Daggett, Haycock, and Price (1999) compared neuropsychological tests results of male offenders deemed competent and incompetent. They found that defendants considered incompetent scored significantly worse than those considered competent on measures of intelligence, memory, attention, and concentration.

An important aspect of legal competence is the ability to assist one's attorney in preparing a defense. Schmidt, Reppucci, and Woolard (2003) compared the responses of adult and juvenile detainees' responses to a hypothetical attorney–client vignette, as well as their self-reported decision making. The results indicated that juveniles were more likely than adults to suggest not talking to their attorney and recommend denying involvement in the crime and less likely to recommend honest communication with one's attorney. They also found that, in their decision making, juveniles were more likely to mention consequences that involve immediate gains, such as ending the questioning or returning home. These response patterns diminished with age. Interestingly, standardized measures of adjudicative competence did not significantly predict participants' recommendations in regard to communication with an attorney or their self-reported decision making. Other studies have found that younger defendants fail to account for factors such as the strength of the evidence against them in making their plea decisions (Viljoen, Klaver, & Roesch, 2005).

Another important aspect of competence is the issue of whether defendants can be restored to competence through training. For persons with cognitive disabilities, Pinals (2005) noted that many individuals may never have been competent to start with and thus competence "attainment," rather than competence "restoration" is more apt. To wit, Anderson and Hewitt (2002) examined the effect of competency-restoration training on 75 defendants with intellectual disabilities and found that most (two thirds) defendants did not significantly improve. Efforts that focus on educational-restoration training for youths have shown similar results. For example, D. K. Cooper (1997), in examining the effect of training on juvenile offenders' competence to stand trial, discovered that before training, only two out of 112 children ages 13 to 16 years were considered competent; after training (i.e., an educational competency training videotape), only 12 juveniles reached a score that indicated competence. Overall, research suggests that persons known to be at risk of competence-related deficits are unlikely to understand and play a meaningful role in their defense, even with substantial training.

Jurors' perceptions of whether defendants are competent have no legal standing. But like perceptions of interrogation capabilities, perceived legal understanding and related aspects may influence culpability and guilt decisions. Among the three populations addressed here, the majority of research has been done on juveniles. Competence-related perceptions of defendants with mental illness and intellectual disabilities have not been studied at length, to our knowledge.

In studying the perceived competence of juveniles, researchers often hypothesize that perceived competence and legal understanding would increase with defendant age (as indicated by the literature on actual capabilities). However, these hypotheses have not always been supported. Rather, age of the defendant often interacts with other factors to influence perceptions. For example, Ghetti and Redlich (2001) surveyed mock jurors about the perceived legal competence of juveniles under varying conditions, which included the defendant's age (11, 14, or 17), whether the victim died or was injured, and whether the crime was arson or a shooting. They found an interesting, albeit somewhat complex, interaction: When the juvenile was 11 years old and the victim died by shooting, participants viewed the 11-year-old's competence as equal to that of a 17-year-old who had shot and injured, but not killed, the victim. Redlich, Quas, and Ghetti (2008) also found a significant interaction between defendant age and juror gender in regard to perceptions of legal competence. When faced with a 14-year-old defendant, men perceived the defendant to have significantly more legal understanding than did women. This interaction between men and women's perceptions did not emerge for 11-year-old defendants. Although more research is needed, these findings suggest that situational factors in addition to dispositional factors can influence perceived competence, which may in turn influence verdict decisions.

In summary, juveniles and individuals with cognitive impairments are at increased risk under investigation, in the interrogation room, and at trial. Research has shown that these suspects are less likely to comprehend and invoke their legal rights and more likely to make false incriminating statements. Given the tremendous strength of confession evidence in securing convictions, vulnerable defendants' adjudicative competency becomes even more vital. Unfortunately, studies indicate that many defendants in this category may be left unprotected at trial, as they are less likely to understand the proceedings and less capable of assisting in their attorneys in preparing a defense. Together, the vulnerabilities of certain defendants during investigation and trial increase the risk of becoming victims of serious miscarriages of justice.

APPLICATION OF RESEARCH ON THE VULNERABILITY–WRONGFUL CONVICTION RELATION

In the earlier sections, we provided scientific and anecdotal evidence that demonstrate that youth and persons with cognitive impairments are at risk of wrongful convictions, as well as evidence for the possible reasons that underlie this increased risk. As stated in the white paper on interrogations,

> There is a strong consensus among psychologists, legal scholars, and practitioners that juveniles and individuals with cognitive impairments or psychological disorders are particularly susceptible to false confession under pressure. Yet little action has been taken to modulate the methods by which these vulnerable groups are questioned when placed into custody as crime suspects. (Kassin et al., 2010, p. 30)

This statement is most certainly true in the United States, in which there are no extraordinary protections in place for vulnerable suspects. In contrast, in other countries, most notably, Great Britain, vulnerable suspects are afforded special rights, including the presence of an appropriate adult during interrogation and special cautions to jurors under certain circumstances (Gudjonsson, 2003). The rights against self-incrimination and to the presence of an informed advocate (an attorney) are not rights equally available to all if these rights are not understood, appreciated, or invoked by all.

In addition, an important policy and legal issue has arisen in regard to competence, one that has implications for wrongful convictions. Specifically, competence assessments and subsequent restorations, when necessary, often do not proceed in a timely manner (Miller, 2003). Individuals suspected of being incompetent can languish in jail until an evaluation can be conducted, many times longer than if they had simply pled out on time served (Pinals, 2005). Determining what is in the best interest of their clients—for instance, deciding whether to raise competence issues or to allow a person who is likely to be incompetent to take a plea and get out of jail—is rarely easy for defense attorneys, particularly when innocent defendants are involved. Some innocent defendants will plead guilty to get out of jail rather than risk a much harsher sentence at trial (Gross et al., 2005; Redlich, 2010). Thus, persons who are innocent and incompetent are arguably at the greatest risk of miscarriages of justice.

The potential for the application of research to affect policy is high. The need to protect vulnerable suspects in the interrogation and adjudication phases goes beyond simply that it is the right thing to do, but rather it extends to the notion of protecting society at large from those perpetrators who were left undetected and free to commit more crimes.

CONCLUSION

Throughout this chapter, we have highlighted the characteristics of juveniles and persons with mental impairment that can contribute to their overrepresentation among the wrongfully arrested and convicted. We concentrated on susceptibilities that can arise in the interrogation room and at adjudication. However, it is foreseeable that vulnerable persons are at risk of wrongful convictions through other means. An examination of the to-date 261 Innocence Project wrongful conviction cases shows quite clearly that multiple factors often need be present to convict persons of a crime they did not do.

We close the chapter with a brief discussion of *Colorado v. Connelly* (1986), one of the most noteworthy U.S. Supreme Court cases relevant to interrogation and confession. In this case, Francis Barry Connelly, a paranoid schizophrenic, heard voices telling him to turn himself into the police and confess to a murder he had claimed to have committed several months earlier. Though the Colorado Supreme Court had held that Connelly was incapable of competently waiving his Miranda rights, the higher court reversed this decision, maintaining that "coercive police activity is a necessary predicate to the finding that a confession is not 'voluntary'" and that valid Miranda waivers should be free of police overreaching but need not be free of coercion from other sources (e.g., voices in one's head). Judge Rehnquist in the majority opinion stated that the U.S. Constitution does not afford the "right of a criminal defendant to confess to his crime only when totally rational and properly motivated."

Recently, Pizzi (2009) questioned the factual guilt of Connelly. In doing so, he quoted from Justice Brennan's 1986 dissenting opinion:

> The record is barren of any corroboration of the mentally ill defendant's confession. No physical evidence links the defendant to the alleged crime. Police did not identify the alleged victim's body as the woman named by the defendant. Mr. Connelly identified the alleged scene of the crime, but it has not been verified that the unidentified body was found there or that a crime actually occurred there. There is not a shred of competent evidence in this record linking the defendant to the charged homicide. There is only Mr. Connelly's confession.

Although Pizzi (2009) argued that there was evidence of Connelly's guilt, Justice Brennan's statement is nonetheless compelling. As described by Pizzi, after the Supreme Court decision did not come down in his favor, Connelly could have gone to trial and most likely would have been found not guilty by reason of insanity. However, an insanity acquittal could mean indefinite hospitalization. Thus, Connelly (who had earlier been deemed incompetent but then restored) accepted a plea and served a total of 5 years and 10 months, the majority of which he had already served preplea. In some ways, Connelly's case exemplifies the increased risk of miscarriages of justice among vulnerable defendants: a stand-alone confession from an unarguably mentally ill man and a plea taken in part to avoid institutionalization when he was in a legal sense not responsible.

We are not in a position to argue that Connelly was wrongly convicted, but we do disagree with the court's majority opinion and the rationale that underlies it. Coercion is necessarily subjective, and the perception of coercion is likely to differ between those who have and those who lack full understanding of their legal rights. As we as a society continue to grapple with the conviction of those who are factually innocent, we must also institute better protections for the large number of vulnerable individuals who enter the criminal justice system daily and who are at increased risk of these most egregious of errors. The safeguards currently in place in the interrogation room and during adjudication are woefully insufficient.

REFERENCES

Anderson, S. D., & Hewitt, J. (2002). The effect of competency restoration training on defendants with mental retardation found not competent to proceed. *Law and Human Behavior, 26,* 343–351. doi:10.1023/A:1015328505884

Appelbaum, K. L., & Appelbaum, P. S. (1994). Criminal justice-related competencies in defendants with mental retardation. *The Journal of Psychiatry & Law, 22,* 483–503.

Arizona v. Fulminante, 499 U.S. 279 (1991).

Atkins v. Virginia, 536 U.S. 304 (2002).

Billings, F. J., Taylor, T., Burns, J., Corey, D. L., Garven, S., & Wood, J. M. (2007). Can reinforcement induce children to falsely incriminate themselves? *Law and Human Behavior, 31,* 125–139. doi:10.1007/s10979-006-9049-5

Bonnie, R. (1992). The competence of criminal defendants: A theoretical reformulation. *Behavioral Sciences & the Law, 10,* 291–316. doi:10.1002/bsl.2370100303

Cialdini, R. B. (2001). *Influence: Science and practice.* New York, NY: Harper Collins.

Clare, I. C. H., & Gudjonsson, G. H. (1995). The vulnerability of suspects with intellectual disabilities during police interviews: A review and experimental study of decision-making. *Mental Handicap Research, 8,* 110–128. doi:10.1111/j.1468-3148.1995.tb00149.x

Colorado v. Connelly, 479 U.S. 157 (1986).

Cooper, D. K. (1997). Juveniles' understanding of trial-related information: Are they competent defendants? *Behavioral Sciences & the Law, 15,* 167–180. doi:10.1002/(SICI)1099-0798(199721)15:2<167::AID-BSL266>3.0.CO;2-E

Cooper, V. G., & Zapf, P. A. (2003). Predictor variables in competency to stand trial decisions. *Law and Human Behavior, 27,* 423–436. doi:10.1023/A:1024089117535

Drizin, S. A., & Leo, R. A. (2004). The problem of false confessions in the post-DNA world. *North Carolina Law Review, 82,* 891–1008.

Ericson, K. I., & Perlman, N. B. (2001). Knowledge of legal terminology and court proceedings in adults with developmental disabilities. *Law and Human Behavior, 25,* 529–545. doi:10.1023/A:1012896916825

Everington, C., & Fulero, S. M. (1999). Competence to confess: Measuring understanding and suggestibility of defendants with mental retardation. *Mental Retardation, 37,* 212–220. doi:10.1352/0047-6765(1999)037<0212:CTCMUA>2.0.CO;2

Federal Bureau of Investigation. (2008). *Crime in the United States.* Washington, DC: U.S. Department of Justice.

Ghetti, S., & Redlich, A. D. (2001). Reactions to youth crime: Perceptions of accountability and competency. *Behavioral Sciences & the Law, 19,* 33–52. doi:10.1002/bsl.426

Grisso, T. (1981). *Juvenile's waiver of rights: Legal and psychological competence.* New York NY: Plenum.

Grisso, T., Steinberg, L., Woolard, J., Cauffman, E., Scott, E., Graham, S., . . . Schwartz, R. (2003). Juveniles' competence to stand trial: A comparison of adolescents' and adults' capacities as trial defendants. *Law and Human Behavior, 27,* 333–363. doi:10.1023/A:1024065015717

Gross, S. R., Jacoby, K., Matheson, D. J., Montgomery, N., & Patil, S. (2005). Exonerations in the United States 1989 through 2003. *The Journal of Criminal Law and Criminology, 95,* 523-560. doi: 0091-4169/05/9502-0523

Gudjonsson, G. H. (2003). *The psychology of interrogations and confessions.* Chichester, England: Wiley.

Heller, K. J. (2006). The cognitive psychology of circumstantial evidence. *Michigan Law Review, 105,* 241–305.

Hoge, S. K., Poythress, N. G., Bonnie, R. J., Monahan, J., Eisenberg, M., & Feucht-Haviar, T. (1997). The MacArthur adjudicative competence study: Diagnosis, psychopathology, and competence-related abilities. *Behavioral Sciences and the Law, 15,* 329-345. doi: CCC 0735-3936/97/030329-17.

Inbau, F. E., Reid, J. E., Buckley, J. P., & Jayne, B. C. (2001). *Criminal interrogation and confessions* (4th ed.). Gaithersburg, MD: Aspen.

Innocence Project Report. (2007). *200 exonerated: Too many wrongfully convicted.* New York, NY: Benjamin N. Cardozo School of Law, Yeshiva University.

Johnson, K., & Seaman, A. (2008, May 28). Mentally incompetent defendants on rise. *USA Today*. Retrieved from http://www.usatoday.com/news/washington/judicial/2008-05-28-Incompetent_N.htm

Kassin, S. M., Drizin, S. A., Grisso, T., Gudjonsson, G. H., Leo, R. A., & Redlich, A. D. (2010). Police-induced confessions: Risk factors and recommendations. *Law and Human Behavior, 34*, 3–38. doi:10.1007/s10979-009-9188-6

Kassin, S. M., & Kiechel, K. L. (1996). The social psychology of false confessions: Compliance, internalization, and confabulation. *Psychological Science, 7*, 125–128. doi:10.1111/j.1467-9280.1996.tb00344.x

Kassin, S. M., & Neumann, K. (1997). On the power of confession evidence: An experimental test of the fundamental difference hypothesis. *Law and Human Behavior, 21*, 469–484. doi:10.1023/A:1024871622490

Kassin, S. M., & Wrightsman, L. S. (1980). Prior confessions and mock juror verdicts. *Journal of Applied Social Psychology, 10*, 133–146. doi:10.1111/j.1559-1816.1980.tb00698.x

Kostelnik, J. O., & Reppucci, N. D. (2009). Reid training and sensitivity to developmental maturity in interrogation: Results from a national survey of police. *Behavioral Sciences & the Law, 27*, 361–379. doi:10.1002/bsl.871

Meyer, J. R., & Reppucci, N. D. (2007). Police practices and perceptions regarding juvenile interrogation and interrogative suggestibility. *Behavioral Sciences & the Law, 25*, 757–780. doi:10.1002/bsl.774

Miller, R. D. (2003). Hospitalization of criminal defendants for evaluation of competence to stand trial or for restoration of competence: Clinical and legal issues. *Behavioral Sciences & the Law, 21*, 369–391. doi:10.1002/bsl.546

Najdowski, C. J., Bottoms, B. L., & Vargas, M. C. (2009). Jurors' perceptions of juvenile defendants: The influence of intellectual disability, abuse history, and confession evidence. *Behavioral Sciences & the Law, 27*, 401–430. doi:10.1002/bsl.873

National GAINS Center for People with Co-Occurring Disorders in the Justice System. (2006). The prevalence of co-occurring mental illness and substance use disorders in jails. *Fact Sheet Series*. Delmar, NY: The National GAINS Center.

Nestor, P. G., Daggett, D., Haycock, J., & Price, M. (1999). Competence to stand trial: A neuropsychological inquiry. *Law and Human Behavior, 23*, 397–412. doi:10.1023/A:1022339130582

Owen-Kostelnik, J., Reppucci, N. D., & Meyer, J. R. (2006). Testimony and interrogation of minors: Assumptions about maturity and morality. *American Psychologist, 61*, 286–304. doi:10.1037/0003-066X.61.4.286

Panetti v. Quarterman, 127 S.Ct. 2842 (2007).

Perfect, T. J., & Moon, H. C. (2005). The own-age effect in face recognition. In J. Duncan, P. McLeod, & L. H. Phillips (Eds.), *Measuring the mind: Speed, control and age* (pp. 317–340). Oxford, England: Oxford University Press.

Perske, R. (2004). Understanding persons with intellectual disabilities in the criminal justice system: Indicators of progress? *Mental Retardation, 42,* 484–487. doi:10.1352/0047-6765(2004)42<484:UPWIDI>2.0.CO;2

Pinals, D. A. (2005). Where two roads meet: Restoration of competence to stand trial from a clinical perspective. *New England School of Law, 31,* 81–108.

Pizzi, W. T. (2009). Colorado v. Connelly: What really happened? *Ohio State Law Journal, 7,* 377–389.

Redlich, A. D. (2004). Mental illness, police interrogations, and the potential for false confession. *Psychiatric Services, 55,* 19–21. doi:10.1176/appi.ps.55.1.19

Redlich, A. D. (2010). False confessions, false guilty pleas: Similarities and differences. In G. D. Lassiter & C. Meissner (Eds.), *Interrogations and confessions: Current research, practice, and policy* (pp. 49–66). Washington, DC: APA Books. doi:10.1037/12085-003

Redlich, A. D., & Goodman, G. S. (2003). Taking responsibility for an act not committed: The influence of age and suggestibility. *Law and Human Behavior, 27,* 141–156. doi:10.1023/A:1022543012851

Redlich, A. D., Ghetti, S., & Quas, J. A. (2008). Perceptions of children during a police interview: A comparison of alleged victims and suspects. *Journal of Applied Social Psychology, 38,* 705–735. doi:10.1111/j.1559-1816.2007.00323.x

Redlich, A. D., Quas, J. A., & Ghetti, S. (2008). Perceptions of children during a police interview: Guilt, confessions, and interview fairness. *Psychology, Crime & Law, 14,* 201–223. doi:10.1080/10683160701652542

Redlich, A. D., Silverman, M., & Steiner, H. (2003). Pre-adjudicative and adjudicative competence in juveniles and young adults. *Behavioral Sciences & the Law, 21,* 393–410. doi:10.1002/bsl.543

Roesch, R., Zapf, P., & Eaves, D. (2006). *FIT-R Fitness Interview Test—Revised: A structured interview for assessing competency to stand trial.* Sarasota, FL: Professional Resource Press.

Rogers, R., Harrison, K. S., Hazelwood, L. L., & Sewell, K. W. (2007). Knowing and intelligent: A study of Miranda warnings in mentally disordered defendants. *Law and Human Behavior, 31,* 401–418. doi:10.1007/s10979-006-9070-8

Rogers, R., Harrison, K. S., Shuman, D., Sewell, K. W., & Hazelwood, L. L. (2007). An analysis of *Miranda* warnings and waivers: Comprehension and coverage. *Law and Human Behavior, 31,* 177–192. doi:10.1007/s10979-006-9054-8

Roper v. Simmons, 543 U.S. 551 (2005).

Schmidt, M. G., Reppucci, N. D., & Woolard, J. L. (2003). Effectiveness of participation as a defendant: The attorney-juvenile client relationship. *Behavioral Sciences & the Law, 21,* 175–198. doi:10.1002/bsl.532

Ternes, M., & Yuille, J. C. (2008). Eyewitness memory and eyewitness identification performance in adults with intellectual disabilities. *Journal of Applied Research in Intellectual Disabilities, 21,* 519–531. doi:10.1111/j.1468-3148.2008.00425.x

U.S. Office of Juvenile Justice and Delinquency Prevention. (2007). *Statistical briefing book*. Retrieved from http://www.ojjdp.ncjrs.gov/ojstatbb/default.asp

Viljoen, J. L., Klaver, J., & Roesch, R. (2005). Legal decisions of preadolescent and adolescent defendants: Predictors of confessions, pleas, communication with attorneys, and appeals. *Law and Human Behavior, 29,* 253–277. doi:10.1007/s10979-005-3613-2

Woolard, J. L., Clearly, H. M. D., Harvell, S. A. S., & Chen, R. (2008). Examining adolescents' and their parents' conceptual and practical knowledge of police interrogation: A family dyad approach. *Journal of Youth and Adolescence, 37,* 685–698. doi:10.1007/s10964-008-9288-5

II

THE INVESTIGATORS

2

DETECTING DECEPTION

AMY-MAY LEACH

Mistaken eyewitness identifications and false confessions have been identified as leading factors in convictions of the innocent (Innocence Project, 2010). However, there may be another cause of wrongful conviction: the inability to detect deception. In 100% of wrongful conviction cases, the truth—that the person did not commit the crime—was overlooked. Thus, fundamentally, every single case in which an innocent person has been convicted of a crime has involved a deception-detection error.

Law enforcement officials are charged with a difficult task: They must decide whether a person committed a crime by weighing the evidence. Although certain types of evidence (e.g., DNA) are strongly indicative of guilt, they are not always available. In turn, suspects' accounts—whether in the form of alibis or descriptions of events—may strongly influence officials' decisions. Generally, individuals who are thought to be telling the truth when denying involvement in the crime are released; lie tellers are pursued and detained. In the majority of actual innocence cases, individuals denied having committed the crime. Thus, members of the justice system (e.g., police officers, prosecutors, judges, jury members) were unable to accurately detect truth telling. Had they been able to do so, these innocent individuals would have been dismissed as suspects and never convicted at trial.

Labeling an individual as a lie teller also, indirectly, sets the stage for conviction. For example, police officers may search for evidence that confirms their belief that the suspect committed the crime (see Chapter 14, this volume). In addition, suspects may be subjected to guilt-presumptive interrogations to elicit confessions. Innocence may actually be a risk factor: Innocent people may be more likely to waive essential rights (e.g., Miranda rights) and elicit confrontational interrogations (Kassin, 2005). Approximately 20% to 25% of actual innocence cases featured a false confession (Innocence Project, 2010). Thus, the truth was not detected. Instead, the presence of a confession may have overridden all other evidence and dramatically increased the likelihood of conviction (see Chapter 3, this volume). Thus, the relationship between deception detection and wrongful conviction may be mediated by investigative processes.

Moreover, deception detection does not end with the interrogation. To date, little attention has been paid to deceptive witnesses and officials. However, law enforcement officials, forensic experts, accomplices, jail-house informants, and eyewitnesses might also be highly motivated to lie. For example, accomplices and jailhouse informants have been known to lie (i.e., implicate the suspect) in exchange for reduced sentences (see Chapter 10, this volume; Innocence Project, 2010). In addition, if there are no other means to convict a suspect, police might alter evidence or a witness might be compelled to alter an account. For example, Romeo Phillion was wrongfully convicted of murder when an officer allegedly intentionally misplaced excul-patory evidence (Association in Defence of the Wrongly Convicted, 2010). Recent research has suggested that traditional safeguards in the justice system, such as cross-examination, may not be effective against deceptive witnesses (Greathouse, 2009). In turn, these individuals might contribute to wrongful conviction.

In summary, there are several direct and indirect ways in which the inability to discriminate between lie and truth tellers can lead to conviction. Thus, working knowledge of the current state of research on deception detection is an important component to understanding wrongful conviction.

SCIENTIFIC PSYCHOLOGICAL FOUNDATIONS OF DECEPTION DETECTION

Deception-detection research has a long history. Even Hugo Münsterberg's (1915) seminal work, *On the Witness Stand,* made note of the importance of differentiating between lie tellers and truth tellers. Since then, hundreds of articles have been produced on the topic. Research on deception detection is grounded in social and cognitive psychology.

Deception detection can fall in the domains of interpersonal communication, person perception, and decision making. More recently, researchers have used signal detection theory to more precisely characterize deception detection (e.g., Meissner & Kassin, 2002). As in other areas of cognitive psychology and psychophysics, deception-detection accuracy is now thought to reflect two separate dimensions of the decision-making process: (a) discrimination between lie tellers and truth tellers and (b) bias (i.e., the tendency to favor a particular response, such as indicating that all individuals are telling the truth).

THEORIES OF DECEPTION DETECTION

There are few established theories of deception detection. However, lie production and detection are invariably intertwined. Thus, our understanding of lie tellers can be used to improve deception detection. Perspectives on deception have emerged from several different areas in psychology. For example, several deception-detection researchers have also studied primary emotions (e.g., Ekman, Sorenson, & Friesen, 1969). Conceptualizations of emotions often involve considerations of underlying physiological patterns and cognition (e.g., Schachter & Singer, 1962); both of these are involved in deception. Examining the cognitive components (e.g., creation of the lie) and, in particular, the physiological correlates of lie telling may better reveal deceit. Moreover, a few researchers (e.g., Ekman & O'Sullivan, 1991) have argued that individuals who are proficient at identifying fleeting expressions of emotion (i.e., microexpressions) are better at detecting deception.

Researchers have also examined deception from a self-presentation perspective (e.g., DePaulo, 1992). In many areas (e.g., employment interviews, interpersonal relationships), individuals might attempt to manipulate others' impressions of them. Deception is one means to this end. To achieve this goal, deceivers must mask behaviors that could reveal the lie and display cues that are believed to be indicative of truth telling. Given the many incorrect notions about deception, focusing on cues that are not intuitively associated with truth telling (e.g., spontaneous corrections) could improve deception detection (DePaulo et al., 2003).

In more recent times, theories have focused on the role of cognition in deception. Increasing cognitive load (i.e., taxing cognitive resources, such as working memory and attention) can negatively affect performance on several types of tasks (e.g., Kahneman, 1973). The same is likely true for deception. A lie teller must create and remember the lie, actively conceal the truth, and consciously control nonverbal and verbal behaviors. Thus, lie telling may be more cognitively demanding than truth telling (Zuckerman, DePaulo, & Rosenthal, 1981). Researchers suggest that placing additional cognitive demands on lie tellers should further impair deception (Vrij, Fisher, Mann, & Leal, 2006).

Cognitive dissonance theory, which emerged from research on attitudes and persuasion, also offers an interesting perspective on deception. Inconsistencies between cognitions and behavior can produce psychological discomfort and physiological arousal (Croyle & Cooper, 1983). It is likely that during deception individuals experience a discrepancy between their cognitions ("lying is wrong") and behaviors (actually telling a lie), resulting in the expression of physiological arousal. As a result, manipulating lie tellers' cognitions about deception may improve detection (Leach, 2009).

SCIENTIFIC METHODS USED IN THE RESEARCH ON DECEPTION DETECTION

Typically, deception-detection researchers use experimental or quasi-experimental research designs. These experiments involve a two-step process: lie production and lie detection.

Lie-Production Paradigms

First, researchers create a scenario in which individuals will lie or tell the truth. Given the importance of establishing ground truth (i.e., individuals in the truth-telling condition are, in fact, telling the truth and individuals in the lie-telling condition are lying), the majority of the research is conducted in laboratory settings. In a typical study, a participant—usually a university student—is explicitly instructed to lie or tell the truth about opinions (e.g., Ekman, O'Sullivan, & Frank, 1999), life events (e.g., Leach et al., 2009), or witnessed events (e.g., Ekman & O'Sullivan, 1991). For example, Ekman and Friesen (1974) collected video footage of student nurses who were instructed to describe a nature film. Half of the participants had in fact been watching pleasant nature images (truth-telling condition), whereas the rest had been watching stressful medical-training scenes (lie-telling condition). Although a few researchers have attempted to approximate high-stakes scenarios by instructing participants to engage in mock crimes (e.g., theft), this approach is much less common (e.g., Kassin & Fong, 1999; Vrij et al., 2008).

There is some disagreement about the best way to produce deception. Paradigms are often criticized for their lack of experimental realism and external validity. However, in the field of deception detection, these arguments can be conceptualized as two separate issues: low versus high stakes and experimentally manipulated versus naturalistic deception. First, the majority of studies involve *low-stakes deception*. That is, there are no rewards associated with successful deception and few consequences associated with detection. Participants in these scenarios may not be as motivated as real-life suspects who are trying to avoid incarceration for serious crimes (e.g., murder). Research has shown that motivated lie tellers' deception is easier to detect (e.g., DePaulo, Lanier, & Davis, 1983); thus, assessments of lie detection accuracy that are based on low-stakes deception might underestimate true ability.

Second, deception is often experimentally manipulated. Typically, participants are informed that they are taking part in a deception study before being instructed to lie or tell the truth. Ekman (1997) argued that a key component of deception is that the listener is unaware of the deceiver's intent; thus, "an actor is not a liar." However, in the majority of deception paradigms, the listener is the experimenter (i.e., the person who orchestrated the lie). Thus, these paradigms may simply produce acting rather than lying. In addition, the deceiver's awareness of the purpose of the study ought to lessen guilt and any other emotional and physiological reactions associated with lying because the experimenter has explicitly endorsed deception. In fact, there is some evidence that experimentally manipulated scenarios and *naturalistic* scenarios —in which individuals were not aware that they were part of a deception study and were not instructed to lie or tell the truth—produce different deception-detection rates (Leach et al., 2009).

Ideally, researchers would want to use paradigms that involve high-stakes and naturalistic deception. However, these scenarios are often more difficult to design and carry out. Naturalistic deception relies on participants who decide, on their own, to commit a transgression and lie about it. Although the resulting deception is more ecologically valid, it can be more time consuming to produce, and it raises several of the same concerns that are associated with quasi-experimental research (e.g., underlying differences between self-selected lie tellers and truth tellers). Moreover, participants are expected to experience greater levels of physiological arousal and guilt in high-stakes, naturalistic scenarios. Thus, many of these paradigms produce ethical challenges for researchers and research ethics boards: the more involving and realistic the scenario, the more distress a participant will experience. One might assume that simply using video footage of real police interrogations might circumvent all of these issues. In fact, observers are more accurate when detecting the deception of real suspects being interviewed about actual crimes, such as arson, theft, and murder, than experimentally manipulated scenarios (e.g., Mann, Vrij, & Bull, 2004). However, given the difficulty in gaining access to these videos and establishing ground truth, this approach is rarely used. Thus, there is no gold-standard approach to producing deception; each researcher has his or her own preferred paradigm and must assume the benefits and costs associated with that choice.

Lie-Detection Paradigms

Researchers have attempted to uncover differences between lie tellers and truth tellers in several ways. First, deception detection can occur online (i.e., as the person is lying or telling the truth) or after a delay (i.e., footage and transcripts are analyzed after the fact). Second, approaches vary in terms of the training and equipment required which, in turn, affects whether lie detection occurs in the laboratory or in the field. Third, researchers may focus on the specific cues that are indicative of deception (e.g., using the polygraph) or more global judgments (e.g., using implicit deception detection).

Polygraph

The polygraph may be the most widely recognized deception-detection tool—perhaps due to its being dubbed the "lie detector." The underlying assumption in polygraph research is that the guilt or fear of detection experienced during deception produces changes in autonomic arousal (e.g., electrodermal response, heart rate, respiration). Thus, monitoring changes in individuals' physiological arousal across questions can reveal deception. Using the control question technique, participants are asked a series of irrelevant questions (e.g., "Are you 21 years old?"), control questions (e.g., "Have you ever lied?"), and crime-relevant questions (e.g., "Did you steal money from the bank?"). Guilty individuals are thought to experience greater amounts of physiological arousal when responding to crime-relevant (vs. control) questions. Using another technique, the guilty knowledge test, individuals are asked a series of questions about a particular aspect of the crime that only the guilty party should know (e.g., "Was the gun a shotgun? a revolver?"). Guilty individuals are expected to exhibit increased physiological responses when denying a true (vs. untrue) element of the crime.

Although, overall, the polygraph can accurately discriminate between lie tellers and truth tellers, the number of false positives (i.e., innocent suspects who are deemed guilty) is quite high (e.g., Ben-Shakhar & Elaad, 2003; Kircher, Horowitz, & Raskin, 1988). In addition, physical and mental countermeasures (e.g., biting the tongue, counting backward) can be effectively used to falsify patterns of arousal (Honts, Raskin, & Kircher, 1994). Currently, polygraph tests may be used as an investigative tool, but results are inadmissible in Canadian and some American courts (*R v. Béland*, 1987; *United States v. Scheffer*, 1998).

Neuroimaging Techniques

More recently, neuroscientists have begun to use neuroimaging techniques to detect deception. For example, functional magnetic resonance imaging (fMRI) has been used to track changes in brain activity during deception.

Researchers have suggested that examining particular brain regions (e.g., the right anterior cingulate gyrus) might allow for better discrimination between lie tellers and truth tellers (e.g., Kozel, Padgett, & George, 2004). In a similar vein, researchers are examining whether event-related potentials can be used to reveal deception. Using the guilty knowledge test paradigm, researchers suggest that the P300 amplitude associated with concealed information (e.g., the location of the crime) is larger than that observed in response to novel items (e.g., Farwell & Donchin, 1991).

Although initial reports are promising, the application of neuroimaging techniques to deception detection is still in its infancy. To date, research in the area has been limited, and the techniques' reliability and generalizability are unknown. In addition, neuroimaging techniques share many of the same weaknesses as the polygraph due to their reliance on the guilty knowledge test paradigm. Neuroimaging techniques involve presenting a series of stimuli to an individual; the expectation is that brain activity will change when that individual recognizes and denies critical elements of the crime. Thus, this approach relies on crime-relevant information being known only by the guilty party. However, in many cases, it is difficult to conceal this evidence from suspects and the general public. Currently, these tests cannot discriminate between a guilty individual who recognizes information because he or she committed the crime and an innocent individual who simply obtained the information elsewhere (e.g., heard it on the news). As a result of all of these weaknesses, the use of neuroimaging evidence in deception detection is not yet widely accepted by the scientific community, and its admissibility in courts remains unclear (Moriarty, 2008).

Statement Analysis

Alternative deception-detection approaches rely on analyses of the verbal content of statements rather than technology. Criteria-based content analysis (CBCA) involves training coders to use 19 different criteria (e.g., the types of details provided) to analyze individuals' statements (for full reviews, see Ruby & Brigham, 1997; Vrij, 2005). Truth telling is expected to elicit higher CBCA scores than lie telling. Using another approach—reality monitoring (RM)—researchers also suggest that memories for experienced and imagined events differ in terms of contextual information (e.g., temporal information), sensory information (e.g., visual details), semantic information, and cognitive operations (e.g., inclusion of thoughts; e.g., Masip, Sporer, Garrido, & Herrero, 2005). Analyses of CBCA and RM approaches indicate that both tools can be used to detect deception well above the level of chance (Vrij & Mann, 2004). Although these results are encouraging, the significant training requirements, combined with the time-consuming transcription and scoring procedures, render CBCA and RM inaccessible to most law enforcement officials.

Intuitive Deception Detection

The simplest, most common approach used by investigators and researchers is intuitive deception detection. As a result, it is the focus of the remainder of this chapter. In these paradigms, video footage of lie tellers and truth tellers is shown to observers. Although these studies are often conducted in the laboratory, research with expert populations (e.g., police officers) can take place in the field. In a typical experiment, an observer is asked to view a series of video clips of speakers who are communicating either truthful or deceptive information. After each clip, the observer must decide whether the speaker was lying or telling the truth. Observers may make upward of 40 such lie detection decisions (e.g., Leach et al., 2004); however, the majority of studies feature fewer than 20 targets (e.g., Ekman & O'Sullivan, 1991). At the end of the session, the individual's lie-detection accuracy is calculated.

There is some disagreement among researchers about the best way to assess intuitive lie-detection accuracy. Typically, individuals are deemed good or poor lie detectors based on their discrimination between a small number of lie tellers and truth tellers during a single session. This presents several challenges. Guessing might have a greater effect on performance when a small number of judgments is required (e.g., it is easier to obtain 2/2 than 100/100). In fact, lie detection performance is artificially inflated when there are few targets (Bond & DePaulo, 2008).

Researchers also vary in terms of their approach to stimulus sampling. Specifically, a few researchers include only poor lie tellers, or those whose deception was readily observable (e.g., Ekman & O'Sullivan, 1991; Ekman et al., 1999). This approach should lead to the best-case scenario: If observers cannot detect deception even under ideal conditions (i.e., when there are objective differences between groups), then it is evident that they are very poor lie detectors. Conversely, restricting the stimuli may decrease external validity because there is a full range of deceptive ability in the real world. In fact, poor lie tellers might lie less often than proficient lie tellers because they are more likely to be detected. Thus, current approaches that include only poor lie tellers might lead to overestimations of true lie-detection ability. Generally, despite the variability in approaches to stimulus sampling, there are few differences across studies in terms of lie-detection accuracy. Although these findings might suggest that the stimuli do not affect performance, it is more likely that lie-detection ability is so abysmal that differences in stimuli can have little effect.

RELEVANT RESEARCH ON DECEPTION DETECTION

Before examining deception-detection accuracy, it is important to establish that there are discernable differences between lie tellers and truth tellers. There are distinct verbal and behavioral cues that are associated with deception (DePaulo et al., 2003). However, there is no proverbial Pinocchio's nose; that is, there is no single cue that is exhibited by lie tellers and not exhibited by truth tellers. Rather, there are certain cues (e.g., vocal tension) that are exhibited more frequently by lie tellers (or truth tellers; DePaulo et al., 2003). Thus, theoretically, deception detection should be possible.

However, cues to deception must be readily apparent to observers. Several behaviors associated with deception, such as increased pupil dilation, are detectable only by using specialized equipment because they are virtually indistinguishable to the naked eye. In addition, other successful approaches (e.g., CBCA) require extensive analyses and training on the part of the observer. Even easily observable cues might be missed because the majority of laypersons and law enforcement officials have incorrect beliefs about the cues to deception (Akehurst, Köhnken, Vrij, & Bull, 1996). Thus, despite the existence of diagnostic cues, it is unclear that they can be easily recognized and correctly used by observers.

Deception-Detection Accuracy

Deception detection should be severely hampered if observers rely on irrelevant cues. In fact, the average lie-detection accuracy for laypersons is 54%, which is near chance levels (Bond & DePaulo, 2006). This finding might be unsurprising given laypersons' lack of specialized training. However, even law enforcement officials who have extensive lie-detection experience (e.g., police officers, customs officials, Federal Bureau of Investigations agents) perform at chance levels (e.g., Ekman & O'Sullivan, 1991; Kraut & Poe, 1980). A few law enforcement groups (e.g., Secret Service agents, Central Intelligence Agency agents, sheriffs) are significantly more accurate than chance (Ekman et al., 1999; Ekman & O'Sullivan, 1991). However, these tend to be the exception rather than the rule; the majority of groups that have been examined are not proficient at detecting deception.

It is too simplistic to dismiss deception detection as an impossible task due to poor group performance. In fact, there are individual differences in accuracy. For example, in a recent study by Leach et al. (2009), average accuracy among laypersons was at chance levels; however, their performance ranged from 29% to 75%. Thus, deception detection might follow a normal distribution similar to other traits (O'Sullivan, 2007). There are several explanations for variations in overall performance within groups. Individual differences might be because of underlying factors that improve or hinder performance. However, the majority of characteristics that have been studied (e.g., age, cognitive ability, extraversion, gender, self-monitoring, shyness) have no significant effects on deception detection (e.g., Porter, Campbell, Stapleton, & Birt, 2002; Zuckerman et al., 1981). Moreover, factors that do appear to be associated with accuracy (e.g., left-handedness, social anxiety) cannot account for the wide variability in performance (DePaulo & Tang, 1994; Porter et al., 2002). O'Sullivan and Ekman (2004) discussed the existence of lie detection "wizards." To date, these researchers have discovered 29 people (out of over 10,000 who have been studied) who reliably detected deception at high levels of accuracy. Researchers would be interested in studying wizards' backgrounds and strategies to determine ways to better detect deception. However, there remains considerable controversy about the existence of these high-performing lie detectors. For example, Bond and Uysal (2007) argued that these findings represent a fluke, or chance responding. Regardless of the statistical explanation for high-performing wizards, there is mounting evidence that certain individuals are better lie detectors.

However, the reliance on single-session observations has made it difficult to assess whether lie detection performance is trait like or simply the result of a series of (lucky or unlucky) guesses. Typically, researchers draw conclusions about an individual's long-term lie-detection performance after one lie-detection session. If deception detection is based on an innate ability, then performance should be stable over time. However, new research— in which observers' accuracy was assessed over several sessions—indicates that lie-detection performance is not reliable under a variety of conditions (Leach et al., 2009; Vrij, Mann, Robbins, & Robinson, 2006). These findings suggest that when making lie-detection decisions, observers might merely be guessing.

Accuracy and Confidence

Although the majority of individuals are poor lie detectors, their performance appears to have little impact on their confidence. Despite being no more proficient than untrained observers, law enforcement groups express greater confidence in their ability to detect deception than laypersons (e.g., Leach, Talwar, Lee, Bala, & Lindsay, 2004). Moreover, these officials have a tendency to overestimate their accuracy: In one international survey, police officers indicated that their average accuracy was 77% (Kassin et al., 2007). Given the inability to accurately assess one's own performance, it is unsurprising that a meta-analysis has shown that there is no relationship between confidence and accuracy (DePaulo, Charlton, Cooper, Lindsay, & Muhlenbruck, 1997).

Training

One reason for law enforcement officials' poor lie-detection performance may be their training. This argument might appear counterintuitive, as lie-detection training is intended to improve, nor worsen, accuracy. A significant proportion of law enforcement officials in North America are trained using the Reid technique (Inbau, Reid, Buckley, & Jayne, 2001). The first part of the technique involves establishing that a suspect is lying (or telling the truth) using the Behavior Analysis Interview (BAI; John E. Reid and Associates, 2010). As part of this interview, officers are instructed to ask specific questions that will evoke different verbal and nonverbal responses from truth and lie tellers. Two troubling findings have emerged from analyses of this approach. First, Inbau et al. (2001) specified verbal and nonverbal cues that they stated were indicative of lying (e.g., increased eye contact); however, these cues are not empirically associated with deception (DePaulo et al., 2003). Second, a primary prediction of the BAI—that truth tellers will exhibit higher scores than lie tellers—is incorrect (Vrij, Mann, & Fisher, 2007). In fact, lie tellers appear to be more concerned with impression management and thus exhibit the opposite pattern of behaviors than expected by Inbau et al. (e.g., more helpfulness, less nervousness). Thus, the fundamental assumptions of the BAI run contrary to scientific evidence and are considerably flawed.

Perhaps it is not surprising that Reid training can have a devastating impact on lie-detection accuracy. Higher officer endorsement of Reid cues has been associated with lower levels of lie-detection accuracy (Mann, Vrij, & Bull, 2004). Reid training also appears to unjustifiably bolster confidence: When researchers trained individuals in the portions of the Reid technique that pertained to deception detection, they became less accurate but more confident in their decisions (Kassin & Fong, 1999). However, providing an alternative training approach may be challenging (e.g., Frank & Feeley, 2003). Given that the predominant training technique hinders deception detection, researchers continue to search for viable alternatives.

APPLICATION OF RESEARCH ON DECEPTION DETECTION

Unlike other areas in forensic psychology (e.g., eyewitness identifications), the deception-detection literature has had little impact on policy. There are several reasons why this might be the case. First, deception detection is a common occurrence. If individuals tell a lie, on average, once per day, opportunities for lie detection are abundant (DePaulo, Kashy, Kirkendol, Wyer, & Epstein, 1996). Given that people have detected deception their entire lives, it may be difficult to override their notions about the cues to deception and their own accuracy. For a variety of reasons (e.g., self-preservation, self-esteem), individuals might fail to seek out feedback because they do not wish to acknowledge that they might have been fooled. Thus, incorrect beliefs are maintained and strengthened over time. In turn, there is no perceived need for policy changes because current deception-detection tactics are thought to be appropriate. Dispelling this notion may be even more difficult when addressing law enforcement officials for whom deception detection is a primary occupational task. Although anecdotal evidence suggests that many law enforcement officials are aware of the inherent difficulties involved in detecting deception, administrators are wary of claims that their officers perform as poorly as untrained university students. Thus, there may be some reluctance at the administrative level to acknowledge that current training procedures are not effective.

Second, it has been challenging for empirically based training programs to compete with the Reid technique. As noted, the Reid technique is implemented worldwide. Thus, the descriptive norm that is conveyed to law enforcement officials is that other agencies endorse this technique (and they should, too!). In addition, John E. Reid & Associates (2010) make very impressive claims: Individuals trained to use the BAI are reported to correctly identify deception 85% of the time. At the time of this publication, there is no competing training paradigm available that makes similar promises of improvement. Thus, law enforcement agencies may be reluctant to adopt untried paradigms that increase accuracy to 60%. Although research suggests that the Reid technique should be abandoned because of its harmful effects, until researchers can produce a more compelling alternative, there may be little direct impact on policy and procedures.

Many officers already, intuitively, use interviewing techniques that will improve performance; however, it is still important to examine these approaches empirically. There are two main ways to increase accuracy: (a) making deception more difficult for lie tellers, and (b) improving lie-detection tactics. One recent approach involved increasing lie tellers' cognitive load (Vrij, Fisher, et al., 2006). Lying is known to be cognitively taxing. Thus, increasing cognitive load, such as by making suspects provide accounts in reverse chronological order, makes deception more difficult to conceal (Vrij et al., 2008). Newer research has focused on manipulating lie tellers' attributions about the source of their arousal to reveal deception (e.g., Leach, 2009).

Another approach is to improve observers' ability to detect deception. For example, Hartwig, Granhag, Stromwell, and Vrij (2005) advocated in favor of the strategic use of evidence. When interrogators withheld key pieces of evidence, suspects were more likely to implicate themselves, improving deception detection. Changing the focus of investigators might also improve deception detection. Specifically, thin slicing (i.e., judgments based on exposure to short segments of behavior) and rapid judgments result in more accurate deception detection, perhaps because observers are less likely to overanalyze their decisions (e.g., Albrechtsen, Meissner, & Susa, 2009; Vrij, Evans, Akehurst, & Mann, 2004). Moreover, given that lie tellers appear to think harder than truth tellers because of increases in cognitive load, asking investigators whether suspects were "thinking hard" rather than "lying" has also been deemed effective (Vrij, Edward, & Bull, 2001). All of these techniques are quick, easy, cost-effective ways for law enforcement officials to make deception easier to detect.

Although it is important for agencies to implement new, empirically validated approaches to deception detection, the greatest impact of deception-detection research might be to introduce caution. Currently, officers receive very little feedback about their lie-detection performance. As a result, they may have drawn incorrect conclusions about their proficiency. Officers (and agencies) should be made aware of their poor accuracy and actively discouraged from relying on their own intuitions. Instead, officers should be trained to focus solely on objective evidence and hypothesis testing. Certainly, this does not mean that we should do away with interrogations. However, additional caution should be introduced into the process, such that individuals charged with deception detection—whether it be officers or jury members—should be aware that there is a strong likelihood that they will be inaccurate.

CONCLUSION

Improvements in detection accuracy would certainly impact wrongful conviction. Currently, lie-detection accuracy is abysmal. This is problematic at all steps of the legal process.

Law enforcement officials might rely on incorrect intuitions rather than evidence. In turn, their inaccurate determinations of guilt may lead to tunnel vision and intense interrogations, which place innocents at risk of false confession. It is also important to note that poor deception detection is not one sided: In many cases, neither interrogators nor suspects can detect each other's lies. Thus, when interrogators present false evidence (e.g., claim that DNA places the suspect at the scene), it is unlikely that the suspect will be able to detect the deception. This might account for why false evidence can increase the likelihood of internalization and false confession (e.g., Kassin, 2005). Therefore, the failure to detect deception has several negative implications for innocent suspects prior to trial.

Moreover, deception-detection errors extend beyond the interrogation room. Defense attorneys and prosecutors may not be able to correctly evaluate the veracity of witnesses' statements and each other's claims. More important, judges and jury members may be unlikely to detect the deceptive testimony of witnesses (e.g., informants, alibi witnesses, eyewitnesses, experts) and the truthful testimony or false confessions of innocent defendants. Although there is limited research on deception detection in the courtroom, decades of research suggest that it could contribute to wrongful conviction (e.g., Bond & DePaulo, 2006).

A failure of truth detection lies at the heart of wrongful conviction. However, law enforcement officials and researchers have focused their efforts primarily on detecting deceit. Although truth and lie detection might be considered to be two sides of the same coin, recent research has shown that perspective matters. Overriding individuals' long-held incorrect notions about deception might simply be too difficult. In fact, reframing training to focus on truth detection actually increases accuracy more than traditional lie-detection approaches (Masip, Alonso, Garrido, & Herrero, 2009). More research on this topic is needed; a better understanding of truth detection might decrease wrongful conviction.

At many levels in the justice system, the inability to detect deception can lead to wrongful conviction. Unfortunately, there is no quick fix. However, agencies must be made aware of new, empirically supported lie-detection techniques. More important, they should consider that a deception-detection decision is a very poor, subjective, unsubstantiated piece of information. It should not be considered evidence or accorded any significant weight in conclusions about a suspect's guilt.

REFERENCES

Akehurst, L., Köhnken, G., Vrij, A., & Bull, R. (1996). Lay persons' and police officers' beliefs regarding deceptive behavior. *Applied Cognitive Psychology, 10,* 461–471. doi:10.1002/(SICI)1099-0720(199612)10:6<461::AID-ACP413>3.0.CO;2-2

Albrechtsen, J. S., Meissner, C. A., & Susa, K. J. (2009). Can intuition improve deception detection performance? *Journal of Experimental Social Psychology, 45,* 1052–1055. doi:10.1016/j.jesp.2009.05.017

Association in Defence of the Wrongly Convicted. (2010). Retrieved from http://www.aidwyc.org/

Ben-Shakhar, G., & Elaad, E. (2003). The validity of psychophysiological detection of information with the guilty knowledge test: A meta-analytic review. *Journal of Applied Psychology, 88,* 131–151. doi:10.1037/0021-9010.88.1.131

Bond, C. F., Jr., & DePaulo, B. M. (2006). Accuracy of deception judgments. *Personality and Social Psychology Review, 10,* 214–234. doi:10.1207/s15327957pspr1003_2

Bond, C. F., Jr., & DePaulo, B. M. (2008). Individual differences in judging deception: Accuracy and bias. *Psychological Bulletin, 134,* 477–492. doi:10.1037/0033-2909. 134.4.477

Bond, C. F., Jr., & Uysal, A. (2007). On lie detection "wizards." *Law and Human Behavior, 31,* 109–115. doi:10.1007/s10979-006-9016-1

Croyle, R. T., & Cooper, J. (1983). Dissonance arousal: Physiological evidence. *Journal of Personality and Social Psychology, 45,* 782–791. doi:10.1037/0022-3514.45.4.782.

DePaulo, B. M. (1992). Nonverbal behaviour and self-presentation. *Psychological Bulletin, 111,* 203–243. doi:10.1037/0033-2909.111.2.203

DePaulo, B. M., Charlton, K., Cooper, H., Lindsay, J. J., & Muhlenbruck, L. (1997). The accuracy-confidence correlation in the detection of deception. *Personality and Social Psychology Review, 1,* 346–357. doi:10.1207/s15327957pspr0104_5

DePaulo, B. M., Kashy, D. A., Kirkendol, S. E., Wyer, M. M., & Epstein, J. A. (1996). Lying in everyday life. *Journal of Personality and Social Psychology, 70,* 979–995. doi:10.1037/0022-3514.70.5.979

DePaulo, B. M., Lanier, K., & Davis, T. (1983). Detecting the deceit of the motivated liar. *Journal of Personality and Social Psychology, 45,* 1096–1103. doi:10.1037/0022-3514.45.5.1096

DePaulo, B. M., Lindsay, J. J., Malone, B. E., Muhlenbruck, L., Charlton, K., & Cooper, H. (2003). Cues to deception. *Psychological Bulletin, 129,* 74–118. doi:10.1037/0033-2909.129.1.74

DePaulo, B. M., & Tang, J. (1994). Social anxiety and social judgment: The example of detecting deception. *Journal of Research in Personality, 28,* 142–153. doi:10.1006/jrpe.1994.1012

Ekman, P. (1997). Lying and deception. In N. L. Stein, P. A. Ornstein, B. Tversky, & C. Brainerd (Eds.), *Memory of everyday and emotional events* (pp. 333–347). Mahwah, NJ: Erlbaum.

Ekman, P., & Friesen, W. V. (1974). Detection deception from the body or face. *Journal of Personality and Social Psychology, 29,* 288–298. doi:10.1037/h0036006

Ekman, P., & O'Sullivan, M. (1991). Who can catch a liar? *American Psychologist, 46,* 913–920. doi:10.1037/0003-066X.46.9.913

Ekman, P., O'Sullivan, M., & Frank, M. G. (1999). A few can catch a liar. *Psychological Science, 10,* 263–266. doi:10.1111/1467-9280.00147

Ekman, P., Sorenson, E. R., & Friesen, W. V. (1969, April 4). Pan-cultural elements in facial displays of emotion. *Science, 164,* 86–88. doi:10.1126/science.164.3875.86

Farwell, L. A., & Donchin, E. (1991). The truth will out: Interrogative polygraph ("lie detection") with event-related potentials. *Psychophysiology, 28,* 531–547. doi:10.1111/j.1469-8986.1991.tb01990.x

Frank, M. G., & Feeley, T. H. (2003). To catch a liar: Challenges for research in lie detection training. *Journal of Applied Communication Research, 31,* 58–75. doi:10.1080/00909880305377

Greathouse, S. M. (2009). *Does cross-examination help jurors detect deception?* (Unpublished doctoral dissertation). The City University of New York, New York.

Hartwig, M., Granhag, P. A., Stromwell, L. A., & Vrij, A. (2005). *Detecting deception via strategic disclosure of evidence, 29,* 469–484. doi: 10.1007/s10979-005-5521-x

Honts, C. R., Raskin, D. C., & Kircher, J. C. (1994). Mental and physical counter-measures reduce the accuracy of polygraph tests. *Journal of Applied Psychology, 79,* 252–259. doi:10.1037/0021-9010.79.2.252

Inbau, F. E., Reid, J. E., Buckley, J. P., & Jayne, B. C. (2001). *Criminal interrogation and confessions* (4th ed.). Gaithersburg, MD: Aspen.

Innocence Project. (2010). Retrieved from http://www.innocenceproject.org

John E. Reid and Associates. (2010). Retrieved from http://www.reid.com/services/r_behavior.html

Kahneman, D. (1973). *Attention and effort.* Englewood Cliffs, NJ: Prentice-Hall.

Kassin, S. M. (2005). On the psychology of confessions: Does innocence put inno-cents at risk? *American Psychologist, 60,* 215–228. doi:10.1037/0003-066X.60.3.215

Kassin, S. M., & Fong, C. T. (1999). "I'm innocent!" Effects of training on judgments of truth and deception in the interrogation room. *Law and Human Behavior, 23,* 499–516. doi:10.1023/A:1022330011811

Kassin, S. M., Leo, R. A., Meissner, C. A., Richman, K. D., Colwell, L. H., Leach, A.-M., & LaFon, D. (2007). Police interviewing and interrogation: A self-report survey of police practices and beliefs. *Law and Human Behavior, 31,* 381–400. doi:10.1007/s10979-006-9073-5

Kircher, J. C., Horowitz, S. W., & Raskin, D. C. (1988). Meta-analysis of mock crime studies of the control question polygraph technique. *Law and Human Behavior, 12,* 79–90. doi:10.1007/BF01064275

Kozel, F. A., Padgett, T. M., & George, M. S. (2004). A replication study of the neural correlates of deception. *Behavioral Neuroscience, 118,* 852–856. doi:10.1037/0735-7044.118.4.852

Kraut, R. E., & Poe, D. (1980). Behavioral roots of person perception: The deception judgments of customs inspectors and laypersons. *Journal of Personality and Social Psychology, 39,* 784–798. doi:10.1037/0022-3514.39.5.784

Leach, A.-M. (2009, July). *A new look at deception: Revisiting cognitive dissonance theory.* Paper presented at the Biennial Meeting of the Society for Applied Research in Memory and Cognition, Kyoto, Japan.

Leach, A.-M., Lindsay, R. C. L., Koehler, R., Beaudry, J. L., Bala, N. C., Lee, K., & Talwar, V. (2009). The reliability of lie detection performance. *Law and Human Behavior, 33,* 96–109. doi:10.1007/s10979-008-9137-9

Leach, A.-M., Talwar, V., Lee, K., Bala, N. C., & Lindsay, R. C. L. (2004). Intuitive lie detection of children's deception by law enforcement officials and university students. *Law and Human Behavior, 28,* 661–685.

Mann, S., Vrij, A., & Bull, R. (2004). Detecting true lies: Police officers' ability to detect suspects' lies. *Journal of Applied Psychology, 89,* 137–149. doi:10.1037/0021-9010.89.1.137

Masip, J., Alonso, H., Garrido, E., & Herrero, C. (2009). Training to detect what? The biasing effects of training on veracity judgments. *Applied Cognitive Psychology, 23,* 1282–1296. doi:10.1002/acp.1535

Masip, J., Sporer, S. L., Garrido, E., & Herrero, C. (2005). The detection of deception with the reality monitoring approach: A review of the empirical evidence. *Psychology, Crime & Law, 11,* 99–122. doi:10.1080/10683160410001726356

Meissner, C. A., & Kassin, S. M. (2002). "He's guilty!": Investigator bias in judgments of truth and deception. *Law and Human Behavior, 26,* 469–480. doi:10.1023/A:1020278620751

Moriarty, J. C. (2008). Neuroimaging evidence in the U.S. courts. *Behavioral Sciences & the Law, 26,* 29–49. doi:10.1002/bsl.795

Münsterberg, H. (1915). *On the witness stand.* New York, NY: Doubleday, Page & Company. doi:10.1037/10854-000

O'Sullivan, M. (2007). Unicorns or Tiger Woods: Are lie detection experts myths or rarities? A response to *On Lie Detection "Wizards"* by Bond and Uysal. *Law and Human Behavior, 31,* 117–123. doi:10.1007/s10979-006-9058-4

O'Sullivan, M., & Ekman, P. (2004). The wizards of deception detection. In P. A. Granhag & L. A. Stromwell (Eds.), *The detection of deception in forensic contexts* (pp. 269–286). New York, NY: Cambridge University Press.

Porter, S., Campbell, M. A., Stapleton, J., & Birt, A. R. (2002). The influence of judge, target, and stimulus characteristics on the accuracy of detecting deceit. *Canadian Journal of Behavioural Science, 34,* 172–185. doi:10.1037/h0087170

R v. Béland, 2 S. C. R 398 (1987).

Ruby, C. L., & Brigham, J. C. (1997). The usefulness of the criteria-based content analysis technique in distinguishing between truthful and fabricated allegations. *Psychology, Public Policy, and Law, 3,* 705–737. doi:10.1037/1076-8971.3.4.705

Schachter, S., & Singer, J. (1962). Cognitive, social, and physiological determinants of emotional state. *Psychological Review, 69,* 379–399. doi:10.1037/h0046234

United States v. Scheffer, 188 S. Ct. 1261 (1998).

Vrij, A. (2005). Criteria-based content analysis: A qualitative review of the first 37 studies. *Psychology, Public Policy, and Law, 11,* 3–41. doi:10.1037/1076-8971.11.1.3

Vrij, A., Edward, K., & Bull, R. (2001). Police officers' ability to detect deceit: The benefit of indirect deception detection measures. *Legal and Criminological Psychology, 6,* 185–196. doi:10.1348/135532501168271

Vrij, A., Evans, H., Akehurst, L., & Mann, S. (2004). Rapid judgements in assessing verbal and nonverbal cues: Their potential for deception researchers and lie detection. *Applied Cognitive Psychology, 18,* 283–296. doi:10.1002/acp.964

Vrij, A., Fisher, R., Mann, S., & Leal, S. (2006). Detecting deception by manipulating cognitive load. *Trends in Cognitive Sciences, 10,* 141–142. doi:10.1016/j.tics.2006.02.003

Vrij, A., & Mann, S. (2004). Detecting deception: The benefit of looking at a combination of behavioral, auditory and speech content related cues in a systematic manner. *Group Decision and Negotiation, 13,* 61–79. doi:10.1023/B:GRUP.0000011946.74290.bc

Vrij, A., Mann, S., & Fisher, R. (2007). An empirical test of the Behaviour Analysis Interview. *Law and Human Behavior, 30,* 329–345. doi:10.1007/s10979-006-9014-3

Vrij, A., Mann, S., Fisher, R. P., Leal, S., Milne, R., & Bull, R. (2008). Increasing cognitive load to facilitate lie detection: The benefit of recalling an event in reverse order. *Law and Human Behavior, 32,* 253–265. doi:10.1007/s10979-007-9103-y

Vrij, A., Mann, S., Robbins, E., & Robinson, M. (2006). Police officers' ability to detect deception in high stakes situations and in repeated lie detection tests. *Applied Cognitive Psychology, 20,* 741–755. doi:10.1002/acp.1200

Zuckerman, M., DePaulo, B. M., & Rosenthal, R. (1981). Verbal and nonverbal communication of deception. In L. Berkowitz (Ed.), *Advances in experimental social psychology* (Vol. 14, pp. 1–59). New York, NY: Academic Press.

3

FALSE CONFESSIONS

LISA E. HASEL AND SAUL M. KASSIN

In criminal law, confession evidence is a highly potent weapon of prosecution, so potent it has been suggested that "the introduction of a confession makes the other aspects of a trial in court superfluous" (McCormick, 1972, p. 316). Over the years, confessions have played a vital role in law enforcement and crime control. They are also fallible, however, and are a source of recurring controversy, with questions often arising about whether a statement is authentic, voluntarily given, the product of a competent waiver of rights, and in accord with the law. For all of these reasons, confessions have been described as "troubling" (Brooks, 2000).

Many instances contradict the myth that people do not confess to crimes they did not commit. Throughout American history, as far back as the Salem witch trials of 1692, men and women have been wrongfully prosecuted, convicted, imprisoned, and sometimes even sentenced to death as a result of false confessions. The prevalence rate is unknown and, we would argue, unknowable. But out of more than 250 individuals thus far exonerated by postconviction DNA testing and released from prison, false confessions were a contributing factor in nearly 25% of those cases (Garrett, 2008; http://www.innocenceproject.org). Although DNA-based exonerations are relatively new to criminal justice, researchers and legal scholars have, in other ways, long documented the problem of false confessions in the annals of wrongful convictions (Borchard, 1932; Leo, 2005). Indeed, psychology's interest can also be traced to its early days as a science. More than 100 years ago, in *On the Witness Stand*, Hugo Munsterberg (1908) devoted an entire chapter to the topic of "Untrue Confessions."

Although the prevalence of false confessions cannot be quantified with any precision, Kassin and Wrightsman (1985) initially proposed, and most researchers agree, that there are three types of false confessions. *Voluntary false confessions* are those in which people claim responsibility for crimes they did not commit without prompting or pressure from police. Often this occurs in high profile cases. When Charles Lindbergh's infant son was kidnapped in 1932, 200 people confessed. When "Black Dahlia" actress Elizabeth Short was murdered in 1947, more than 50 men and women confessed. In 2006, John Mark Karr volunteered a detailed confession to the unsolved murder of young JonBenet Ramsey. The charges against Karr were dropped when physical evidence failed to corroborate his claim. There are many reasons why innocent people voluntarily confess—such as a pathological need for attention or self-punishment; feelings of guilt; delusions of their own involvement; the perception of tangible gain; or the desire to protect a parent, child, or someone else.

In other cases, suspects are induced to confess through the processes of police interrogation. In *compliant false confessions*, the suspect agrees to the demand for a confession to escape a stressful situation, avoid an expected punishment, or gain a promised or implied reward. As in the classic form of social influence observed in Asch's (1956) conformity studies, this type of confession is a mere act of public compliance by a suspect who believes that the short-term benefits of confession outweigh the long-term costs. This type of false confession was multiply illustrated in the 1989 Central Park Jogger case, in which five New York City teenagers confessed after lengthy interrogations, each claiming he expected to go home afterward. On the basis of these confessions, the boys were convicted and sent to prison but then exonerated in 2002 when the real rapist gave a confession that was confirmed by the original DNA evidence (*New York v. Wise, Richardson, McCray, Salaam, & Santana*, 2002; Saulny, 2002).

Internalized false confessions are those in which innocent but vulnerable suspects (often juveniles, who may be mentally ill or intellectually impaired—see Chapter 1 of this volume) exposed to highly suggestive interrogation tactics, come not only to confess but also to believe that they committed the crime in question, sometimes confabulating false memories in the process (for a description of the process, see Kassin, 2007). Gudjonsson and MacKeith (1982) argued that this phenomenon stems from *memory distrust syndrome*, whereby people come to distrust their memory, rendering them vulnerable to misinformation from external sources. The case of 14-year-old Michael Crowe, whose sister Stephanie was stabbed to death in her bedroom, is a case in point. Although Crowe adamantly asserted his innocence, police targeted him for suspicion. After a series of interrogation sessions, during which time he was deceived into thinking there was substantial physical evidence of guilt, Crowe concluded that he was a killer, saying, "I'm not sure how I did it. All I know is I did it." Eventually, he was convinced that he had a split personality—that "bad Michael" acted out of a jealous rage while "good Michael" blocked the incident from consciousness. The charges against Crowe were later dropped when a drifter in the neighborhood that night was found with Stephanie's blood on his clothing.

Three important and often overlooked points are worth noting about false confessions. First, the numbers of known cases represent the tip of an iceberg because they do not include the countless false confessions that are uncovered by police and prosecutors, causing them to drop the charges; those made to lesser crimes, which often result in guilty pleas and receive no postconviction scrutiny, and those in juvenile proceedings that contain confidentiality provisions (for a discussion, see Drizin & Leo, 2004; Gross, Jacoby, Matheson, Montgomery, & Patel, 2004). Second, despite the recent interest in the problem, false confessions are not a new or uniquely American phenomenon. Although most individual and aggregated case studies have been based in the United States and England, proven false confessions have been documented throughout history and in countries all over the world (Kassin et al., 2010). Third, every time an innocent confessor is arrested, tried, and found guilty, the true perpetrator remains free to harm additional victims. This consequence is an unintended but costly flip side of every wrongful conviction. In the Central Park jogger case briefly described above, five boys' confessions closed the New York Police Department investigation of the case. As a result, Matias Reyes, the actual culprit, went on to rape three more women in the area, killing one in the process.

PSYCHOLOGICAL FOUNDATIONS FOR THE STUDY OF FALSE CONFESSIONS

Although there was little empirical research on confession evidence until the 1980s, behavioral scientists have been studying relevant psychological processes for more than 100 years. Current knowledge of the processes of interrogations and the effects on suspects is firmly grounded in universally accepted core principles of psychology. In this section, we focus on the principles of reinforcement and decision making; social influence research on compliance, obedience, and other forms of social impact; and recent work on memory misattributions and other errors. (For an examination of interrogation techniques from a procedural fairness perspective, see Chapter 4, this volume.)

Principles of Reinforcement and Decision Making

Dating back to Thorndike's (1911) law of effect, behaviorists, and other psychologists have long known that people are highly responsive to reinforcement and subject to the laws of conditioning. Additionally, behavior is influenced more by immediate short-term consequences than by future long-term consequences—both of which are strategically manipulated by trained police investigators. Of relevance to a psychological analysis of interrogation are the hundreds of experiments on operant conditioning in animals and humans; studies of reinforcement schedules; the effects of punishment; and appetitive, avoidance, and escape learning (Herrnstein, 1970; Skinner, 1938). The principles derived from this operant conditioning research tradition have been used to modify behavior in hospitals, schools, the military, workplaces, and other applied settings. Interrogations that evoke confessions often function in similar ways, with police leading suspects to confess to a particular narrative account as if they were rats in a Skinner box (Kassin, 2007).

Similarly relevant to an analysis of choice behavior in the interrogation room are more recent studies of human decision making in the behavioral economics paradigm. A substantial body of research has shown that people make choices designed to maximize their well-being given the constraints they face, making the best of the situation they are in—a phenomenon that Herrnstein, Rachlin, and Laibson (1997) called the "matching law." Animals and humans also clearly prefer delayed punishment to immediate aversive stimulation (e.g., Deluty, 1978). With respect to a suspect's response to interrogation, studies on the discounting of rewards and costs show that people tend to be myopic in their orientation, preferring outcomes that are immediate rather than delayed, and the subjective value of delayed punishment depreciates over time (Rachlin, 2000). This tendency is particularly evident in juvenile populations as well as among cigarette smokers, alcoholics, and other substance users (see Bickel & Marsch, 2001).

Social Influence Effects

Over the years, social psychologists have observed that people are inherently social beings and, hence, highly vulnerable to influence from change agents, particularly those in positions of authority, who seek their compliance. Latané's (1981) social impact theory provides a predictive model that can account for the influence of police interrogators—who bring power, proximity, and number to bear on their exchange with suspects. Of direct relevance to an analysis of interrogation are the extensive literatures on attitudes and persuasion (Petty & Cacioppo, 1986), informational and normative influences (e.g., Asch, 1956; Sherif, 1936), the use of sequential request strategies, as in the foot-in-the door effect (Cialdini, 2001), and the gradual escalation of commands, issued by figures of authority, to effectively obtain self- and other-defeating acts of obedience (Burger, 2009; Milgram, 1974). Police interrogators are trained in the use of various social influence techniques (e.g., Inbau, Reid, Buckley, & Jayne, 2001), so the confessions they elicit can be scrutinized from a range of social psychological perspectives (e.g., see Bem, 1966; Davis & O'Donohue, 2003; Zimbardo, 1967).

Memory Alterations and Errors

A third set of core principles consists of the "sins of memory" that Schacter (2001) summarized from cognitive and neuroscience research— a list that includes memory transience, misattribution effects, suggestibility, and bias. In 1985, Kassin and Wrightsman noted that some false confessors, under intense interrogation, begin to question their own innocence and internalize a belief in their own guilt, sometimes confabulating false memories in the process. At the time, existing models of memory could not account for the phenomenon whereby innocent suspects would come to internalize responsibility for crimes they did not commit. These cases occur when a suspect is dispositionally or situationally rendered vulnerable to manipulation and the interrogator then misrepresents the evidence, a common ploy. This type of internalization bears close resemblance to well-documented suggestibility effects in children (Bruck & Ceci, 1999), the suggestibility effects produced within hypnosis (McConkey & Sheehan, 1995), the creation of false memories in laboratory subjects (Loftus, 2005), the "thought reform" methods of indoctrination in prisoners of war (Lifton, 1956; Schein, Schneier, & Barker, 1961), and the so-called recovery of repressed false trauma memories in psychotherapy patients (de Rivera, 1997). In addition, a source-monitoring perspective has been proposed to explain the conditions under which people can be induced to distort recollections and internalize guilt for a crime they did not commit by incorrectly attributing the origins of their externally induced beliefs to their presence at the crime scene (see Henkel & Coffman, 2004).

RESEARCH METHODS USED IN THE STUDY OF CONFESSIONS

Inspired by tales of false confessions that resulted in miscarriages of justice, empirical research has focused on three sets of questions: Why are innocent people often misidentified for interrogation? What factors put innocent suspects at risk to confess? and, How are confessions perceived by police, juries, judges, and others? This research has drawn on a wide range of methodologies—including case studies, self-report measures, observational studies, and laboratory experiments (Kassin, 2008).

The case study method has proved particularly informative, concerning the problem of false confessions in the real world. Over the years, researchers have reported on numerous accounts of proven false confessions, producing a vast literature of individual and aggregated case studies. As reported in books, newspapers, TV documentaries, and in analyses of actual case files, these stories reveal that false confessions occur with some unknown frequency, that they share certain common features, and that they seem more common in some types of people and under some conditions more than others (e.g., see Gudjonsson, 2003). For example, Drizin and Leo (2004) described the characteristics of 125 cases of proven false confession in the United States and found that 81% occurred in murder cases, 30% involved false confessions from multiple suspects, and 32% of false confessors were under 18 years old. Analyzing the contents of 33 false confessions from the Innocence Project files of DNA exonerations, Garrett (2010) found that 32 contained accurate details about the crime, the victim, and the setting that were not in the public domain.

Other research methods are also common. Naturalistic observations of live and recorded interrogations have been used to study the processes and outcomes of police interrogations in the United States (Leo, 1996) and in Great Britain (e.g., Moston, Stephenson, & Williamson, 1992). Self-report methods have also been used to examine correlations between various personal suspect characteristics—such as interrogative compliance, suggestibility, and mental illness—and the tendency to confess or resist confession (e.g., Gudjonsson, Sigurdsson, & Sigfusdottir, 2009; Redlich, Summers, & Hoover, 2010). Last but not least, experimental paradigms have been developed for causal hypothesis testing—to assess how accurately investigators make pre-interrogation judgments of truth and deception (Hartwig, Granhag, Strömwall, & Vrij, 2005; Kassin & Fong, 1999; Vrij, Mann, & Fisher, 2006; for reviews, see Chapter 2, this volume); to determine the effects of various interrogation tactics on the probability of confession (e.g., Kassin & Kiechel, 1996; Nash & Wade, 2009; Russano, Meissner, Narchet, & Kassin, 2005); and to assess the impact of confession evidence on juries (e.g., Kassin & Sukel, 1997; Lassiter, Geers, Handley, Weiland, & Munhall, 2002), judges (Lassiter, Diamond, Schmidt, & Elek, 2007; Wallace & Kassin, 2009), and eyewitnesses (Hasel & Kassin, 2009).

In conducting meaningful laboratory experiments, the challenge is threefold: to recreate in a realistic manner the elements of an interview or interrogation, to mimic the short-term and long-term decision-making consequences for mock suspects, and to achieve these goals in a manner that captures experimental realism without violating ethical standards of conduct concerning the treatment of human subjects. In the first laboratory paradigm developed in false confessions research, Kassin and Kiechel (1996) had participants engage in a typing task, accused them of causing the computer to crash by pressing a key they were specifically instructed to avoid, and asked them to sign a confession. All participants were innocent, and all initially denied the charge. In some sessions, a confederate (i.e., "an aide of the experimenter who poses as a participant"; American Psychological Association, 2007) told the experimenter that she witnessed the participant hit the forbidden key; in other sessions, she said she did not see what happened. This false evidence nearly doubled the number of students who signed a written confession, from 48% to 94%. Some of these students also went on to internalize the belief in their own guilt, and a subsample of this group confabulated memories of how it happened. This method of eliciting false confessions has since been used by several researchers (e.g., Horselenberg et al., 2006; Redlich & Goodman, 2003; Swanner, Beike, & Cole, 2010).

The computer crash paradigm has provided a reliable means of assessing the causes of false confessions. It is ecologically limited, however, by the fact that the behavior for which participants are induced to confess is an alleged accident, not a willful and deliberate action, and by the fact that all participants are innocent, making it impossible to compare true and false confession rates. To address these issues, Russano et al. (2005) developed a cheating paradigm in which they paired participants with a confederate for a problem-solving study. Violating the terms of the experiment, half were induced by the confederate to provide assistance on a problem that was supposed to be solved alone. The experimenter later "discovered" the similarity in their solutions, accused the participant of cheating, and tried to extract a signed confession. This study showed that two tactics—minimization and a promise of leniency— increased false confession rates more than true confession rates, thereby lowering the diagnosticity of interrogation outcomes. This paradigm has also been used in research on the effects of false evidence lies and bluffs on true and false confessions (Perillo & Kassin, in press).

RESEARCH ON FACTORS THAT INDUCE FALSE CONFESSIONS

Empirical research on confessions has focused on three aspects of confession evidence: (a) why innocent people are often misidentified for interrogation, (b) what dispositional and situational factors put innocent suspects at risk to confess, and (c) how accurate juries and others are at judging confession evidence.

Why Innocent People Are Misidentified for Interrogation

Typically, the confrontational and often coercive process of interrogation is preceded by an information-gathering interview conducted by police to determine whether a suspect is truthful or deceptive. Sometimes, that initial judgment is reasonably based on witnesses, informants, or other extrinsic evidence. Often, however, it is based on a personal impression, a hunch formed during the preinterrogation interview. Presenting the Reid technique, Inbau et al. (2001) thus advised police on how to use verbal cues, nonverbal cues, and behavioral attitudes to divine deception—they claimed, at exceedingly high levels of accuracy.

To help investigators determine whether their suspects are telling the truth or lying, Inbau et al. (2001) trained investigators in the use of the Behavior Analysis Interview, or BAI. Using this approach, investigators are advised to ask a series of special "behavior provoking questions" the responses to which are presumed to be indicative of guilt and innocence (e.g., "What do you think should happen to the person who took the money?") and then to observe changes in the suspect's verbal and nonverbal behavior (e.g., eye contact, pauses, posture, fidgeting) to determine whether he or she is telling the truth. For a person under suspicion, an investigator's judgment at this stage becomes a pivotal choice point, determining whether the suspect is interrogated or sent home.

On the basis of a single study, Inbau et al. (2001) claimed that training in the Reid technique produces a high 85% level of accuracy. Yet this claim is out of step with basic science. Research has consistently shown that people are only modestly accurate in judging truth and deception; that training produces little, if any, improvement compared with naive control groups; and that police investigators and other professionals perform only slightly better than laypeople, if at all (for reviews, see Chapter 2, this volume; Vrij, 2008).

In studies aimed at evaluating the Reid technique approach to lie detection, the results are not supportive of the claims made by Inbau et al. (2001). Assessing the diagnostic value of the behavior provoking questions, Vrij et al. (2006) had some subjects but not others commit a mock crime they were motivated to deny. All subjects were then interviewed using the BAI interview protocol. The results showed that responses to the behavior provoking questions were not significantly different between truth tellers and liars in the predicted manner (e.g., the liars were not more anxious or less helpful). There is also no evidence to support the idea that the particular verbal and nonverbal behavioral cues that investigators are trained to observe are actually indicative of deception. For example, Kassin and Fong (1999) randomly trained some college students but not others in the use of "behavioral symptoms" cited by the Reid technique. All students then watched videotaped interviews of mock suspects, some of whom committed one of four mock crimes (shoplifting, breaking and entering, vandalism, and computer break-in), others of whom did not. On questioning, all suspects denied their involvement. As in nonforensic laboratory experiments, observers did not reliably differentiate between the two groups of suspects. In fact, those who underwent training were significantly less accurate, more confident, and biased toward making false positive errors with regard to detecting deception. Using these same taped interviews, Meissner and Kassin (2002) tested experienced police detectives and found that they exhibited these same tendencies. Other research suggests that police tend to, with confidence, make prejudgments of guilt, which are frequently in error (e.g., Garrido, Masip, & Herrero, 2004).

Recent forensic research on deception detection has focused on two sets of issues. The first concerns whether certain individuals are uniquely gifted in their deception–detection skills. To be sure, the distribution of lie-detection accuracy scores suggests that some individuals are intuitively and consistently more accurate than others (Ekman, O'Sullivan, & Frank, 1999; O'Sullivan & Ekman, 2004). After testing thousands of people in different tasks, O'Sullivan and Ekman identified 15 "wizards" of lie detection who achieved at least an 80% level of accuracy in two of three tests. However, Bond and Uysal (2007) challenged both the poorly controlled procedures through which these scores were derived and the statistical significance of the wizards' performance given the number of people tested (for a rejoinder, see O'Sullivan, 2007). Clearly, more research is needed on this issue. Another important research direction concerns whether it is possible to improve deception-detection performance. In one program of research, Hartwig and colleagues (2005) found that interviewers make more accurate judgments by withholding crime details while questioning suspects, a strategy that traps guilty liars in inconsistencies when these facts are later disclosed. In a second approach to improving performance, Vrij and his colleagues (2008, 2009) have conducted a series of studies designed to "outsmart liars." Reasoning that lying requires more concentration and effort than telling the truth, they proposed that interviewers should tax a suspect's cognitive load and then attend to cues that betray effort. Hence, when interviewers had truth tellers and liars recount their stories in reverse chronological order, or when they asked more challenging and unanticipated questions, they became more accurate in their ability to distinguish between the truthful and deceptive accounts.

Dispositional and Situational Factors That Put Innocent People at Risk

Observational studies have shown that because police are legally prohibited from taking confessions through torture, violence, threats of harm or punishment, or promises of leniency, police interrogation tends to be psychologically oriented (e.g., Leo, 1996). In a survey that illustrates the point, 631 police investigators from the United States and Canada estimated that the tactics they most often use are to physically isolate the suspect from family and friends, typically in a small private room; identify contradictions in the suspect's denials; try to establish rapport to gain the suspect's trust; confront the suspect with incriminating evidence; and appeal to the suspect's self-interest (Kassin et al., 2007). In the annals of wrongful convictions, two themes are inherent in stories about false confessions: Some involve suspects who are weak, malleable, and uniquely vulnerable to manipulation; others involve psychologically coercive police interrogation tactics. On the basis of their review of the literature, Kassin and Gudjonsson (2004) thus concluded that both personal and situational risk factors may be sufficient, but neither is necessary, to increase the risk of a false confession.

Some Suspects Are Uniquely Vulnerable to Manipulation

Some suspects are dispositionally more vulnerable to influence than others and more likely to confess during the course of an interrogation (for a review of risk factors, see Chapter 1, this volume). Focusing on personality traits, Gudjonsson (2003) found that individuals who are prone to *compliance* in social situations are especially vulnerable because of their eagerness to please others and a desire to avoid confrontation, particularly with those in authority. Individuals who are prone to *suggestibility*—whose memories can be altered by misleading questions and negative feedback—are also more likely to confess under interrogation. Of even greater concern, Gudjonsson noted that people who are highly anxious, fearful, depressed, delusional, or otherwise psychologically disordered are often at a heightened risk to confess under pressure. Redlich (2007) found that offenders with mental illness self-reported a 22% lifetime false confession rate—notably higher than the 12% found in samples of prison inmates without mental illness (Sigurdsson & Gudjonsson, 1996; see also Redlich et al., 2010).

Juveniles are also more prone than adults to police-induced false confessions, which can be seen in the disproportionate number of juveniles who populate the list of false confessors. In a database of 125 proven false confessions, for example, Drizin and Leo (2004) found that 33% involved juveniles, most of whom had confessed to a murder. In addition, although an estimated 14% to 25% of all wrongful convictions historically have involved false confessions, 44% of exonerated juveniles are wrongly convicted because of false confessions—75% among the youngest juveniles, 12 to 15 years old (Gross et al., 2004). These statistics are supported by a substantial body of research. In an experiment that used the computer crash paradigm, for example, Redlich and Goodman (2003) accused participants of pressing the forbidden key and found that juveniles ages 12 and 13, and 15 and 16, were more likely to confess despite innocence than 18- to 26-year-old adults—especially when confronted with false evidence of their culpability. As to what makes juveniles vulnerable, Owen-Kostelnik, Reppucci, and Meyer (2006) reviewed numerous developmental studies that together indicate that adolescents are more compliant and suggestible than adults and that their decision making is characterized by an *immaturity of judgment*—a pattern of behavior that is impulsive, directed at immediate gratification, and lacking in future orientation and perceptions of risk. To the adolescent whose focus is on short-term outcomes, confession under stress produces a powerful form of immediate gratification—escape from an aversive situation.

People who are intellectually impaired are also highly susceptible to influence during an interrogation. Drizin and Leo (2004) reported that at least 22% of exonerees in their sample were mentally retarded as measured by standard IQ tests. This result is not surprising. Research shows that individuals with mental retardation have significant deficits in their understanding and appreciation of Miranda warnings (O'Connell, Garmoe, & Goldstein, 2005). They tend to exhibit an acquiescence response bias that leads them to say "yes" to a range of questions, even when such a response is absurd (Finlay & Lyons, 2002). They are also highly suggestible, as measured by the degree to which they are influenced by leading and misleading questions. People who are mentally retarded score higher than average on the Gudjonsson Suggestibility Scale (Gudjonsson, 2003), a commonly used test of interrogative suggestibility.

Some Interrogation Techniques Can Be Hazardous to Innocent Suspects

As a consequence of the two-step process by which police interview suspects to make a confident judgment of truth and deception, and then interrogate only those deemed to be lying, interrogation is by definition a guilt-presumptive process potentially confounded by a number of cognitive and behavioral confirmation biases (Kassin, Goldstein, & Savitsky, 2003). As recommended in popular training manuals (Inbau et al., 2001), and as observed in practice (e.g., Kassin et al., 2007; Leo, 1996), American police interrogation is a psychologically oriented multistep process that involves use of a number of specific techniques. Essentially, the process is reducible to three factors: (a) isolation, often in a special interrogation room, which is designed to increase a suspect's anxiety and incentive to escape; (b) positive confrontation, in which the suspect is accused of the crime, presented with evidence, real or manufactured, and blocked from denial; and (c) minimization, in which the crime is morally excused, justified, and normalized by a sympathetic interrogator, leading suspects to infer that confession is a possible means of gaining leniency (for reviews, see Kassin, 1997, 2005; Leo, 2008).

As noted earlier, a long history of basic research indicates that people are responsive to reinforcement, influenced more by immediate than delayed consequences, and highly vulnerable to influence from social impact agents in positions of authority. With regard to studies specifically aimed at testing the tactics of interrogation, research has implicated two tactics that can lead innocent people to confess. One pertains to the presentation of false evidence. Once suspects are isolated, interrogators confront them with bold and confident assertions of guilt, assertions that may be accompanied by outright lies about the evidence (e.g., pretending to have the suspect's fingerprints, a blood or hair sample, an eyewitness identification, or a failed polygraph). In the United States, this false evidence ploy, which is apparent in numerous false confession cases, is permissible by law (*Frazier v. Cupp*, 1969).

The persuasive impact of false evidence, even on innocent people, is not surprising. Crime suspects report that feeling trapped by the weight of evidence against them is the primary reason why they ultimately confess (e.g., Moston et al., 1992). In addition, classic psychological research across a range of nonforensic domains has shown that that misleading people about reality—using confederates, counterfeit test results, bogus norms, false autonomic feedback, misleading postevent information, and other manipulations— can substantially alter people's visual perceptions (Asch, 1956; Sherif, 1935), emotional states (Schachter & Singer, 1962), memories (Loftus, 2005), and even certain medical outcomes seen in studies of the placebo effect (Price, Finniss, & Benedetti, 2008). In the Kassin and Kiechel (1996) computer crash experiment described earlier, the presence of a false witness substantially increased the number of innocent participants who signed a confession; many of them internalized guilt for that outcome they did not produce. In follow-up studies, this effect persisted even when confession would result in financial penalty (e.g., Horselenberg et al., 2006). Within a wholly different paradigm, Nash and Wade (2009) used digital editing software to fabricate video evidence in a computerized gambling experiment of participants who were "stealing" money from the "bank" during a losing round. Confronted with this presentation, all participants confessed and most internalized the belief in their own guilt. In short, scientific evidence for the effects of false evidence on perceptions, thoughts, feelings, decision making, and behavior is broad and pervasive.

It is important to realize that the false evidence effect is not a mere laboratory phenomenon. Consider the 1989 case against 17-year-old Marty Tankleff, who was accused of murdering his parents despite the absence of evidence against him. Tankleff vehemently denied the charges for several hours until the lead detective told him that his hair was found within his mother's grasp and that his comatose father had regained consciousness and identified Marty as his assailant. Both of these allegations were untrue. Yet they caused him to become temporarily disoriented and to confess. Solely on the basis of that confession, which the detective handwrote and which Tankleff recanted moments later and did not sign, he was convicted. After 19 years in prison, his wrongful conviction was vacated and the charges were dismissed (Firstman & Salpeter, 2008).

A second commonplace interrogation tactic that has received research attention concerns the use of minimization. Once interrogators have driven a suspect to feel trapped by the weight of evidence, they proceed to minimize the crime through *theme development*, a process by which they provide moral justification and face-saving excuses, making a confession seem like an expedient means of escape. Using minimization, interrogators will suggest that the crime was spontaneous, accidental, provoked, pressured by peers, drug induced, hormone induced, or otherwise justified by circumstances.

It is important to realize that most courts over the years have rejected as involuntary confessions taken by promises of leniency on the ground that such promises can put innocent people at risk and compromise the reliability of the resulting confessions. But are promises of leniency implied by minimization, even if not explicitly stated? Drawing on cognitive research on the psychology of pragmatic implication (Chan & McDermott, 2006), Kassin and McNall (1991) had participants read a transcript of a murder interrogation. Three versions were produced in which the detective (a) made a conditional promise of leniency, (b) used the technique of minimization by blaming the victim, or (c) used neither technique. Participants read one version and estimated the sentence that they thought would be imposed on the suspect on confession. The result: Minimization lowered sentencing expectations—as if an explicit promise had been made.

To measure the behavioral effects of minimization, Russano et al. (2005) devised the cheating paradigm described earlier in which participants in a problem-solving study were paired with a confederate who in some sessions sought help on a problem that was supposed to be solved alone. A suspicious experimenter then separated the two, accused the participant of cheating, and tried to get the participant to sign an admission by promising leniency (research credit in exchange for a return session without penalty), making minimizing remarks ("I'm sure you didn't realize what a big deal it was"), using both tactics, or using no tactics. Overall, the confession rate was higher among guilty participants when leniency was promised and when minimization was used. It is important to note that the results showed that minimization by itself increased not only the desirable rate of true confessions (from 46% to 81%) but also the undesirable rate of false confessions as well (from 6% to 18%). In short, minimization serves as the implicit functional equivalent to a promise of leniency, increasing the possibility of a false confession.

The Many Impacts of Confession Evidence

Every tragic tale that involves a false confession-based wrongful conviction reveals a series of failures within the criminal justice system. This failure begins with the police, who often close investigations rather than pursue exculpatory evidence and other possible suspects (Leo & Ofshe, 1998) and extends to prosecutors, who often maintain their belief in a confessor's guilt even after DNA testing has indicated otherwise (Findley & Scott, 2006; see Chapter 14, this volume). To make matters worse, confessions are especially devastating in court. When a suspect retracts his or her confession, pleads not guilty, and goes to trial, a judge determines whether the confession was voluntary and hence admissible as evidence. A jury, hearing the admissible confession, then determines whether the defendant is guilty beyond a reasonable doubt. However, are people accurate judges of confessions? What effect does this evidence have on juries?

Research on the impact of confessions is not encouraging. Research has shown that confessions are seen as more incriminating than other potent forms of human evidence, such as eyewitness and character testimony (Kassin & Neumann, 1997). People cannot accurately distinguish between true and false confessions (Kassin, Meissner, & Norwick, 2005). Moreover, people inherently seem to trust confessions and do not fully discount such evidence even when it is logically and legally appropriate to do so. In one study, for example, mock jurors were heavily influenced by a defendant's confession even if it was indisputably induced by an explicit promise of leniency (Kassin & Wrightsman, 1980). In a second study, mock jurors were influenced by an indirect or "secondary confession" reported by an accomplice or jailhouse informant—even when told that this cooperating witness had an incentive to claim that the defendant had confessed (Neuschatz, Lawson, Swanner, Meissner, & Neuschatz, 2008; for a review, see Chapter 10, this volume).

In a mock jury experiment that well illustrates the power of confessions, Kassin and Sukel (1997) presented subjects with one of three versions of a murder trial transcript. In a low-pressure version, the defendant was said to have confessed to police immediately on questioning. In a high-pressure version, participants read that the suspect was in pain and interrogated intensely and aggressively before confessing. A control version contained no confession. Participants presented with the high-pressure confession judged the statement to be involuntary and said it did not influence their decisions. Yet with regard to verdicts, this same confession significantly increased the conviction rate. This increase occurred even among participants who were specifically admonished to disregard confessions they found to be coerced. This point concerning the power of confession evidence is bolstered by archival analyses of actual cases, which show that when proven false confessors pled not guilty and proceeded to trial, the jury typically votes for conviction— a finding that led Drizin and Leo (2004) to describe a confession as "inherently prejudicial and highly damaging to a defendant, even if it is the product of coercive interrogation, even if it is supported by no other evidence, and even if it is ultimately proven false beyond any reasonable doubt" (p. 959).

It is clear that confessions are powerful in part because they are trusted by juries as a matter of common sense. Indeed, most people reasonably believe that they would never confess to a crime they did not commit and have little understanding of the dispositional and situational factors that would lead someone to do so (Henkel, Coffman, & Dailey, 2008). The problem is exacerbated, however, by the fact that confessions can corrupt other evidence, further enhancing the illusion of factual guilt. Two studies illustrate the point. Dror and Charlton (2006; see also Chapter 12, this volume) presented five latent fingerprint experts with pairs of prints from a crime scene and suspect in an actual case in which they had previously made a match or exclusion judgment. The prints were accompanied either by no extraneous information, an instruction that the suspect had confessed (suggesting a match), or an instruction that the suspect was in custody at the time (suggesting an exclusion). The misinformation produced a change in 17% of the original, previously correct judgments. Hasel and Kassin (2009) staged a theft and obtained photo line-up identification decisions from mock eyewitnesses. One week later, individual witnesses were told that the person they had identified denied guilt, or that he confessed, or that another line-up member had confessed. As predicted, many witnesses went on to change their identification decisions most often selecting the confessor and doing so with confidence when given the opportunity to do so.

APPLICATIONS OF FALSE CONFESSION RESEARCH IN POLICY AND PRACTICE

In light of the many false confession cases that have surfaced in recent years, many researchers are wondering whether the highly confrontational approach to interrogation that is commonly used is flawed and whether it is possible to reform current practices without undermining effective police work. As a matter of policy and practice, two possible approaches to reform have been proposed (Kassin et al., 2010). The first and most important is to require the electronic recording of all suspect interviews and interrogations. In the United States, the proposal for taping can be traced to *Convicting the*

Innocent, Edwin Borchard's (1932) classic study of wrongful convictions. There are many possible advantages to a videotaping policy. To begin, the presence of a camera will serve to deter interrogators from using their most aggressive tactics—and deter frivolous defense claims of coercion where none existed. In addition, a videotaped record provides trial judges and juries with a full, objective, and accurate record of the process by which a statement was taken—a common source of dispute.

For many years, the law enforcement community opposed video recording on the basis of various assumptions (e.g., that suspects will refuse to talk on camera and that judges and juries will see the process as coercive). In recent years, however, practices have changed and opposition has softened. Without any legislative or judicial compulsion, police departments in many states now routinely record interviews and interrogations, at least in major felony investigations. Without exception, they have expressed favorable views of this practice. By interviewing law enforcement officials from hundreds of police and sheriff's departments that have recorded custodial interrogations, Sullivan (2004) found that police enthusiastically embraced the practice and reported the following collateral benefits: that recording (a) permits detectives to focus on the suspect rather than take copious notes, (b) provides an instant replay of the suspect's statement that sometimes reveals incriminating comments that were initially overlooked, (c) reduces the amount of time detectives spend in court defending their interrogation practices, and (d) increases public trust in law enforcement.

As more and more numbers of police departments record interrogations, researchers have sought to examine how juries are affected by these tapes. In a series of studies initiated by Lassiter and Irvine (1986), people have been shown mock interrogations from three different camera angles so that the suspect only, the interrogator only, or both were in frontal view. Consistently, those who were focused on the suspect judged the situation as less coercive than those focused on the interrogator or on both parties. By directing visual attention toward the accused, the camera thus leads jurors to underestimate the pressures brought to bear by the hidden detective. Additional studies have confirmed that people are more attuned to the situational factors that prompt confessions whenever the interrogator is on camera than when the focus is solely on the suspect. With both parties on camera, juries can make more informed attributions of voluntariness and guilt (Lassiter et al., 2002).

A second implication of the research literature on false confessions is that certain interrogation techniques, even if they are lawful, can lead innocent people to confess to crimes they did not commit. In a recent scientific review paper, Kassin et al. (2010) suggested two ways to approach questions of reform to the practice of interrogation. One is to completely reconceptualize the model at a macro level and propose that the "confrontational" approach of the Reid technique be replaced by the softer "investigative" approach used in Great Britain. Several years ago, after a number of high-profile false confessions, the British adopted a process of "investigative interviewing," the primary purpose of which is fact finding, not the elicitation of confession (for a description of this model, see Williamson, 2006). On the reasonable question of whether investigative interviewing is an effective replacement for confrontational interrogation, the research evidence is thus far encouraging. In Great Britain, naturalistic observation suggests that such investigative interviews enable police to inculpate offenders—and youthful suspects as well (Lamb, Orbach, Hershkowitz, Horowitz, & Abbot, 2007)—by obtaining useful, incriminating information from them about the crime (for reviews, see Bull & Soukara, 2010; Williamson, 2006).

A second approach to the question of reform is to address the specific risk factors within the confrontational framework for interrogation. On the basis of the research described in this chapter, it is clear that two lines of reform discussion are necessary. First, it is clear that certain types of suspects (i.e., juveniles and people who are cognitively impaired or psychologically disordered) need to be protected—perhaps through the mandatory presence of an attorney; perhaps as well through the use of law enforcement personnel specially trained to question high-risk individuals who are young and immature, mentally retarded, psychologically disordered, or in other ways vulnerable to manipulation. Second, certain interrogation tactics, although lawful, can be hazardous to the innocent suspect. From a convergence of sources, there is strong empirical support for the proposition that the false evidence ploy can get innocent people to confess by leading them to feel confused and trapped by the inevitability of evidence against them. Similarly, a good deal of research indicates that the promises implied by certain minimization themes can get innocent people to confess by leading them to perceive that the only way to lessen or escape punishment is to comply with the interrogator's demand for confession. In short, we believe that serious discussion is warranted by the data on the question of whether these particular interrogation tactics should somehow be limited or altogether banned (for additional discussion, see Kassin et al., 2010).

CONCLUSION

With mounting numbers of DNA exonerations putting a spotlight on the problem of false confessions, psychologists and other researchers have sought to understand the processes by which police interview suspects in an effort to distinguish truth tellers from liars, the dispositional and situational factors during interrogation that increase the tendency to confess, and the effects of confession evidence on juries and other decision-making individuals in the legal system. The review presented in this chapter is by no means comprehensive. Additional research has focused on the variability in language and practical utility of Miranda rights (Rogers, Harrison, Shuman, Sewell, & Hazelwood, 2007), on the ways in which juvenile suspects may remain unprotected in an interrogation despite the presence of a guardian (Oberlander & Goldstein, 2001), on the phenomenology of innocence and how it may put innocent persons at risk to waive their rights and confess (Kassin & Norwick, 2004), and on the ways in which perceptions of video-taped confessions are biased by camera perspective (Lassiter et al., 2002), to name a few.

Now that some of the problems with confession evidence have been identified, researchers are poised to propose possible improvements. Ideally, this next phase of discourse will bring together social scientists, law enforcement professionals, and policymakers in a collaborative effort to create more effective methods of interviewing and interrogating suspects and then presenting the process and their statements in court. Everyone agrees that the surgical objective is to produce outcomes that are diagnostic—namely, the conviction of offenders, not of innocents. Toward this end, we believe that the continued study of wrongful convictions, informed by core principles of psychology as well-focused laboratory and field experiments, and other means of research, are needed to establish causal connections, minimize error and bias, and increase the accuracy of outcomes.

REFERENCES

American Psychological Association. (2007). *APA dictionary of psychology*. Washington, DC: Author.

Asch, S. E. (1956). Studies of independence and conformity: A minority of one against a unanimous majority. *Psychological Monographs, 70*, 416.

Bem, D. J. (1966). Inducing belief in false confessions. *Journal of Personality and Social Psychology, 3*, 707–710. doi:10.1037/h0023226

Bickel, W. K., & Marsch, L. A. (2001). Toward a behavioral economic understanding of drug dependence: Delay discounting processes. *Addiction, 96*, 73–86. doi: 10.1046/j.1360-0443.2001.961736.x

Bond, C. F., & Uysal, A. (2007). On lie detection "wizards." *Law and Human Behavior, 31*, 109–115. doi:10.1007/s10979-006-9016-1

Borchard, E. M. (1932). *Convicting the innocent: Errors of criminal justice*. New Haven, CT: Yale University Press.

Brooks, P. (2000). *Troubling confessions: Speaking guilt in law and literature*. Chicago, IL: University of Chicago Press.

Bruck, M., & Ceci, S. J. (1999). The suggestibility of children's memory. *Annual Review of Psychology, 50,* 419–439. doi:10.1146/annurev.psych.50.1.419

Bull, R., & Soukara, S. (2010). Four studies of what really happens in police interviews. In G. D. Lassiter & C. A. Meissner (Eds.), *Police interrogations and false confessions: Current research, practice, and policy recommendations* (pp. 81–95). Washington, DC: American Psychological Association.

Burger, J. M. (2009). Replicating Milgram: Would people still obey today? *American Psychologist, 64,* 1–11. doi:10.1037/a0010932

Chan, J. C. K., & McDermott, K. B. (2006). Remembering pragmatic inferences. *Applied Cognitive Psychology, 20,* 633–639. doi:10.1002/acp.1215

Cialdini, R. B. (2001). *Influence: Science and practice* (4th ed.). Needham Heights, MA: Allyn & Bacon.

Davis, D., & O'Donohue, W. (2003). The road to perdition: "Extreme influence" tactics in the interrogation room. In W. O'Donohue, P. Laws, & C. Hollin (Eds.), *Handbook of forensic psychology* (pp. 897–996). New York, NY: Basic Books.

Deluty, M. Z. (1978). Self-control and impulsiveness involving aversive events. *Journal of Experimental Psychology. Animal Behavior Processes, 4,* 250–266. doi:10.1037/0097-7403.4.3.250

de Rivera, J. (1997). The construction of false memory syndrome: The experience of retractors. *Psychological Inquiry, 8,* 271–292. doi:10.1207/s15327965pli0804_1

Drizin, S. A., & Leo, R. A. (2004). The problem of false confessions in the post-DNA world. *North Carolina Law Review, 82,* 891–1007.

Dror, I. E., & Charlton, D. (2006). Why experts make errors. *Journal of Forensic Identification, 56,* 600–616.

Ekman, P., O'Sullivan, M., & Frank, M. G. (1999). A few can catch a liar. *Psychological Science, 10,* 263–266. doi:10.1111/1467-9280.00147

Findley, K. A., & Scott, M. S. (2006). The multiple dimensions of tunnel vision in criminal cases. *Wisconsin Law Review, 2006,* 291–397.

Finlay, W. M. L., & Lyons, E. (2002). Acquiescence in interviews with people who have mental retardation. *Mental Retardation, 40,* 14–29. doi:10.1352/0047-6765(2002)040<0014:AIIWPW>2.0.CO;2

Firstman, R., & Salpeter, J. (2008). *A criminal injustice: A true crime, a false confession, and the fight to free Marty Tankleff.* New York, NY: Ballantine Books.

Frazier v. Cupp, 394 U.S. 731 (1969).

Garrett, B. (2008). Judging innocence. *Columbia Law Review, 108,* 55–142.

Garrett, B. L. (2010). The substance of false confessions. *Stanford Law Review, 62,* in press. Currently available at SSRN: http://ssrn.com/abstract=1280254

Garrido, E., Masip, J., & Herrero, C. (2004). Police officers' credibility judgments: Accuracy and estimated ability. *International Journal of Psychology, 39,* 254–275. doi:10.1080/00207590344000411

Gross, S. R., Jacoby, K., Matheson, D. J., Montgomery, N., & Patel, S. (2004). Exonerations in the United States, 1989 through 2003. *The Journal of Criminal Law & Criminology, 95*, 523–553.

Gudjonsson, G. H. (2003). *The psychology of interrogations and confessions: A handbook.* Chicester, England: Wiley.

Gudjonsson, G. H., & MacKeith, J. A. C. (1982). False confessions: Psychological effects of interrogation. In A. Trankell (Ed.), *Reconstructing the past: The role of psychologists in criminal trials* (pp. 253–269). Deventer, the Netherlands: Kluwer.

Gudjonsson, G. H., Sigurdsson, J. F., & Sigfusdottir, I. D. (2009). Interrogation and false confessions among adolescents in seven European countries. What background and psychological variables best discriminate between false confessors and non-false confessors? *Psychology, Crime & Law, 15*, 711–728. doi:10.1080/10683160802516257

Hartwig, M., Granhag, P. A., Strömwall, L. A., & Vrij, A. (2005). Detecting deception via strategic disclosure of evidence. *Law and Human Behavior, 29*, 469–484. doi:10.1007/s10979-005-5521-x

Hasel, L. E., & Kassin, S. M. (2009). On the presumption of evidentiary independence: Can confessions corrupt eyewitness identifications? *Psychological Science, 20*, 122–126. doi:10.1111/j.1467-9280.2008.02262.x

Henkel, L. A., & Coffman, K. A. (2004). Memory distortions in coerced false confessions: A source monitoring framework analysis. *Applied Cognitive Psychology, 18*, 567–588. doi:10.1002/acp.1026

Henkel, L. A., Coffman, K. A. J., & Dailey, E. M. (2008). A survey of people's attitudes and beliefs about false confessions. *Behavioral Sciences & the Law, 26*, 555–584. doi:10.1002/bsl.826

Herrnstein, R. J. (1970). On the law of effect. *Journal of the Experimental Analysis of Behavior, 13*, 243–266. doi:10.1901/jeab.1970.13-243

Herrnstein, R. J., Rachlin, H., & Laibson, D. I. (Eds.). (1997). *The matching law: Papers in psychology and economics.* New York, NY: Russell Sage Foundation.

Horselenberg, R., Merckelbach, H., Smeets, T., Franssens, D., Ygram Peters, G.-J., & Zeles, G. (2006). False confessions in the lab: Do plausibility and consequences matter? *Psychology, Crime & Law, 12*, 61–75. doi:10.1080/1068310042000303076

Inbau, F. E., Reid, J. E., Buckley, J. P., & Jayne, B. C. (2001). *Criminal interrogation and confessions* (4th ed.). Gaithersburg, MD: Aspen.

Kassin, S. M. (1997). The psychology of confession evidence. *American Psychologist, 52*, 221–233. doi:10.1037/0003-066X.52.3.221

Kassin, S. M. (2005). On the psychology of confessions: Does innocence put innocents at risk? *American Psychologist, 60*, 215–228. doi:10.1037/0003-066X.60.3.215

Kassin, S. M. (2007). Expert testimony on the psychology of confessions: A pyramidal model of the relevant science. In E. Borgida & S. T. Fiske (Eds.), *Psychological science in court: Beyond common knowledge* (pp. 185–218). Oxford, England: Blackwell.

Kassin, S. M. (2008). The psychology of confessions. *Annual Review of Law and Social Science, 4*, 193–217. doi:10.1146/annurev.lawsocsci.4.110707.172410

Kassin, S. M., Drizin, S. A., Grisso, T., Gudjonsson, G. H., Leo, R. A., & Redlich, A. D. (2010). Police-induced confessions: Risk factors and recommendations. *Law and Human Behavior, 34*, 49–52. doi:10.1007/s10979-010-9217-5

Kassin, S. M., & Fong, C. T. (1999). "I'm innocent!": Effects of training on judgments of truth and deception in the interrogation room. *Law and Human Behavior, 23*, 499–516. doi:10.1023/A:1022330011811

Kassin, S. M., Goldstein, C. J., & Savitsky, K. (2003). Behavioral confirmation in the interrogation room: On the dangers of presuming guilt. *Law and Human Behavior, 27*, 187–203. doi:10.1023/A:1022599230598

Kassin, S. M., & Gudjonsson, G. H. (2004). The psychology of confession evidence: A review of the literature and issues. *Psychological Science in the Public Interest, 5*, 33–67. doi:10.1111/j.1529-1006.2004.00016.x

Kassin, S. M., & Kiechel, K. L. (1996). The social psychology of false confessions: Compliance, internalization, and confabulation. *Psychological Science, 7*, 125–128. doi:10.1111/j.1467-9280.1996.tb00344.x

Kassin, S. M., Leo, R. A., Meissner, C. A., Richman, K. D., Colwell, L. H., Leach, A., & La Fon, D. (2007). Police interviewing and interrogation: A self-report survey of police practices and beliefs. *Law and Human Behavior, 31*, 381–400. doi:10.1007/s10979-006-9073-5

Kassin, S. M., & McNall, K. (1991). Police interrogations and confessions: Communicating promises and threats by pragmatic implication. *Law and Human Behavior, 15*, 233–251. doi:10.1007/BF01061711

Kassin, S. M., Meissner, C. A., & Norwick, R. J. (2005). "I'd know a false confession if I saw one": A comparative study of college students and police investigators. *Law and Human Behavior, 29*, 211–227. doi:10.1007/s10979-005-2416-9

Kassin, S. M., & Neumann, K. (1997). On the power of confession evidence: An experimental test of the "fundamental difference" hypothesis. *Law and Human Behavior, 21*, 469–484. doi:10.1023/A:1024871622490

Kassin, S. M., & Norwick, R. J. (2004). Why suspects waive their Miranda rights: The power of innocence. *Law and Human Behavior, 28*, 211–221. doi:10.1023/B:LAHU.0000022323.74584.f5

Kassin, S. M., & Sukel, H. (1997). Coerced confessions and the jury: An experimental test of the "harmless error" rule. *Law and Human Behavior, 21*, 27–46. doi:10.1023/A:1024814009769

Kassin, S. M., & Wrightsman, L. S. (1980). Prior confessions and mock juror verdicts. *Journal of Applied Social Psychology, 10*, 133–146. doi:10.1111/j.1559-1816.1980.tb00698.x

Kassin, S. M., & Wrightsman, L. S. (1985). Confession evidence. In S. Kassin & L. Wrightsman (Eds.), *The psychology of evidence and trial procedure* (pp. 67–94). Beverly Hills, CA: Sage.

Lamb, M. E., Orbach, Y., Hershkowitz, I., Horowitz, D., & Abbott, C. B. (2007). Does the type of prompt affect the accuracy of information provided by alleged victims of abuse in forensic interviews? *Applied Cognitive Psychology, 21*, 1117–1130. doi:10.1002/acp.1318

Lassiter, G. D., Diamond, S. S., Schmidt, H. C., & Elek, J. K. (2007). Evaluating videotaped confessions: Expertise provides no defense against the camera-perspective effect. *Psychological Science, 18*, 224–226. doi:10.1111/j.1467-9280.2007.01879.x

Lassiter, G. D., Geers, A. L., Handley, I. M., Weiland, P. E., & Munhall, P. J. (2002). Videotaped confessions and interrogations: A change in camera perspective alters verdicts in simulated trials. *Journal of Applied Psychology, 87*, 867–874. doi:10.1037/0021-9010.87.5.867

Lassiter, G. D., & Irvine, A. A. (1986). Videotaped confessions: The impact of camera point of view on judgments of coercion. *Journal of Applied Social Psychology, 16*, 268–276. doi:10.1111/j.1559-1816.1986.tb01139.x

Latané, B. (1981). The psychology of social impact. *American Psychologist, 36*, 343–356. doi:10.1037/0003-066X.36.4.343

Leo, R. A. (1996). Inside the interrogation room. *The Journal of Criminal Law & Criminology, 86*, 266–303. doi:10.2307/1144028

Leo, R. A. (2005). Re-thinking the study of miscarriages of justice: Developing a criminology of wrongful conviction. *Journal of Contemporary Criminal Justice, 21*, 201–223. doi:10.1177/1043986205277477

Leo, R. A. (2008). *Police interrogation and American justice.* Cambridge, MA: Harvard University Press.

Leo, R. A., & Ofshe, R. J. (1998). The consequences of false confessions: Deprivations of liberty and miscarriages of justice in the age of psychological interrogation. *The Journal of Criminal Law & Criminology, 88*, 429–496. doi:10.2307/1144288

Lifton, R. J. (1956). Thought reform of western civilizations in Chinese communist prisons. *Psychiatry, 19*, 173–195.

Loftus, E. F. (2005). Planting misinformation in the human mind: A 30-year investigation of the malleability of memory. *Learning & Memory, 12*, 361–366. doi:10.1101/lm.94705

McConkey, K. M., & Sheehan, P. W. (1995). *Hypnosis, memory, and behavior in criminal investigation.* New York, NY: Guilford Press.

McCormick, C. T. (1972). *Handbook of the law of evidence* (2nd ed.). St. Paul, MN: West.

Meissner, C. A., & Kassin, S. M. (2002). "He's guilty!": Investigator bias in judgments of truth and deception. *Law and Human Behavior, 26*, 469–480. doi:10.1023/A:1020278620751

Milgram, S. (1974). *Obedience to authority: An experimental view.* New York, NY: Harper & Row.

Moston, S., Stephenson, G. M., & Williamson, T. M. (1992). The effects of case characteristics on suspect behaviour during questioning. *The British Journal of Criminology, 32*, 23–40.

Munsterberg, H. (1908). *On the witness stand.* Garden City, NY: Doubleday.

Nash, R. A., & Wade, K. A. (2009). Innocent but proven guilty: Using false video evidence to elicit false confessions and create false beliefs. *Applied Cognitive Psychology, 23*, 624–637. doi:10.1002/acp.1500

Neuschatz, J. S., Lawson, D. S., Swanner, J. K., Meissner, C. A., & Neuschatz, J. S. (2008). The effects of accomplice witnesses and jailhouse informants on jury decision making. *Law and Human Behavior, 32*, 137–149. doi:10.1007/s10979-007-9100-1

New York v. Kharey Wise, Kevin Richardson, Antron McCray, Yusef Salaam, & Raymond Santana: Affirmation in response to motion to vacate judgment of conviction (2002). Indictment No. 4762/89, December 5, 2002.

Oberlander, L. B., & Goldstein, N. E. (2001). A review and update on the practice of evaluating Miranda comprehension. *Behavioral Sciences & the Law, 19*, 453–471. doi:10.1002/bsl.453

O'Connell, M. J., Garmoe, W., & Goldstein, N. E. S. (2005). Miranda comprehension in adults with mental retardation and the effects of feedback style on suggestibility. *Law and Human Behavior, 29*, 359–369. doi:10.1007/s10979-005-2965-y

O'Sullivan, M. (2007). Unicorns or Tiger Woods: Are lie detection experts myths or rarities? A response to on lie detection "wizards" by Bond and Uysal. *Law and Human Behavior, 31*, 117–123. doi:10.1007/s10979-006-9058-4

O'Sullivan, M., & Ekman, P. (2004). The wizards of deception detection. In P. A. Granhag & L. A. Stromwall (Eds.), *Deception detection in forensic contexts* (pp. 269–286). Cambridge, England: Cambridge University Press.

Owen-Kostelnik, J., Reppucci, N. D., & Meyer, J. R. (2006). Testimony and interrogation of minors: Assumptions about maturity and morality. *American Psychologist, 61*, 286–304. doi:10.1037/0003-066X.61.4.286

Perillo, J. T., & Kassin, S. M. (in press). Inside interrogation: The lie, the bluff, and false confessions. *Law and Human Behavior.*

Petty, R. E., & Cacioppo, J. T. (1986). *Communication and persuasion: Central and peripheral routes to attitude change.* New York, NY: Springer.

Price, D. D., Finniss, D. G., & Benedetti, F. (2008). A comprehensive review of the placebo effect: Recent advances and current thought. *Annual Review of Psychology, 59*, 565–590. doi:10.1146/annurev.psych.59.113006.095941

Rachlin, H. (2000). *The science of self-control.* Cambridge, MA: Harvard University Press.

Redlich, A. D. (2007). Double jeopardy in the interrogation room: Young age and mental illness. *American Psychologist, 62*, 609–611. doi:10.1037/0003-066X62.6.609

Redlich, A. D., & Goodman, G. S. (2003). Taking responsibility for an act not committed: Influence of age and suggestibility. *Law and Human Behavior, 27,* 141–156. doi:10.1023/A:1022543012851

Redlich, A. D., Summers, A., & Hoover, S. (2010). Self-reported false confessions and false guilty pleas among offenders with mental illness. *Law and Human Behavior, 34,* 79–90. doi:10.1007/s10979-009-9194-8

Rogers, R., Harrison, K., Shuman, D., Sewell, K., & Hazelwood, L. (2007). An analysis of Miranda warnings and waivers: Comprehension and coverage. *Law and Human Behavior, 31,* 177–192. doi:10.1007/s10979-006-9054-8

Russano, M. B., Meissner, C. A., Narchet, F. M., & Kassin, S. M. (2005). Investigating true and false confessions within a novel experimental paradigm. *Psychological Science, 16,* 481–486. doi:10.1111/j.0956-7976.2005.01560.x

Saulny, S. (2002, December 8). Why confess to what you didn't do? *The New York Times,* Section 4. Retrieved from http://www.nytimes.com/2002/12/08/week inreview/ideas-trends-why-confess-to-what-you-didn-t-do.html

Schachter, S., & Singer, J. (1962). Cognitive, social, and physiological determinants of emotional state. *Psychological Review, 69,* 379–399. doi:10.1037/h0046234

Schacter, D. L. (2001). *The seven sins of memory: How the mind forgets and remembers.* Boston, MA: Houghton Mifflin.

Schein, E., Schneier, I., & Barker, C. H. (1961). *Coercive pressure.* New York, NY: Norton.

Sherif, M. (1935). A study of some social factors in perception. *Archives of Psychology, 187,* 60.

Sherif, M. (1936). *The psychology of social norms.* New York, NY: Harper.

Sigurdsson, J. F., & Gudjonsson, G. H. (1996). The psychological characteristics of "false confessors": A study among Icelandic prison inmates and juvenile offenders. *Personality and Individual Differences, 20,* 321–329. doi:10.1016/0191-8869 (95)00184-0

Skinner, B. F. (1938). *The behavior of organisms.* New York, NY: Appleton-Century-Crofts.

Sullivan, T. P. (2004). *Police experiences with recording custodial interrogations.* Chicago, IL: Northwestern University Law School, Center on Wrongful Convictions.

Swanner, J. K., Beike, D. R., & Cole, A. T. (2010). Snitching, lies, and computer crashes: An experimental investigation of secondary confessions. *Law and Human Behavior, 34,* 53–65. doi:10.1007/s10979-008-9173-5

Thorndike, E. L. (1911). *Animal intelligence: Experimental studies.* New York, NY: MacMillan.

Vrij, A. (2008). *Detecting lies and deceit: Pitfalls and opportunities.* Chichester, England: Wiley.

Vrij, A., Leal, S., Granhag, P. A., Mann, S., Fisher, R. P., Hillman, J., & Sperry, K. (2009). Outsmarting the liars: The benefit of asking unanticipated questions. *Law and Human Behavior, 33,* 159–166. doi:10.1007/s10979-008-9143-y

Vrij, A., Mann, S., & Fisher, R. P. (2006). An empirical test of the Behaviour Analysis Interview. *Law and Human Behavior, 30,* 329–345. doi:10.1007/s10979-006-9014-3

Vrij, A., Mann, S., Fisher, R. P., Leal, S., Milne, R., & Bull, R. (2008). Increasing cognitive load to facilitate lie detection: The benefit of recalling an event in reverse order. *Law and Human Behavior, 32,* 253–265. doi:10.1007/s10979-007-9103-y

Wallace, B. D., & Kassin, S. M. (2009, March). Harmless error analysis: Judges' performance with confession errors. Paper presented at the American Psychology-Law Society, San Antonio, TX.

Williamson, T. (Ed.). (2006). *Investigative interviewing: Rights, research, regulation.* Devon, England: Willan.

Zimbardo, P. G. (1967). The psychology of police confessions. *Psychology Today, 1,* 17–20, 25–27.

4

PROCEDURAL JUSTICE EVALUATIONS IN INTERROGATIONS

DIANE SIVASUBRAMANIAM AND LARRY HEUER

Data from the Innocence Project have shown that in 25% of cases in which people have been wrongfully convicted, those innocent people had confessed to the crime of which they were accused. Much research has centered on this finding, investigating the factors that would lead innocent suspects to confess to these very serious crimes. A large body of research has focused on the interrogation procedures used by police officers and the way that particular interrogation techniques can increase the risk that innocent suspects will falsely confess to crimes. Studies have demonstrated that particular methods used in the Reid technique (Inbau, Reid, Buckley, & Jayne, 2001) can increase the risk that innocent suspects will make confessions during police interrogations (Kassin & Fong, 1999; Kassin, Goldstein, & Savitsky, 2003), thereby placing these innocent suspects at risk of wrongful conviction. The Reid technique outlines two primary stages of interrogation: (a) the preinterrogation interview and (b) the interrogation.

The work described in this chapter was funded by the National Science Foundation Grant SES-0550495.

THE REID TECHNIQUE: THE PREINTERROGATION
INTERVIEW PHASE

The preinterrogation interview is a process through which interrogators determine whether a suspect is being truthful or deceptive. As outlined in Chapter 3 of this volume, there are a number of reasons to be skeptical of interrogators' ability to accurately sort the guilty from the innocent during the preinterrogation interview. Research has shown that people trained in deception detection according to the Reid technique are more confident but less accurate in their judgments of the target's guilt (Kassin & Fong, 1999), and police officers are more likely than naïve students to display what Meissner and Kassin (2002) referred to as *investigator response bias*, an exaggerated tendency to judge the target as deceptive. As routinely practiced, the pre-interrogation interview phase of the Reid technique puts suspects in danger of being judged deceptive by interrogators who are low on lie-detection accuracy, high in confidence, and biased toward judging innocent targets as deceptive.

THE REID TECHNIQUE: THE INTERROGATION PHASE

Those suspects judged by interrogators to be deceptive, or guilty of the crime of which they are accused, are moved on to the interrogation stage. Thus, the Reid technique is guilt presumptive; the interrogator has already confidently determined during the preinterrogation interview that the suspect is guilty. The interrogation phase provides further potential for wrongful conviction, through the use of particular confrontational interrogation tactics. During the interrogation phase, the interrogator attempts to elicit a confession from the suspect using a nine-step procedure (Inbau et al., 2001), which Kassin and Gudjonsson (2006) characterized as tapping three primary methods of psychological influence: isolation, confrontation, and minimization (for a detailed description of these interrogation procedures and how they may lead to false confessions, refer to Chapter 3, this volume). Converging findings from an extensive body of laboratory and field studies (for a review, see Kassin & Gudjonsson, 2006) as well as an ample and growing record of overturned convictions (http://www.innocenceproject.org/) paint a discouraging picture regarding the prospect for miscarriages of justice to result from these coercive and hostile procedures. Accordingly, many psychology and law researchers have challenged the propriety of these interrogation techniques and have called for reform of interrogation procedures. Despite this, interrogators continue to use and endorse the Reid technique and other coercive interrogation practices.

THE DECISION MAKERS' PERSPECTIVE

With evidence amassing that coercive interrogation procedures place the innocent at risk of wrongful conviction, we must ask why interrogators continue to use these procedures. There is a need to examine the design and use of interrogation procedures from the perspective of the interrogators. What motivates interrogators to use coercive interrogation procedures that involve hostility and deception when dealing with suspects in a criminal investigation, despite the documented risk that such procedures present of wrongful conviction of the innocent?

Central to this question is the principle that the Reid technique interrogator begins the interrogation phase with a certainty that the suspect in the interrogation room is not innocent—that the suspect is guilty and the interrogator's task is to elicit a confession and ultimately a conviction. In this chapter, we argue that this belief in the suspect's guilt fundamentally influences the procedures that interrogators will use and endorse for dealing with the suspect. We consider three possible ways in which this belief in the suspect's guilt might influence the interrogator's view of the interrogation procedure:

1. Interrogators believe that the suspect is not deserving of respectful treatment and the interrogation itself functions as part of the punishment of the offender, who may have yet to stand trial but whom the interrogator has determined (with high confidence) to be guilty.
2. Interrogators are less concerned with treating a suspect respectfully than they are with obtaining the correct outcome—the outcome in which the suspect in their custody, whom they have determined to be guilty, is convicted of the crime.
3. Interrogators differ from others (suspects, observers) in the way that they evaluate the fairness of an interrogation procedure and its methods. Interrogators judge the coercive interrogation procedure to be fair and expect that it will lead to a fair outcome.

In this chapter, we examine the interrogator's perspective on the fairness of police interrogation procedures and present evidence that suggests that all three of the mechanisms just noted contribute to the use and endorsement of coercive interrogation procedures by legal authorities. We begin by reviewing previous literature on procedural justice evaluations, outlining the variety of methodologies and contexts in which these effects have been demonstrated. We then outline more recent evidence indicating that the meaning and importance of procedural justice may be moderated by one's perspective when rendering a justice judgment. In particular, we focus on recent research suggesting that the factors that influence procedural justice and satisfaction judgments are quite different depending on whether one is issuing the justice judgment from the perspective of an authority or the subordinate in legal (and other) procedures. We review recent studies that begin to investigate why this discrepancy between decision makers and non–decision makers may occur, and then we go on to discuss the implications of this discrepancy for our understanding of the use of coercive interrogation procedures by interrogators. Finally, we identify some directions for future investigation, with an eye toward generating a better understanding of interrogators' continued use and endorsement of coercive interrogation procedures, despite the risk that they present to innocent suspects.

SCIENTIFIC FOUNDATIONS OF PROCEDURAL JUSTICE RESEARCH

Procedural justice refers to judgments that people make about the fairness of treatment experienced during a decision-making procedure, and *distributive justice* (or *outcome fairness*) refers to the fairness of the outcomes derived from those decision-making procedures (Tyler, Degoey, & Smith, 1996). There is a large body of literature that examines the way in which people make these decisions about the fairness of the treatment they experience and the outcomes that they receive, with many studies investigating the way that particular features of legal decision-making procedures affect people's procedural and distributive justice judgments.

The first systematic research that applied this body of work to the legal system was conducted by Thibaut and Walker (1975, 1978). Their findings suggested that, in legal disputes, people's satisfaction with the resolution of their conflicts is strongly influenced by the treatment they receive from authorities (e.g., judges), as well as the outcomes they receive from those authorities. Thibaut and Walker also distinguished between two types of control that are available to disputants in decision-making procedures: *process control* and *decision control* (Houlden, LaTour, Walker, & Thibaut, 1978; Thibaut & Walker, 1975, 1978). Process control refers to the level of control that disputants have over aspects of the procedure used to make a decision. It encompasses the amount of input disputants have into the procedure and the degree to which they are able to control, for example, the presentation of evidence. Process control is often referred to as *voice* (Folger, 1977). Decision control refers to the degree to which disputants are able to control the outcome of the decision-making procedure. For example, in the adversarial justice system, disputants are allowed process control (they are able to present evidence in support of their case and have input into the procedure itself), but they do not have decision control. In the traditional, adversarial court procedure, an independent third party (e.g., judge, jury) makes the final decision about the outcome of the case. So, in an adversarial court procedure, disputants retain process control, but they have relinquished decision control to a third party.

Thibaut and Walker (1975, 1978) and Houlden et al. (1978) proposed that people's beliefs about procedural justice are influenced by the distribution of process control and decision control in a conflict resolution procedure. In cases of intractable conflict, where disputants are unable to resolve a dispute themselves, they turn to a third party (e.g., decision makers in the legal system) to assist them in the resolution of the dispute, often asking this third party to administer a binding decision. In other words, these disputants in intractable conflict are willing to relinquish decision control. However, even when disputants are willing to relinquish decision control, they still value process control or voice. Disputants judge legal decision-making procedures and their outcomes to be fairer when they are allowed voice (or input or process control) in a procedure than when they are not permitted to have voice in a procedure (Houlden et al., 1978; Thibaut & Walker, 1975, 1978). Thus, Thibaut and Walker's early findings are significant because they demonstrate that in legal disputes (a) disputants' judgments about procedural justice are not influenced solely by outcomes but also by voice or process control, and (b) voice increases disputants' satisfaction with the outcomes that they receive from those decision-making procedures. This finding, that voice increases satisfaction with outcomes, has come to be known as the *fair process effect* and has been replicated across a number of studies in a variety of contexts (Greenberg & Folger, 1983).

Thibaut and Walker (1975) advocated an instrumental interpretation for these findings, arguing that ultimately voice was important to disputants because they believed that it would increase their chances of obtaining fair outcomes. They argued that in situations in which disputants had relinquished decision control to a third party, voice was seen as a mechanism by which a decision maker could be influenced to deliver a fair outcome. However, some later findings did not fit well with this instrumental interpretation. Lind, Kanfer, and Earley (1990) demonstrated that people value voice even when there is no possibility that it can lead to improved outcomes. Their study manipulated voice on three levels: (a) no voice—in this condition, participants were not allowed to express an opinion about the workload involved in a task that they would have to complete; (b) predecision voice—in this condition, participants were permitted to express an opinion about their workload and then the experimenter delivered a workload decision to the participant; and (c) postdecision voice—in this condition, participants were told that the workload decision had already been made, but they were still invited to express an opinion about the workload requirement. Findings from this study showed that participants judged procedural justice to be highest in the condition in which they were allowed predecision voice but that participants considered the decision-making procedure to be fairer in the postdecision voice condition than they did in the no-voice condition. In other words, even when participants knew that their voice could not influence the experimenter's decision, they still valued voice and judged the decision-making procedure to be fairer when they were invited to express their voice than when they were not invited to do so. These findings did not fit well with Thibaut and Walker's (1975) instrumental interpretation of the importance of voice because these data suggested that voice is important for noninstrumental reasons: People value voice independently of its ability to shape outcomes.

Findings like those of Lind et al. (1990) led to the formulation of the group value model of procedural justice (Lind & Tyler, 1988; Tyler, 1989; Tyler & Lind, 1992), which outlines a relational, rather than instrumental, explanation for the importance of voice in justice reasoning. The group value model emphasizes people's concern with their social relationships. On the basis of social identity theory (Tajfel, 1982; Tajfel & Turner, 1986), the group value model posits that people are motivated to discern whether they are valued members of the social groups that are important to them. When we interact with those social groups and the authorities that represent them, we look for signs to indicate to us that the social group values us. Voice (or process control) is one such sign. If authorities are asking for our input, this is a signal that we are held in high regard by our social group.

These authors also suggested that voice is one of a few variables that are central in shaping procedural justice judgments. Trustworthy authorities, neutral procedures, and respectful treatment are also variables that communicate favorable standing in a social group and therefore serve to enhance judgments of procedural justice. These three variables (trust, neutrality, respect) are commonly referred to as the *relational variables* (Tyler & Lind, 1992). Therefore, if an authority in a procedure is trustworthy (appearing to have our best interests in mind: trust), if the procedure itself is neutral (allowing for all of the relevant evidence to be presented: neutrality), if our rights are generally respected in the procedure (respect), and if we are invited to express our opinion and version of events during the procedure (voice), these aspects of the procedure convey to us that we are valued and respected by the social group. According to the group value model, when procedures convey to us that we are valued members of the social group and that we are held in high regard by that group, we judge those procedures to be fair.

It is important to note that the central claim of the group value model is that we do not judge procedures to be fair because they carry the promise of instrumentality, and we do not value voice because it enhances the possibility of instrumentality. Rather, we judge procedures to be fair when they convey to us that we are socially valued, and we value voice because it is an indication to us that we are held in high regard by the social group. The group value model is a very influential theory, with much of the justice literature shaped around it and an extensive body of research that provides strong support for the group value model's central claims (De Cremer & Blader, 2006; Tyler & Lind, 1992).

SCIENTIFIC METHODS IN PROCEDURAL JUSTICE RESEARCH

From its earliest roots in equity theory and distributive justice research, scholars of the psychology of justice have used laboratory experiments, manipulating particular independent variables to test their effects on people's justice-related behavior and their procedural and distributive justice judgments. The procedures used in these experiments have varied and have included asking children to think about justice problems or asking participants to imagine themselves in fictitious legal disputes. Although some vignette studies examined these questions in legal contexts (Austin, Walster, & Utne, 1976; Utne, 1974), many other studies posed psychologically equivalent justice problems across a range of nonlegal settings, establishing the generalizability of these effects across contexts (e.g., Walster, Berscheid, & Walster, 1976). Thibaut and Walker's (1975, 1978) research program, which demonstrated the importance of process control, was largely experimental, as were the studies by Lind et al. (1990) that subsequently demonstrated that the importance of process control was not because of its instrumental value.

However, since these early studies were conducted, the field of procedural justice research has expanded to incorporate a variety of methodologies that test its central research questions, and the procedural justice literature is notable for the breadth of methodologies encompassed within the field. Laboratory experiments are ongoing, using deception as well as asking participants to read fictitious vignettes and imagine themselves in particular scenarios. However, field surveys are also regularly used, with cross-sectional data that demonstrates that procedural justice affects legitimacy and compliance (Tyler, 1989, 1990; Tyler & Huo, 2002) in real citizen encounters with police as well as in laboratory experiments. Concerns about causal direction in these cross-sectional field studies are alleviated in two ways. First, the causal statements made by researchers in these studies are well supported by laboratory experiments that manipulated these independent variables to demonstrate causality. Second, panel data show that fair procedures (incorporating the relational variables of trust, neutrality, and respect) at one time point increase perceptions of legitimacy and self-reported compliance among citizens at a later time point and that fair procedures are a better predictor of later legitimacy and compliance than are concerns with economic benefit (Murphy, 2005).

Quasi-experiments in field settings are also regularly used, as are true experiments in field settings. Many of these field experiments convincingly demonstrate the generalizability of findings from laboratory studies to real-life regulatory settings. For example, Wenzel (2006) tested procedural justice effects among 2,000 Australian taxpayers who were late to file a tax declaration. These taxpayers were randomly assigned to read one of three kinds of reminder letters: (a) a control letter; (b) an informational letter, including information about the reason for the letter and the penalties for late payment; or (c) an interpersonal letter, which indicated a concern for the taxpayer's welfare and trust in their honesty. In addition, Wenzel (2006) found that the interpersonal letter increased compliance with tax regulations significantly more than either the informational or control letters.

A number of studies have demonstrated that perceived procedural justice has positive effects on satisfaction with legal procedures and legal authorities, compliance with the law, and cooperation with legal institutions. Aside from these legal contexts (e.g., Tyler, 1990; Tyler & Huo, 2002), procedural justice research has been conducted in organizational (e.g., Cohen-Charash & Spector, 2001), educational (Tyler & Caine, 1981), political (Leung, Tong, & Lind, 2007), medical (Poythress, Schumacher, Wiener, & Murrin, 1993), family (Brubacher, Fondacaro, Brank, Brown, & Miller, 2009), and interpersonal (Davis-Lipman, Tyler, & Andersen, 2007) contexts, using a variety of populations. The procedural features that are manipulated as independent variables in these studies (or monitored in nonexperimental field studies) include voice (van Prooijen, van den Bos, & Wilke, 2002), respect (Heuer, Blumenthal, Douglas, & Weinblatt, 1999), neutrality (Heuer, Penrod, Hafer, & Cohn, 2002), and accuracy (De Cremer, 2004), and when procedural justice is measured as a dependent variable it is variously conceptualized as general fair process (e.g., judgments about whether one was treated fairly in a procedure; Heuer et al., 2002), or specific features of process criteria (e.g., objectivity, impartiality, and trust in the authority figure; van Prooijen et al., 2002). Other dependent variables, themselves important consequences of procedural justice, that are often measured in the procedural justice literature are satisfaction with procedures (Heuer et al., 2002), positive behaviors such as good organizational citizenship (van Prooijen et al., 2008), compliance with laws and regulations (Sunshine & Tyler, 2003), and negative behaviors such as stealing (Colquitt & Greenberg, 2003). Despite the large diversity in the variables included and range of questions addressed in procedural justice research, the findings in regard to the importance of treatment and process concerns in justice and satisfaction judgments, and their consequences, have been remarkably consistent. These numerous findings across methodologies, contexts, participants, independent variables, and dependent measures, strengthen the claim of procedural justice research to external validity beyond the laboratory context in which it originated.

The Emergence of Moderators of Justice Effects

A more nuanced understanding of justice reasoning is emerging as moderators of these effects are discovered. Meta-analyses of procedural justice research provide quantitative analyses of effects across a large number of procedural justice studies (e.g., Cohen-Charash & Spector, 2001, 2002; Skitka, Winquist, & Hutchinson, 2003). These meta-analyses have served to confirm the consistency of procedural justice effects across contexts and types of participants but have also more rigorously tested the potential moderators of justice effects across the field of research.

For example, previous work by Brockner and Wiesenfeld (1996) demonstrated that outcome favorability moderates the effect of procedural features on people's reactions to encounters with others. When one receives an outcome that is favorable at the end of a procedure, the positive effects of fair processes are weaker, but fair process effects are stronger when one receives an outcome that is unfavorable. While Brockner and Wiesenfeld (1996) demonstrated that the effects of procedural factors on people's reactions to procedures were more nuanced than previously thought, their analysis consisted of simply observing and tallying effects across a number of justice studies. A subsequent meta-analysis by Skitka, Winquist, and Hutchinson (2003) used a finer distinction with regard to outcomes by distinguishing the effects of outcome favorability and outcome fairness. This analysis revealed that fair process effects are less likely to emerge when people hold clear standards for outcome fairness—when they have a clear belief about what the outcome of the procedure should be (Skitka, 2002). For example, when people feel confident that they know a defendant's guilt or innocence, their procedural justice judgments are based solely on whether the verdict matches their belief about culpability. When people lack confidence in their knowledge of culpability, the fair process effect becomes evident, with justice judgments determined by procedural considerations (Skitka & Houston, 2001). Although outcome favorability moderates the fair process effect (i.e., the fair process effect is diminished when outcome favorability is high and enhanced when favorability is low), outcome fairness diminishes the fair process effect (i.e., procedural effects on satisfaction are reduced when outcome fairness is unambiguous—that is, when participants have clear beliefs in regard to an appropriate outcome; Skitka et al., 2003).

Weaknesses in Procedural Justice Research

In this way, meta-analyses have shed some light on factors that moderate the importance of fair treatment for procedural judgments and have highlighted some limitations in the field. Skitka et al. (2003) noted that researchers often combine measures of outcome fairness and outcome favorability when testing research questions about outcomes. Other researchers have also noted that there is very little measurement research devoted to the development of valid measures of constructs in justice research, leaving great inconsistency in the manipulation of independent variables and measurement of dependent variables in the field (Reisig, Bratton, & Gertz, 2007). One concern raised by the findings of Skitka et al. (2003) is the importance of consistency and rigor in the operational definitions of variables in justice research, as subtle differences between constructs (e.g., outcome favorability vs. outcome fairness) can produce important differences in justice effects. Some of the work in this field does pay careful attention to measurement concerns, testing the structure of key justice variables (e.g., Blader & Tyler, 2003). However, this is one aspect of procedural justice research that needs to be developed further, allowing for advances in the field based on a consistent understanding of major constructs and theoretical validity of key dependent variables across studies.

The Decision Maker–Decision Recipient Disparity

Evidence has shown that factors other than outcome fairness can diminish the effects and importance of fair procedures. Early studies showed that decision makers in employment (Lissak & Sheppard, 1983) and legal (Houlden et al., 1978) contexts were more strongly influenced by instrumental criteria (like financial considerations and control over decisions) than they were by relational criteria (such as trustworthiness and respectful treatment). More recent research has expanded the scope of inquiry into decision makers in the legal system, examining the justice perceptions of judges. Judges describe their own legal decision making as a process of utilitarian balancing of outcome concerns, weighing societal benefits against individual harms (Monahan & Walker, 1994). This cost–benefit characterization of judicial reasoning does not fit well with the research on procedural justice, which emphasizes the importance of treatment and relational concerns for people's decisions about the fairness and acceptability of procedures (e.g., Tyler, 1994). However, this procedural justice research, which often asserts the dominance of procedures in people's justice concerns (e.g., Lind & Tyler, 1988), has not examined the justice reasoning of decision makers such as employers, police officers, or judges.

The procedural justice research has focused overwhelmingly on the justice reasoning of decision recipients, such as employees in interactions with employers, citizens in interactions with police, or disputants in court. The role in which participants operate when they make justice judgments may account for this discrepancy between reported judicial reasoning and the findings of much procedural justice research. In four studies, Heuer, Penrod, and Kattan (2007) examined the justice reasoning of decision makers and decision recipients, and they found a disparity in the weight accorded to procedures versus outcomes by individuals in these two different roles.

In two studies, judges (appellate court judges in Study 1 and state trial court judges in Study 2) read a fictitious summary of an appellate court case, in which a defendant was stopped and searched before boarding a flight because a voice stress analysis indicated that he was deceptive in answering security questions. On searching the passenger, federal agents discovered illegal items in the passenger's possession, and the defendant was charged and ultimately convicted. The judges in these studies read a summary description of the defendant's appeal of this conviction, on the grounds that his Fourth Amendment right to protection against unreasonable search and seizure had been violated. This summary included a description of the search procedure as well as the outcome of the search. The judges were randomly assigned to receive one of the four versions of the summary used to manipulate two variables: whether the procedure was conducted in a respectful or disrespectful manner, and whether the search procedure produced an outcome of high societal benefit (in this case, a .45 caliber pistol, which the defendant had been trying to carry illegally onto the flight) or an outcome of low societal benefit (one marijuana cigarette in Study 1 or stolen credit cards in Study 2). Judges then answered questions about the fairness of the search procedure as well as their likely decisions about the appeal.

In these two studies, no evidence was found to indicate that the respectfulness of the search procedure influenced the judges' decisions or procedural evaluations once the outcome of the search was known. This result stands in contrast to much of the research in the procedural justice field, which emphasizes the importance of respectful treatment on people's procedural evaluations. Rather, the judges' decision about whether to uphold the conviction was influenced by their perception of distributive justice, which depended on the societal benefit of the outcome of the search procedure. When societal benefit was high (the search produced a weapon that the defendant had been trying to carry illegally onto the flight), judges in this study considered the outcome of the procedure to be more fair and were more likely to uphold the appellant's conviction.

These findings suggest that decision makers (appellate and state court judges) emphasize outcome concerns more than respectful treatment in their judgments about the fairness and acceptability of procedures. However, both of these studies examined the justice judgments of decision makers, without comparing these to the justice judgments of nondecision makers. A third study addressed this shortcoming, randomly assigning participants to either a decision maker or nondecision maker role in an experimental design. Undergraduate participants read a fictional scenario about an undergraduate in student housing whose room had been searched by a resident assistant. When a violation of campus housing regulations was discovered, the resident assistant reported the student, who was then sanctioned by the university. Participants read that the offending student was appealing this sanction on the grounds that the search procedure was inappropriate. Three variables were manipulated in this study: role, outcome, and respectful treatment. Participants were told that appeal decisions were made by a board composed of student housing residents, residence assistants, and a campus administrator. Role was manipulated by assigning participants to consider this case from the perspective of a decision maker or a nondecision maker. Decision makers read the story from the perspective of a member of the board who was a resident advisor, whereas nondecision makers read the case from the perspective of either the offending student who was appealing their sanction, a student representative on the appellant board, or another student resident of university housing who was learning about the case from a report in the campus newspaper. Outcome was manipulated by telling participants in the high benefit condition that the search procedure had revealed cocaine in the student's room and telling participants in the low benefit condition that the search had revealed burning incense in the student's room. Finally, participants were told that the search procedure had been conducted either respectfully or disrespectfully.

The findings were consistent with those of the first two studies that involved state and appellate court judges. Procedural justice influenced the decisions of people in the nonauthority role significantly more than it did those of people in the authority role (the resident advisor member of the decision-making board). Among participants who were in this authority role, the outcome of the search procedure (cocaine vs. burning incense) had a stronger effect on the decision to uphold or overturn the sanction than did the manner in which the search procedure was conducted. However, among non–decision makers, the manner in which the search was conducted had a stronger effect on the recommendation to uphold or overturn the sanction than did the outcome of the search.

The final study in this article by Heuer et al. (2007) examined justice judgments in a field setting and also extended this investigation to a different situation. In the three studies described above, the outcome of the case was known to the participants as they made their responses: Participants (judges in Studies 1 and 2, and undergraduate students in Study 3) were making justice judgments about a procedure that had been successfully applied—the target of the procedure had violated a law or regulation, and the procedure had been effective at detecting this violation. Study 4 asked participants to evaluate the fairness of a procedure whose outcome (and therefore effectiveness) was uncertain. In Study 4, restaurant managers and employees were asked to respond to a fictional newspaper article about a procedure that had been proposed by health officials to prevent a hepatitis A threat. Two independent variables were manipulated in the stories: threat and treatment. Participants in the high-threat condition were told that the disease was very serious, was transmitted easily, and that few restaurants in the city would be able to survive the lawsuit that would result if contamination occurred; participants in the low-threat condition were told that the disease was not serious, was very difficult to transmit, and that any lawsuits that might be attempted after a contamination case were unlikely to succeed. In the manipulation of treatment, participants in the respectful procedure condition were told that the proposed procedure entailed restaurant employees signing a contract pledging to wash their hands after visiting the restroom. Participants in the disrespectful procedure condition were told that the proposed procedure entailed employees being followed into the restroom by a manager or designated employee, who would be required to observe the employee washing his or her hands after a visit to the restroom.

The findings of this study indicated that restaurant employees were more concerned than restaurant managers were about the respectfulness of the proposed procedure: Their approval for the procedure was more strongly influenced by judgments of the fairness of the procedure than it was for restaurant managers, and in turn, judgments of the fairness of the procedure were more strongly influenced by respectful treatment among restaurant employees than they were among restaurant managers. The results also indicated that restaurant managers were more concerned than employees were about the effectiveness of the proposed procedure: Perceived effectiveness of the procedure affected procedural justice judgments and support for the procedure among restaurant managers but not among restaurant employees.

Potential Limits to the Influence of Relational Variables

In four studies, Heuer et al. (2007) demonstrated that authorities or people in a decision-making role emphasized outcome concerns when evaluating the fairness of procedures and making judgments about approval of their use. This stands in stark contrast to non–decision makers, who have been shown by a large body of procedural justice research to place a stronger emphasis on respectful treatment when evaluating procedures. There are several possible reasons for the discrepancy between the findings of Heuer et al. (2007) and the findings of previous research on decision recipients, and these reasons center on the motivational assumptions that underlie the group value model.

Responsibility to Protect the Group

As outlined earlier in this chapter, the group value model posits that people judge procedures to be fair when those procedures engender a sense that one is valued and held in high regard by the social group (Lind & Tyler, 1988; Tyler & Lind, 1992). Respectful treatment is important because it conveys information about one's group standing. This motivational analysis is well suited to subordinates who are contemplating their interactions with authorities (e.g., the employee who interacts with an employer) and seeking information about their group standing from the authority figure representing the social group. However, this group value explanation might be less well suited to authorities who are interacting with subordinates. Decision makers or authority figures may be less concerned with their group standing (which is clearly high) and motivated by different concerns. Motivation to protect the group is likely to be a particularly salient concern for group authorities (including authorities in legal, political, and organizational contexts) and has been described as a primary human motivation (Stangor & Leary, 2006). Authorities often hold their high status positions specifically for the purpose of protecting a social group. For example, a senior manager is responsible for the financial viability of a company in a way that a midlevel employee is not, and a police officer is responsible for the safety of his or her jurisdiction in a way that an ordinary citizen is not. This increased concern with group protection may be one feature that differentiates decision makers and non-decision makers, resulting in differing motivations that drive the procedural evaluations of these two groups.

Deservingness

Another explanation that has been proposed for harsh treatment by suspects at the hands of interrogators is the possibility that interrogators view suspects as being undeserving of respectful treatment. This deservingness-based explanation is supported by research that shows that the effect of respectful treatment on procedural justice judgments is moderated by deservingness; respectful treatment increases procedural justice judgments when the target of that treatment is judged to deserve respect but not when the target of the procedure is judged to be undeserving of respectful treatment (Heuer et al., 1999). Further, research shows that ordinary citizens' support for harsh interrogation techniques is driven by retributive motives (Carlsmith & Sood, 2009). The possibility that interrogators endorse coercive interrogation tactics because they view suspects as undeserving of respectful treatment is consistent with the findings of Studies 1–3 by Heuer et al. (2007), in which decision makers are relatively unconcerned with the treatment of an offender who has been discovered violating a regulation or law.

However, in the fourth study by Heuer et al. (2007), the discrepancy in the justice reasoning of authorities and subordinates does remain in regard to a preventive procedure. In this study, authorities or decision makers were considering the use and fairness of a precautionary procedure when there was no suggestion of wrongdoing by the target of the procedure, rendering a retribution motive an unlikely one in this context. Therefore, when considering explanations for the discrepancy between decision makers and decision recipients in the importance of respectful treatment for their procedural evaluations, we must also consider other possible explanations.

The Source–Decision Maker Confound

Among decision makers and decision recipients in natural settings, a confound usually occurs, which may explain the different degrees of concern shown by each for procedures compared with outcomes. Typically, decision makers are the source, rather than the target, of a procedure being enacted. For example, in Study 4 by Heuer et al. (2007), the employee was the target of the handwashing procedure under consideration. Thus, when restaurant managers and restaurant employees evaluate this procedure, restaurant managers are evaluating a procedure that will treat another person respectfully or disrespectfully, whereas restaurant employees are considering a procedure that will treat them respectfully or disrespectfully. This source–target variable offers another explanation for the moderation effects observed in this study. It is possible that this distinction drives the reduced concern shown by decision makers for respectful treatment—people are more concerned about respect when they are evaluating their own treatment than when they are evaluating another person's treatment. However, the design of the studies by Heuer et al. (2007) does not allow us to disentangle the causal role of these two confounded variables. Further research is needed to determine whether decision-maker status itself leads to a reduced concern with respectful treatment, independent of this source–decision maker confound.

Procedural Evaluations by Authorities in an Interrogation Context

Evidence is emerging to indicate that this focus on outcomes by authorities who are making evaluations about the fairness and acceptability of procedures extends to settings that involve interrogation procedures. Sivasubramaniam, Heuer, Schmidt, and Silva (2009) examined the way that authorities in interrogation procedures (interrogating officers) evaluate the fairness of coercive interrogation procedures. Participants completed the study online, in exchange for payment. In this study, participants read a fictitious newspaper story, describing a crime that they were told had been recently committed. The stimulus materials described a modified version of an actual crime in which a Central Park jogger was viciously attacked and raped in 1989. The description ended by noting that two suspects, a male and a female, had been detained and were being interrogated. Participants then read a description of the interrogation of the female suspect, who was accused of keeping watch while her male companion assaulted and raped the victim. In the description of the interrogation procedure, four variables were manipulated in a between-subjects design: role, procedure, accuracy, and confidence. As they read the materials, participants imagined themselves as the police officer conducting the interrogation (interrogator), the female suspect accused of keeping watch while her companion attacked the victim (suspect), or a jogger who routinely jogs in the park where the attack took place (neutral observer). In the manipulation of the interrogation procedure, participants were either told that coercive interrogation tactics were used (e.g., the suspect was inter-rogated for 8 hr, the police officer lied about the evidence, the police officer offered a false promise of leniency), or that noncoercive interrogation tactics were used (e.g., the suspect was interrogated for 1 hr, and the police officer was honest about the evidence). In the high-accuracy condition, participants were told that the tactics used by the interrogator are known to produce false confession rates of about 1%, and in the low-accuracy condition, participants were told that the tactics used by the interrogator are known to produce false confession rates of about 20%. Participants in the high-confidence conditions were told that the interrogator was convinced that the suspect was guilty, and those in the low-confidence condition were told that the interrogator thought the suspect was guilty but would not stake their reputation on it. Manipulation checks showed that all of these manipulations were successful, and participants completed a questionnaire that measured four primary depend-ent variables: the fairness of the interrogation procedure, satisfaction with the interrogation procedure, expectation that the procedure would result in a fair outcome, and satisfaction with the interrogation outcome.

Results were supportive of our predictions that role would interact with procedure to influence the participant's judgments of fairness and satisfaction, as the role and procedure manipulations interacted to affect all four depend-ent variables. The procedural justice judgments of the suspects and neutral observers were strongly affected by the procedure manipulation. They judged the coercive interrogation procedure to be less fair than the noncoercive interrogation procedure. However, although procedures also affected the interrogators' procedural justice judgments, this effect was weaker for this group. Similarly, suspects and observers were less satisfied with the coercive inter-rogation procedure and the outcomes that it would produce than they were with the noncoercive procedure and its outcomes, whereas interrogators were equally satisfied with the use of the coercive and noncoerceive interrogation procedures and their outcomes. The findings of this experimental laboratory study therefore replicated those of Heuer et al. (2007), demonstrating that the treatment of the suspect in the interrogation procedure is more important for the procedural justice and satisfaction judgments of suspects and observers than it is for the justice and satisfaction judgments of interrogators.

Importantly, interrogators also differed from suspects and observers on their judgments of distributive justice. Interrogators thought that the outcome produced by a coercive interrogation procedure would be as fair as that produced by a noncoercive procedure, whereas suspects and observers considered that the coercive interrogation procedure would produce an outcome that would be less fair. This finding suggests that interrogators are not simply willing to tolerate coercive procedures and potentially unfair outcomes in exchange for other valued goals, such as resolution and closure of a case. Rather, it appears that interrogators expect that the coercive procedures will produce just outcomes.

An additional contribution of this study lies in its examination of neutral observers, in addition to suspects and interrogators. The justice judgments of these neutral observers can assist in teasing apart competing explanations for the reduced emphasis on respectful treatment among decision makers. Earlier in this chapter, we pointed to the source–decision maker confound, and we noted the possibility that what we have hypothesized as a decision maker–decision recipient effect might actually be a source-target effect. Our finding in this study was that both the suspect (the actual target of the interrogation) and the observer (who was not a target) responded similarly to the respectfulness of the interrogation procedure. Although this does not entirely disambiguate the confound, it argues against the source-target variable as a sufficient explanation for the moderation we have observed. The inclusion of neutral observers in this study therefore clarifies an important issue in regard to the underlying mechanism that drives the discrepancy between the justice judgments of decision makers and decision recipients. The reduced concern for respectful treatment among decision makers is not simply due to the fact that they are not the targets of that treatment, because neutral observers (who are also not the targets of that treatment) do not show this reduced concern for treatment. The underlying motivation that leads decision makers to emphasize outcomes over treatment in their procedural evaluations therefore appears to be, at least in part, unique to their decision-making status in the situation.

IMPLICATIONS OF RESEARCH ON PROCEDURAL JUSTICE AND INTERROGATION TECHNIQUES

The research described here demonstrates important differences between the procedural evaluations of decision makers and non–decision makers, which extend to the evaluation of interrogation procedures. In the following sections, we consider the implications these differences have for research on interrogations and for current interrogation practices and policy.

Implications for Research on Interrogations

Random assignment is an important methodological feature of the studies described in this chapter. Participants were randomly assigned to one of two (Heuer et al., 2007) or three (Sivasubramaniam et al., 2009) roles, and this produced differences between authorities and subordinates in justice reasoning. Simply asking people to take the perspective of the decision maker or interrogating officer in these scenarios changes the way that these participants consider the justice of a procedure and its outcomes and the way that they determine approval of its use. This is an important contribution to the research on interrogation procedures: When people step into the role of an authority figure, or decision maker, this changes what they find to be acceptable and fair in an interrogation procedure. The studies described above therefore highlight the importance of considering the influence of one's role in a procedure as we attempt to better understand the reasons for the evidently high level of support among police officers for procedures that violate standards of procedural justice strongly endorsed by the vast majority of the population. The research described in this chapter suggests that decision makers, who are in a position of responsibility for protecting the wider social group, are less concerned than non–decision makers are about the respectfulness of treatment that these procedures involve and more concerned with obtaining a just and correct outcome from these procedure. The role or perspective that people take when considering legal decision making and interrogation procedures affects the way that they evaluate the fairness of that procedure, and it also affects the factors that they take into consideration when determining whether they endorse the procedure and approve of its use.

This research highlights a key point for psychology and law researchers who have amply documented the injustices that result from such coercive interrogation procedures. It is not that decision makers tolerate what they perceive to be otherwise objectionable procedures for the purpose of resolving a case. Rather, authorities in interrogation procedures evidently construe the fairness of these procedures differently than do suspects and neutral observers. Rather than arguing that decision makers in interrogation procedures are using unfair procedures, research on interrogations in psychology and law might benefit from more work devoted to understanding decision makers' perceptions of justice, which are more outcome driven than others' justice perceptions, and to changing decision makers' evaluations of these interrogation procedures. When behavior change is the goal among a particular population, interventions are more effective when they accurately target the determinants of that behavior (Michie, Johnston, Francis, Hardeman, & Eccles, 2008). The research reviewed in this chapter suggests that the fact that these procedures are coercive or disrespectful is less important to decision makers than to others; what is important to decision makers is the procedure's ability to obtain or produce the correct outcome. Decision makers will be less likely to endorse the use of such procedures not when they are convinced that it is procedurally unfair to use them but when they are convinced that they are not effective in obtaining just outcomes. Therefore, the research reviewed in this chapter suggests that any interventions designed to prevent interrogators from using coercive or unfair procedures should not focus on convincing interrogators of the disrespectfulness or impropriety of such procedures. Rather, these interventions should center on either establishing procedural safeguards to ensure that decision makers do not violate procedural fairness concerns even if they do not value them or on working to make decision makers more aware of unjust outcomes that result from coercive interrogation procedures.

Implications for Interrogation Practice and Policy

As noted earlier in this chapter, the interrogation phase of the Reid technique is a guilt-presumptive procedure. Interrogators enter this phase having made the determination that the suspect in their custody has broken the law and thus poses a threat to the security of a community of individuals. The research reviewed here suggests that authorities or decision makers in this situation will endorse and use procedures that they believe will lead to the just or correct outcome (in this case, the conviction of the suspect they have already determined to be guilty) rather than be concerned with treating a suspect respectfully or deem procedures to be appropriate because they comprise procedural justice criteria, such as suspect voice, neutrality in the interrogation procedure, and trustworthiness of the interrogator. In the context of the Reid interrogation procedure, a just outcome is always a confession, and interrogators will determine the fairness or propriety of a procedure according to its ability to elicit that confession (i.e., obtain the "correct" outcome), with less consideration than others (e.g., suspects, neutral observers) for the nature of the procedure itself.

CONCLUSION

In this chapter, we have examined the ways in which interrogators, suspects, and community observers evaluate the justice of police interrogation procedures. Previous research on procedural justice has demonstrated, across a variety of contexts and methodologies, the importance of respectful treatment to procedural evaluations.

Interrogators as Decision Makers

The work described in this chapter suggests that the meaning and importance of procedural justice are moderated by perspective. It is important to note, however, that this decision maker—decision recipient disparity has far wider implications. Whereas interrogators are decision makers in interrogation procedures, other actors serve as decision makers at various stages of the legal process. The procedural justice research that we have reviewed in this chapter is plausibly applicable to legal actors who assume the authority role at any stage of the investigation, interrogation, or trial process, and any legal actor who is responsible for the welfare of the social group may be subject to the same outcome focus that drives the fairness and satisfaction judgments of interrogators. In this way, decision making or authority status may lead people to consider the use of suggestive eyewitness identification procedures (see Chapter 6, this volume) or unreliable informants (see Chapter 10, this volume) to be more appropriate than do non–decision makers. Through the responsibility of the decision maker to protect the community, decision-making status may intensify the tendency to engage in tunnel vision (see Chapter 14, this volume). Decision makers at any stage of the conviction process who infer the guilt of the suspect or defendant may be susceptible to this focus on obtaining a just outcome—and when guilt is inferred, a just outcome is ultimately equivalent to a conviction. Thus, for decision makers at all stages of the legal system, procedures will be judged fair and appropriate not to the extent that they are neutral or respectful but to the extent that they secure the "just" outcome—the conviction.

Directions for Future Research

New and emerging research on procedural evaluations by decision makers is focused on discerning the reasons for this discrepancy between decision makers and non–decision makers. Some of the proposed mechanisms that drive this effect have been outlined in this chapter, including judgments of deservingness of the suspect and an increased responsibility by decision makers for protecting the wider social group. However, many potential differences between the motivations of decision makers and non–decision makers remain to be explored. For example, as well as being responsible for protecting the welfare of the social group, decision makers are also more accountable to that social group for the decisions that they make, whereas non–decision makers are often anonymous and make evaluations (e.g., personal opinions) that do not have consequences for the welfare of the wider social group. Current research is examining whether this increased accountability explains decision makers' focus on obtaining correct outcomes, rather than using fair procedures.

It is important that future research continue to explore these motivations that drive the procedural justice judgments and evaluations of decision makers. By doing this, we can generate an improved understanding of interrogators' procedural evaluations and better discern ways to change these evaluations. If we can determine the best ways to convince decision makers in the legal system that coercive interrogation procedures and their outcomes are unfair, we can discourage their use, thereby reducing the risk that these coercive interrogation procedures present to innocent suspects.

REFERENCES

Austin, W., Walster, E., & Utne, M. K. (1976). Equity and the law: The effect of a harmdoer's "suffering in the act" on liking and assigned punishment. In L. Berkowitz & E. Walster (Eds.), *Advances in experimental social psychology* (Vol. 9, pp. 163–190). New York, NY: Academic Press.

Blader, S. L., & Tyler, T. R. (2003). A four-component model of procedural justice: Defining the meaning of a "fair" process. *Personality and Social Psychology Bulletin*, *29*, 747–758. doi:10.1177/0146167203029006007

Brockner, J., & Wiesenfeld, B. M. (1996). An integrative framework for explaining reactions to decisions: Interactive effects of outcomes and procedures. *Psychological Bulletin*, *120*, 189–208. doi:10.1037/0033-2909.120.2.189

Brubacher, M. R., Fondacaro, M. R., Brank, E. M., Brown, V. E., & Miller, S. A. (2009). Procedural justice in resolving family disputes: Implications for childhood bullying. *Psychology, Public Policy, and Law*, *15*, 149–167. doi:10.1037/a0016839

Carlsmith, K. M., & Sood, A. M. (2009). The fine line between interrogation and retribution. *Journal of Experimental Social Psychology*, *45*, 191–196. doi:10.1016/j.jesp.2008.08.025

Cohen-Charash, Y., & Spector, P. E. (2001). The role of justice in organizations: A meta-analysis. *Organizational Behavior and Human Decision Processes*, *86*, 278–321. doi:10.1006/obhd.2001.2958

Cohen-Charash, Y., & Spector, P. E. (2002). Erratum to "The role of justice in organizations: A meta-analysis." *Organizational Behavior and Human Decision Processes*, *89*, 1215. doi:10.1016/S0749-5978(02)00040-7

Colquitt, J. A., & Greenberg, J. (2003). Organizational justice: A fair assessment of the state of the literature. In J. Greenberg (Ed.), *Organizational behavior: The state of the science* (2nd ed., pp. 165–210). Mahwah, NJ: Erlbaum.

Davis-Lipman, A., Tyler, T. R., & Andersen, S. M. (2007). Building community one relationship at a time: Consequences for the seeking and acceptance of help. *Social Justice Research*, *20*, 181–206. doi:10.1007/s11211-007-0038-8

De Cremer, D. (2004). The influence of accuracy as a function of leader's bias: The role of trustworthiness in the psychology of procedural justice. *Personality and Social Psychology Bulletin, 30,* 293–304. doi:10.1177/0146167203256969

De Cremer, D., & Blader, S. L. (2006). Why do people care about procedural fairness? The importance of belongingness in responding and attending to procedures. *European Journal of Social Psychology, 36,* 211–228. doi:10.1002/ejsp.290

Folger, R. (1977). Distributive and procedural justice: Combined impact of voice and improvement on experienced inequity. *Journal of Personality and Social Psychology, 35,* 108–119. doi:10.1037/0022-3514.35.2.108

Greenberg, J., & Folger, R. (1983). Procedural justice, participation, and the fair process effect in groups and organizations. In P. B. Paulus (Ed.), *Basic group processes* (pp. 235–256). New York, NY: Springer.

Heuer, L., Blumenthal, E., Douglas, A., & Weinblatt, T. (1999). A deservingness approach to respect as a relationally based fairness judgment. *Personality and Social Psychology Bulletin, 25,* 1279–1292. doi:10.1177/0146167299258009

Heuer, L., Penrod, S. D., Hafer, C. L., & Cohn, I. (2002). The role of resource and relational concerns for procedural justice. *Personality and Social Psychology Bulletin, 28,* 1468–1482. doi:10.1177/014616702237575

Heuer, L., Penrod, S. D., & Kattan, A. (2007). The role of societal benefits and fairness concerns among decision makers and decision recipients. *Law and Human Behavior, 31,* 573–610. doi:10.1007/s10979-006-9084-2

Houlden, P., LaTour, S., Walker, L., & Thibaut, J. (1978). Preference for modes of dispute resolution as a function of process and decision control. *Journal of Experimental Social Psychology, 14,* 13–30. doi:10.1016/0022-1031(78)90057-4

Inbau, F. E., Reid, J. E., Buckley, J. P., & Jayne, B. C. (2001). *Criminal interrogation and confessions* (4th ed.). Gaithersburg, MD: Aspen.

Kassin, S. M., & Fong, C. T. (1999). "I'm innocent!" Effects of training on judgments of truth and deception in the interrogation room. *Law and Human Behavior, 23,* 499–516. doi:10.1023/A:1022330011811

Kassin, S. M., Goldstein, C. J., & Savitsky, K. (2003). Behavioral confirmation in the interrogation room: On the dangers of presuming guilt. *Law and Human Behavior, 27,* 187–203. doi:10.1023/A:1022599230598

Kassin, S. M., & Gudjonsson, G. H. (2006). The psychology of confessions: A review of the literature and issues [Special issue]. *Psychological Science in the Public Interest, 5,* 33–67. doi: 10.1111/j.1529-1006.2004.00016.x

Leung, K., Tong, K.-K., & Lind, E. (2007). Realpolitik versus fair process: Moderating effects of group identification on acceptance of political decisions. *Journal of Personality and Social Psychology, 92,* 476–489. doi:10.1037/0022-3514.92.3.476

Lind, E. A., Kanfer, R., & Earley, P. C. (1990). Voice, control, and procedural justice: Instrumental and noninstrumental concerns in fairness judgments. *Journal of Personality and Social Psychology, 59,* 952–959. doi:10.1037/0022-3514.59.5.952

Lind, E. A., & Tyler, T. R. (1988). *The social psychology of procedural justice.* New York, NY: Plenum Press.

Lissak, R. I., & Sheppard, B. H. (1983). Beyond fairness: The criterion problem in research on dispute intervention. *Journal of Applied Social Psychology, 13*, 45–65. doi:10.1111/j.1559-1816.1983.tb00886.x

Meissner, C. A., & Kassin, S. M. (2002). "He's guilty!": Investigator bias in judgments of truth and deception. *Law and Human Behavior, 26*, 469–480. doi:10.1023/A:1020278620751

Michie, S., Johnston, S., Francis, J., Hardeman, W., & Eccles, M. (2008). From theory to intervention: Mapping theoretically derived behavioural determinants to behaviour change techniques. *Applied Psychology, 57*, 660–680. doi:10.1111/j.1464-0597.2008.00341.x

Monahan, J., & Walker, L. (1994). *Social science and law: Cases and materials* (3rd ed.). Mineola, NY: Foundation Press.

Murphy, K. (2005). Regulating more effectively: The relationship between procedural justice, legitimacy, and tax non-compliance. *Journal of Law and Society, 32*, 562–589. doi:10.1111/j.1467-6478.2005.00338.x

Poythress, N. G., Schumacher, J., Wiener, R., & Murrin, M. (1993). Procedural justice judgments of alternative procedures for resolving medical malpractice claims. *Journal of Applied Social Psychology, 23*, 1639–1658. doi:10.1111/j.1559-1816.1993.tb01059.x

Reisig, M. D., Bratton, J., & Gertz, M. G. (2007). The construct validity and refinement of process-based policing measures. *Criminal Justice and Behavior, 34*, 1005–1028. doi:10.1177/0093854807301275

Sivasubramaniam, D., Heuer, L., Schmidt, H., & Silva, H. (2009, March). Authorities' perceptions of fairness as a cause of wrongful conviction. Paper presented at the annual meeting of the American Psychology-Law Society, San Antonio, TX.

Skitka, L. J. (2002). Do the means always justify the ends or do the ends sometimes justify the means? A value model of justice reasoning. *Personality and Social Psychology Bulletin, 28*, 588–597. doi:10.1177/0146167202288003

Skitka, L. J., & Houston, D. A. (2001). When due process is of no consequence: Moral mandates and presumed defendant guilt or innocence. *Social Justice Research, 14*, 305–326. doi:10.1023/A:1014372008257

Skitka, L., Winquist, J., & Hutchinson, S. (2003). Are outcome fairness and outcome favorability distinguishable psychological constructs? A meta-analytic review. *Social Justice Research, 16*, 309–341. doi:10.1023/A:1026336131206

Stangor, C., & Leary, S. P. (2006). Intergroup beliefs: Investigations from the social side. In M. Zanna (Ed.), *Advances in experimental social psychology* (Vol. 38, pp. 243–281). San Diego, CA: Elsevier Academic.

Sunshine, J., & Tyler, T. R. (2003). The role of procedural justice and legitimacy in shaping public support for policing. *Law & Society Review, 37*, 513–548. doi:10.1111/1540-5893.3703002

Tajfel, H. (1982). The social psychology of intergroup relations. *Annual Review of Psychology, 33*, 1–39. doi:10.1146/annurev.ps.33.020182.000245

Tajfel, H., & Turner, J. (1986). The social identity theory of intergroup behavior. In S. Worchel (Ed.), *Psychology of intergroup relations* (pp. 7–24). Chicago, IL: Nelson Hall.

Thibaut, J., & Walker, L. (1975). *Procedural justice: A psychological analysis.* Hillsdale, NJ: Erlbaum.

Thibaut, J., & Walker, L. (1978). A theory of procedure. *California Law Review, 66,* 541–566. doi:10.2307/3480099

Tyler, T. R. (1989). The psychology of procedural justice: A test of the group-value model. *Journal of Personality and Social Psychology, 57,* 830–838. doi:10.1037/0022-3514.57.5.830

Tyler, T. R. (1990). *Why people obey the law.* New Haven, CT: Yale University Press.

Tyler, T. R. (1994). Psychological models of the justice motive: Antecedents of distributive and procedural justice. *Journal of Personality and Social Psychology, 67,* 850–863. doi:10.1037/0022-3514.67.5.850

Tyler, T. R., & Caine, A. (1981). The influence of outcomes and procedures on satisfaction with formal leaders. *Journal of Personality and Social Psychology, 41,* 642–655. doi:10.1037/0022-3514.41.4.642

Tyler, T. R., Degoey, P., & Smith, H. J. (1996). Understanding why the justice of group procedures matters: A test of the psychological dynamics of the group value model. *Journal of Personality and Social Psychology, 70,* 913–930. doi:10.1037/0022-3514.70.5.913

Tyler, T. R., & Huo, Y. J. (2002). *Trust in the law.* New York, NY: Russell Sage Foundation.

Tyler, T. R., & Lind, E. A. (1992). A relational model of authority in groups. In M. P. Zanna (Ed.), *Advances in experimental social psychology* (Vol. 25, pp. 115–192). New York, NY: Academic Press.

Utne, M. K. (1974). *Functions of expressions of liking in response to inequity.* Unpublished master's thesis, University of Wisconsin-Madison, Madison, WI.

van Prooijen, J. W., De Cremer, D., van Beest, I., Ståhl, T., van Dijke, M., & Van Lange, P. A. (2008). The egocentric nature of procedural justice: Social value orientation as moderator of reactions to decision-making procedures. *Journal of Experimental Social Psychology, 44,* 1303–1315. doi:10.1016/j.jesp.2008.05.006

van Prooijen, J. W., van den Bos, K., & Wilke, H. A. (2002). Procedural justice and status: Status salience as antecedent of procedural fairness effects. *Journal of Personality and Social Psychology, 83,* 1353–1361. doi:10.1037/0022-3514.83.6.1353

Walster, E., Berscheid, E., & Walster, G. W. (1976). New directions in equity research. In L. Berkowitz (Ed.), *Advances in experimental social psychology* (Vol. 9, pp. 1–42). New York, NY: Academic Press.

Wenzel, M. (2006). A letter from the tax office: Compliance effects of informational and interpersonal justice. *Social Justice Research, 19,* 345–364. doi:10.1007/s11211-006-0011-y

III

THE EYEWITNESSES

5

FALLIBLE EYEWITNESS MEMORY AND IDENTIFICATION

KATHY PEZDEK

Some eyewitness identifications are accurate identifications of guilty individuals, and some eyewitness identifications are misidentifications of innocent individuals. The focus of this chapter is on determining when eyewitness identification is more likely to be correct or incorrect, and what methods of inquiry and empirical evidence best inform this decision. The research is clear that although the majority of jurors and judges consider eyewitness identification to be the most persuasive type of evidence administered in criminal cases (Chapter 9, this volume; Wells & Olson, 2003), there is a growing body of research that highlights the fallibility of eyewitness memory. For example, the forensic research on postconviction DNA exonerations has revealed that of the first 239 cases evaluated, 175 (73%) involved eyewitness misidentification, with 25% of these involving two eyewitnesses and 13% involving three or more eyewitnesses (http://www.innocenceproject.org/understand/Eyewitness-Misidentification.php). One might argue that forensic and legal practices are especially careful in capital cases. However, Radelet, Bedau, and Putnam

I am grateful to Iris Blandon-Gitlin, Matthew O'Brien, and Stacia Stolzenberg for their review of this chapter. E-mail correspondence regarding this chapter to Kathy.Pezdek@cgu.edu.

(1992) reviewed 400 wrongful convictions in capital cases and reported, "As for the causes of the errors, our research has shown that the two most frequent are perjury by prosecution witnesses and mistaken eyewitness testimony" (p. 18). It is clear that eyewitness misidentifications play a critical role in the study of wrongful convictions of the innocent.

Although these recent cases of wrongful conviction are compelling, the fallibility of eyewitness memory is not a new subject among psychologists (Munsterberg, 1908). The history of the role of psychologists in the court is important because it reflects basic perceptions of the role of science in legal decision making. In his book, *On the Witness Stand,* Hugo Munsterberg (1908) presented scientific research demonstrating the unreliability of eyewitness perception and memory, and he argued that scientific psychology had much to offer the legal community. Attorneys and legal scholars were outraged with Munsterberg's suggestion that legal decisions should be influenced by psychological research. For example, Attorney Charles C. Moore (1907) wrote,

> Among the legal professions it is familiar learning that experiments are valuable only when the conditions are fairly identical with those attending the occurrence under investigation. . . . Imagine him [Munsterberg] butting in with his so-called scientific experiments to appraise the testimony of a witness. (p. 127)

Relevant to the thesis of this chapter, Moore's principal argument concerned the value of the scientific method and whether it contributed anything more valuable than the common sense. "On almost every topic that has a proximate and practical relation to the trustworthiness of testimony delivered in court, the judges have the psychologists 'beaten a mile'" [sic] (p. 40). Similar views were also presented by John Henry Wigmore, a leading jurist and expert in the law of evidence in the early 20th century. Wigmore (1909) argued against the utility of the methods available to psychologists for evaluating the reliability of eyewitness accounts. Although today Munsterberg receives high praise for his research on eyewitness memory, in fact, Wigmore and Moore apparently won the debate against Munsterberg at the time: The period from the 1920s to the 1960s was largely devoid of eyewitness memory research, and expert testimony on this topic in courts of law did not obtain general acceptance until the 1990s.

SCIENTIFIC PSYCHOLOGICAL FOUNDATIONS AND SCIENTIFIC METHODS USED IN EYEWITNESS MEMORY RESEARCH

The purpose of this chapter is to examine the research methods that have been used by eyewitness memory researchers and summarize the findings of this research, regarding the factors that affect the accuracy of eyewitness memory and identification. To do this, we should first briefly consider the question of why scientific research is needed to assess when eyewitness identifications are more likely to be correct or incorrect. Isn't this a matter of common sense? In fact, judges regularly rule to exclude the testimony of eyewitness expert witnesses because they consider many components of their testimony to be common sense and known by the jury (Benton, Ross, Bradshaw, Thomas, & Bradshaw, 2006). However, people make different "commonsense assumptions" about the reliability of eyewitness evidence. In addition, although jurors typically find eyewitness evidence especially compelling, and prosecutors tend to rely on the general veracity of eyewitness evidence, defense attorneys tend to be more suspicious about the reliability of eyewitness evidence (for a review, see Read & Desmarais, 2009). Thus, in the absence of commonsense agreement, it is important to have an objective system for determining when an eyewitness is more or less likely to be reliable. Empirical scientific research provides this objective system.

What are the scientific research methods that have been used by eyewitness memory researchers? Most of the research on this topic has been conducted by using the experimental method, whereby independent variables are manipulated to study their effect on specific dependent variables, usually correct identification rates (e.g., hit rate data) and incorrect identification rates (e.g., false-alarm rate data). Although the experimental method is the gold standard for scientists, for reasons explained below, other methods that are more directly linked to real eyewitnesses in real crimes are often considered more convincing to jurors and legal professionals. This chapter focuses on three methods for conducting eyewitness memory research: (a) the case study, (b) archival methods, and (c) experimental methods and meta-analyses thereof.

The Case Study

A *case study* is an in-depth study of a single individual or incident. Cognitive psychologists know that people find case studies to be especially compelling and remember them far better than the results of scientific experiments. But is the case study method a reliable one for identifying generalizable information regarding factors that affect the reliability of eyewitness memory? One of the most highly cited case studies in eyewitness memory and identification is the study by Yuille and Cutshall (1986). Yuille and Cutshall analyzed the verbatim accounts of the eyewitnesses to a gun-shooting incident that occurred on a spring afternoon outside of a gun shop in Burnaby, British Columbia. A thief, who entered the gun shop in full view of several witnesses, tied up the proprietor and stole money and several guns. As the thief ran away, the proprietor freed himself and ran outside to get the license number of his car. However, the thief had not yet entered his car, and he fired two shots at the store owner.

Seconds later, the store owner discharged all six shots from his revolver and killed the thief. Witnesses to the event viewed the incident from along the street, from adjacent buildings and from passing automobiles. There were 21 witnesses who were interviewed by the police shortly after the incident. Thirteen of these witnesses were also interviewed by the researchers 4 to 5 months later. This case was available for research purposes because the thief was dead, the police files were closed, and the research study did not interfere with the judicial process. This case was also selected because numerous witnesses had observed the incident, and the veracity of their statements could be assessed in light of other forensic evidence that was available.

The primary results were that the eyewitnesses' descriptions were very accurate and there was little change in memory over the 5-month period (note that this study did not involve eyewitness identification because recognition memory for the thief was never tested). This is not to say, however, that eyewitness memory is always accurate. When the findings of this case study were broken down more specifically in an attempt to identify specific factors that might predict when eyewitness memory is more or less reliable, the findings were not very helpful. For example, it is important to understand whether high levels of stress enhance or diminish the reliability of eyewitness memory, and there is a great deal of research on this point (see, e.g., Deffenbacher, Bornstein, Penrod, & McCorty, 2004). Yuille and Cutshall (1986) reported that "self-reports of event related stress were unrelated to memory" (p. 300), and prosecutors are quick to use this quote to argue that eyewitnesses are no less accurate when they are reporting a highly stressful event. However, in Yuille and Cutshall's case study, the witnesses who reported a high level of stress were closer to and more involved in the violence than those who reported a lower level of stress. That stress and involvement in the incident were confounded in this study (i.e., they vary together and both affect eyewitness memory) renders any conclusions about the effect of stress on memory invalid.

The above conundrum is a methodological problem inherent in case study research. That is, the effect of specific eyewitness conditions—alone or in interaction with each other—can rarely be isolated because in any real-world event these conditions tend to be confounded with other contextual factors. Another difficulty in case study research is that a single event can only involve a limited set of conditions and a limited number of eyewitnesses. Thus, the generalizability of the findings from any one case study to other cases is limited.

Archival Methods

If conclusions from case studies of a single event are of limited value, perhaps value can be added by examining results from across many real-world cases. However, such cases will only be of value if the *ground truth* (i.e., the facts of each witnessed event including who the perpetrator was) for each case is known, and with real-world criminal cases, this is often not possible. With this in mind, Behrman and Davey (2001) analyzed 271 actual police cases in Sacramento, California, and categorized the conditions under which "suspect identifications" were more or less likely to occur. These are cases in which the suspect—who may or may not have been the perpetrator—was identified by an eyewitness. However, in few, if any, of these cases was the ground truth known, and in fact some of their findings were inconsistent with results reported elsewhere in the research literature. For example, they reported that suspect identifications from photographic lineups were higher for cross-race (i.e., the race of the witness and the perpetrator are different) than same-race identifications. The majority of the previous experimental research indicates that cross-race identifications are less reliable than same-race identifications.

Although it is rarely possible to confirm accurate eyewitness identifications in real-world cases, that is, to determine which individuals identified by eyewitnesses are actually guilty, it is relatively easy to confirm inaccurate eyewitness identifications (or which identified individuals are actually innocent). Several archival studies of eyewitness accuracy have focused on cases in which eyewitnesses positively identify from a lineup one of the filler individuals. Often the filler individuals are people who were actually incarcerated at the time of the crime, so selecting one of these individuals is clearly a misidentification. Several archival studies have been published that assessed patterns of misidentifications of filler individuals in lineups. Wright and McDaid (1996) analyzed the outcomes of 1,561 lineups in London and found that 19.9% of the eyewitness identifications were of fillers. One result by Behrman and Davey (2001) is relevant here. They reported that 24% of live lineup identifications were selections of fillers. This is similar to the reports of Valentine, Pickering, and Darling (2003), who analyzed 119 lineups in London and found that 21.6% of the eyewitnesses identified fillers. Although archival studies of cases of filler identifications are useful in documenting that misidentifications are quite common in real-world criminal cases and cause for concern, results from such studies do little to help us understand the conditions under which eyewitnesses are more or less likely to be accurate.

Another body of archival research from which more informative findings have resulted is the forensic research on postconviction DNA exonerations by the Innocence Project referenced earlier in this chapter. This research not only documents that eyewitness identifications are likely to occur (of the first 239 cases evaluated, 73% involved eyewitness misidentification) but also, given the data available, that researchers are beginning to assemble and statistically analyze data sets to assess factors most likely to be associated with inaccurate eyewitness identifications (Garrett, 2008). These findings will help predict eyewitness identification accuracy for individual real-world cases.

Experimental Methods

An *experimental study* is one in which the effect of specific independent variables (e.g., exposure time, time delay, prior familiarity with the perpetrator) on specific dependent variables (e.g., correct identification of the perpetrator, false-alarm rate to innocent fillers) is assessed under conditions in which the confounding effect of other extraneous variables is controlled. Further, in an experimental study, participants are randomly assigned to conditions to exclude the confounding effect of subject variability. Only if researchers conduct an experimental study can they draw causal conclusions, and causal conclusions permit more accurate prediction. This is why the experimental methodology is the gold standard in science.

Why are causal conclusions important? The purpose of science is to help understand the relationships among variables so that some variables can be used to predict others. Assume that we are interested in predicting what changes to our diet will result in weight loss. One research approach to assessing this relationship would involve doing a large cross-cultural assessment of which cultural groups tend to have thin builds and which do not and then assessing dietary differences among these groups. In such an analysis, a researcher might find that Japanese people tend to be thin, and they eat significantly more tofu than do other cultural groups. This would be a correlational study because no variable is manipulated under controlled conditions. Another research approach would be to test the hypothesis that, for example, a lower calorie diet leads to more weight loss. In this approach, half of the participants would be randomly assigned to one treatment group in which, for example, they would be limited to a 2,500-calorie-a-day diet; the other half would be randomly assigned to another treatment group and limited to a 1,800-calorie-a-day diet. Over time, the two groups would be compared on weight loss. In such an analysis, a researcher is likely to find that people in the lower calorie condition had more weight loss than those in the higher calorie condition. This would be an experimental research design.

The results of the correlational study suggest that if people eat more tofu then they will lose weight, but this conclusion is incorrect. The reason Japanese people tend to be thin is because they eat a lower calorie diet, not because they eat more tofu, per se. In other words, eating more tofu does not cause one to lose weight. On the other hand, the results of the experimental study suggest that if people eat a lower calorie diet then they will lose weight, and this conclusion is correct. In the experimental design, extraneous variables have been excluded so that a causal relationship between the independent variable (diet) and the dependent variable (weight loss) can be concluded. Causal relationships permit prediction. In this case, it can be predicted that eating a lower calorie diet will lead to weight loss.

What is the advantage of doing eyewitness memory research by using an experimental design? In other words, why does it matter in eyewitness memory research whether we can make causal conclusions or not? A good example of how not using an experimental study can be misleading is the archival study by Valentine et al. (2003), mentioned previously. They analyzed 119 lineups conducted in London and reported that cross-race identification, weapon focus, and time delay had no significant effect on identification rates for foils or suspects. These findings are inconsistent with the results of numerous experimental studies. Does this mean that experimental studies are not reliable and archival studies are reliable? This is probably not the conclusion. Rather, the findings of Valentine et al. likely resulted because in the specific cases included in their data base other extraneous variables confounded these conditions and eliminated the effects. This would occur, for example, if in the cross-race cases sampled, eyewitnesses tended to have more time to observe the perpetrator than in the same-race cases. In a later section of this chapter, Relevant Research on Eyewitness Memory, the major findings on this topic are presented, findings primarily from studies in which experimental methods have been used.

The major limitation of eyewitness memory studies conducted by using the experimental method is ecological validity. That is, based on differences between the circumstances of real-world crimes and the circumstances in typical eyewitness memory studies, the results of the research studies may be of limited generalizability. However, experimental tests of this claim have received little support. For example, several critics are concerned that results of studies with college students may not generalize to those of typical crime victims. However, O'Rourke, Penrod, Cutler, and Stuve (1989) compared the effect of numerous eyewitness factors across student and nonstudent samples, ranging in age from 18 to 74 years old. O'Rourke et al. (1989) found consistent findings across subject populations. Also, in Bornstein's (1999) meta-analysis, 21 of the 26 jury decision-making studies, sampling both undergraduates and community representative mock jurors, found no main effect of participant sample; and of the five studies that did show an effect, the differences were inconsistent. Others have been concerned that mock trials may be a poor approximate to real trials for assessing the effectiveness of certain types of testimony. However, Pezdek, Avila-Mora, and Sperry (2010) reported no differences in mock jurors' perceptions or verdicts as a function of trial presentation modality. Thus, although there are certainly differences between real-world crimes and the circumstances in typical eyewitness memory studies, it appears that these differences are not likely to interact with experimental variables manipulated and thus are not likely to limit the generalizability of the findings.

Meta-Analyses of Experimental Findings

Forensic scholars should also be familiar with another methodology: meta-analysis. If numerous experimental studies have been conducted on a particular topic, with perhaps some studies finding a strong effect, others finding a weak effect, and still others finding no effect, it will be useful to do a statistical analysis pooling results across these studies to see (a) how strong the effect is on average and (b) what secondary variables are associated with the strength of the effect. For example, numerous studies have examined eyewitness identification accuracy in same- versus cross-race conditions, and although same-race identifications tend to be more accurate than cross-race identifications the effect is inconsistent across studies. To help clarify the conclusions across these studies, Meissner and Brigham (2001) reviewed 39 research studies on cross-race identification. In terms of correct identifications, averaged across these studies, eyewitnesses were 1.4 times more likely to correctly identify *someone from their own race* whom they had previously viewed than *someone from a race other than their own* whom they had previously viewed. In terms of misidentifications, selection of the wrong suspect was 1.56 times more likely with other-race individuals than with same-race individuals. This meta-analysis, therefore, allows conclusions that are likely to be more reliable than the results of any of the 39 single studies that contributed to it. Meissner and Brigham also found that, across studies, certain factors such as exposure time influence the magnitude of the cross-race effect.

Numerous meta-analyses have been published to assess the strength of eyewitness memory factors. Some of these are mentioned in the section on Relevant Research on Eyewitness Memory. On a large scale, Shapiro and Penrod (1986) conducted a meta-analysis of all facial identification studies published at that time. These included 128 eyewitness identification and facial recognition studies that included 960 experimental conditions and 16,950 subjects. In this analysis, the effect size for each of 19 different independent variables was assessed and pooled across studies. Conclusions were then made about which of these variables were significant in predicting correct hit rates to targets and false-alarm rates to nontargets, and further, the size of the effect of each variable was assessed.

There are several statistical methods for conducting meta-analyses (for an easy-to-understand summary of these methods, see Cutler & Penrod, 1995). Typically, though, meta-analyses involve effect-size analyses expressed in d units (i.e., the difference in means between conditions divided by the standard deviation). A d value of 0.00 indicates no effect; an absolute value larger than 0.00 indicates better recognition in one condition than another. Although meta-analyses allow researchers to draw conclusions that are likely to be more generalizable than those drawn from any single study, it should be considered that the value of a meta-analysis ultimately depends on the validity of the results of the individual studies pooled.

RELEVANT RESEARCH ON EYEWITNESS MEMORY

The research on eyewitness memory typically focuses on specific psychological factors that affect the accuracy of eyewitness memory either alone (i.e., statistical main effects) or in interaction with other factors (i.e., statistical interactions). Although most of this research focuses on the main effects of these factors, in this analysis readers are encouraged to consider how these factors are likely to interact as well. The eyewitness factors are generally divided into two classes of variables: *estimator variables* and *system variables*. Estimator variables are those that are not under the control of the criminal justice system and include characteristics of the witness and characteristics of the observed event. System variables are those that are under the control of the criminal justice system and relate to how a witness was interviewed and the conditions under which an identification was made. There are excellent reviews of the research on factors that affect the accuracy of eyewitness memory, including the meta-analysis by Shapiro and Penrod (1986), and reviews by Wells, Memon, and Penrod (2006) and Wells and Olson (2003). In the remainder of this chapter, I summarize this research and focus on conceptualizations of the interactive effects that these factors are likely to have. First, as background, I summarize the independent effects of these psychological factors. However, because the research on system variables is covered elsewhere (see Chapter 6, this volume), this research is not presented here.

Estimator Variables That Are Characteristics of the Observed Event

It is generally true that characteristics of the observed event have a greater impact on eyewitness memory than characteristics of the eyewitness. This is because even eyewitnesses with excellent visual memory are nonetheless likely to have impaired memory for a perpetrator if they observe him under poor conditions and are not tested until weeks or months later. It should be pointed out that most eyewitness identifications occur from a photographic lineup, in which the face of a suspect is presented along with five filler faces. Thus, at the most basic level, eyewitness identification is going to be affected by how clearly the eyewitness sees the perpetrator's face to begin with. This is called the *perception stage* of memory. The perception stage is primarily affected by how long the eyewitness has to look at the face of the perpetrator, at what distance, and under what lighting conditions.

Exposure Time, Distance, and Lighting

Although few would disagree that an individual cannot be observed in detail when seen from several hundred feet away, after dark, or if the source of lighting is behind the perpetrator's face, the effect of brief exposure time is less obvious. If, for example, individuals incorrectly believed that eyewitness memory works like a camera, then they might assume that whether an eyewitness viewed a person for a long time or a brief duration, the eyewitness's "picture" would still be preserved in memory. This assumption is incorrect. A wealth of research exists on the effects of exposure time on eyewitness memory. In their meta-analysis of facial identification studies, Shapiro and Penrod (1986) reported a linear trend between exposure time to a face and the probability of correctly identifying the face. Memon, Hope, and Bull (2003) demonstrated this effect under reasonably ecologically valid conditions. They had mock witnesses view a realistic videotape of a crime in which the perpetrator was visible for either 12 or 45 s. Tested only 40 min later, the probability of a correct identification in the target-present arrays (the real perpetrator was included in the lineup) was vastly higher in the 45-s than in the 12-s condition (90% vs. 32%), and the probability of an incorrect identification (i.e., a false alarm) in the target-absent arrays (the real perpetrator was not included in the lineup) was significantly higher in the 12-s than in the 45-s condition (85% vs. 41%). However, if an eyewitness observed a shooter for 45 s, but the eyewitness was 150 feet away after sunset, together, the interaction of these factors would not favor an accurate identification.

Weapon Focus

Weapon focus refers to the fact that when an eyewitness's attention is drawn away from a perpetrator's face to a weapon, this decreases the probability that the perpetrator will be correctly identified later. A weapon is an especially salient form of distraction that consequently decreases exposure time to the perpetrator's face. Loftus, Loftus, and Messo (1987) recorded subjects' eye movements when they looked at a series of slides depicting an event in a fast-food restaurant. When a handgun was present in the slides, eyewitnesses made more fixations on the gun, and the fixations were of longer duration than when the gun was replaced by a bank account check. Subsequently, when eyewitness memory was tested with a 12-person photographic lineup, eyewitnesses were significantly less likely to identify the perpetrator in the gun (.15) than the check (.35) condition. This effect was also confirmed by Steblay's (1992) meta-analysis of 19 studies on weapon focus. This analysis indicated that the weapon focus effect was larger in target-absent lineups (higher false alarm rates to filler faces when the perpetrator was not in the lineup) and when memory was impaired by other conditions, such as the factors discussed in this chapter. This is another example of how eyewitness factors interact to affect identification accuracy.

Disguise

Often people try to disguise their appearance when they commit a crime, by wearing a hat, sunglasses, or a hood. In a number of research studies it has been reported that even these relatively commonplace disguises effectively reduce eyewitness identification accuracy. In one such study (Cutler, Penrod, & Martens, 1987), individuals viewed a videotape of a store robbery in which the robber wore a knit cap that covered his hair and hairline or had no cap. In a later videotaped lineup, the robber was less accurately identified when wearing the cap than not (hit rate = .27 vs. .45). Findings in Shapiro and Penrod's (1986) meta-analysis confirm that any alteration in a face from when it was initially viewed until it was presented in a lineup will impair eyewitness identification accuracy (this is the variable that they call *transformation*). However, disguises to upper facial features (i.e., eyes, forehead, hairline) are more likely to impair eyewitness memory than those to lower facial features (i.e., mouth, chin, nose) because upper facial features tend to play a more critical role in face perception and are more likely to be recognized later (Davies, Shepherd, & Ellis, 1979).

Time Delay

Regardless of how well an eyewitness perceives an individual initially, the chance of an accurate identification will dissipate with the passage of time. Knowing this, police officers typically work diligently to apprehend a suspect in the hours and days immediately following a crime while eyewitness memory is more likely to be preserved. The results of a large number of studies support the detrimental effect of time delay on eyewitness memory. It is clear from Shapiro and Penrod's (1986) meta-analysis that longer delays led to fewer correct identifications and more false identification.

A lesser known fact about the relation between time delay and memory is an effect known as *Jost's law* (see Britt & Bunch, 1934). According to Jost's law, weaker memories fade more quickly than stronger ones. Given that older memories are weaker than newer memories, this suggests that the passage of time following a crime will have a greater effect on eyewitness memory for faces perceived poorly and with less detail than for those perceived more clearly and with more detail. This is an example of the interactive effect of psychological factors on eyewitness memory.

Estimator Variables That Are Characteristics of the Witness

Although characteristics of the eyewitness generally have a lesser impact on eyewitness memory than characteristics of the observed event, several characteristics of the witness are significant and should be taken into consideration.

Witness Confidence

A case is more likely to go to trial if the eyewitnesses are confident in their identifications, because attorneys know that confident witnesses are perceived to be more compelling to jurors. However, is it true that more confident eyewitnesses are likely to be more accurate eyewitnesses? In a meta-analysis of the research on the accuracy–confidence relationship, Sporer, Penrod, Read, and Cutler (1995) found that across 30 studies on this topic, the accuracy–confidence relationship was $r = .29$. Although this correlation is statistically significant, it accounts for only 8% of the variance in eyewitness accuracy.

However, Sporer et al. (1995) reported a stronger accuracy–confidence relationship when they limited their analysis only to individuals who chose to make identifications. The accuracy–confidence rate for these "choosers" is more forensically relevant because the individuals who are more likely to testify in court are those who chose someone from a prior lineup, field showup, or some other type of identification test.[1] Among the choosers, the accuracy–confidence relationship was $r = .41$. How can an eyewitness expert help a jury understand what a .41 correlation means? Wells, Olson, and Charman (2002) suggested that one way to think about this correlation is to draw the comparison to a similar relationship for which the correlation is in this same range. Using U.S. Department of Health and Human Services data, they reported that the correlation between a person's height and gender is $r = .43$. Thus, if we assume that eyewitnesses make accurate identifications about 50% of the time, encountering a highly confident misidentification would be about as common as encountering a tall female or a short male person. Presenting the accuracy–confidence relationship to a jury in these terms would help diminish the sanctity of a highly confident eyewitness.

It is also important to recognize that witness confidence is malleable. Typically, given that witness memory declines with the passage of time, it would be predicted that witness confidence decreases as well. However, occasionally witness confidence increases over time, for example, from an identification at a field showup ("He looks like the perpetrator") to the live lineup ("I think that's him; yes, that's him") to testimony at the trial ("I'm sure that's the man who robbed me at the ATM"). When this occurs, it is usually a red flag that something in addition to eyewitness memory is at play. For example, it has been reported that repeatedly questioning eyewitnesses inflates their confidence without affecting the accuracy of memory (Shaw, 1996). Also, if after making an identification (whether correct or incorrect), eyewitnesses

---

[1] A *field showup* is the identification procedure most often used by police, in which an eyewitness is presented a suspect and asked if he or she can identify this suspect. Statistically, this is similar to a true–false test, where you have a 50% chance of being correct if you just guess. The advantage of a field showup is that it can be conducted quickly to avoid time delay.

are provided feedback that they are good witnesses, their subsequent confidence is likely to increase (Chapter 7, this volume; Wells & Bradfield, 1999). By the time that most witnesses testify in court, they have been questioned multiple times, and it would not be surprising to learn that along the way they have either inadvertently or directly received feedback that they "picked the right guy." This alone can explain why many eyewitnesses are so confident in their identification in court in front of the jury.

Cross-Race Identification

One of the strongest witness characteristics associated with identification accuracy is whether the race or ethnicity of the eyewitness and the perpetrator is the same or different. This conclusion follows from the meta-analysis of Meissner and Brigham (2001) discussed earlier in the section on meta-analyses. The cross-race effect has also been reported to be consistent across age. Pezdek, Blandon-Gitlin, and Moore (2003) compared kindergarten children, third graders, and young adults in their ability to identify a Black and a White individual from a six-person lineup after a 1-day delay. Similar sized cross-race effects were reported at each age level.

Meisner and Brigham's (2001) meta-analysis of the cross-race memory research also identified several variables that moderate the cross-race effect. For example, people often want to know whether the cross-race effect is greater for individuals who have lived in racially segregated areas than for those who have lived in racially mixed areas. Although the cross-race effect is somewhat reduced by exposure to other-race individuals, the effect of other-race contact on reducing the false-alarm rate to other-race faces is modest. People also wonder whether the cross-race effect is related to one's racial attitudes. There is no evidence of a direct influence of racial attitudes on the ability to recognize other-race faces. There is, however, a significant interaction of the cross-race effect with exposure time to the target faces. Meissner and Brigham (2001) reported that increased viewing time reduced the disadvantage for cross-race faces; that is, when a witness had more time to view a perpetrator, the false-alarm rate to other-race faces decreased. The cross-race factor influences false-alarm rates less when the other-race target face is observed for a longer period of time. This finding is interesting because it suggests an interaction among eyewitness factors such that eyewitness identification accuracy would be expected to be especially unreliable when multiple deleterious eyewitness factors co-occur.

Eyewitness Stress

In presenting an eyewitness to a jury, the prosecutor frequently claims that certainly the eyewitness would be reliable given the high rate of stress that focused her attention during the incident. Ironically, the research evidence clearly suggests that under high levels of stress, eyewitness memory is less—not more—reliable. This conclusion follows from a meta-analysis by Deffenbacher et al. (2004). Included in the meta-analysis were 36 tests of the effects of stress on recall of crime-related details and 27 tests of stress on person identification. High levels of stress significantly impaired both types of memory, and the effect of stress was greater on (a) reducing correct identification rates than (b) increasing false-alarm rates.

Prosecutors also frequently argue that findings of impaired memory under high levels of stress are restricted to laboratory tests of face recognition memory and have little to do with the high stress of a real crime. This does not appear to be true. First, in the meta-analysis by Deffenbacher et al. (2004), the effects of stress were actually significantly higher in eyewitness identification studies that involved staged crimes than in those that involved laboratory face recognition tasks. Also, in one of the most impressive real-world studies of the effects of high stress on face recognition accuracy (Morgan et al., 2004), high levels of stress impaired eyewitness memory. In their study, more than 500 active duty military personnel were tested on their ability to recognize two individuals, each of whom had interrogated them for 40 min as part of a prisoner-of-war survival training program. After 12 hr of confinement, each participant experienced both (a) a high-stress interrogation in which questioning was accompanied by physical confrontation, and (b) a low-stress interrogation without physical confrontation. A different individual had interrogated them in each condition. One day later, after recovering from sleep and food deprivation, each participant was tested on memory for the two interrogators by using a live lineup or a photographic lineup. Correct identifications were significantly lower and incorrect identifications were significantly higher under the high- than the low-stress condition.

Intoxication of Witness

It has long been known that alcohol consumption impairs cognitive functioning, including memory (Parker & Noble, 1977), but how does alcohol affect eyewitness memory? It is not unusual for an eyewitness to a crime to be intoxicated; this would be common in late-night fights, drug deals that have gone bad, and home-invasion robberies. The results of two studies suggest that alcohol impairs eyewitness memory and identification. In the first of these studies, the eyewitnesses were intoxicated or sober only at the time that they observed the perpetrator. In this study, Read, Yuille, and Tollestrup (1992) had intoxicated and sober individuals view a staged crime, and then 1 week later (when sober) they tested their memories for the perpetrator by using a six-person lineup. Overall, alcohol reduced the probability of correctly identifying the target individual but did not affect false-identification rates. In a second study, Dysart, Lindsay, MacDonald, and Wicke (2002) reported that intoxicated eyewitnesses were less reliable than sober eyewitnesses, especially if they were intoxicated both at the time of observation and test. This would occur, for example, if an intoxicated eyewitness was presented a field showup shortly after observing an incident. They reported that under these conditions, although blood-alcohol level was not significantly related to correct identification of the target individual when the eyewitness was shown a target-present showup, when presented a target-absent showup, the false identification rate was vastly higher in the high (52% misidentification) than the low (22% misidentification) blood-alcohol level condition. From these two studies it is clear that sober eyewitnesses are more accurate than intoxicated eyewitnesses, whether they are tested with a one-person showup or a six-person lineup, and whether they are intoxicated or sober when tested. However, additional research is necessary to flesh out the mechanisms by which alcohol affects eyewitness memory.

In another study, Assefi and Garry (2003) assessed the effect of alcohol on the suggestibility of eyewitness memory. Individuals drank plain tonic water, but half were told that it was vodka and tonic. They all then participated in an eyewitness memory experiment in which misleading postevent information was suggested. Individuals who were told that they had consumed vodka were significantly more likely to be swayed by the suggested information than were control subjects. This finding suggests that eyewitnesses who simply believe that they are intoxicated are more likely to be misled by information that they heard from other eyewitnesses or police officers than are eyewitnesses who believe that they are sober.

Interactive Effects of Eyewitness Memory Factors

Every eyewitness case involves the role of numerous variables, each of which is likely to affect the accuracy of eyewitness memory alone (i.e., a statistical main effect) and in interaction with other variables (i.e., a statistical interaction). First, consider the interactive effect of several estimator variables operating together (some of these have been discussed earlier in this chapter). As a general rule, eyewitness identification accuracy would be expected to be especially unreliable when multiple deleterious eyewitness factors co-occur. For example, we discussed Meissner and Brigham's (2001) finding that the cross-race effect was especially detrimental to the accuracy of eyewitness memory when the viewing time was relatively short. If an eyewitness observed a perpetrator for a relatively brief time, the probability of being able to correctly identify the perpetrator is reduced but especially so if the perpetrator and the eyewitness are of different races. Also, as we discussed previously, if the briefly observed perpetrator was 100 feet away rather than 10 feet away, the probability of correctly identifying the individual is even worse.

The delay factor also interacts with other estimator variables. As discussed above, based on Jost's law it can be predicted that weaker memories will fade more quickly than stronger memories. Thus, if, for example, an eyewitness is tested 3 months after a crime, this relatively long time delay will detrimentally affect memory more for a cross-race individual seen only briefly than for a same-race individual with whom the eyewitness had a face-to-face conversation for 15 min. Whether the combined effect of multiple estimator variables is cumulative (i.e., simply the sum of the effect of each variable alone) or interactive (i.e., the combined effect of the variables is some more complex function) is yet to be determined empirically. Nonetheless, in predicting the probability that an eyewitness identification is accurate, it is important to consider the full list of psychological factors operating in the case and the combined effect of these factors. It is rare that the accuracy of an eyewitness identification will rest with an appraisal of a single factor.

What about the interactive effect of estimator variables and system variables? As a general rule, when eyewitness memory is weak, system variables are likely to have a stronger impact. Consider the situation in which two coworkers in a doctor's office are having lunch. The office is closed, so when they hear some noise in the adjacent room, they walk over to see who might be there. When they see an unfamiliar man packing up a box, they ask him what he is doing. He claims to be looking for the restroom and leaves when confronted. The coworkers call the police, who have a suspect apprehended within 30 min. Both coworkers, standing together, confidently identify the defendant at a field show up at which they are told, "We've got him." Under the conditions of observation in this situation, these eyewitnesses would be expected to have a strong memory for the perpetrator—they were close to him, the lighting was good, they were face-to-face talking to him for about 45 s, their attention was directed to the perpetrator by the witnesses' suspicion, and they identified him only 30 min later. The witnesses should have been tested independently, and they should not have been given the biased comment "We've got him." Nonetheless, we have sufficient reason to believe that these witnesses have a strong and enduring memory for the perpetrator's face, and such a memory is less likely to be influenced by flawed system variables.

APPLICATIONS OF RESEARCH ON EYEWITNESS MEMORY

Psychological research on factors that affect the accuracy of eyewitness memory and identification can be used by the legal system in various ways that serve to increase conviction rates for individuals more likely to be guilty and decrease conviction rates for individuals more likely to be innocent. Two such applications are presented here. The most obvious way that these research findings are applied is through eyewitness expert testimony. According to Federal Rule of Evidence 702, an *expert witness* is an expert in his or her field who by virtue of education, training, skill or experience has specialized knowledge in a particular area that has been determined to be beyond the stock of common knowledge and potentially of assistance to the jury. Basically, an eyewitness expert witness is usually called by the defense to testify during a trial in which the prosecution's case against a defendant involves eyewitness evidence, evidence that is deemed dubious by the defense.

Most of the substance of the eyewitness-expert testimony pertains to what is referred to in the landmark California eyewitness case of *People v. McDonald* (1984) as "the psychological factors that may have impaired the accuracy of a typical eyewitness identification, . . . with supporting references to experimental studies of such phenomena." Generally, this is done by having the expert present the estimator variables and system variables that are likely to have affected the reliability of the eyewitness identifications. For a detailed discussion of how eyewitness expert witnesses work with attorneys and what type of testimony they tend to give, see Pezdek (2009).

Another way that research findings on the accuracy of eyewitness memory and identification can be applied is through continuing education of prosecution and defense attorneys. Although the Sixth Amendment of the U.S. Constitution guarantees all criminal defendants the right to a trial, in fact, the majority of criminal cases do not result in a trial. Approximately 90% of criminal cases are resolved through plea bargaining, and it is crucial to assure that such bargains produce justice on both sides of the bar. Legal scholars suggest that attorneys' decisions in regard to whether to plea bargain a case are largely based on the strength of the evidence against the defendant (Burke, 2007; Pritchard, 1986). When the evidence is weak, prosecutors are more likely to offer a plea bargain; when the evidence is strong, defense attorneys are more likely to recommend a plea bargain. However, in eyewitness identification cases, attorneys are not always accurately assessing the strength of the eyewitness evidence, because they are unfamiliar with the eyewitness memory research. Knowing what factors tend to be associated with accurate versus inaccurate eyewitness identification, prosecution and defense attorneys are more likely to discriminate accurately between strong and weak eyewitness evidence and thus avoid proceeding to trial with cases that might lead to convictions of the innocent. Police officers can also apply this knowledge in their investigations. With a better understanding of eyewitness memory, perhaps they would follow fewer false leads and put together stronger cases for prosecutors.

CONCLUSION

Eyewitness evidence is the leading cause of erroneous convictions of innocent individuals. Fortunately, there is now considerable scientific research on this topic, research conducted using rigorous scientific methods. This research, if effectively disseminated to jurors as well as prosecution and defense attorneys, could reduce conviction rates for the innocent. Although attorneys and forensic practitioners have historically been difficult to impress with scientific evidence, this is less likely to be true today. The impressive scope of the psychological research on eyewitness memory and identification has bolstered the admissibility of eyewitness expert testimony in court and expanded forensic continuing education opportunities in this area.

REFERENCES

Assefi, S. L., & Garry, M. (2003). Absolut memory distortions: Alcohol placebos influence the misinformation effect. *Psychological Science, 14,* 77–80. doi:10.1111/1467-9280.01422

Behrman, B. W., & Davey, S. L. (2001). Eyewitness identification in actual criminal cases: An archival analysis. *Law and Human Behavior, 25,* 475–491. doi: 0147-7307/01/1000-0475

Benton, T. R., Ross, D. F., Bradshaw, E., Thomas, W. N., & Bradshaw, G. S. (2006). Eyewitness memory is still not common sense: Comparing jurors, judges, and law enforcement to eyewitness experts. *Applied Cognitive Psychology, 20,* 115–129. doi:10.1002/acp.1171

Bornstein, B. H. (1999). The ecological validity of jury simulations: Is the jury still out? *Law and Human Behavior, 23,* 75–91. doi:10.1023/A:1022326807441

Britt, S. H., & Bunch, M. E. (1934). Jost's law and retroactive inhibition. *The American Journal of Psychology, 46,* 299–308. doi:10.2307/1416562

Burke, A. S. (2007). Prosecutorial passion, cognitive bias, and plea bargaining. *Marquette Law Review, 91,* 183–212.

Cutler, B. L., & Penrod, S. D. (1995). *Mistaken identification: The eyewitness, psychology, and the law.* Cambridge, MA: Cambridge University Press.

Cutler, B. L., Penrod, S. D., & Martens, T. K. (1987) The reliability of eyewitness identifications: The role of system and estimator variables. *Law and Human Behavior, 11,* 223-258. doi: 0147-7307/87/0900-0233

Davies, G. M., Shepherd, J. W., & Ellis, H. D. (1979). Similarity effects in face recognition. *The American Journal of Psychology, 92,* 507–523. doi:10.2307/1421569

Deffenbacher, K. A., Bornstein, B. H., Penrod, S. D., & McCorty, E. K. (2004). A meta-analytic review of the effects of high stress on eyewitness memory. *Law and Human Behavior, 28,* 687–706. doi:10.1007/s10979-004-0565-x

Dysart, J. E., Lindsay, R. C. L., MacDonald, T. K., & Wicke, D. (2002). The intoxicated witness: Effects of alcohol on identification accuracy from showups. *Journal of Applied Psychology, 87,* 170–175. doi:10.1037/0021-9010.87.1.170

Garrett, B. L. (2008, January). Judging innocence. *Columbia Law Review.* Retrieved from http://ssrn.com/abstract=999984

Loftus, E. F., Loftus, G. R., & Messo, J. (1987). Some facts about "weapon focus." *Law and Human Behavior, 11,* 55–62. doi:10.1007/BF01044839

Meissner, C. A., & Brigham, J. C. (2001). Twenty years of investigating the own-race bias in memory for faces: A meta-analytic review. *Psychology, Public Policy, and Law, 7,* 3–5. doi:10.1037/1076-8971.7.1.3

Memon, A., Hope, L., & Bull, R. (2003). Exposure duration: Effects on eyewitness accuracy and confidence. *The British Journal of Psychology, 94,* 339–354. doi:10.1348/000712603767876262

Moore, D. (1907). Yellow psychology. *Law Notes, 11,* 125–127.

Morgan, C. A., III, Hazlett, G., Doran, A., Garrett, S., Hoyt, G., Thomas, P., . . . Southwick, S. M. (2004). Accuracy of eyewitness memory for persons encountered during exposure to highly intense stress. *International Journal of Law and Psychiatry, 27,* 265–279. doi:10.1016/j.ijlp.2004.03.004

Munsterberg, H. (1908). *On the witness stand: Essays on psychology and crime.* Garden City, NY: Doubleday.

O'Rourke, T. E., Penrod, S. D., Cutler, B. L., & Stuve, T. E. (1989). The external validity of eyewitness identification research: Generalizing across subject populations. *Law and Human Behavior, 13,* 385–395. doi:10.1007/BF01056410

Parker, E. S., & Noble, E. P. (1977). Alcohol consumption and cognitive functioning in social drinkers. *Journal of Studies on Alcohol, 38,* 1224–1232.

People v. McDonald, 37 Cal.3d 351, 690 P.2d 709, 716, 208. Cal. Rptr. 236, 245 (1984).

Pezdek, K. (2009). Content, form and ethical issues concerning expert psychological testimony on eyewitness identification. In B. L. Cutler (Ed.), *Expert testimony on the psychology of eyewitness identification* (pp. 29–51). New York, NY: Oxford University Press. doi:10.1093/acprof:oso/9780195331974.003.002

Pezdek, K., Avila-Mora, E., & Sperry, K. (2010). Does trial presentation medium matter in jury simulation research? Evaluating the effectiveness of eyewitness expert testimony. *Applied Cognitive Psychology, 24,* 673–690.

Pezdek, K., Blandon-Gitlin, I., & Moore, C. (2003). Children's face recognition memory: More evidence for the cross-race effect. *Journal of Applied Psychology, 88,* 760–763. doi:10.1037/0021-9010.88.4.760

Pritchard, D. (1986). Homicide and bargained justice: The agenda setting effect of crime news on prosecutors. *Public Opinion Quarterly, 50,* 143–159. doi:10.1086/268971

Radelet, M. L., Bedau, H. A., & Putnam, C. E. (1992). *In spite of innocence: Erroneous convictions in capital cases.* Boston, MA: Northeastern University Press.

Read, J. D., & Desmarais, S. L. (2009). Expert psychology testimony on eyewitness identification: A matter of common sense? In B. L. Cutler (Ed.), *Expert testimony on the psychology of eyewitness identification* (pp. 115–141). Oxford, England: Oxford University Press. doi:10.1093/acprof:oso/9780195331974.003.006

Read, J. D., Yuille, J. C., & Tollestrup, P. (1992). Recollections of a robbery: Effects of arousal and alcohol upon recall and person identification. *Law and Human Behavior, 16,* 425–446. doi:10.1007/BF02352268

Shapiro, P. N., & Penrod, S. (1986). Meta-analysis of facial identification studies. *Psychological Bulletin, 100,* 139–156. doi:10.1037/0033-2909.100.2.139

Shaw, J. S., III. (1996). Increases in eyewitness confidence resulting from postevent questioning. *Journal of Experimental Psychology: Applied, 2,* 126–146. doi:10.1037/1076-898X.2.2.126

Sporer, S. L., Penrod, S., Read, J. D., & Cutler, B. (1995). Choosing, confidence, and accuracy: A meta-analysis of the confidence-accuracy relation in eyewitness identification studies. *Psychological Bulletin, 118,* 315–327. doi:10.1037/0033-2909.118.3.315

Steblay, N. M. (1992). A meta-analytic review of the weapon focus effect. *Law and Human Behavior, 16,* 413–424. doi:10.1007/BF02352267

Valentine, T., Pickering, A., & Darling, S. (2003). Characteristics of eyewitness identification that predict the outcome of real lineups. *Applied Cognitive Psychology, 17,* 969–993. doi:10.1002/acp.939

Wells, G. L., & Bradfield, A. L. (1999). Distortions in eyewitnesses' recollections: Can the postidentification-feedback effect be moderated? *Psychological Science, 10,* 138–144. doi:10.1111/1467-9280.00121

Wells, G. L., Memon, A., & Penrod, S. D. (2006). Eyewitness evidence: Improving its probative value. *Psychological Science in the Public Interest, 7,* 45–75. doi:10.1111/j.1529-1006.2006.00027.x

Wells, G. L., & Olson, E. A. (2003). Eyewitness testimony. *Annual Review of Psychology, 54,* 277–295. doi:10.1146/annurev.psych.54.101601.145028

Wells, G. L., Olson, E. A., & Charman, S. D. (2002). The confidence of eyewitnesses in their identifications from lineups. *Current Directions in Psychological Science, 11,* 151–154. doi:10.1111/1467-8721.00189

Wigmore, J. H. (1909). Professor Munsterburg and the psychology of testimony. *Illinois Law Review, 3,* 399–445.

Wright, D. B., & McDaid, A. T. (1996). Comparing system and estimator variables using data from real lineups. *Applied Cognitive Psychology, 10,* 75–84. doi:10.1002/(SICI)1099-0720(199602)10:1<75::AID-ACP364>3.0.CO;2-E

Yuille, J. C., & Cutshall, J. (1986). A case study of eyewitnesses' memory of a crime. *Journal of Applied Psychology, 71,* 291–301. doi:10.1037/0021-9010.71.2.291

6

SUGGESTIVE EYEWITNESS IDENTIFICATION PROCEDURES

DAVID M. ZIMMERMAN, JACQUELINE L. AUSTIN,
AND MARGARET BULL KOVERA

In 1986, Thomas McGowan was convicted of aggravated sexual assault and burglary on the basis of the victim's identification of him as the man who had raped her. The victim was first shown a live lineup that contained three suspects, one of whom was McGowan, and three fillers (or foils). After the victim failed to identify anyone from that lineup, the police showed her a photo array that contained seven photos; McGowan's photo was presented with six other filler photos, only three of which were marked as being from Richardson County where the crime took place. Of the remaining four photos, one was in color like the Richardson county photos but indicated that it had been taken of someone arrested in a different county, and the other three were black-and-white pictures. The photographs were presented to the victim simultaneously in a horizontal array, and the investigators did not instruct the victim that the perpetrator may or may not be in the lineup. Additionally, the lineup administrator knew which lineup member was the suspect. The victim–witness picked McGowan from the lineup even though he was not the man who raped her. Although she initially said she was not certain that the man in the photo was her attacker, the police officer who administered the lineup told her that she had to be sure if she were to make an identification, at which point the victim said that McGowan was definitely the perpetrator. Only after serving 23 years in prison was McGowan exonerated by DNA evidence (for full information on the case, see http://www.innocenceproject.org or http://www.thejusticeproject.org).

RELEVANCE OF SUGGESTIVE EYEWITNESS IDENTIFICATION PROCEDURES TO CONVICTION OF THE INNOCENT

When collecting eyewitness identification evidence in the McGowan case, the police used procedures that have been deemed *suggestive* by leading scholars of eyewitness reliability (Wells et al., 1998). The instructions given to the victim in the McGowan case did not include a warning that the perpetrator may or may not be in the lineup. Instructions that fail to warn the witness that the perpetrator may not be in the lineup have been termed *biased instructions* because witnesses may implicitly assume the perpetrator must be in the lineup, even if nobody is a match to their memory, otherwise the police would not have asked the witness to make an identification. Further, any explicit suggestion by the administrator that the perpetrator is in the lineup might reinforce this belief (Wells & Quinlivan, 2009). Also, the lineup composition in the McGowan case clearly narrowed the victim's viable choices— only four of the seven lineup members were represented by color photos, and of these color photos only three had the lineup members holding placards indicating that they had been arrested in the relevant county. Research has shown that other differences in lineup composition (e.g., fillers that do not match the witness's description of the perpetrator) increase the suggestiveness of the lineup procedure, in turn increasing misidentifications (e.g., Clark & Tunnicliff, 2001; Wells, Rydell, & Seelau, 1993). The police in the McGowan case did not use a double-blind lineup procedure in which the lineup administrator (usually a detective) is unaware of the suspect's identity (Wells et al., 1998). The lineup administrator in the McGowan case knew which lineup member was the suspect and may have emitted subtle cues that led the victim to initially pick McGowan. Moreover, the administrator's suggestion that the victim had to be certain about her identification likely produced the victim's inflated confidence in the accuracy of her identification.

Two other procedures also could have played a role in the victim's misidentification of McGowan. The police presented the lineup members to the victim–witness *simultaneously*, as opposed to *sequentially*, with the witness making a separate yes–no decision after the presentation of each lineup member. Simultaneous lineups may encourage witnesses to make relative judgments, leading them to pick whichever lineup member is most similar to their memories of the perpetrator (Lindsay & Wells, 1985). In contrast, a sequential procedure does not allow witnesses to make direct comparisons among the lineup members, forcing them to compare each lineup member against their memory of the perpetrator. Although there is some debate about whether sequential lineups reduce mistaken identifications because they reduce relative judgments or increase witnesses' criterion for choosing a person from a lineup (Meissner, Tredoux, Parker, & MacLin, 2005), a large body of research comparing simultaneous and sequential procedures demonstrates that sequential procedures significantly reduce false identifications with a relatively smaller reduction in correct identification of guilty perpetrators (for a meta-analytic review, see Steblay, Dysart, & Wells, in press). Finally, McGowan's appearance in multiple lineup presentations may also have contributed to the victim's incorrect identification, as it is possible that the witness found McGowan familiar when viewing the photo array because she had seen him previously in the live lineup, an effect known as *transference* (Deffenbacher, Bornstein, & Penrod, 2006).

The McGowan case contained most of the possible suggestive procedures that can occur during the administration of a lineup, and the presence of these suggestive procedures is common in DNA exoneration cases (http://www.innocenceproject.org). Nearly 75% of DNA exoneration cases involved at least one witness misidentification, and it is likely that many of these wrongful convictions could have been prevented with less suggestive police procedures. In the remainder of this chapter, we review the psychological foundations, research methodologies, and relevant research on suggestive eyewitness identifications procedures, followed by an examination of the policy implications and future directions for research in this important domain.

SCIENTIFIC PSYCHOLOGICAL FOUNDATIONS OF SUGGESTIVE EYEWITNESS IDENTIFICATION PROCEDURES

Wells and Luus (1990) argued that

> although substantive theory in social psychology has had some impact on the practical research literature on eyewitness identification, it has been the theory of what constitutes a sound social psychological experiment that has directed most of the advances in this area. (p. 107)

Conducting lineups is akin to psychological experimentation, in which the police officer represents the experimenter, and various other components of the lineup procedure represent elements of an experiment. In this framework witnesses are considered the study participants, lineup members are the stimuli, instructions to witnesses are the experimental protocol, and eyewitness behaviors (e.g., choosing, accuracy, confidence) are the dependent variables.

Moreover, police have hypotheses about the suspect that they test using a design (e.g., the lineup containing a suspect and some number of fillers) and procedure—just as social psychologists test their theories.

Given the parallel logic of experiments and eyewitness lineup procedures, the "lineups as experiments" analogy—more than any specific social psychological theory—has influenced the study of suggestive eyewitness lineup procedures. Because experimental stimuli can create demand characteristics (i.e., communicate to the participant the hypothesis of the experiment), researchers have studied lineup composition and whether varying methods of choosing lineup fillers are more likely to communicate to the witness which lineup member is the suspect. The lineup administrators' instructions to witnesses can also communicate biasing information, just as instructions in experiments have the potential for demand characteristics. Different methods of presenting lineup members to witnesses may encourage different decision-making processes. Finally, just as it is possible for experimenters who know the study hypothesis to communicate that hypothesis to participants who wittingly or unwittingly change their behaviors to conform to the experimenters' expectations (i.e., experimenter expectancy effects), lineup administrators who know which lineup member is the suspect may communicate that information to the witness, intentionally or unintentionally. Thus, there are many similarities between conducting an identification procedure and conducting an experiment, and the same principles used to evaluate the internal validity of an experiment may be used to evaluate the quality of lineup procedures.

SCIENTIFIC METHODS USED IN THE RESEARCH ON SUGGESTIVE EYEWITNESS IDENTIFICATION PROCEDURES

Researchers primarily use one of two standard paradigms for studying eyewitness phenomena. In both field and laboratory simulation paradigms, participants watch a staged or filmed event (e.g., a theft, an unusual event in a classroom), after which the witnesses participate in some type of identification procedure. Researchers may manipulate variables associated with the lineup procedure (e.g., sequential vs. simultaneous lineup, instruction type) or composition (e.g., how fillers are chosen) to determine whether they increase or decrease suggestiveness. One common manipulation is whether the actual perpetrator is present in the lineup. When the perpetrator is present (a target-present lineup), the study will provide information about the effects of procedural changes on the rate of correct identifications of the perpetrator and two types of mistakes: filler identifications and incorrect rejections of the lineup (e.g., a failure to identify the perpetrator). Target-absent lineups, which do not contain the perpetrator, provide information about rates of correct rejections of the lineup as well as mistaken identifications of the innocent suspect or fillers. The primary benefits of field and laboratory simulations are tight experimental control and the experimenters' unequivocal knowledge of the perpetrator's identity.

In archival studies, researchers examine case files that contain information about the identifications made by witnesses to actual crimes. They may code the cases for information about the witnessing conditions (e.g., witness and perpetrator race, presence of a weapon), witness confidence, and characteristics of the identification procedure (e.g., method of presenting lineup members). Because it is often impossible to determine whether the suspect is the true perpetrator, the identification decisions in these studies are normally limited to whether the witness identified the suspect, identified a filler, or rejected the lineup (i.e., failed to choose a lineup member). Although the identification of a filler is a known mistake, as the filler is definitely not the perpetrator, the identification of a suspect may be a correct decision or a mistake. Although authors of some archival studies may attempt to estimate the likelihood that the identification of a particular suspect is a mistake or a correct identification by evaluating the extent to which the identification is corroborated by other evidence, in the absence of DNA evidence implicating the suspect, there normally remains doubt about whether a particular suspect is the perpetrator. Not even convictions provide certain proof of suspect guilt given the number of defendants who have been wrongfully convicted on the basis of faulty eyewitness evidence.

Some have argued (e.g., Mecklenburg, 2006) that typical field and laboratory simulations lack external validity. More specifically, critics have argued that such simulations do not adequately mimic conditions that occur in *actual* crimes, limiting the generalizability of the observed effects. Relatively few archival studies have been conducted, in part because it is difficult to evaluate the effects of lineup procedures on accuracy using archival methods. Archival methods are problematic not only because it is difficult to establish ground truth but also because the lack of random assignment and the inability to control for the influence of unmeasured procedural variations in archival studies make establishing the causal role of identification procedures in mistaken identifications virtually impossible. In contrast, experimental simulations— whether conducted in the laboratory or the field—allow for strong inferences about the causal relationships between identification procedures and witness accuracy. Finally, critics of laboratory and field simulations appear to be a minority among established researchers, as many top experts agree that simulation research is generalizable (Kassin, 2001; see also Chapter 5, this volume, for a discussion of scientific methods used in eyewitness research).

RELEVANT RESEARCH ON SUGGESTIVE EYEWITNESS IDENTIFICATION PROCEDURES

Scholars have used these research methods to examine whether characteristics of the identification procedure used to collect eyewitness evidence influence the accuracy of the resulting eyewitness identifications. The characteristics that have received the most empirical scrutiny are the instructions given to witnesses about the lineup procedure, lineup composition (e.g., how lineup members are chosen), administrator knowledge of which lineup member is the suspect, and the method of presenting lineup members to the witness.

Lineup Instructions

The importance of administering unbiased instructions was first demonstrated by using a laboratory simulation in which witnesses watched a staged act of vandalism and then attempted to make identifications (Malpass & Devine, 1981). Participants viewed either a target-present or target-absent live lineup and heard either biased or unbiased instructions. Specifically, the unbiased instructions contained a warning that the perpetrator may not be in the lineup, whereas the biased instructions communicated to the witness that the administrator believed the perpetrator was in the lineup and asked the witness to tell the administrator which lineup member was the perpetrator. Overall, participants who received biased instructions were more likely than participants who received unbiased instructions to make a selection from the lineup regardless of whether it contained the perpetrator. This higher choosing rate increased the rate of mistaken identifications in target-absent lineups. Overall, the number of correct identifications did not differ between instruction types (Malpass & Devine, 1981).

A meta-analysis of 18 studies examining the influence of biased police lineup instructions supported the reliability of these findings. Across studies, choosing rates were higher when the witnesses received biased instruction (Steblay, 1997). When the perpetrator was present in the lineup, biased instructions did not affect the proportion of correct identifications obtained. However, when biased instructions were used in target-absent lineups, the increased rate of choosing increased the rate of mistaken identifications (Steblay, 1997). Therefore, although there were no benefits of using unbiased instructions when the perpetrator was present, there were benefits when the perpetrator was absent. Because police are rarely certain of a perpetrator's identity at the time of the lineup (otherwise there would be little need to conduct the identification procedure), these findings provide support for police use of unbiased instructions.

A critic of this meta-analysis noted that the effects of biased instructions in target-present and target-absent lineups should follow different patterns than observed and suggested that the conclusions taken from Steblay's analysis may be wrong (Clark, 2005). In target-absent lineups, an increase in choosing rates should result in an equivalent drop in accurate rejection rates. In target-present lineups, an increase in choosing rates should result in a $1/N$ fractional increase of correct identifications, where $N =$ the number of lineup members. As a side note, these effects would be observed only with the use of fair lineups; however, research shows that lineups are often unfair such that the suspect has a greater than $1/N$ chance of being chosen from the lineup (Brigham, Meissner, & Wasserman, 1999; Valentine & Heaton, 1999; Wells & Bradfield, 1999). To better understand why these effects were not observed, Clark (2005) reexamined the studies contained in the meta-analysis. He found that many of the studies used in Steblay's meta-analysis suffered from ceiling effects, a methodological artifact known to reduce sensitivity and restrict the ability to detect significant differences. Therefore, he provided a cautionary warning about the conclusions drawn from Steblay's meta-analysis and further encouraged researchers to pursue research to address these methodological issues.

Generally, scholars have advocated the use of unbiased lineup instructions in which administrators warn witnesses that the perpetrator may or may not be in the lineup (Technical Working Group for Eyewitness Evidence, 1999; Wells et al., 1998). Scholars have also made other recommendations to further improve lineup instructions. For example, one group of scholars suggested that law enforcement officers tell witnesses that the lineup administrator is blind to the identity of the suspect (Wells et al., 1998). A different group of scholars recommended instructing law enforcement officers to provide witnesses with a cautionary warning that the perpetrator may have changed appearance since committing the crime and that it is just as important to free innocent suspects as it is to identify guilty ones (Technical Working Group for Eyewitness Evidence, 1999).

Although there remains no published empirical evidence to support the efficacy of the instruction that the lineup administrator is blind to the suspect's identity or the warning about the importance of setting innocent suspects free, there has been one published study that tests the effects of the change of appearance instruction. Specifically, researchers tested the hypothesis that this change of appearance instruction would lead witnesses to lower their criterion for choosing a lineup member when making an identification because the instruction would cause them to assume that their memory of the perpetrator may not exactly match how the suspect looks at the time of the identification (Charman & Wells, 2007). To test this hypothesis, participants viewed a videotaped mock crime of four perpetrators breaking and entering a garage and later attempted to identify the perpetrators from a photo array. All participants were told that the perpetrator may or may not be in the lineup. Half of the participants were also given appearance change instruction. Each witness attempted identifications from four separate line-ups, one for each perpetrator. Two of the lineups were target present and two were target absent. Witnesses were more likely to identify one of the lineup members as the perpetrator when they had received appearance change instructions. This increase in choosing rates produced increased rates of filler identifications in both target-present and target-absent lineups. However, appearance change instructions did not increase the rates of accurate identifications in target-present lineups. Although further research and replication is necessary, these initial results do not support the inclusion of this warning as it did not increase correct identifications but did increase the likelihood of mistaken identifications.

Lineup Composition

The composition of a lineup affects the extent to which the lineup communicates to the witness who the suspect is. It is obvious that a lineup with a light-skinned suspect and darker skinned fillers provides the witness with a clue as to the suspect's identity (especially if the perpetrator was light skinned), but this is an extreme example. Researchers investigating the fairness of lineup composition in real cases provide naïve participants with the description of the perpetrator provided by the actual witness, after which the naïve participants view the lineup and attempt to identify the perpetrator. The lineup is suggestive if participants identify the suspect at rates that are greater than chance (Doob & Kirshenbaum, 1973). Studies using this methodology have shown bias in the lineups that the police use in their investigations, with naïve participants choosing suspects at over twice the rate that would be expected by chance (Brigham et al., 1999; Py, Demarchi, Ginet, & Wasiak, 2003; Wells & Bradfield, 1999). In sum, it appears that unfair lineups are not uncommon in criminal justice practice.

Are there methods of constructing a lineup that decrease the likelihood that witnesses would choose the suspect through guessing or deduction rather than because the suspect matches their memory of the perpetrator? A primary purpose of providing fillers—lineup members who are known to be innocent—in lineups is to reduce the likelihood that a witness who is guessing will identify the suspect as the perpetrator (Wells & Quinlivan, 2009). Additionally, fillers can serve as a test for the quality of witnesses' memory of the event, because choosing a filler from a lineup is a mistake that establishes that a witness's memory for the perpetrator is unreliable. The quality of lineup fillers is related to the suggestiveness of the procedures, which in turn can lead witnesses to misidentify innocent suspects from target-absent lineups. If the suspect stands out from the fillers because the photos of the fillers have different labels, markings, or photographic quality than the photo of the suspect (as was the case in the photo array used to identify McGowan), these differences may narrow witnesses' focus to a smaller subset of lineup members. Not only can physical differences between the photos of the suspect and fillers call attention to the suspect but also the selection of fillers themselves can narrow the number of viable choices a lineup contains, such as when fillers do not match the witness's description of the perpetrator. When examining the influence of lineup composition on witness accuracy, some researchers have focused their theoretical attention and empirical efforts on this issue of filler selection.

Lineups that contain fillers that do not match the physical characteristics of the perpetrator can increase false identifications. In one study, participants viewed a staged crime, after which they had an opportunity to identify the perpetrator from a six-person photo array (Lindsay & Wells, 1980). The target-present and target-absent (with an innocent suspect) arrays contained fillers chosen to be similar to witnesses' descriptions of the perpetrator ("fair" lineups) or to be dissimilar ("unfair" lineups). Subjects were less likely to pick either the perpetrator or the innocent suspect from fair lineups that contained fillers that were similar to descriptions of the perpetrator than from lineups with fillers that were dissimilar to witness descriptions of the perpetrator. The reduction in identifications of the suspect was significantly greater for lineups that contained the innocent suspect than for lineups that contained the perpetrator.

Similar results were obtained in a more ecologically valid experiment, in which witnesses believed they were participating in an actual case (Wells et al., 1993). The lineups presented to witnesses contained fillers that either matched the suspect's appearance or matched the witness's description of the perpetrator. Matching fillers to the witness's description of the perpetrator resulted in significantly fewer false identifications than did matching fillers to suspects. Moreover, the efficacy of other procedural safeguards may be contingent on lineup composition. Sequential presentation of lineups—as opposed to simultaneous presentation—reduced witnesses' mistaken identifications of innocent suspects only in unfair lineups (Carlson, Gronlund, & Clark, 2008). These findings underscore the importance of lineup composition, especially as some jurisdictions have resisted adopting sequential presentation of lineups.

What is the best way to pick fillers to ensure a fair, nonsuggestive lineup? The match-to-suspect technique involves picking fillers based on their similarity to the suspect, but it does not specify discrete parameters for matching the fillers. In contrast, a match-to-description strategy involves picking fillers based on the attributes provided in the original description by the witness (Luus & Wells, 1991). Luus and Wells (1991) argued that the match-to-suspect method may sometimes yield a lineup of suspect clones, with so little variation in the physical characteristics of the lineup members that the witness is left with no distinguishing features to assist their identification attempt. In contrast, with a match-to-description method of choosing fillers, lineup members match the perpetrator on the characteristics that the witness mentioned in his or her description of the perpetrator but vary on attributes not explicitly mentioned in the description. Matching fillers on characteristics mentioned by the witness should reduce the ability of the witness to deduce which lineup member is the suspect. Allowing the lineup members to vary on other dimensions provides witnesses with some characteristics that would allow them to differentiate among the lineup members. Because the match-to-description technique contains both of these qualities, it should produce more accurate identifications.

Studies that examine the differences between a match-to-suspect and match-to description strategy have yielded mixed results. In one study, witnesses attempted identifications from lineups created by using a match-to-description strategy, match-to-suspect strategy, or a mismatch-description method (i.e., the filler failed to match one physical characteristic from the description; Wells, Rydell, & Seelau, 1993). Match-to description lineups minimized false identifications and maximized correct identifications. In comparison, the match-to-suspect lineups produced fewer correct identifications, and the mismatch-description lineups increased mistaken identifications. Some studies have replicated the finding that match-to-suspect lineups produce increases in false identifications (Clark & Tunnicliff, 2001), whereas others have failed to find an advantage of match-to-description lineups (Darling, Valentine, & Memon, 2008; Tunnicliff & Clark, 2000). Although the match-to-description method does not consistently improve accuracy rates, this method does not reduce eyewitness accuracy rates, and thus the match-to-description method should be the preferred strategy for composing lineups.

However, it is increasingly clear that single-suspect lineups with multiple fillers are less suggestive than a single-suspect lineup, also referred to as a *showup*. A showup is a procedure in which a witness is shown a single person or photograph (invariably the suspect) without any fillers at all. Although not as commonly studied as lineups, showups are quite common in criminal justice practice (Steblay, Dysart, Fulero, & Lindsay, 2003). Despite the frequent use of showups in police investigations, there is a significant problem with them in that all positive identification errors represent false identifications of innocent suspects. Lineups, on the other hand, distribute false identifications among the suspect and fillers, assuming that the lineup's composition is unbiased. On their face, showups are suggestive because witnesses are undoubtedly aware of who is suspected of committing the witnessed crime.

A meta-analysis of 12 tests of the relative suggestiveness of showups and lineups confirms that showups are more suggestive than are lineups (Steblay et al., 2003). For target-present identification procedures, showups and lineups produced approximately equal rates of correct identification. Because witnesses were less likely to make a positive identification (i.e., a choice) from a showup than from a lineup, showups resulted in more correct rejections when the target was absent than did lineups. Rates of mistaken identifications of innocent suspects were equal for showups and lineups. However, innocent suspects who closely resembled the perpetrator were at greater risk of being falsely identified from a showup than from a lineup. These results suggest that witness identifications from a showup, although often less accurate than identifications from a nonsuggestive lineup that has viable fillers, will still be more accurate than identifications made from suggestive lineups that have only one or two viable fillers (Wells & Quinlivan, 2009).

Administrator Knowledge of a Suspect's Identity

Scholars have advocated the use of double-blind procedures when conducting identification tasks, in contrast to more typical single-blind procedures in which the lineup administrator knows the suspect's identity (Wells et al., 1998). This recommendation was based on a robust literature on experimenter expectancy effects, demonstrating that an experimenter's knowledge of a study's hypothesis can influence the behavior of participants in that study (Rosenthal, 1994, 2002; Rosenthal & Rubin, 1978). Just like experimenters who may unintentionally communicate their research hypothesis to their participants, lineup administrators may unintentionally leak their hypothesis that a particular lineup member—the suspect—is the perpetrator or they may interpret the witnesses' responses to the lineup in a manner that is consistent with their hypothesis. A few studies have specifically examined the effects of lineup administrator knowledge about the suspect's identity on eyewitness identification accuracy (Greathouse & Kovera, 2009; Haw & Fisher, 2004; Phillips, McAuliff, Kovera, & Cutler, 1999; Russano, Dickinson, Greathouse, & Kovera, 2006; for a discussion of effects of administrator feedback on witness confidence, see Chapter 7, this volume).

In the first study to examine the effects of double-blind administration on eyewitness accuracy, participant administrators presented witnesses to a staged crime, involving two perpetrators with two sequential target-absent photospreads or two simultaneous target-absent photospreads, one for each perpetrator (Phillips et al., 1999). The administrators knew the identity of the suspect (i.e., single-blind administration) in only one of the two photospreads. Additionally, there was an observer present for half of the administrations, to mimic the presence of a defense attorney who might be present to observe an attempted identification of his or her client. Administrators' knowledge of which photo represented the suspect increased the likelihood that witnesses would pick the innocent suspect when administrators presented the photos sequentially and an observer was present.

Because some studies have failed to find effects of double-blind lineup administration (Russano et al., 2006), it is possible that moderator variables influence the extent to which single-blind administrators influence the identifications that witnesses make. For example, biased lineup instructions suggest that the perpetrator is present. When witnesses do not easily find the perpetrator among the lineup members but have received instructions that the perpetrator is there, they may look for cues regarding which lineup member is the suspect. If administrators know the suspect's identity, they might provide those cues. Similarly, the simultaneous presentation of a lineup may increase the likelihood that witnesses will notice differential behaviors toward the lineup members. Thus, lineup instructions and presentation may moderate the effects of administrator knowledge because they facilitate the influence of administrators' behavioral cues. In a test of this hypothesis, participant administrators—half who knew the suspect's identity and half who did not—presented target-absent or target-present photospreads to witnesses (Greathouse & Kovera, 2009). The administrators delivered biased or unbiased instructions and presented the photospread simultaneously or sequentially. Results supported the predicted pattern of moderation; witnesses who received biased instructions and simultaneous lineups were more likely to pick the suspect when the administrator knew the suspect's identity than when the administrator was blind to the suspect's identity. Further, identifications made from double-blind lineups were twice as diagnostic of the suspect's guilt than were identifications made from single-blind lineups.

When the same investigator administers a lineup to multiple witnesses, even double-blind lineup administration may not be enough to minimize administrator influence. In one study, participant administrators who did not know which photo in an array represented the suspect (e.g., they were blind to the suspect's identity) presented target-absent sequential photo arrays to confederate witnesses who identified a photo from the array with high or low confidence (Douglass, Smith, & Fraser-Thill, 2005). Subsequently, administrators presented the same target-absent photo array to nonconfederate witnesses who had witnessed a videotaped crime and were attempting to make an identification of the perpetrator of that crime. If the confederate witness had reported low confidence in his or her identification to the administrator, nonconfederate witnesses were more likely to pick the same photo in the second photo array that the administrator conducted than were witnesses paired with an administrator who had previously administered to a confederate witness who made a highly confident identification. Independent observers rated the identification task to be more difficult in the low-confidence condition than in the high-confidence condition. Perhaps administrators in the low-confidence condition were more likely to believe that the identification task was difficult and that the witnesses needed assistance in making an identification than were administrators in the high-confidence condition. Because of these differences in perceived task difficulty, administrators might have been more likely to emit cues during the second administration to assist the witnesses. Although this study does not provide direct evidence about whether administrators' perceptions mediate the effects of previous witness confidence on the choices other witnesses make in subsequent identification tasks administered by the same administrator, these findings suggest that even a double-blind administrator should not conduct multiple identification tasks within a single investigation.

A different method of reducing the influence of an administrator's knowledge of the suspect's identity on witness behavior is to limit the amount of contact that the administrator has with the witness during the identification task. Single-blind administrators, in one study, had an incentive to obtain suspect identifications, but for half of the administrations the administrators had only limited contact with the witnesses (e.g., they stood behind the witnesses while they viewed the photos either simultaneously or sequentially; Haw & Fisher, 2004). When the photo arrays were presented simultaneously, the administrators that were allowed high contact with the witnesses were more likely to obtain identifications of the innocent suspect than were those in the low-contact condition; level of administrator contact did not influence witnesses' identifications of innocent suspects from sequentially presented photo arrays. Similarly, level of contact did not affect the correct identification rates.

Given the relatively small number of studies on the effects of lineup administrator knowledge of the suspect's identity on the accuracy of witness identifications, more research on double-blind administration is needed. For now, the more recent research suggests that double-blind administration may be more protective when the lineup or photo array is presented simultaneously than when it is presented sequentially, in part because rates of misidentification are already lowered by the sequential presentation. Moreover, it is clear that double-blind administration does not harm innocent suspects, and it likely helps them as identifications produced by using double-blind administration were twice as diagnostic as those from single-blind administrations (Greathouse & Kovera, 2009).

Simultaneous Versus Sequential Lineup Presentation

Police can use one of two methods to present lineup members or photos to a witness: a simultaneous method in which the witness is shown all lineup members or photos at the same time or a sequential method in which the witness is shown lineup members or photos one at a time. The sequential presentation of lineup members has, at times, been paired with other procedural variations from the standard simultaneous method for lineup presentation. In some operationalizations of sequential presentation, witnesses are allowed to view each lineup member only once whereas other operationalizations allow witnesses additional passes through the sequence of lineup members. A second possible variant of the sequential procedure is whether the presentation of lineup members ceases after the witness makes an identification or continues, which allows for the identification of multiple lineup members. In all variants of the sequential method, the witness must make a fixed judgment as to whether or not each lineup member is the perpetrator before the administrator presents the next person or photograph (Lindsay, Lea, & Fulford, 1991; Lindsay & Wells, 1985).

Although simultaneous presentation is the traditional method used by law enforcement, researchers have criticized its use, suggesting that during a simultaneous lineup witnesses may compare and contrast lineup members to choose the person who best matches their memory of the perpetrator rather than making an absolute judgment that the person in the lineup matches their memory of the perpetrator (Wells, 1984). Given that police are rarely certain that the true perpetrator is the suspect in the lineup, this kind of relative judgment can be extremely problematic for innocent suspects because it could lead witnesses to identify whichever lineup member is the best match for the perpetrator, even if the match is not particularly close. The purported strength of the sequential method—if witnesses are prevented from reviewing the lineup members a second time—is that it compels witnesses to make identifications only when the lineup member matches their memory of the perpetrator (Lindsay & Wells, 1985).

To test whether sequential presentation improves the accuracy of eyewitness identification, participants attempted to identify the perpetrator from a target-present or target-absent lineup after watching an act of staged vandalism (Lindsay & Wells, 1985). The lineup presentation method also varied, with witnesses viewing either a simultaneous or a sequential lineup. Participants in the sequential condition (a) made an immediate yes–no decision about whether the person in the photograph was the perpetrator, (b) could not return and review any photos, and (c) did not know how many photos would be shown. Their data demonstrated that when the perpetrator was in the lineup, there were no significant differences in identification accuracy. However, when the perpetrator was absent from the lineup, 43% of participants shown a simultaneous lineup made a false identification, whereas only 17% of participants shown a sequential lineup made a false identification (Lindsay & Wells, 1985). This study was merely the first demonstration of the *sequential-superiority effect*—that sequential lineups decrease false identifications with little-to-no declines in correct identification rates. Other studies have replicated and extended these findings (Cutler & Penrod, 1988; Lindsay, Lea, & Fulford, 1991; Lindsay, Lea, Nosworthy, et al., 1991; Sporer, 1993).

An early meta-analysis provided support for the sequential-superiority effect (Steblay, Dysart, Fulero, & Lindsay, 2001). In this analysis, the authors pooled data from 23 studies that compared the effects of sequential and simultaneous lineups on identification accuracy. Looking at the collective data for witness performance with target-present and target-absent lineups, sequential lineups are superior in that they result in more correct decisions (i.e., a combination of correct rejections and accurate identifications). However, if examining the data for target-present and target-absent lineups separately, the simultaneous procedure demonstrates an advantage in target-present lineups in that there were more correct identifications and fewer false rejections for simultaneous than for sequential procedures. In target-absent lineups, however, the sequential lineup procedure was superior because there were more correct rejections of the lineup and fewer false identifications. The analysis revealed that support for the sequential superiority effect came primarily from one laboratory and that unpublished studies were less likely to support the sequential superiority effect—suggesting potential publication bias. Due to these issues, and because the demonstrated effects could be unreliable because they are based on a relatively small number of studies, some scholars have expressed concern that others prematurely have advocated for policy reform to require sequential presentation (McQuiston & Malpass, 2002; McQuiston-Surrett, Malpass, & Tredoux, 2006).

Although sequential presentation has consistently demonstrated positive outcomes in laboratory studies, some researchers are hesitant to recommend that police adopt the procedures because the sequential method may be more prone to administrator bias unless double-blind procedures are used in tandem with sequential presentation. These researchers fear that with a sequential presentation the administrator may have more opportunities to steer the witness toward an identification of the suspect because only one person or photograph is presented at a time (Wells et al., 1998). Even though this concern may not be warranted given the recent findings that administrator knowledge of the suspect's identity and greater administrator contact with the witness are more likely to increase mistaken identifications in simultaneous lineups, researchers appear hesitant to encourage a procedure that may increase problems until double-blind procedures become the norm (Wells et al., 2000). Furthermore, police are likely concerned about the slight drop in accurate identifications that occur with the sequential method. Therefore, a policy shift toward sequential presentation has not been unanimously recommended.

Another reason that scholars have not unanimously supported recommending sequential presentation is because the psychological mechanisms that underlie the sequential superiority effect are not fully understood. Some have argued that the effect was primarily due to the absolute judgment strategy employed in the sequential method (Gronlund, 2004; Lindsay, Lea, & Fulford, 1991; Lindsay & Wells, 1985; Wells, 1993); others have expressed concern with the reduced number of correct identifications in target-present lineups, suggesting that a lowered response criterion reduces choosing rates, which produces the sequential superiority effect (Ebbesen & Flowe, 2002). Indeed, one study that used signal detection theory to examine the influence of simultaneous versus sequential presentation on the response criterion that witnesses adopted when reporting whether they had seen a series of faces before demonstrated that witnesses adopted higher response criterions when the faces to be identified were presented sequentially than when they were presented simultaneously (Meissner, Tredoux, Parker, & MacLin, 2005). It is important to understand whether sequential presentation reduces false identification by encouraging absolute judgments or because it reduces choosing rates because the former mechanism should leave the correct identification rate untouched but the latter mechanism should produce a concomitant decrease in correct identifications. If sequential presentation produces a significant drop in correct identifications, recommendations for a policy shift toward sequential presentation are likely to meet resistance from those in law enforcement circles.

Multiple Presentations of the Suspect

Recent qualitative and quantitative reviews have recognized the suggestiveness of presenting a suspect in multiple lineups (e.g., Deffenbacher et al, 2006; Wells & Quinlivan, 2009). Witness memory is prone to errors produced by exposure to postevent information (Loftus, 1975; Loftus, Miller, & Burns, 1978), sometimes because of source-confusion errors in which a witness misremembers the witnessed event as the source of postevent information (Johnson, Hashtroudi, & Lindsay, 1993). When the police present witnesses with a lineup that contains a suspect and then subsequently present the same witnesses with another identification task that contains the same suspect, they have introduced the possibility that the witnesses will confuse their memory for the suspect with their memory for the perpetrator.

In an early study of the effects of multiple presentations of the suspect on witness accuracy, participants witnessed a confederate who interrupted a classroom lecture, after which they were either shown a series of target-absent mug shots or dismissed without seeing any mug shots (Gorenstein & Ellsworth, 1980). Two days later subjects were presented a six-person photo array and attempted to identify the confederate. Witnesses exposed to intervening mugshots chose the confederate with less accuracy than did those who did not see any intervening photos. Although another study that used a similar paradigm found the same effect of intervening lineups (Brigham & Cairns, 1988), neither of these studies provided information about whether multiple presentations of an innocent suspect are suggestive because they both tested only target-present photo arrays, precluding any analysis of effects on false identification rates.

Several studies have tested whether multiple presentations of an innocent suspect influence mistaken identifications from target-absent arrays. In one study, participants viewed a target face for 60 s and then 1 week later viewed a target-absent lineup with or without a repeated distracter face (RDF; Hinz & Pezdek, 2001). After another 2 days passed, participants attempted an identification from a lineup that contained the target face and RDF, the RDF but not the target face, or just the target face. Target hit rates (i.e., correct identifications) were higher when the RDF was absent from the test lineup; false identifications of the RDF were higher when the target face was absent from the test lineup. This outcome supports the notion that multiple viewings of an innocent suspect can increase the likelihood of false identification. Other research demonstrated that this effect may be more likely when memory for the perpetrator is poor (Pezdek & Blandon-Gitlin, 2005).

A meta-analysis by Deffenbacher et al. (2006) examined a variety of intervening mug shot effects, including the possibility of transference effects. A transference effect occurs "if a previously seen non-target face is chosen from a fair lineup, ordinarily a target absent one, at a significantly greater rate than for previously unfamiliar foils" (Deffenbacher et al., 2006, p. 288). The non-target person may be present as a bystander during the target event (e.g., the crime) or presented to the witness through their review of mugshots shortly after the target event. Transference effects reliably occur in experiments designed to elicit them, with a small-to-moderate effect size. Transference effects were more than twice as large when exposure to the innocent person occurred through intervening mug shots than when the innocent person was a bystander to the target event (Deffenbacher et al., 2006). These results further support the conclusion that multiple presentations of an innocent suspect can increase the likelihood that witnesses will mistakenly identify the suspect.

APPLICATION OF RESEARCH ON SUGGESTIVE EYEWITNESS LINEUP PROCEDURES

A panel of experts convened by the Executive Committee of the American Psychology-Law Society (APLS) made four recommendations to improve eyewitness lineup procedures, based primarily on the relevant research available at that time (Wells et al., 1998). First, the panel recommended that police conduct lineups, using double-blind procedures, in which neither the administrator nor the witness knows the identity of the suspect. Second, they recommended an instruction that indicated that the perpetrator may or may not be in the lineup, as well as an instruction that the lineup administrator does not know the identity of the suspect. Third, the lineup construction should not make the suspect more salient than other members of the lineup based on the witness's given description of the perpetrator. Finally, they recommended that administrators immediately record witness confidence after a witness makes an identification before they give any feedback to the witness. These guidelines did not include a recommendation for the use of sequential versus simultaneous lineups, mainly due to concerns regarding increased suggestiveness of nonblind administrators in sequential lineups.

Around the same time that the APLS panel of experts was developing their white paper describing best practices in lineup administration, then Attorney General Janet Reno, under the auspices of the National Institute of Justice, convened a group of scientists, prosecutors, defense attorneys, and police officers to create guidelines for the collection of eyewitness evidence (Technical Working Group on Eyewitness Evidence, 1999). Many of the recommended guidelines were evidence based, including their recommendations for using unbiased lineup instructions, including a warning that the perpetrator may not be in the lineup and that the fillers should be chosen to match the witness's description of the perpetrator. Other recommendations, however, had no empirical support at the time the recommendation was made. For example, the NIJ guidelines instruct law enforcement officers to provide witnesses with a cautionary warning that the perpetrator may have changed appearance since committing the crime and that it is just as important to free innocent suspects as it is to identify guilty ones (Technical Working Group for Eyewitness Evidence, 1999). Since the NIJ guidelines were developed, there has been one study published that tested the effects of the change of appearance instruction supporting the notion that change of appearance instructions lower the criterion for choosing and thus increase the rates of mistaken eyewitness identifications (Charman & Wells, 2007).

In contrast to the APLS panel recommendations, the NIJ guidelines did not recommend the use of a double-blind procedure, which was noted to be a significant shortcoming of the NIJ guidelines by the researchers in the working group (Wells et al., 2000). Like the APLS white paper on best practices, the NIJ guidelines did not favor the use of sequential lineup procedures over simultaneous lineup procedures, despite the research showing that it reduces mistaken identification. So far, nine states have taken action to reform eyewitness lineup procedures, and some states (e.g., New Jersey, North Carolina) have mandated their use.

CONCLUSION

The results of laboratory studies on eyewitness identification procedures provide suggestions for policy changes that could reduce the frequency of mistaken identifications, which presumably would also reduce the number of wrongful convictions (see Chapter 9, this volume, for a discussion of how mistaken identifications could result in wrongful convictions because of jurors' belief in eyewitness accounts). Because biased instructions increase the likelihood of mistaken identifications in perpetrator-absent lineups, instructions to witnesses should include a statement that indicates that the culprit might not be in the lineup (Clark, 2005; Steblay, 1997; Wells & Quinlivan, 2009). Lineups should also include plausible fillers that do not direct undue attention toward the suspect, and showups should be avoided if possible (Lindsay & Wells, 1980; Steblay et al., 2003; Wells et al., 1993, 1998). Double-blind lineup administration increases the diagnosticity of witness identifications (Greathouse & Kovera, 2009). Despite controversy surrounding the degree and nature of the sequential superiority effect, there is reliable evidence that sequential lineup presentation reduces the mistaken identification of innocent suspects (Steblay et al., in press, 2001). Finally, the repeated presentation of suspects to the same witnesses should be avoided because it increases the probability that witnesses will mistakenly identify innocent suspects (Deffenbacher et al., 2006; Hinz & Pezdek, 2001; Pezdek & Blandon-Gitlin, 2005).

These conclusions are based largely on laboratory experiments that use an eyewitness simulation paradigm. Valid field research on the suggestiveness of lineup procedures is scarce. Field studies have demonstrated that some procedures increase the identification of fillers (e.g., Slater, 1994; Wright & McDaid, 1996; Wright & Skagerberg, 2007), which are known errors but are necessarily silent on the issue of false identification rates as it is only known if the suspect and the perpetrator are truly the same person when there are verifiable crime details or DNA to exonerate or implicate the suspect. One field study examined the identification decisions that 206 witnesses made from 280 sequential, double-blind lineups (Klobuchar, Steblay, & Caligiuri, 2006). The study did not provide for an evaluation of the effects of presentation style or double-blind administration, but it did suggest that the repeated viewing of sequential arrays was suggestive, as people who viewed an array once identified fillers less frequently (3%) than did those who viewed an array twice (13%) or three times (29%). Another field study in Illinois (Mecklenburg, 2006) compared double-blind sequential lineups with single-blind simultaneous lineups. Although witnesses were more likely to identify the suspect from single-blind simultaneous lineups than from double-blind sequential lineups, this study has largely been discredited because it confounded the manipulation of presentation style and administrator knowledge of the suspect's identity (Schacter et al., 2008). Further, a recent analysis of the Illinois data indicated that nonrandom assignment to groups created favorable conditions for people who make identifications in the nonblind simultaneous condition. For example, eyewitnesses in the nonblind simultaneous condition were more likely to know the suspect than those in the double-blind sequential group (Steblay, 2010). It does appear, however, that law enforcement groups are eager for field data on the effectiveness of these proposed remedies for lineup suggestiveness (e.g., sequential presentation and double-blind administration) before widely adopting these less suggestive procedures.

REFERENCES

Brigham, J. C., & Cairns, D. (1988). The effect of mugshot inspections on eyewitness identification accuracy. *Journal of Applied Social Psychology, 18*, 1394–1410. doi:10.1111/j.1559-1816.1988.tb01214.x

Brigham, J. C., Meissner, C. A., & Wasserman, A. W. (1999). Applied issues in the construction and expert assessment of photo lineups. *Applied Cognitive Psychology, 13*, S73–S92. doi:10.1002/(SICI)1099-0720(199911)13:1+<S73::AID-ACP631>3.3.CO;2-W

Carlson, C. A., Gronlund, S. D., & Clark, S. E. (2008). Lineup composition, suspect position, and the sequential lineup advantage. *Journal of Experimental Psychology: Applied, 14*, 118–128. doi:10.1037/1076-898X.14.2.118

Charman, S. D., & Wells, G. L. (2007). Eyewitness lineups: Is the appearance change instruction a good idea? *Law and Human Behavior, 31*, 3–22. doi:10.1007/s10979-006-9006-3

Clark, S. E. (2005). A re-examination of the effects of biased lineup instructions in eyewitness identification. *Law and Human Behavior, 29*, 575–604. doi:10.1007/s10979-005-7121-1

Clark, S. E., & Tunnicliff, J. L. (2001). Selecting lineup foils in eyewitness identification experiments: Experimental control and real-world simulation. *Law and Human Behavior, 25*, 199–216. doi:10.1023/A:1010753809988

Cutler, B. L., & Penrod, S. D. (1988). Improving the reliability of eyewitness identification: Lineup construction and presentation. *Journal of Applied Psychology, 73*, 2, 281–290.

Cutler, B. L., & Penrod, S. D. (1995). *Mistaken identifications: The eyewitness, psychology, and the law*. New York, NY: Cambridge University Press.

Darling, S., Valentine, T., & Memon, A. (2008). Selection of lineup foils in operational contexts. *Applied Cognitive Psychology, 22*, 159–169. doi:10.1002/acp.1366

Deffenbacher, K. A., Bornstein, B. H., & Penrod, S. H. (2006). Mugshot exposure effects: Retroactive interference, mugshot commitment, source confusion, and unconscious transference. *Law and Human Behavior, 30,* 287–307. doi:10.1007/s10979-006-9008-1

Doob, A. N., & Kirshenbaum, H. M. (1973). Bias in police lineups—partial remembering. *Journal of Police Science and Administration, 1,* 287–293.

Douglass, A. B., Smith, C., & Fraser-Thill, R. (2005). A problem with double-blind photospread procedures: Photospread administrators use one eyewitness's confidence to influence the identification of another eyewitness. *Law and Human Behavior, 29,* 543–562. doi:10.1007/s10979-005-6830-9

Ebbesen, E. E., & Flowe, H. D. (2002) *Simultaneous v. sequential lineups: What do we really know?* Unpublished manuscript, University of California, San Diego. Retrieved from http://www.psy.ucsd.edu/~eebbesen/SimSeq.htm

Gorenstein, G. W., & Ellsworth, P. C. (1980). Effect of choosing an incorrect photograph on a later identification by and eyewitness. *Journal of Applied Psychology, 65,* 616–622. doi:10.1037/0021-9010.65.5.616

Greathouse, S. M., & Kovera, M. B. (2009). Instruction bias and lineup presentation moderate the effects of administrator knowledge on eyewitness identification. *Law and Human Behavior, 33,* 70–82. doi:10.1007/s10979-008-9136-x

Gronlund, S. D. (2004). Sequential lineups: Shift in decision criterion or decision strategy? *Journal of Applied Psychology, 89,* 362–368. doi:10.1037/0021-9010.89.2.362

Haw, R. M., & Fisher, R. P. (2004). Effects administrator-witness contact on eyewitness identification accuracy. *Journal of Applied Psychology, 89,* 1106–1112. doi:10.1037/0021-9010.89.6.1106.

Hinz, T., & Pezdek, K. (2001). The effect of exposure to multiple lineups on face identification accuracy. *Law and Human Behavior, 25,* 185–198. doi:10.1023/A:1005697431830

Johnson, M. K., Hashtroudi, S., & Lindsay, D. S. (1993). Source monitoring. *Psychological Bulletin, 114,* 3–28. doi:10.1037/0033-2909.114.1.3

Klobuchar, A., Steblay, N., & Caligiuri, H. L. (2006). Symposium: Reforming eyewitness identification: Convicting the guilty, protecting the innocent: Improving eyewitness identifications: Hennepin County's blind sequential lineup pilot project. *Cardoza Public Law, Policy, and Ethics Journal, 4,* 381–413.

Lindsay, R. C. L., Lea, J. A., & Fulford, J. A. (1991). Sequential lineup presentation: Technique matters. *Journal of Applied Psychology, 76,* 741–745. doi:10.1037/0021-9010.76.5.741

Lindsay, R. C. L., Lea, J. A., Nosworthy, G. J., Fulford, J. A., Hector, J., LeVan, V., & Seabrook, C. (1991). Biased lineups: Sequential presentation reduces the problem. *Journal of Applied Psychology, 76,* 796–802. doi:10.1037/0021-9010.76.6.796

Lindsay, R. C. L., & Wells, G. L. (1980). What price justice? Exploring the relationship between lineup fairness and identification accuracy. *Law and Human Behavior, 4,* 303–313. doi:10.1007/BF01040622

Lindsay, R. C. L., & Wells, G. L. (1985). Improving eyewitness identifications from lineups: Simultaneous versus sequential lineup presentation. *Journal of Applied Psychology, 70*, 556–564. doi:10.1037/0021-9010.70.3.556

Loftus, E. F. (1975). Leading question and the eyewitness report. *Cognitive Psychology, 7*, 560–572. doi:10.1016/0010-0285(75)90023-7

Loftus, E. F., Miller, D. G., & Burns, H. J. (1978). Semantic integration of visual information into visual memory. *Journal of Experimental Psychology: Human Learning and Memory, 4*, 19–31. doi:10.1037/0278-7393.4.1.19

Luus, C. A. E., & Wells, G. L. (1991). Eyewitness identification and the selection of distracters for lineups. *Law and Human Behavior, 15*, 43–57. doi:10.1007/BF01044829

Malpass, R. S., & Devine, P. G. (1981). Eyewitness identification: Lineup instructions and the absence of the offender. *Journal of Applied Psychology, 66*, 482–489. doi:10.1037/0021-9010.66.4.482

McQuiston, D. E., & Malpass, R. S. (2002). Validity of the mockwitness paradigm: Testing the assumptions. *Law and Human Behavior, 26*, 439–453. doi:10.1023/A:1016383305868

McQuiston-Surrett, D., Malpass, R. S., & Tredoux, C. G. (2006). Sequential vs. simultaneous lineups: A review of methods, data, and theory. *Psychology, Public Policy, and Law, 12*, 137–169. doi:10.1037/1076-8971.12.2.137

Mecklenburg, S. H. (2006). *Report to the legislature of the state of Illinois: The Illinois pilot program on double-blind, sequential lineup procedures.* Retrieved from http://www.psychology.iastate.edu/faculty/gwells/Illinois_Report.pdf

Meissner, C. A., Tredoux, C. G., Parker, J. F., & MacLin, O. H. (2005). Eyewitness decisions in simultaneous and sequential lineups: A dual-process signal detection theory analysis. *Memory & Cognition, 33*, 783–792.

Penrod, S. D., & Kovera, M. B. (2009). Recent developments in North American identification science and practice. In R. Bull, T. Valentine, & T. Williamson (Eds.), *Handbook of psychology of investigative interviewing: Current developments and future directions* (pp. 257–283). Chichester, England: Wiley-Blackwell. doi:10.1002/9780470747599.ch15

Pezdek, K., & Blandon-Gitlin. (2005). When is an intervening lineup most likely to affect eyewitness identification accuracy? *Legal and Criminological Psychology, 10*, 247–263. doi:10.1348/135532505X49846

Phillips, M. R., McAuliff, B. D., Kovera, M. B., & Cutler, B. L. (1999). Double-blind photoarray administration as a safeguard against investigator bias. *Journal of Applied Psychology, 84*, 940–951. doi:10.1037/0021-9010.84.6.940

Py, J., Demarchi, S., Ginet, M., & Wasiak, L. (2003). *"Who is the suspect?" A complimentary instruction standard to the standard mock witness paradigm.* Paper presented at the American Psychology-Law Society and European Association of Psychology and Law Conference, Edinburgh, Scotland.

Rosenthal, R. (1994). Interpersonal expectancy effects: A 30-year perspective. *Current Directions in Psychological Science, 3*, 176–179. doi:10.1111/1467-8721.ep10770698

Rosenthal, R. (2002). Covert communication in classrooms, clinics, courtrooms, and cubicles. *American Psychologist, 57,* 839–849. doi:10.1037/0003-066X.57.11.839

Rosenthal, R., & Rubin, D. B. (1978). Interpersonal expectancy effects: The first 345 studies. *The Behavioral and Brain Sciences, 1,* 377–386. doi:10.1017/S0140525X00075506

Russano, M. B., Dickinson, J. J., Greathouse, S. M., & Kovera, M. B. (2006). Why don't you take another look at number three: Investigator knowledge and its effects on eyewitness confidence and identification decisions. *Cardozo Public Law, Policy, and Ethics Journal, 4,* 355–379.

Slater, A. (1994). *Identification parades: A scientific evaluation.* London, England: Police Research Group, Home Office.

Sporer, S. L. (1993). Eyewitness identification accuracy, confidence, and decision times in simultaneous and sequential lineups. *Journal of Applied Psychology, 78,* 22–33. doi:10.1037/0021-9010.78.1.22

Steblay, N. M. (1997). Social influence in eyewitness recall: A meta-analytic review of lineup instructions effects. *Law and Human Behavior, 21,* 283–297. doi:10.1023/A:1024890732059

Steblay, N. M. (2011). What we know now: The Evanston Illinois field lineups. *Law and Human Behavior, 35,* 1–12. doi: 10.1007/s10979-009-9207-7

Steblay, N., Dysart, J., Fulero, S., & Lindsay, R. C. L. (2001). Eyewitness accuracy rates in sequential and simultaneous lineup presentations: A meta-analytic comparison. *Law and Human Behavior, 25,* 459–473. doi:10.1023/A:1012888715007

Steblay, N., Dysart, J., Fulero, S., & Lindsay, R. C. L. (2003). Eyewitness accuracy rates in police showup and lineup presentations: A meta-analytic comparison. *Law and Human Behavior, 27,* 523–540. doi:10.1023/A:1025438223608

Steblay, N. K., Dysart, J. E., & Wells, G. L. (in press). Seventy-two tests of the sequential lineup superiority effect: A meta-analysis and policy discussion. *Psychology, Public Policy, and Law.*

Technical Working Group for Eyewitness Evidence. (1999). *Eyewitness evidence: A guide for law enforcement (NCJ 178240).* Washington, DC: National Institute of Justice, U.S. Department of Justice.

Tunnicliff, J. L., & Clark, S. (2000). Foils for identification lineups: Matching suspects or descriptions? *Law and Human Behavior, 24,* 231–258. doi:10.1023/A:1005463020252

Valentine, T., & Heaton, P. (1999). An evaluation of the fairness of police lineups and video identifications. *Applied Cognitive Psychology, 13,* S59–S72. doi:10.1002/(SICI)1099-0720(199911)13:1+<S59::AID-ACP679>3.0.CO;2-Y

Wells, G. L. (1984). The psychology of lineup identifications. *Journal of Applied Social Psychology, 14,* 89–103. doi:10.1111/j.1559-1816.1984.tb02223.x

Wells, G. L. (1993). What do we know about eyewitness identification. *American Psychologist, 48,* 553–571. doi:10.1037/0003-066X.48.5.553

Wells, G. L., & Bradfield, A. L. (1999). Measuring the goodness of lineups: Parameter estimation, question effects, and limits to the mock witness paradigm. *Applied Cognitive Psychology, 13*, S27–S39. doi:10.1002/(SICI)1099-0720(199911)13:1+<S27::AID-ACP635>3.3.CO;2-D

Wells, G. L., & Luus, C. E. (1990). Police lineups as experiments: Social methodology as a framework for properly conducted lineups. *Personality and Social Psychology Bulletin, 16, 1,* 106–117.

Wells, G. L., Malpass, R. S., Lindsay, R. C. L., Fisher, R. P., Turtle, J. W., & Fulero, S. M. (2000). From the lab to the police station: A successful application of eyewitness research. *American Psychologist, 55,* 581–598. doi:10.1037/0003-066X.55.6.581

Wells, G. L., Small, M., Penrod, S., Malpass, R. S., Fulero, S. M., & Brimacombe, C. A. E. (1998). Eyewitness identification procedures: Recommendations for lineups and photospreads. *Law and Human Behavior, 22,* 603–647. doi:10.1023/A:1025750605807

Wells, G. L., & Quinlivan, D. S. (2009). Suggestive eyewitness identification procedures and the Supreme Court's reliability test in light of eyewitness science: 30 years later. *Law and Human Behavior, 33,* 1–24. doi:10.1007/s10979-008-9130-3

Wells, G. L., Rydell, S. M., & Seelau, E. P. (1993). The selection of distracters for eyewitness lineups. *Journal of Applied Psychology, 78,* 835–844. doi:10.1037/0021-9010.78.5.835

Wright, D. B., & McDaid, A. T. (1996). Comparing system and estimator variables using data from real lineups. *Applied Cognitive Psychology, 10,* 75–84. doi:10.1002/(SICI)1099-0720(199602)10:1<75::AID-ACP364>3.0.CO;2-E

Wright, D. B., & Skagerberg, E. M. (2007). Post-identification feedback affects real eyewitnesses. *Psychological Science, 18,* 172–178. doi:10.1111/j.1467-9280.2007.01868.x

7

EYEWITNESS CONFIDENCE MALLEABILITY

AMY BRADFIELD DOUGLASS AND AFTON PAVLETIC

No subjective feeling of certainty can be an objective criterion for the desired truth.

—Munsterberg (1908, p. 49)

Imagine an eyewitness has made a mistaken identification. In spite of her mistake, she delivers her testimony to the jury with confidence. She asserts that she is "positive" she has identified the culprit and reports being "100% certain" about details of the crime. Under cross-examination, she maintains her high confidence, refusing to acknowledge any doubt in either her identification or the details of the crime. To avoid conviction, an innocent defendant must convince jurors that the eyewitness is wrong. In doing so, the defendant must ask jurors to ignore their natural tendencies to use confidence as a cue to accuracy (e.g., Cutler, Penrod, & Dexter, 1990). This challenge is insurmountable for many innocent defendants and presents a puzzling dilemma: How could a witness be so confident and yet so wrong?

The apparent contradiction of a very confident but incorrect witness is explained by the dynamic nature of confidence reports: They are subject to change long after a decision has been made or details have been reported. Psychological researchers refer to this phenomenon as *confidence malleability*. Confidence malleability occurs in the context of confidence about both identification decisions and crime scene details. It occurs in the context of current confidence reports (i.e., "How confident are you about your identification now?") and retrospective confidence reports (i.e., "How confident were you when you made your identification?"). Of greatest relevance to judges, jurors, and defendants is that these changes in confidence occur in the absence of any corresponding changes in accuracy.

Psychological scientists are nearly unanimous in their recognition of confidence malleability as a problem. In a survey of eyewitness experts, 95% agreed that confidence can be manipulated independent of accuracy. Agreement on this item was among the highest of all 30 items surveyed, behind only agreement about the influence of lineup instructions on an eyewitness's willingness to testify and the wording of questions on witnesses' responses (Kassin, Tubb, Hosch, & Memon, 2001). In the legal community, the possibility for confidence to change over time has been recognized by at least some U.S. Supreme Court justices, as noted in the dissenting opinion in *Manson v. Braithwaite* (1977), written by Justice Marshall (for an excellent analysis of this case, see Chapter 8, this volume; Wells & Quinlivan, 2009).

Instances of confidence malleability from DNA exonerations cases are easy to find. As one example, consider Ryan Matthews, who was convicted of murder in 1999 after an eyewitness identified him as the perpetrator of a convenience store shooting (http://www.innocenceproject.org). Although Matthews was initially sentenced to death, he was eventually exonerated in 2004. Postconviction analysis of Matthews's case revealed important changes in the confidence of one eyewitness. In her initial identification, the eyewitness was "tentative"; at trial, she was "positive" Matthews was the culprit. Given that there was virtually no other substantial evidence to support a guilty verdict, it is likely that this confident witness was largely responsible for Matthews's conviction.

In another case, Earl Charles was mistakenly identified by a witness who, in describing how confident she was that she had identified the right person testified to the "impossibility of forgetting the looks of a man who had stuck a gun in her face" (Radelet, Bedau, & Putnam, 1992, p. 240). These cases do not represent an isolated problem (Doyle, 2005).

One explanation for the confidence expressed by these witnesses is that they strategically inflated their confidence, knowing that higher confidence would make them more credible. Although there is no question that witnesses sometimes lie on the stand to make themselves appear more credible (e.g., see Chapter 10, this volume), our primary concern in this chapter is with witnesses whose high confidence is genuinely reported but connected to a mistaken identification or erroneous crime report details. Although we briefly address sources of confidence malleability that arise as a function of witnesses' self-presentation concerns, most of the relevant research focuses on genuine witness errors. In concentrating on genuine witness errors, we review research showing how high-confidence reports can be produced even though the underlying identification decision or crime report details are completely inaccurate. We also review the basic research methodology used to study these questions and the few available strategies for preventing (or occasionally reversing) confidence malleability.

The problems generated by confidence malleability are very clear if one substitutes "DNA evidence" for "confidence report." Imagine that a crime scene analysis finds a 50% match between the suspect's DNA and the culprit's DNA. Time passes. Before the trial, the analysis is repeated, using the exact same methodology, with a new result of a 90% match. A forensic expert testifies at trial about the 90% match. The jury never hears about the earlier results indicating a 50% match. In this scenario, it is clear that testimony about the 90% match presents the jury with an incomplete—and overly positive—picture of the evidence against the defendant. The degree of match between the defendant and the culprit should not have changed between the initial analysis and the trial when the exact same methodology is used to evaluate the evidence. Such an arbitrary change in the quality of the DNA evidence against a defendant would immediately trouble any trier of fact. Unfortunately, the problems that result from changeable confidence reports are twofold. First, juries rarely hear about initial confidence reports. All they are likely to hear is the confident testimony of the witness on the stand. Second, judges and juries tend to ignore evidence of confidence inflation, even if it is present (e.g., Bradfield & McQuiston, 2004).

The distinction between memory evidence and other forensic evidence was noted by one of the original scholars of psychology and law, Hugo Munsterberg. In Munsterberg's (1908) book, *On the Witness Stand,* he argued for the application of psychology to the legal system. For Munsterberg, careful treatment of forensic evidence was a natural part of an investigation, whereas memory evidence was treated more casually:

> No juryman would be expected to follow his general impressions in the question as to whether the blood on the murderer's shirt is human or animal. But he is expected to make up his mind as to whether the memory ideas of a witness are objective reproductions of earlier experience or are mixed up with associations and suggestions. (Munsterberg, 1908, p. 45).

In the remaining sections of this chapter, we articulate research supporting Munsterberg's contention that memory evidence, especially as it is connected to confidence judgments, should be treated with the utmost care.

Eyewitness confidence influences three categories of people in the criminal justice system: jurors, cowitnesses, and investigators. In the first category, confidence reports form the foundation of juror evaluations of eyewitnesses.

In one study, jurors ignored valid cues to an eyewitness's accuracy, such as the culprit's disguise and how much time passed between the witnessed event and the identification. Instead, they focused exclusively on how confident the eyewitness was (Cutler et al., 1990). Jurors intuitively assume that high confidence is an appropriate indication of accuracy, an intuition supported by the U.S. Supreme Court recommendations for evaluation of eyewitnesses (e.g., Neil v. Biggers, 1972).

In the second category, confidence guides cowitnesses' memory reports. The best evidence for this comes from a study in which participants watched a crime alone and then discussed what they saw with a partner (Wright, Self, & Justice, 2000). The experimenters manipulated the presence of an accomplice in the event: One member of each pair saw an accomplice, the other member of the pair did not. Even so, 15 out of 19 pairs reached consensus on whether an accomplice was present. How did the partners decide which account prevailed? Confidence was the key. The witness who was more confident about the presence or absence of an accomplice persuaded his or her partner to accept that account.

Finally, investigators also use an eyewitness's confidence. At the most basic level, they decide whether to pursue a lead based at least in part on how confident the eyewitness is in his or her identification (e.g., Boyce, Lindsay, & Brimacombe, 2008). On a more subtle level, the confidence of an eyewitness can change the investigator's behavior with subsequent witnesses. In one study, a participant investigator showed a target-absent photospread to a confederate eyewitness who made identification with either high confidence or low confidence (the confederate always identified the same innocent suspect). The investigator then showed the same target-absent photospread to an actual eyewitness. When the confederate's confidence was low, the investigator obtained more identifications of the innocent suspect from the real eyewitness than when the confederate's confidence was high (Douglass, Smith, & Fraser-Thill, 2005). This study shows that a witness's confidence can shift an investigator's behavior with subsequent witnesses, even to the point of increasing the likelihood that an innocent suspect is identified.

The role of confidence in jury deliberations, cowitness discussions, and investigator decisions makes sense because in many situations confidence does provide a useful cue to accuracy. Indeed, when an eyewitness's confidence is derived from internal cues, such as the match between the lineup photo and the eyewitness's memory (e.g., Bradfield, Wells, & Olson, 2002; Leippe, Eisenstadt, & Rauch, 2009), there is a nontrivial relationship between confidence and accuracy. The problem for innocent suspects is that confidence is an imperfect cue to accuracy. Strong correlations between confidence and accuracy notwithstanding, high-confidence reports can be driven almost entirely by external variables that are completely unrelated to the accuracy of witness reports. It is important to note that people who evaluate these witnesses do not realize that confidence has been rendered useless as a cue to accuracy. These witnesses represent a real tragedy for innocent suspects because in the absence of external influences, they likely would have reported low confidence and, therefore, would have been easier to overcome in convincing triers of fact to acquit.

SCIENTIFIC FOUNDATION OF CONFIDENCE MALLEABILITY EFFECTS

Prior to clear demonstrations of confidence malleability, psychological scientists thought of confidence as the result of a simple cognitive process wherein witnesses' confidence was determined by either (a) the degree to which the identified photo matched their memory (i.e., ecphoric similarity; Tulving, 1981) or (b) the ease with which report details came to mind (e.g., Shaw & McClure, 1996). However, repeated demonstrations of confidence malleability required psychological scientists to consider other research as a source of understanding witness confidence judgments.

Important foundational research also comes from the literature on inference processes, for example, self-perception (Bem, 1967). For example, if confirming feedback suggests that memory is good, witnesses may assume that they should produce a high-confidence report to be consistent with the positive feedback. According to this perspective, a confidence report reflects a witness's judgment of what level of confidence is appropriate, rather than any match between stimulus and memory or ease of retrieval. One study that supports this perspective obtained identifications from participants after giving them positive feedback about their memory for the details of the witnessed event. Witnesses who heard they scored in the 90th percentile of witnesses on the memory test produced significantly higher identification confidence compared with witnesses who heard either no information or that they scored in the 21st percentile (Leippe et al., 2009).

In other instances, assumptions about inferences processes are most clearly supported by postidentification feedback paradigms in which participants receive feedback and then are asked to recall how confident they were when they made their identification. At that point, witnesses construct a confidence judgment through the lens of the outcome information they received (e.g., Wells & Bradfield, 1998). Witnesses who think about or make a confidence report before learning feedback presumably can skip this inference process because they have a memory for how confident they were before feedback was delivered (e.g., Neuschatz et al., 2007; Wells & Bradfield, 1999).

This "inoculation" is temporary, though. When a 1-week delay occurs between initial confidence report and feedback, witness confidence reports are just as malleable compared with witnesses who made no initial confidence report (Quinlivan et al., 2009).

Basic research on social influence is also useful in providing a framework for confidence malleability effects. For example, some witnesses are likely to change their confidence in direct response to information about cowitness decisions. In that case, the relevant question is whether the witness's goal is to be accurate (i.e., informational influence) or to fit in (i.e., normative influence; Deutsch & Gerard, 1955). The difficulty and importance of an eyewitness's task can determine which of these motivations takes precedence. In a clever study that mimicked Asch's (1955) classic conformity experiment, Baron, Vandello, and Brunsman (1996) demonstrated that people conform readily when a task is important but difficult. When a task is important but easy, conformity drops significantly. When the task is unimportant, difficulty does not affect conformity. This research highlights the motivational underpinnings of confidence reports. As discussed later, Shaw and colleagues' research on different confidence levels in public versus private also suggests a strong motivational component of some witnesses' confidence reports (e.g., Shaw, Appio, Zerr, & Pontoski, 2007; Shaw, Zerr, & Woythaler, 2001).

Research on confidence malleability is best informed by an awareness of multiple basic research areas. As one example, consider a situation in which a witness receives feedback from an investigator and uses that information to make a judgment about how familiar a stimulus photo is. In this case, a social factor (e.g., postidentification feedback) prompts a distorted cognitive process (e.g., generating a confidence report based on a faulty sense of familiarity).

SCIENTIFIC METHODS USED IN CONFIDENCE MALLEABILITY RESEARCH

Most studies on confidence malleability use a basic experimental paradigm. In the first part of the paradigm, participants witness a live staged crime or a videotaped event. In general, participants do not know that they will be asked to identify anyone (for one exception, see Douglass, Brewer, & Semmler, 2009). After the event is over, participants typically see a target-absent photospread, one in which the real culprit is not present (for one exception, see Bradfield et al., 2002). In designing this research, psychologists weigh the tradeoff between internal and external validity with experiments running the gamut of the range between tightly controlled experiments (e.g., Luus & Wells, 1994) and field studies (e.g., Wright & Skagerberg, 2007).

As in any scientific field, results are not always consistent across experiments. One example of this inconsistency comes from two studies that measured confidence malleability in accurate identifications versus inaccurate identifications. One study showed that confidence in accurate identifications is not malleable, whereas confidence in inaccurate identifications is easy to inflate (Bradfield et al., 2002). A study with similar methodology showed that confidence in accurate and inaccurate identifications is equally malleable (Semmler, Brewer, & Wells, 2004). As discussed in Semmler et al. (2004), it is possible that these different results are due to variations in stimuli shown to participants. Although varying stimuli is a crucial part of expanding ecological validity of laboratory studies, it can complicate efforts to aggregate results.

RELEVANT RESEARCH ON CONFIDENCE MALLEABILITY

In this section, we discuss variables that affect witness confidence statements: report context, investigators, and cowitnesses. *Report context* refers to the environment in which witnesses provide a confidence judgment. Witnesses who state their confidence judgments out loud in front of a group of other research participants report higher confidence estimates compared with witnesses who record their confidence on anonymous forms. These effects occur even though accuracy levels are similar in the two groups (Shaw et al., 2001). An interesting exception to this pattern occurs in situations in which cowitnesses exist. If other witnesses can challenge accuracy, public confidence is lower than private confidence. In contrast, if the other witnesses cannot challenge accuracy (e.g., because they did not view the same set of faces), public confidence is higher than private confidence (Shaw et al., 2007). Again, these differences occur despite that accuracy is equivalent in the public and private confidence report groups.

The second category of variables that influence eyewitness confidence reports comes from investigators. Investigators who perform the most basic of duties related to collecting information from witnesses can influence confidence reports. In one study, witnesses were interviewed according to the Cognitive Interview, a standard interview, or not at all. Then, all witnesses took a memory test and indicated how confident they were in their answers. Witnesses who were interviewed produced higher confidence ratings than did witnesses in the control condition. These inflated confidence levels appeared in spite of equal levels of accuracy across the three experimental groups (Granhag, Jonsson, & Allwood, 2004). Granhag et al. (2004) argued that reiterating answers could be responsible for the confidence inflation. This argument is consistent with other research showing that witnesses who are queried repeatedly about the details of a crime produce increased confidence ratings over time, even though the accuracy of their report details stays the same (e.g., Shaw & McClure, 1996).

Investigators sometimes go beyond querying witnesses about what they have seen. On occasion, they help witnesses prepare for trial. If that preparation includes instructions designed to motivate the witnesses, changes in confidence levels could result. In one experiment, motivation was operationalized by telling some witnesses that they could win a prize for accuracy. Among those told this, higher confidence ratings were obtained than in a group without that incentive. The actual report accuracy was identical in the two groups of witnesses (Shaw & Zerr, 2003).

The effect of investigators on eyewitness confidence is measureable even when investigators' only task is to show a set of photos to an eyewitness. For example, in one experiment, participant investigators learned who the suspect was before showing the target-absent photo array to a witness. If the witness confirmed the investigator's expectation by identifying the "correct" photo, the witness's confidence was higher than witnesses in a control condition (where the investigator had no information about who the suspect was). In contrast, if the witness identified someone who looked very different from the photo the investigator thought the suspect was the photo, the witness's confidence ratings declined, compared with the control condition (Garrioch & Brimacombe, 2001). These effects occurred even though 100% of the investigators in the Garrioch and Brimacombe (2001) study reported not providing any feedback information to witnesses.

Finally, when crimes occur in public places there are often multiple witnesses to the event. In such a situation, conversations among witnesses about the culprit's appearance and event details are difficult to avoid. Indeed, data from real eyewitnesses in the United Kingdom suggest that witnessing an event with at least one other person is common, as is talking about the event. Among 60 real witnesses, 88% reported witnessing an event with another person. On average, these witnesses experienced the event with approximately four other people (Skagerberg & Wright, 2008). Because it is impossible to know what transpired in a real-crime situation or what cowitnesses discussed, researchers cannot determine precisely how real cowitnesses influence each other (for a very useful general discussion of cowitnesses, see Wright, Memon, Skagerberg, & Gabbert, 2009).

The first empirical test of confidence malleability as a function of cowitness information was reported in Luus and Wells (1994). These researchers paired witnesses for a live staged crime. After the crime was over, witnesses independently made an identification from a target-absent lineup. Then, they were randomly assigned to hear information about their cowitness's decision. The primary dependent variable was the witnesses' confidence. Because witnesses were randomly assigned to condition, the average confidence level across condition should have been equivalent. In stark contrast, confidence levels varied widely, according to the information presented about a cowitness's decision.

There were eight versions of the cowitness manipulation. With one exception, every iteration of the manipulation significantly changed witnesses' confidence compared with a no cowitness control. Witnesses who heard that a cowitness identified the same person or an implausible person inflated their confidence; witnesses who heard that a cowitness identified a different (but plausible) person lowered their confidence. It is important to note that witnesses in Luus and Wells (1994) did not learn anything about the actual accuracy of their own decision; the fact that a cowitness identified the same person does not necessarily mean that a witness's own identification was accurate. Even so, research participants took cowitness information as confirming (or disconfirming) evidence of their choice and adjusted their confidence correspondingly (see also Semmler et al., 2004).

Are witnesses merely making an appropriate adjustment to their confidence when it inflates in response to cowitness confirmation? After all, witnesses do not blindly adjust confidence reports in response to external information. In one study, witnesses' confidence ratings were unaffected by the knowledge that 97% of a sample of children made the same identification they did (Skagerberg & Wright, 2009). These witnesses produced the same confidence ratings as those who heard that only 4% of a sample of children made the same identification. Another seemingly rational adjustment comes from a study in which witnesses who learned that a confession was obtained from the person they identified increased their confidence; witnesses who learned that the person they identified denied perpetrating the crime decreased their confidence (Hasel & Kassin, 2009).

In spite of rational explanations for some witness behavior, changes in confidence cannot be seen as entirely rational. First, in the case of cowitness information, witnesses fail to update their confidence reports again when the cowitness information turns out to be erroneous (Luus & Wells, 1994). Second, as discussed later, disconfirming and confirming postidentification feedback do not produce symmetric changes in retrospective confidence reports ("How certain do you remember being when you first made your identification?"). Witnesses' reports are more sensitive to influence from confirming feedback than from disconfirming feedback (Douglass & Steblay, 2006).

The malleability of retrospective certainty reports was first examined in a simple study by Wells and Bradfield (1998). In that experiment, witnesses watched a videotape, made an identification from a target-absent photospread, and received one of three types of feedback about their identification.

Some witnesses heard confirming feedback (i.e., "Good, you identified the suspect"). Others heard disconfirming feedback (i.e., "The actual suspect was number __" [a photo not identified by the witness]). The final group of witnesses heard no information about their identification accuracy. Next, witnesses were queried about their recollections. The first question was how certain they remembered being when they made their identification. It is important that this question asked witnesses to recall their state of mind before feedback was delivered, that is, before they knew whether they were right or wrong about their identification. Even so, feedback dramatically distorted witnesses' recollections in predictable ways.

Compared with the control condition, confirming feedback inflated witnesses' memories of how confident they were when they made their identification. Confidence inflation as a function of confirming feedback has been extensively examined since the original postidentification feedback experiments were reported in 1998. In these subsequent experiments, the effect has been routinely observed in a number of variations. Some of those variations include using earwitnesses (Quinlivan et al., 2009), witnesses to real events (Douglass et al., 2009; Wright & Skagerberg, 2007), and unbiased instructions in which it is not suggested to witnesses that the culprit is present (Semmler et al., 2004). Malleability effects are easily eliminated when participants think privately about their certainty before receiving feedback. This inoculation presumably occurs because witnesses did not need to undergo an inference process to determine their confidence. They simply recalled the judgment they thought about before feedback was known (Wells & Bradfield, 1999).

APPLICATION OF RESEARCH ON CONFIDENCE MALLEABILITY

The most obvious recommendation derived from research on confidence malleability is to mandate immediate collection of confidence judgments. The benefits of such a recommendation are twofold. First, the mere act of producing a confidence report can inoculate witnesses against subsequent influence by some external variables (e.g., Neuschatz et al., 2007; Wells & Bradfield, 1999). This is no panacea because other sources of malleability, for example, repeated questioning (Shaw & McClure, 1996), occur in spite of immediate confidence reports. The second benefit of collecting immediate confidence reports is that any inflation can be challenged in court. Although mock jurors do not automatically discredit eyewitnesses whose confidence has increased (e.g., Bradfield & McQuiston, 2004), having a clear means for a defense attorney to challenge a witness puts innocent defendants in a better position than they are in now.

Psychological researchers have another important opportunity to examine the application of confidence malleability research. In two separate cases, the U.S. Supreme Court singled out eyewitness confidence as a critical component in judgments of identification accuracy (*Manson v. Braithwaite*, 1977; *Neil v. Biggers*, 1972). The Supreme Court has not yet revisited this recommendation even though decades of psychological research and over 250 DNA exonerations suggest that emphasizing confidence reports can lead to disastrous consequences. Even more troubling is the finding that certainty reports—which can easily be distorted—influence evaluations of other testimony-relevant judgments. In one study, participants who evaluated a highly confident witness concluded that the witness also gave a good description, even though no information about the description was provided (Bradfield & Wells, 2000). These collateral effects are worrying because the quality of the witness's description is also suggested by the Supreme Court for use in judgments of eyewitness accuracy.

The Supreme Court's recommendation to use confidence as a cue to accuracy fails to disentangle situations in which confidence is useful from those in which it is misleading (e.g., if postidentification feedback has been introduced). Although this is clearly problematic from the standpoint of an innocent defendant, it is perhaps even more so from an innocent *suspect's* perspective. In the *Biggers* decision, the Court stipulated that a suggestive procedure (e.g., a showup) was not sufficient to exclude an identification from court as long as the witness's reports on five criteria exceeded a threshold of acceptability. These five criteria are the witness's certainty, how good the view was, how much attention the witness reports paying, how much time passed between the event and the witness's identification, and the degree to which the witness's description matched the defendant's appearance. This reliability analysis, designed to evaluate the suggestiveness of identification procedures, is practically useless when the procedures themselves, for example, biased lineups, affect the content of the reports (Chapter 8, this volume; Wells & Quinlivan, 2009).

Beyond laying the groundwork for judges who may reference psychological science in appellate decisions or Supreme Court cases, psychological scientists also have a role in individual court cases. Experts represent one of the last opportunities for innocent defendants to avoid conviction. Unfortunately, this safeguard is notoriously ineffective because juries often completely ignore expert testimony. In one study, jurors were explicitly informed that confidence was not a perfect cue to accuracy. Even so, they judged a highly confident witness as more accurate than a witness with low confidence (Fox & Walters, 1986). Even if expert testimony can improve the plight of innocent defendants in individual cases, it is an incremental approach to change. A better way to protect innocent defendants is to require police forces to collect confidence reports at the earliest possible opportunity.

CONCLUSION

Natural human interactions, such as conversations with cowitnesses and feedback from investigators, can influence witnesses to become highly confident even when their identifications and recall of crime scene details are inaccurate. Most of the variables known to affect eyewitness confidence are difficult to control. Witnesses often ask investigators whether their identification was accurate, making postidentification feedback a predictable part of many cases (e.g., Wells & Bradfield, 1998). Cowitness conversations are difficult, if not impossible, to prevent in real crime situations. Sometimes, police arrive at a crime scene after conversations have already transpired. At other times, cowitnesses have existing relationships and discuss their identifications or the crime in spite of police prohibitions to the contrary. Other procedures that artificially inflate confidence reports, like rehearsing testimony (e.g., Wells, Ferguson, & Lindsay, 1981), are merely sensible suggestions for anxious witnesses who are contemplating cross-examination.

There are many unanswered questions about confidence malleability. One is whether confidence reports are less malleable in response to disconfirming feedback than to confirming feedback. Extant research provides conflicting information on this question. In a meta-analysis of the postidentification feedback effect, comparisons between confirming feedback and control conditions show a robust effect on confidence reports across 11 tests (average Cohen's $d = .79$). In three tests of the difference between disconfirming feedback and control conditions, the effect size estimate was substantially smaller than the effect between confirming feedback and the control condition ($d = .21$; Douglass & Steblay, 2006). In contrast, Luus and Wells (1994) found that negative cowitness information (e.g., learning that the cowitness said "not there") deflated eyewitness confidence reports more than positive cowitness information (e.g., learning that the cowitness identified the same person as the eyewitness) inflated them. Understanding when and why disconfirming or negative information has less impact on witnesses will expand our understanding of how witness memory works and may suggest important solutions to protect witnesses from external influence.

In general, finding ways to inoculate witness confidence reports against external influences would be invaluable. However, because influence occurs so quickly in the context of a casual comment from a lineup administrator or a cowitness conversation, an even more useful solution would be finding ways to uncover the true confidence report after external influence has already been introduced. Research showing that witnesses can produce feedback-free confidence reports after becoming suspicious of the experimenter—even though suspicion is not introduced until after feedback is received—suggests that there could be situations in which an uncontaminated confidence report can be recovered (Neuschatz et al., 2007).

Most research in the previous decades has concentrated on when and how confidence relates to identification or report accuracy. Promising new research expands our understanding of eyewitness confidence reports by connecting them to memory processes, not just accuracy. Witness confidence is an important component in decisions about whether to volunteer fine-grained (i.e., highly detailed) versus coarse-grained answers in response to questions about a witnessed event (e.g., Weber & Brewer, 2008). Confidence in fine-grained answers is particularly helpful in separating accurate from inaccurate responses. Does this mean that confidence in fine-grained answers is not as malleable as confidence in coarse-grained answers? If investigators begin an interview with difficult (i.e., fine-grained) questions, will witnesses conclude that their memory for the event is poor and become less confident in subsequent answers, even if accuracy remains constant? If investigators begin an interview with easy (i.e., coarse grained) questions will witnesses' confidence increase, even if accuracy does not? Answers to these questions can provide critical information about how confidence interacts with memory processes.

One understudied variable is the influence of the nature of a crime on the vulnerability of witness confidence to influence. Some witnesses know they will be asked to identify a perpetrator. For example, witnesses to bank robberies know that police will ask them to attempt an identification. Other witnesses do not realize they have seen a crime until they are approached by police. For example, a convenience store clerk who accepts a forged check might not realize it until the police arrive and ask for an identification. This distinction has not been studied very systematically in the eyewitness literature. Many studies on confidence malleability surprise participant eyewitnesses with an identification task (e.g., Luus & Wells, 1994; Wells & Bradfield, 1998). Others inform witnesses ahead of time that they will be asked to identify a face from a photospread (e.g., Douglass et al., 2009). To date, no studies have manipulated witness knowledge to examine whether it moderates confidence malleability effects. Such research would be informative because real witnesses see culprits in both contexts (Valentine, Pickering, & Darling, 2003).

Innocent defendants have few weapons in their arsenal as they attempt to avoid conviction. A confident eyewitness makes an already difficult task nearly impossible. Given the wide variety of variables responsible for inflating eyewitness confidence, Munsterberg's (1908) dire analysis still applies:

> . . . in a thousand courts at a thousand places all over the world, witnesses
> every day affirm by . . . mixtures of truth and untruth, combinations of

memory and of illusion, of knowledge and of suggestion, of experience and wrong conclusions. (p. 43).

Educating judges, police, and juries can mitigate the problem of inappropriate reliance on distorted confidence reports. However, the only solution capable of completely eliminating the influence of distorted confidence is twofold. First, confidence reports should be obtained immediately after an identification is made or a crime is reported. Recording identification procedures or witness interviews will ensure that any confidence report taken is available for presentation at trial. Second, subsequent confidence reports should not be allowed at trial. To the extent that those reports differ from the original confidence report, empirical data has not conclusively demonstrated that triers of fact are able to appropriately discount inflated confidence (e.g., Bradfield & McQuiston, 2004). To protect innocent defendants, witnesses should be barred from providing evidence about their confidence in trial testimony unless the confidence report was previously recorded, before any external variables could have influenced it. This is a radical solution. However, experts would likely agree that invalid scientific evidence like handwriting analyses should be banned from the courtroom. Confidence reports that have been tampered with, even inadvertently, are worse than unscientific evidence like handwriting. They represent a distortion of a truly valuable piece of evidence—uncontaminated confidence reports—and can lead to dire consequences for innocent defendants.

REFERENCES

Asch, S. E. (1955). Opinions and social pressure. *Scientific American, 193*(5), 31–35. doi:10.1038/scientificamerican1155-31

Baron, R. S., Vandello, J. A., & Brunsman, B. (1996). The forgotten variable in conformity research: Impact of task importance on social influence. *Journal of Personality and Social Psychology, 71*, 915–927. doi:10.1037/0022-3514.71.5.915

Bem, D. J. (1967). Self-perception: An alternative interpretation of cognitive dissonance phenomena. *Psychological Review, 74*, 183–200. doi:10.1037/h0024835

Boyce, M. A., Lindsay, S. D., & Brimacombe, C. A. E. (2008). Investigating investigators: Examining the impact of eyewitness identification evidence on student-investigators. *Law and Human Behavior, 32*, 439–453. doi:10.1007/s10979-007-9125-5

Bradfield, A. L., & McQuiston, D. E. (2004). When does evidence of eyewitness confidence inflation affect judgments in a criminal trial? *Law and Human Behavior, 28*, 369–387. doi:10.1023/B:LAHU.0000039331.54147.ff

Bradfield, A. L., & Wells, G. L. (2000). The perceived validity of eyewitness identification testimony: A test of the five Biggers criteria. *Law and Human Behavior, 24*, 581–594. doi:10.1023/A:1005523129437

Bradfield, A. L., Wells, G. L., & Olson, E. A. (2002). The damaging effect of confirming feedback on the relation between eyewitness certainty and identification accuracy. *Journal of Applied Psychology, 87,* 112–120. doi:10.1037/0021-9010.87.1.112

Cutler, B. L., Penrod, S. D., & Dexter, H. R. (1990). Juror sensitivity to eyewitness identification evidence. *Law and Human Behavior, 14,* 185–191. doi:10.1007/BF01062972

Deutsch, M., & Gerard, H. B. (1955). A study of normative and informational social influences upon individual judgment. *Journal of Abnormal and Social Psychology, 51,* 629–636. doi:10.1037/h0046408

Douglass, A. B., Brewer, N., & Semmler, C. (2009). Moderators of post-identification feedback effects on eyewitnesses' memory reports. *Legal and Criminological Psychology, 15,* 279–292. DOI: 10.1348/135532509X446337

Douglass, A. B., Smith, C., & Fraser-Thill, R. (2005). A problem with double-blind photospread procedures: Photospread administrators use one eyewitness's confidence to influence the identification of another eyewitness. *Law and Human Behavior, 29,* 543–562. doi:10.1007/s10979-005-6830-9

Douglass, A. B., & Steblay, N. (2006). Memory distortion in eyewitnesses: A meta-analysis of the post-identification feedback effect. *Applied Cognitive Psychology, 20,* 859–869. doi:10.1002/acp.1237

Fox, S. G., & Walters, H. A. (1986). The impact of general versus specific expert testimony and eyewitness confidence upon mock juror judgment. *Law and Human Behavior, 10,* 215–228. doi:10.1007/BF01046211

Garrioch, L., & Brimacombe, C. A. E. (2001). Lineup administrators' expectations: Their impact on eyewitness confidence. *Law and Human Behavior, 25,* 299–314. doi:10.1023/A:1010750028643

Granhag, P. A., Jonsson, A., & Allwood, C. M. (2004). The cognitive interview and its effect on witnesses' confidence. *Psychology, Crime & Law, 10,* 37–52. doi: 10.1080/1068316021000030577

Hasel, L. E., & Kassin, S. M. (2009). On the presumption of evidentiary independence: Can confessions corrupt eyewitness identifications? *Psychological Science, 20,* 122–126. doi:10.1111/j.1467-9280.2008.02262.x

Innocence Project. *Know the cases: Ryan Matthews.* Retrieved from http://www.innocenceproject.org/Content/206.php

Kassin, S. M., Tubb, V. A., Hosch, H. M., & Memon, A. (2001). On the "general acceptance" of eyewitness testimony research: A new survey of the experts. *American Psychologist, 56,* 405–416. doi:10.1037/0003-066X.56.5.405

Leippe, M. R., Eisenstadt, D., & Rauch, S. M. (2009). Cueing confidence in eyewitness identifications: Influence of biased lineup instructions and pre-identification memory feedback under varying lineup conditions. *Law and Human Behavior, 33,* 194–212. doi:10.1007/s10979-008-9135-y

Luus, C. A. E., & Wells, G. L. (1994). The malleability of eyewitness confidence: Co-witness and perseverance effects. *Journal of Applied Psychology, 79,* 714–723. doi:10.1037/0021-9010.79.5.714

Manson v. Braithwaite, 432 U.S. 98 (1977).

Munsterberg, H. (1908). *On the witness stand: Essays on psychology and crime.* New York, NY: The McClure Company.

Neil v. Biggers, 409 U.S. 188 (1972).

Neuschatz, J. S., Lawson, D. S., Fairless, A. H., Powers, R. A., Neuschatz, J. S., Goodsell, C. A., & Toglia, M. P. (2007). The mitigating effects of suspicion on post-identification feedback and on retrospective eyewitness memory. *Law and Human Behavior, 31,* 231–247. doi:10.1007/s10979-006-9047-7

Quinlivan, D. S., Neuschatz, J. S., Jimenez, A., Cling, A. D., Douglass, A. B., & Goodsell, C. A. (2009). Do prophylactics prevent inflation? Post-identification feedback and the effectiveness of procedures to protect against confidence-inflation in ear-witnesses. *Law and Human Behavior, 33,* 111–121. doi:10.1007/s10979-008-9132-1

Radelet, M. L., Bedau, H. A., & Putnam, C. E. (1992). *In spite of innocence: Erroneous convictions in capital cases.* Boston, MA: Northeastern University Press.

Semmler, C., Brewer, N., & Wells, G. L. (2004). Effects of postidentification feedback on eyewitness identification and nonidentification confidence. *Journal of Applied Psychology, 89,* 334–346. doi:10.1037/0021-9010.89.2.334

Shaw, J. S., III, Appio, L. M., Zerr, T. K., & Pontoski, K. E. (2007). Public eyewitness confidence can be influenced by the presence of other witnesses. *Law and Human Behavior, 31,* 629–652. doi:10.1007/s10979-006-9080-6

Shaw, J. S., III, & McClure, K. A. (1996). Repeated postevent questioning can lead to elevated levels of eyewitness confidence. *Law and Human Behavior, 20,* 629–653. doi:10.1007/BF01499235

Shaw, J. S., III, & Zerr, T. K. (2003). Extra effort during memory retrieval may be associated with increases in eyewitness confidence. *Law and Human Behavior, 27,* 315–329. doi:10.1023/A:1023487908640

Shaw, J. S., III, Zerr, T. K., & Woythaler, K. A. (2001). Public eyewitness confidence ratings can differ from those held privately. *Law and Human Behavior, 25,* 141–154. doi:10.1023/A:1005641314083

Skagerberg, E. M., & Wright, D. B. (2008). The co-witness misinformation effect: Memory blends or memory compliance? *Memory, 16,* 436–442. doi:10.1080/09658210802019696

Skagerberg, E. M., & Wright, D. B. (2009). Susceptibility to postidentification feedback is affected by source credibility. *Applied Cognitive Psychology, 23,* 506–523. doi:10.1002/acp.1470

Tulving, E. (1981). Similarity relations in recognition. *Journal of Verbal Learning and Verbal Behavior, 20,* 479–496. doi:10.1016/S0022-5371(81)90129-8

Valentine, T., Pickering, A., & Darling, S. (2003). Characteristics of eyewitness identification that predict the outcome of real lineups. *Applied Cognitive Psychology*, *17*, 969–993. doi:10.1002/acp.939

Weber, N., & Brewer, N. (2008). Eyewitness recall: Regulation of grain size and the role of confidence. *Journal of Experimental Psychology: Applied*, *14*, 50–60. doi:10.1037/1076-898X.14.1.50

Wells, G. L., & Bradfield, A. L. (1998). "Good, you identified the suspect": Feedback to eyewitnesses distorts their reports of the witnessing experience. *Journal of Applied Psychology*, *83*, 360–376. doi:10.1037/0021-9010.83.3.360.

Wells, G. L., & Bradfield, A. L. (1999). Distortions in eyewitnesses' recollections: Can the postidentification-feedback effect be moderated? *Psychological Science*, *10*, 138–144. doi:10.1111/1467-9280.00121

Wells, G. L., Ferguson, T. J., & Lindsay, R. C. L. (1981). The tractability of eyewitness confidence and its implications for triers of fact. *Journal of Applied Psychology*, *66*, 688–696. doi:10.1037/0021-9010.66.6.688

Wells, G. L., & Quinlivan, D. S. (2009). Suggestive eyewitness identification procedures and the Supreme Court's reliability test in light of eyewitness science: 30 years later. *Law and Human Behavior*, *33*, 1–24. doi:10.1007/s10979-008-9130-3

Wright, D. B., Memon, A., Skagerberg, E. M., & Gabbert, F. (2009). When eyewitnesses talk. *Current Directions in Psychological Science*, *18*, 174–178. doi:10.1111/j.1467-8721.2009.01631.x.

Wright, D. B., Self, G., & Justice, C. (2000). Memory conformity: Exploring misinformation effects when presented by another person. *The British Journal of Psychology*, *91*, 189–202. doi:10.1348/000712600161781

Wright, D. B., & Skagerberg, E. M. (2007). Post-identification feedback affects real eyewitnesses. *Psychological Science*, *18*, 172–178. doi:10.1111/j.1467-9280.2007.01868.x

8

WHY DO MOTIONS TO SUPPRESS SUGGESTIVE EYEWITNESS IDENTIFICATIONS FAIL?

GARY L. WELLS, SARAH M. GREATHOUSE, AND LAURA SMALARZ

In the American legal system, one of the safeguards against wrongful convictions on the basis of mistaken eyewitness identification is the right of the defense to file motions to suppress suggestive eyewitness identifications. These pretrial motions to suppress eyewitness identification evidence are filed routinely, and yet they almost never succeed, even when the identification procedures are profoundly suggestive. The right to file suppression motions was available to all of the innocent people whose convictions based on mistaken identifications have been overturned using DNA evidence (266 at press, see http://www.innocenceproject.org/), but, of course, none were suppressed.

In this chapter, we describe a number of reasons why eyewitness identification evidence is rarely suppressed. These reasons include (a) flaws in the case law that is used in deciding suppression motions, (b) a tendency of the legal system to underestimate the power of suggestive procedures and overestimate the reliability of witnesses, (c) the great sense of unease about a system that would seemingly deny victims the right to point out their assailants, (d) the false dichotomy (suppress vs. not suppress) trap that courts have taken, and (e) the ineffectiveness of defense attorneys who fail to do their homework and their tendency to file "boilerplate" motions.

We discuss each of these six problems that, when considered in totality, seem to shift the question from "Why do motions to suppress eyewitness identification procedures almost always fail?" to "Why do they ever succeed?" Our intent is not one of assigning blame. But, absent some significant changes in domains that are under the control of the criminal justice system, there is no reason to be optimistic about the ability of motions to suppress to serve as a safeguard against wrongful convictions. Key corrections to these problems, in contrast, can have two important effects. One effect is to help weed out unreliable identifications at the time of the motion-to-suppress hearing. The other effect, which is related to the first, is that these changes will (a) provide an incentive to police to eliminate suggestive procedures so as to avoid the risk that the identification will be suppressed, (b) serve as justification for permitting expert testimony, or (c) trigger jury instructions that lower the impact of the evidence.

A BRIEF HISTORY OF THE RIGHT TO FILE MOTIONS TO SUPPRESS IDENTIFICATION EVIDENCE

During the past 50 years, the legal community has gained substantial awareness of the fragile nature of eyewitness identifications. Some of the first judicial attempts to address this issue came in a series of cases in 1967 (*United States v. Wade*, *Gilbert v. California*, *Stovall v. Denno*), which implemented various safeguards designed to increase the reliability of pretrial identifications. The right to file motions to suppress identification evidence is a safeguard still in place today; however, the law that outlines exactly what factors determine whether eyewitness evidence should be suppressed has changed over the years. Prior to 1972, the per se exclusion rule held that the use of unnecessarily suggestive eyewitness identification procedures warranted the exclusion of eyewitness evidence at trial. Such suggestive procedures include using a showup procedure when the police could have conducted a lineup, conducting a lineup in which the suspect stood out, failing to tell eyewitnesses that the culprit might not be in the lineup, showing the witnesses a photo of the suspect before conducting a lineup, telling witnesses that their choice was correct, or conducting a second lineup procedure in which the only person in common was the suspect. Psychological research has since demonstrated the destructive influence of these practices on the accuracy of eyewitness identifications, and their propensity to lead to wrongful convictions (see Chapter 6, this volume).

A new standard for determining the admissibility of identification evidence surfaced as a result of the 1972 Supreme Court case of *Neil v. Biggers*. The new approach, called the *reliability* or the *totality* approach, was based on the idea that the exclusion of eyewitness evidence should not be based solely on whether the procedures involved unnecessary suggestiveness but on whether the identification was nevertheless reliable. This approach was upheld and reaffirmed in *Manson v. Braithwaite* in 1977 (hereafter called *Manson*) and is used today by courts evaluating motions to suppress. The evaluation of the motion consists of a two-pronged assessment. The first component is to determine whether the identification procedure was unnecessarily suggestive. If it was not, the evidence is admitted into court. If the procedure is found to have been suggestive, then the distorting influence of the suggestive procedure is weighed against five criteria intended to assess whether the identification is nevertheless reliable. These factors include the witness's opportunity to view the offender, the witness's degree of attention during the crime, the accuracy of the witness's description of the offender, the time elapsed between the crime and the pretrial identification, and the level of certainty demonstrated at the time of identification. In the event that the court determines that the suggestive procedure created a "very substantial likelihood of irreparable misidentification," the motion to suppress is granted.

THE FLAWS IN *MANSON*

We begin our analysis of why motions to suppress unreliable eyewitness identifications fail with an analysis of the legal architecture of *Manson*.[1] When *Manson* was decided by the U.S. Supreme Court, there was no scientific literature on eyewitness identification. Hence, the *Manson* test for admission of eyewitness identification evidence is based almost exclusively on the common sense of the Supreme Court at that time. In addition, in fact, there is a common sense behind *Manson*. The Supreme Court reasoned that the presence of suggestion in an eyewitness identification should not automatically result in suppression. After all, the critical issue is reliability. Also, if there were clear indications of reliability, then the suggestion is unlikely to have been a problem in the case under consideration. In fact, eyewitness scientists today agree with a variant of this type of reasoning, namely, that if memory is strong enough, suggestion should not affect the witness. Consider an extreme case, for instance, in which suggestive procedures were used to try to get someone to misidentify his or her own spouse. At the extreme, strong memories can indeed trump suggestive procedures. Hence, the idea that a suppression decision should be based on weighing a set of reliability factors against the suggestion is not, in itself, a flawed idea.

---

[1]A more extensive analysis of the problems with *Manson* can be found in Wells and Quinlivan (2009). Also, the dissenting opinion in *Manson v. Braithwaite* (1977) was written by Justice Marshall and is still very much worth reading today. It is interesting to speculate how different the legal treatment of eyewitness identification evidence in the United States would have been over the last 33 years had Marshall's opinion been the majority opinion.

But the flaws in *Manson* begin to unfold when we consider the *Manson* criteria that are used to assess reliability. Recall that the Court listed five criteria: (a) How good was the witness's view during the crime? (b) How much attention did the witness pay to the culprit? (c) How certain was the witness at the time of the identification? (d) How good was the witness's description of the culprit? and (e) How much time passed between witnessing and the identification? Hereafter, we will call these criteria *view*, *attention*, *certainty*, *description*, and *delay*, respectively. Collectively, we will refer to these as the *Manson reliability criteria*.

The first thing to note about these criteria is that three of the five are self-reports from the witness. In effect, the only way to know how to "score" the witness on view, attention, and certainty is to ask him or her. This creates an odd situation in which a witness is asked to assess his or her own reliability. Although there are occasions on which a witness's statement about view might be contrasted with objective measures (e.g., when a witness claims to have been 30 feet away, whereas reconstruction of the crime scene shows the distance to have been 100 feet), view is generally assessed simply by asking witnesses if they had a good view and could make out details of the face. Similarly, attention and certainty are subjective judgments that can never be gauged against objective measures.

There are a number of problems with people's estimates of their view, attention, and certainty (see Chapter 5, this volume). For example, people overestimate the duration of their views, especially when the view was brief (for a more extensive treatment of this, see Wells & Quinlivan, 2009). But our primary concern about these three self-report variables is that research has shown convincingly and repeatedly that eyewitnesses' answers are strongly influenced by prior suggestion (see Chapter 7, this volume). Consider, for example, the postidentification feedback effect. In postidentification feedback effect studies, witnesses to simulated crimes make identification attempts from lineups and are then randomly assigned to receive confirming feedback (e.g., "Good, you identified the suspect") or no feedback. In the original postidentification feedback effect experiments (Wells & Bradfield, 1998), all witnesses who made identifications were mistaken because they were given a perpetrator-absent lineup. Later, witnesses were asked a number of questions of the type that would be asked in a suppression hearing (or later at trial). These included questions about view ("How good was the view you had of the culprit?" "How well could you make out details of the culprit's face?"), attention ("How much attention did you pay to the culprit's face?"), and certainty ("At the time of your identification, how certain were you that you identified the actual culprit?"). Results show that confirming feedback strongly inflates witnesses' estimates of how good their view was, how well they could make out details of the culprit's face, how closely they attended to the culprit during the crime, and how certain they recall having been at the time of the identification. It is important to note that these inflated answers are distortions; after all, the feedback did not occur until after the identification and, through random assignment, both groups were actually equally certain or uncertain, paid the same amount of attention, and got the same view. Since the time it was first demonstrated (Wells & Bradfield, 1998) the postidentification feedback effect has been widely replicated (see Chapter 7, this volume).

The postidentification feedback effect represents a serious challenge to the two-pronged assessment architecture of *Manson*. In *Manson*, the first prong assesses whether or not there was suggestiveness. If there was suggestiveness, then the witness's standing on the *Manson* criteria is assessed. If the witness scores reasonably well on the *Manson* criteria, then the identification testimony is admitted. The problem, of course, is that the witness's score on the *Manson* criteria is inflated by the suggestive procedures themselves. This leads to some absurd consequences. For instance, in the absence of the suggestive event the witness might not have claimed to be certain, might not have said that his or her view was good, and might not have said that he or she paid close attention. Therefore, in what sense do the certainty, view, and attention criteria manage to assess reliability when there have been suggestive procedures? They do not. In fact, the witness's standing on these three important *Manson* criteria is confounded by the very fact that suggestion occurred.

Consider now the other two *Manson* criteria: delay and description. Delay, which is the amount of time that passed between the witnessed event and the identification, is clearly something that can be assessed objectively because the time of the crime is known and the time of any identification procedure is known. Suggestive procedures cannot distort assessments of the delay variable. In addition, there definitely is empirical evidence that indicates that the elapsed time between witnessing an event and later identification accuracy is negatively correlated with accurate identifications and positively correlated with mistaken identifications (see Cutler & Penrod, 1995; Shapiro & Penrod, 1986). However, the myopic focus on the passage of time, per se, is somewhat misplaced given the wealth of evidence that it is what happens during the passage of time, rather than the mere passage of time, that is more important. Eyewitness researchers have documented the very strong effects of events that witnesses experience during the passage of time. The important work of Elizabeth Loftus (1979) and the numerous researchers who have followed her lead exemplifies this emphasis on studying the effects of events that occur during the memory retention interval (see Wells & Loftus, 2003). This research shows that the amount of time that elapsed between the witnessed event and the identification is not, in itself, determinative information about the likely reliability of a given identification.

The description criterion is theoretically an objective criterion rather than a self-report. Although it is true that the description is obtained from the witness, hence it relies on the witness to report it, the description is supposedly taken prior to the identification and needs to match some externally judged criterion level (i.e., similarity to the accused). However, like certainty, view, and attention, even the description can be malleable if it is obtained after the identification is already made. In other words, a description that is given at a suppression hearing could be formulated to closely fit the characteristics of the accused once the witness has already viewed the accused in the lineup or in court at the hearing. In fact, many courts have been sloppy in permitting witnesses to give a more detailed description or change their description at a suppression hearing and then use the modified or elaborated description to argue that the witness gave a good description. This happens despite the clarity in *Manson* that the description criterion refers to the witness's initial description (prior to the identification attempt). However, even preidentification descriptions tend to show little-to-no correlation to identification accuracy, whether they are measured in terms of completeness of description or in terms of congruence (similarity or fit) to the identified person (Pigott & Brigham, 1985; Wells, 1985). Furthermore, eyewitnesses tend to select the person who looks most like their memory of the culprit (Wells, 1984) and will readily select an innocent person if that person fits the eyewitness's prelineup description better than do the lineup fillers (e.g., Lindsay & Wells, 1980; Wells, Rydell, & Seelau, 1993). In other words, when misidentifications occur, they tend to be of lineup members who fit the eyewitness's prelineup description of the culprit. Hence, finding that the description fits the identified person may indicate nothing more than the propensity of witnesses to identify someone who fits the description. Furthermore, if a lineup is constructed properly, everyone in the lineup should fit the description already (Wells, Rydell, & Seelau, 1993).

Another problem with the *Manson* factors is how they are actually used in a suppression decision. The Supreme Court did not articulate any clear decision rule other than the "totality of the circumstances." The Court did not say, for instance, that one of these five factors was more important than others or that the witness needed to have a high standing on four of the five, nor did the Court specify how well the witness had to score on any one of them. As of this writing, there is no systematic study of motions to suppress eyewitness identification evidence in the United States. However, one thing is fairly clear nevertheless: Witnesses can score very poorly on more than one of the criteria and judges will still rule the evidence to be admissible. If there is a pattern to this, it seems to be that witnesses can score extremely poorly on the *Manson* criteria as long as they are highly certain. Consider the time-since-witnessing variable. *Biggers* was identified by using a showup procedure 7 months after the crime; nevertheless, the witness was certain, and the identification was permitted (*Neil v. Biggers*, 1972). Consider the view variable. In a 1997 case, a man was convicted of murder on the basis of the highly certain identification testimony of someone who was 450 feet away, which exceeds the capability of the human visual system (G. R. Loftus & Harley, 2005) by at least 100 feet. Consider the attention factor. In *State v. Ledbetter* (1981), the court said that even a "fleeting glance" might be sufficient and noted the high level of certainty of the witness to justify admission of the identification. In these cases, "totality of circumstances" seems to mean primarily that the witness was certain.

In summary, *Manson v. Brathwaite* (1977) set down the decision-making architecture for courts in regard to how to reason about and make rulings on motions to suppress eyewitness identification evidence. That architecture is still in place nearly 35 years later. Meanwhile, exonerations of factually innocent people based on DNA testing over the last 15 years or so show that mistaken identification testimony accounts for over 75% of these wrongful convictions. Suppressions rarely occur, even for the most egregiously suggestive procedures. Our analysis of *Manson* tells us a lot about why this is the case. Three of the five *Manson* criteria are self-reports from the witness that cannot be substantiated against objective factors, and each of these three can be inflated by suggestive procedures. This is especially important considering that the *Manson* test is used primarily when there were suggestive procedures; hence, it is virtually guaranteed that the witness's scores on three of the five criteria would be inflated by the suggestiveness, thereby confounding the use of these three criteria. Furthermore, none of the five criteria is strongly related to eyewitness identification accuracy even in the absence of suggestiveness. In addition, courts seem to not care that much about any of the criteria except the certainty of the witness, which is the most malleable of all the criteria. In conclusion, the primary reason that suppression motions fail is because the judicial law that governs suppression hearings, *Manson v. Braithwaite* (1977), is flawed in a way that makes it almost certain that the witness will pass the admissibility test.

OVERESTIMATING THE RELIABILITY OF WITNESSES

Another possible reason why motions to suppress suggestive eyewitness identifications fail is that judges underestimate the influence of suggestive procedures. At a broad level, this should not be surprising to psychological scientists. One of the general principles discovered in social psychology is that people underestimate the extent to which situations influence thinking and behavior, which leads to such phenomena as the fundamental attribution error. We see no reason to think that judges would be immune to this tendency. In addition, we do not think that any treatment of the question of why suppression motions fail would be complete without considering the obvious possibility that many judges simply do not think that eyewitnesses make mistaken identifications, or they think that such occurrences are so astronomically rare that they need not seriously consider the possibility in any case that comes before them.

Typically, motions to suppress and suppression hearings are relatively specific to the individual case and are tied closely to legal arguments based on case law (e.g., *Manson*). They are not designed to be a method of teaching judges about reliability problems with eyewitnesses. We believe that suppression hearings could and should be opportunities to educate judges. Here, we make three observations that we think all trial judges should know.

Archival Studies Reveal Error

First, there have been six published studies that have examined large sets of lineups in actual cases (Behrman & Davey, 2001; Behrman, & Richards, 2005; Slater, 1994; Valentine, Pickering, & Darling, 2003; Wright & McDaid, 1996; Wright & Skagerberg, 2007). These are archival studies in which every lineup within a specific time frame is counted (not just those that police or prosecutors or defense attorneys or researchers wanted to look at). The issue of interest is how often eyewitnesses to these serious crimes (whether victim or bystander) pick the suspect, pick a known-innocent filler, or pick no one. When a witness picks the suspect, we cannot be absolutely sure of whether the identification is accurate or not. When the witness picks no one, we do not know if that was because the perpetrator was not in the lineup or because the witness was not confident enough to make an identification. However, when the witness picks a known-innocent filler (someone placed in the lineup merely for the purpose of "filling out" the lineup), we know that the eyewitness made a mistaken identification.[2] In Table 8.1, we report the results of these important archival studies. The first thing to notice is the consistency of the results across these studies. Despite the fact that Berhman and Davey (2001) is based on data from Northern California, whereas Wright and Skagerberg (2007) is based on data from England, for example, their results differ by only a few percentage points. Hence, we focus our analysis here on the overall averages. For our purposes, it is important to note that fully one of every five witnesses (21%) who view a lineup picked a known-innocent filler. Moreover, when we remove those who picked no one, one out of three (33%) picked a known-innocent filler! Every judge should know these findings. These findings, from real eyewitnesses in serious criminal cases, show quite vividly

---

[2]These filler identifications are often "buried" in real cases. If the suspect is not prosecuted, for instance, there is no clear path back to a record to show that a lineup was even done. Many detectives fail to record whether the witness identified no one versus identified one of the fillers and instead merely note that the witness failed to identify the suspect (Behrman & Davey, 2001). Rarely is a witness who did not identify the suspect ever called to court. Hence, the only way to track this important statistic on filler identification rates is through archival studies like these.

TABLE 8.1
Published Archival Studies of Suspect Identification (ID), Filler Identification, and No-Identification Rates From Lineups in Actual Cases

Study	Filler (%)	Suspect (%)	No ID (%)	IDs that are not of suspect (%)
Behrman & Davey (2001)	24	50	26	32
Behrman & Richards (2005)	15	52	33	22
Slater (1994)	22	42	36	34
Valentine et al. (2003)	21	41	39	34
Wright & McDaid (1996)	20	39	41	34
Wright & Skagerberg (2007)	21	58	21	27
Averages	21	47	33	31

that the chances of mistaken identification are not trivial at all. Also, the real rate must be higher than one out of three identifying witnesses because we cannot assume that all identifications of suspects were accurate identifications.

Exoneration Cases Underestimate the Problem

A second important observation based on real eyewitnesses comes from the DNA exoneration cases. As of this writing, there have been 266 exonerations of people wrongfully convicted in U.S. courts, and 203 of these were cases of mistaken eyewitness identification (Innocence Project, 2010). Some critics note that 199 is a small number relative to the large numbers of people convicted every year in the United States. That is true, but the number 199 is a gross underestimate of the real numbers for several reasons. First, it must be kept in mind that these were the "lucky few" who were convicted by juries and then, for some reason, the biological evidence was preserved. In the vast majority of cases in which prisoners claim to have been mistakenly identified, the biological evidence was not collected, it was not collected properly, it deteriorated, it was lost, or it was destroyed. However, there is an even bigger factor involved here: In only a small percentage of cases is there any biological evidence to be analyzed at all, let alone by using DNA tests. In fact, virtually every DNA exoneration case is a case that involved sexual assault. This does not mean that sexual assault witnesses are bad witnesses. In fact, they may be the most reliable single category of eyewitnesses because they usually get a closer view and a longer view of the perpetrator than do most eyewitnesses. However, sexual assault cases, unlike robberies and most other crimes, usually leave behind semen or other biological trace material (e.g., pubic hair with root) that can be analyzed using forensic DNA techniques. Our best estimate at this point is that fewer than 5% of lineups are for sexual assault cases or other cases for which there is likely any DNA evidence. This last estimate alone requires us to multiply the 233 by 20, yielding the number 4,060 for a conservative minimum estimate of the number of people imprisoned in the United States, at press, based on mistaken identification.[3] Also, this is a very conservative estimate because the 199 itself is based only on the subset of DNA-present cases for which the evidence was preserved and for which the claim of innocence has been tested.

The Pleading Effect Changes the Odds

Archival studies indicate that those charged with a crime enter a guilty plea in 80% to 90% of cases (Cole, 1986). For current purposes, we assume the 80% pleading rate (our argument is stronger at 90%). Assume further that those who plead guilty are in fact guilty.[4] In other words, assume that all innocent suspects mistakenly identified in a lineup fight the case rather than plead, and they exercise their rights by filing motions to suppress the identification. That means that 100% of innocent (mistakenly identified) defendants will have a motion to suppress hearing, whereas only 20% of guilty (accurately identified) defendants will have a motion to suppress hearing. These differential base rates in pleading guilty versus maintaining innocence give rise to what has been called the *pleading effect* (Charman & Wells, 2007; Wells, Memon, & Penrod, 2006), and it has a huge effect on the rate of mistaken identifications that judges can encounter at a suppression hearing. Suppose, for example, that 5% of the time witnesses identify an innocent suspect in a lineup, 50% of the time they identify a guilty suspect, 15% of the time they identify a filler, and 30% of the time they identify no one. When no one is identified or when a filler is identified, there is no suppression hearing. When a guilty suspect is identified, 80% of the time the guilty person pleads guilty, which means only 10% (20% of the 50%) try to fight conviction and have a suppression hearing. In addition, based on our prior assumptions, all 5% of the innocent suspects fight conviction and have a suppression hearing. This means that only 15% of the lineups will result in a suppression hearing and one third of those are innocent suspects. This is greatly at odds with an expectation by a judge that the chances of encountering a mistaken identification in a suppression hearing are remote or astronomically low. Of course, there are a lot of assump-

---

[3]The assumption here is that only 1/20 of identifications would have had the possibility for DNA evidence . Hence, unless witnesses were more reliable in crimes with no DNA (e.g., robberies) than they were in crimes that had DNA (sexual assault), the 266 exonerations (at press) based on DNA can only be 1/20 of the mistaken identifications.

[4]In no sense do we intend for this assumption to be interpreted as a denial of the important work of Kassin and Gudjonsson (2004) and other false-confession researchers, who have clearly made a compelling case that innocent people plead guilty.

tions behind this analysis. It assumes, for instance, that the rate of identifying innocent suspects is 5%. We do not really know the number, of course, but many scholars have placed the rate higher. It also assumes that innocent suspects identified from a lineup are actually charged. In some cases there might be exculpating evidence that surfaces after the lineup. Our point is that a judge whose tendency is to think that the chances of mistaken identification in motion to suppress cases are extremely low should carefully consider the pleading effect and other things that we know (e.g., the DNA exonerations and the archival studies of filler identification rates). And, of course, it can be expected that the mistaken witnesses are likely to score well on the *Manson* factors, especially if there was anything suggestive involved in the identification procedure.

DENYING A VICTIM THE "RIGHT" TO IDENTIFY THE PERPETRATOR

Thus far, our discussion of why suppression motions fail has focused on problems with case law (*Manson*) and a lack of appreciation for the propensities of eyewitnesses to mistakenly identify. However, we also believe that there is a natural and understandable reluctance to deny an eyewitness the opportunity to testify in these cases. After all, the honesty of these eyewitnesses is not in question; they are not lying. They are telling the truth as they know it. Consider as well that a large share of eyewitnesses are victim witnesses. Imagine telling a rape victim that her identification of her alleged rapist will not be admitted at trial and that she cannot point him out at trial merely because the police used fillers who did not fit the description she gave of her perpetrator (a highly suggestive identification procedure). Not only victim's rights groups but many others (including the authors of this chapter) would have great difficulty making such a ruling. In fact, such a ruling would likely turn the public and even the press against the judge. Fox News and Bill O'Reilly could make such a case go national. In jurisdictions in which judges are elected, that judge might as well not bother to run in the next election. Perhaps this is an exaggeration, but suppressing any evidence against a criminal defendant, let alone a victim-witness's identification testimony, is considered by a large share of the American public to be part of a left-wing conspiracy to be soft on crime. No matter what judges might claim, they cannot be immune to these sociopolitical considerations. This is a primary reason why we believe that more practical remedies (short of exclusion) need to be considered, and we discuss those in the next section, The False Dichotomy of Suppress Versus Not Suppress.

Contrast the seemingly radical decision to suppress an identification that was riddled with problems with the profoundly easy alternative available to judges, namely, a ruling in which the judge says "let it go to weight." This is the type of language in which a judge acknowledges problems with the identification but simply says that the jury can decide how much weight to attach to the identification. In this case, the judge is fully admitting the testimony and expressing total confidence that the jury can assess the reliability of the identification. For a review of the shortcomings of jurors in their abilities to evaluate eyewitness identification testimony, see Chapter 9 of this volume. A decision to let it go to weight is no decision at all and, hence, its overuse eliminates a fundamental safeguard.

THE FALSE DICHOTOMY OF SUPPRESS VERSUS NOT SUPPRESS

One of the biggest factors that has led to faulty identifications nevertheless being admitted is the treatment of the suppression issue as a dichotomy—full admission versus total exclusion. And yet, nothing in *Manson* or other case law requires this. As we noted in the previous section, the total exclusion option is an extreme one that some judges will simply never exercise regardless of how suggestive the identification procedures are and how unreliable the witness is likely to be. Furthermore, there are many cases in which total exclusion is unwise because the problems, although important, are not sufficient to assume the witness to be definitively unreliable. Fortunately, although rarely used, there are remedies that do not require full exclusion.

Consider two concrete examples. In the first, an eyewitness gave a description of the perpetrator as a White male in his early 20s with short dark hair, no facial hair, and a medium build. Later, the witness picked the suspect from a lineup after a long time studying the lineup. Immediately after making the choice, the detective blurted out "Great! Good job. That is the guy." Later, the witness claims to have been positive all along. In this case, the feedback is a big problem. The witness took a long time to make an identification, suggesting uncertainty, and yet claims now to have been certain all along. We know such feedback inflates retrospective and current certainty, and we know that certainty is not only a central criterion at a suppression hearing but also is important to a jury's decision as to whether to believe the witness. At the same time, the feedback alone is perhaps not sufficient to suppress the identification testimony altogether. Hence, under the dichotomous approach the testimony would simply be admitted. An alternative is clearly available, however. Specifically, because the certainty of the witness was tainted, the certainty of the witness could not be considered a reliability factor at the suppression hearing. This would place more burden on the prosecution to demonstrate reliability through other reliability criteria. Furthermore, the judge could rule that the witness could not testify at trial about her certainty. In other words, although the identification testimony is admitted, it is limited.

In the second example, assume all the same facts except that there was no confirming feedback. Instead, after the identification, the detective shows the witness a picture of a scar on the suspect's chest and says, "You saw him without a shirt and never mentioned this scar. That might be a problem." Later, the witness begins giving descriptions that include the scar. Assuming no problems with the lineup itself, the lineup identification is not necessarily at issue. However, we know that showing the witness the photo of the scar is highly suggestive and problematic. Hence, at a suppression hearing a judge could rule that the witness can testify but can never mention the scar in her testimony. The defense, in contrast, is permitted to argue at trial that the witness never mentioned a scar in her initial descriptions.

Our point is that the apparent suppress–not suppress dichotomy is a false one. There are many case-tailored alternatives that can smartly limit testimony to individual elements that a suggestive procedure might have contaminated. But this failure to break away from dichotomous thinking does not rest solely with trial judges. In fact, it is primarily the responsibility of defense attorneys to fashion meaningful responses, such as to craft motions in limine (a motion to limit rather than totally suppress) on which for judges to rule. There are other remedies for which defense attorneys can ask that are short of full suppression, such as judicial instructions, expert testimony, or both. Treating the suppression hearing as though the only possible outcomes are to suppress the testimony or not suppress the testimony is a myopic and limited view of what can be achieved. Hence, one of the reasons that suppression motions fail is because the defense motion takes the all-or-nothing (suppress–not suppress) approach rather than giving the judge a range of options for dealing with the problematic testimony.

We know of no study that has examined how well or poorly prepared most defense attorneys are as they enter a suppression hearing. It seems likely to us that no such study has ever been done. Hence, our treatment of this matter can only be based on our own impressions. However, as anecdotal as it might be, we do not think it is at all unusual for defense attorneys to do a poor job in eyewitness identification suppression hearings. We see several recurring problems. First, many defense attorneys often use boilerplate written motions that are only slightly rewritten so that they do not appear to be something that was downloaded from the Internet. In many cases, such as with public defenders who have impossible case loads, it just takes too much time to prepare an effective motion to suppress. In addition, there is a defeatist attitude about suppression motions in eyewitness identification cases. Most experienced defense attorneys have had the experience of putting great time and effort into trying to get an egregious identification suppressed, only to have the judge rule that the testimony is admissible. Why put great effort into something that will fail anyway? The attorney has to make a suppression motion, otherwise he or she is not doing her job. But if he or she is not going to get the identification suppressed anyway, what incentive is there to expend time and energy investigating suggestive procedures and drafting a detailed suppression motion? As it stands now, there is none. Ideally, however, the defense should conduct a thorough investigation of the events occurring prior to and following the identification that could have contributed to an unreliable identification.

Whenever possible, for instance, the attorney should review a copy of the 911 call, which will often include a description of the perpetrator. There should be another description in the initial police report. It is absolutely critical that these descriptions be the ones that are used in the suppression hearing, not descriptions that are given later or that the witness gives at the suppression hearing. The prosecution will want to use these later descriptions because they tend to increasingly resemble the defendant. The defense should never allow this to happen; the language of *Manson* is quite clear that it is the initial description of the perpetrator that should be used to assess reliability. However, if the defense attorney does not know what that initial description is, then the attorney is in no position to win that point. Good presuppression homework can also mean visiting the crime scene to see what might be discovered there. At the crime scene, one might be able to measure lighting conditions and measure some distances. If the witness at the hearing claims to have been 15 feet away, but physical measurements show the distance to be 50 feet, this speaks directly to one of the *Manson* criteria (opportunity to view). Furthermore, a careful review of the police report might indicate something about the certainty or uncertainty of the witness at the time of the identification. It is interesting to note that it is very common for police reports on lineups to say nothing about the certainty of the witness at the time of the identification and instead say something like, "Witness indicated number 3." That too is important because it indicates that a strong line of questioning should take place at the hearing as to what the witness has been told or has heard about the defendant since the time of identification. Most witnesses will admit that they have been told something (e.g., case detective said that this was the right guy, prosecutor thanked the witness for helping get this guy off of the streets) that would have the effect of increasing the certainty of the witness. The defense attorney then has to be prepared to make the case that the absence of any record of how certain the witness was at the time of the identification means that witness's confidence cannot be used to argue that the witness is reliable. This is also the chance to argue that if the identification is not suppressed, witnesses should not be permitted to state their certainty at trial because it has been contaminated. But records of initial statements of uncertainty are rarely available and, hence, the witness's inflated postidentification certainty is typically used both in the suppression hearing and at trial.

Many defense attorneys wait until after their motion to suppress is denied and then start thinking about getting an eyewitness expert to testify.

In our view, the suppression hearing is the best place and time to make a case for permitting an expert at trial. The key is to get the expert testimony into the suppression hearing. It is easier to get an eyewitness expert admitted at the suppression hearing than it is to get an eyewitness expert admitted at trial. After all, one of the primary arguments for not permitting an eyewitness expert at trial is that it might influence the jury too much (or invade the province of the jury or be prejudicial). However, there is no jury in a suppression hearing, only the judge. Why would a judge fear hearing from an expert? Once admitted at the suppression hearing, the chances of successful suppression are increased if a good expert is used. But even if the judge rules that the eyewitness evidence is admissible, the use of the expert at the suppression hearing increases the chances that the expert will be admitted at trial. There are two reasons for this. First, many trial judges, if not most, have never heard an eyewitness expert testify, but when they do, they tend to wonder what all the fuss over admissibility was about. Judges who actually hear an eyewitness expert testify usually come to realize that the expert is making reasonable, well-founded statements that are not merely a matter of common sense and that do not invade the province of the jury. In addition, if a judge rules that the eyewitness identification testimony is admissible (i.e., the suppression motion fails), the defense can request at that point that an eyewitness expert be admitted at trial; a sort of "consolation prize."

The general point is that suppression hearings should not be treated in a perfunctory manner. It is true that there is a great deal that defense attorneys cannot know prior to the suppression hearing. Usually, they have no opportunity to interview the witness or the detective in the case before the hearing, and therefore they do not know how the witness or detective will answer many of the questions. Indeed, the extremely useful book by E. F. Loftus, Doyle, and Dysart (2008) argues that a primary reason for filing a motion to suppress and having a suppression hearing is for discovery purposes. A suppression hearing need not result in full suppression to be successful. Parts of testimony might be suppressed (e.g., witness cannot testify about her certainty or witness cannot modify her description of the perpetrator from what she initially said now that she has studied the defendant's characteristics). In addition, the suppression hearing might succeed in getting an expert admitted at trial.

CONCLUSION

In this chapter, we have tried to take a broad view of why motions to suppress suggestive and unreliable eyewitness identifications routinely fail. This is an important issue because the right to file a motion to suppress is considered to be a fundamental safeguard against wrongful convictions. It failed for the

193 individuals who were later exonerated on the basis of forensic DNA testing (which our conservative estimate indicates must be at least 3,840 wrongful convictions from mistaken identification when the percentage of cases in which there is no DNA evidence is considered). These failed motions to suppress identifications in DNA exoneration cases include people like John Briscoe, who was placed in a live lineup dressed in an orange prison jumpsuit while the fillers were dressed in street clothes. If a motion to suppress such a lineup fails, then something is broken. Our analysis argues that much of the problem rests with the architecture of the case law (*Manson v. Braithwaite*, 1977) that permits egregiously suggestive procedures as long as the witness passes a "reliability test": A test that is influenced in a perverse way by the suggestive procedures themselves. But, the failure of suppression hearings to filter out mistaken identifications is also influenced by judges' tendencies to underestimate the power of suggestive procedures and overestimate the reliability of eyewitness identifications. These tendencies are broadly shared outside of the judiciary, but judges are the ones who make the rulings on suppression motions. Judges are in a very difficult position; however, as we explained in our discussion of the profound distaste at the idea of denying a victim witness the opportunity to testify about the identity of his or her assailant. Part of the problem as well is the all-or-nothing manner in which suppression motions are treated. To some extent, the narrative in *Manson* is to blame for this dichotomous suppress–admit approach because nothing in *Manson* even hints at the idea that other remedies fall short of full suppression, such as limiting the testimony, strongly instructing jurors, or admitting expert testimony. Finally, defense attorneys are not blameless in many of the failures to obtain good outcomes in suppression hearings. In part because of the rarity of a successful motion to suppress eyewitness identification evidence, a sense of hopelessness with regard to these issues seems to have set in many years ago. But recent developments, such as the emergence of a powerful scientific literature on eyewitness identification and the uncovering of large numbers of mistaken identifications, can and should be used to help make suppression hearings more effective for innocent defendants. The use of eyewitness experts in suppression hearings and the use of motions in limine can help achieve some success in suppression hearings, even if full suppression is not achieved.

Finally, we note one of the most problematic consequences of the routine failure to suppress suggestive eyewitness identifications, namely, that it permits suggestive identification procedures to continue. In fact, a compelling argument has been made that the excessive permissiveness of *Manson* has not only undermined incentives for law enforcement to jettison suggestive procedures but has actually provided incentives to continue to use suggestive eyewitness identification procedures (Wells & Quinlivan, 2009). Suggestive eyewitness identification procedures not only help to ensure that the eyewitness will identify the person of interest (see Chapter 6, this volume) but also lead the witness to be more credible to the judge and jury (by inflating the witness's certainty, claims of a good view, and claims of close attention; see Chapters 7 and 9, this volume). If the use of suggestive procedures is not going to result in suppression, then it becomes seen by law enforcement as a strategic tool for getting an identification and creating a believable witness rather than something to be avoided.

REFERENCES

Behrman, B. W., & Davey, S. L. (2001). Eyewitness identification in actual criminal cases: An archival analysis. *Law and Human Behavior, 25*, 475–491. doi:10.1023/A:1012840831846

Behrman, B. W., & Richards, R. E. (2005). Suspect/foil identification in actual crimes and in the laboratory: A reality monitoring analysis. *Law and Human Behavior, 29*, 279–301. doi:10.1007/s10979-005-3617-y

Charman, S. D., & Wells, G. L. (2007). Applied lineup theory. In R. C. L. Lindsay, D. F. Ross, J. D. Read, & M. P. Toglia (Eds.), *Handbook of eyewitness psychology: Memory for people* (pp. 219–254). Mahwah, NJ: Erlbaum.

Cole, G. F. (1986). *The American system of criminal justice* (4th ed.). Monterey, CA: Brooks/Cole.

Cutler, B. L., & Penrod, S. D. (1995). *Mistaken identification: The eyewitness, psychology, and the law*. New York, NY: Cambridge University Press.

Gilbert v. California, 388 U.S. 263 (1967).

Innocence Project. (2010). http://www.innocenceproject.org/?gclid=CNPCp6bjq6cCFcbc4AodlSxTCg

Kassin, S. M., & Gudjonsson, G. H. (2004). The psychology of confessions: A review of the literature and issues. *Psychological Science in the Public Interest, 5*, 33–67. doi:10.1111/j.1529-1006.2004.00016.x

Lindsay, R. C. L., & Wells, G. L. (1980). What price justice? Exploring the relationship between lineup fairness and identification accuracy. *Law and Human Behavior, 4*, 303–313. doi:10.1007/BF01040622

Loftus, E. F. (1979). *Eyewitness testimony*. Cambridge, MA: Harvard University Press.

Loftus, E. F., Doyle, J. M., & Dysart, J. E. (2008). *Eyewitness testimony: Civil and criminal*. Charlottesville, VA: Lexis Law Publishing. Loftus, G. R., & Harley, E. M. (2005). Why is it easier to identify someone close than far away? *Psychonomic Bulletin & Review, 12*, 43–65. Retrieved from http://pbr.psychonomic-journals.org/

Loftus, G. R., & Harley, E. M. (2005). Why is it easier to identify someone close than far away? *Psychonomic Bulletin & Review, 12*, 43–65. Retrieved from http://pbr.psychonomic-journals.org/

Manson v. Braithwaite, 432 U.S. 98 (1977).

Neil v. Biggers, 409 U.S. 188 (1972).

Pigott, M. A., & Brigham, J. C. (1985). Relationship between accuracy of prior description and facial recognition. *Journal of Applied Psychology, 70*, 547–555. doi:10.1037/0021-9010.70.3.547

Shapiro, P. N., & Penrod, S. (1986). Meta-analysis of facial identification studies. *Psychological Bulletin, 100*, 139–156. doi:10.1037/0033-2909.100.2.139

Slater, A. (1994). Identification parades: A scientific evaluation. *Police Research Award Scheme*. London, England: Police Research Group, Home Office.

State v. Ledbetter, 441, A.2d 595, Connecticut (1981).

Stovall v. Denno, 388 U.S. 293 (1967).

United States v. Wade, 388 U.S. 218 (1967).

Valentine, T., Pickering, A., & Darling, S. (2003). Characteristics of eyewitness identification that predict the outcome of real lineups. *Applied Cognitive Psychology, 17*, 969–993. doi:10.1002/acp.939

Wells, G. L. (1984). The psychology of lineup identifications. *Journal of Applied Social Psychology, 14*, 89–103. doi:10.1111/j.1559-1816.1984.tb02223.x

Wells, G. L. (1985). Verbal descriptions of faces from memory: Are they diagnostic of identification accuracy? *Journal of Applied Psychology, 70*, 619–626. doi:10.1037/0021-9010.70.4.619

Wells, G. L., & Bradfield, A. L. (1998). "Good, you identified the suspect": Feedback to eyewitnesses distorts their reports of the witnessing experience. *Journal of Applied Psychology, 83*, 360–376. doi:10.1037/0021-9010.83.3.360

Wells, G. L., & Loftus, E. F. (2003). Eyewitness memory for people and events. In A. Goldstein (Ed.), *Comprehensive handbook of psychology: Forensic psychology* (Vol. 11, pp. 149–160). New York, NY: Wiley.

Wells, G. L., Memon, A., & Penrod, S. (2006). Eyewitness evidence: Improving its probative value. *Psychological Science in the Public Interest, 7*, 45–75. doi:10.1111/j.1529-1006.2006.00027.x

Wells, G. L., & Quinlivan, D. S. (2009). Suggestive eyewitness identification procedures and the Supreme Court's reliability test in light of eyewitness science: 30 years later. *Law and Human Behavior, 33*, 1–24. doi:10.1007/s10979-008-9130-3

Wells, G. L., Rydell, S. M., & Seelau, E. P. (1993). On the selection of distractors for eyewitness lineups. *Journal of Applied Psychology, 78*, 835–844. doi:10.1037/0021-9010.78.5.835

Wright, D. B., & McDaid, A. T. (1996). Comparing system and estimator variables using data from real lineups. *Applied Cognitive Psychology, 10*, 75–84. doi:10.1002/(SICI)1099-0720(199602)10:1<75::AID-ACP364>3.0.CO;2-E

Wright, D. B., & Skagerberg, E. M. (2007). Post-identification feedback affects real eyewitnesses. *Psychological Science, 18*, 172–178. doi:10.1111/j.1467-9280.2007.01868.x

9

JURORS BELIEVE EYEWITNESSES

CAROLYN SEMMLER, NEIL BREWER, AND AMY BRADFIELD DOUGLASS

Every day in jurisdictions all over the world police and the courts assess the reliability of eyewitness evidence. Few categories of evidence are as compelling to members of a jury as eyewitness evidence, a fact long acknowledged by judges (Devlin, 1976). The challenge is to carry out these assessments accurately and efficiently so that victims of crime, defendants, and the wider community can have faith in the justice system. Unfortunately, this faith has been shaken as the accuracy of these assessments has been called into question by the fact that many individuals have now been exonerated by DNA evidence that follows convictions strongly influenced by eyewitness evidence. It is not particularly surprising that jurors believe eyewitnesses when they recount the details of an event, describe the features of a perpetrator, and say "that is the man!" when confronted with a lineup. But jurors believing an eyewitness who is completely wrong represents a major problem for the fairness and efficiency of any legal process reliant on eyewitness testimony. The problem of overbelief of inaccurate eyewitnesses has been the focus of detailed

Supported by Australian Research Council Grants DP1093210 and DP1092507 and National Science Foundation Grant 0921193.

empirical examination for over 30 years. It was a focus of the initial research program developed by Wells, Lindsay, and Ferguson (1979) designed to investigate the causes of wrongful conviction and highlight the dangers of eyewitness testimony to the legal system. Yet, it is interesting that the eyewitness testimony literature now contains many more empirical studies focused on testing identification procedures than on trial procedures aimed at reducing the rate of wrongful convictions. This is significant because the impact of identification test-procedure reform on the frequency of false convictions and wrongful acquittals is unlikely to be realized fully unless we also understand how to improve the accuracy of jurors' evaluations of eyewitness evidence (Cutler, Penrod, & Dexter, 1989). Using the evidence presented in court and a commonsense understanding of how memory works, jurors are required to assess the likelihood that the defendant is indeed the perpetrator and whether the charges brought by the prosecution have been proven beyond reasonable doubt. Although at face value it may seem a simple task to work out whether the witnesses' account is reliable and credible, and then to determine whether the charges have been proven, empirical tests show that jurors often reach incorrect conclusions on the basis of eyewitness testimony, particularly when evaluating the accuracy of an identification (Wells et al., 1979). Although the main message from this research has not changed over the years, we now know much more about when eyewitnesses should be believed and when they should not. Much of this knowledge is counterintuitive, and its impact on legal processes is likely to be shaped by psychologists' ability to explain clearly and convincingly how the knowledge was acquired and what it might mean for courtroom judgments. However, the communication to jurors of knowledge of eyewitness memory research findings through expert witness testimony is by itself unlikely to prevent errors of judgment on their part. Indeed, we believe that a fresh approach to improving juror decision making in relation to eyewitness evidence will be required. This will involve exploiting what is known about (a) the cues used by jurors to infer the accuracy of eyewitnesses' memories and (b) the psychological processes that underpin improved judgment and decision making that have not yet been considered in the context of assessing the accuracy of eyewitness identification evidence.

In this chapter, we first introduce the way that the courts expect jurors to evaluate eyewitness testimony across the three main Western legal systems with which we are familiar: the United Kingdom, Australia, and the United States. Second, we review the methods developed to understand what it is that jurors use to determine the accuracy of an eyewitness report and an identification decision, providing a critique of the approaches and methods developed so far. Third, we evaluate how well assumptions that underlie the legal criteria match up with the scientific literature on indices of memory accuracy and the cues that jurors actually use to evaluate the accuracy of eyewitness testimony. Fourth, we examine the effectiveness of legal safeguards against errors likely to be made by eyewitnesses when evaluating eyewitness memory. Finally, we look at some of the key factors that need to be understood to improve the accuracy of juror judgments in regard to eyewitness evidence.

HOW THE COURTS RECOMMEND THAT JURORS EVALUATE EYEWITNESS EVIDENCE

Courts in the United States, the United Kingdom, and Australia operate on assumptions about eyewitness memory and how it works that appear to be based largely on commonsense or intuitive notions. In the United Kingdom and the United States, these assumptions are described in rulings about eyewitness evidence and in the instructions that judges give to jurors at the conclusion of a trial. In all jurisdictions, specific criteria are suggested for evaluating identification evidence. The criteria for evaluating eyewitness accounts of the events and people involved are less specific. The evaluative criteria are also foreshadowed, in part, by the many surveys of judges' and jurors' knowledge of eyewitness testimony that have been carried out by psychologists (Benton, Ross, Bradshaw, Thomas, & Bradshaw, 2006). We briefly review the conclusions from recent surveys in the subsequent section on methodology.

Assessing Identification Accuracy

In a U.S. Supreme Court ruling (*Manson v. Braithwaite*, 1977), five criteria that could be used to assess the reliability of identification evidence were outlined: (a) the opportunity that the witness had to view the offender during the encounter (view); (b) the degree of attention that the witness reported paying to the offender (attention); (c) the degree of detail that the witness could provide when recounting the offender's appearance and whether this matched the suspect or defendant's appearance (detail); (d) the amount of time that had elapsed between the event and the attempt to identify the perpetrator (time); and (e) the degree of certainty expressed by the witness in the identification (certainty). In the United Kingdom, the criteria were set out in *R v. Turnbull* (1976) and in Code D of the Police and Criminal Evidence Act (1984) used by police to conduct and evaluate identification procedures. They include the length of time that the witness had the offender in view, the distance between the witness and the offender, visibility at the time of the offense, whether anything obstructed the view of the witness, whether the witness had reason to remember the incident, and whether the witness would know the offender if the offender was encountered again.

In Australian law, there are similar tests but no single case that is consistently cited as the definitive authority on identification evidence. The two most often cited rulings are found in *Alexander v. The Queen* (1981) and *Domican v. The Queen* (1992). Both cases list distance between the perpetrator and the witness, the amount of time the witness was able to view the perpetrator, the time elapsed between the offense and the identification, and whether the witness knew the offender before the offense was committed as factors that the jury should consider. The majority of judges in Australian courts will give *Domican* directions to a jury if a case involves identification evidence. In particular, they will warn the jury that certainty in an identification is no indication of accuracy and that jurors should pay attention to distance, quality of view, and the delay between the offense and the identification. Across all three jurisdictions, distance, time in view, and time delay before the identification are important factors, representing the commonly held beliefs that distance affects the ability to perceive the details of a stimulus, that seeing something for longer improves one's ability to later remember it, and that memories fade over time. None of these assumptions would be challenged by the basic memory and perception literature. Indeed, studies have confirmed the predicted relations between identification accuracy and viewing distance (Lindsay, Semmler, Weber, Brewer, & Lindsay, 2008), exposure duration (Memon, Hope, & Bull, 2003), and retention interval (Sauer, Brewer, Zweck, & Weber, 2010). However, an exclusive focus on these factors neglects consideration of other factors known to influence eyewitness identification decisions, factors such as cross-race effects, stress, the instructions that the witness received before viewing the lineup, the composition of the lineup, the format or method of presentation, and the impact of information offered to the witness after the identification decision is made (see Chapters 5 and 6, this volume; Brewer & Palmer, 2010).

Another overlooked factor is that the courts' criteria for evaluating the likely accuracy of the identification evidence are often based on self-report, which in many cases may be significantly affected by factors completely unrelated to the accuracy of memory (for a discussion of problems with self-reports, see Chapter 7, this volume). It has now been shown across numerous lab and field studies that identification evidence can be significantly distorted through the provision of feedback information to a witness (Chapter 7, this volume; Semmler, Brewer, & Wells, 2004; Wells & Bradfield, 1998). Nearly all subjective reports, including estimates of quality of view, ease of the identification, amount of attention the witness paid to the perpetrator, time in view, and distance from the perpetrator are affected by feedback to the witness, confirming the identification decision (Chapter 7, this volume; Douglass, Brewer, & Semmler, 2010; Wells & Bradfield, 1998). Whether jurors can detect when testimony has been distorted by feedback is an issue we return to later.

Of course, it is not just evidence of identification from a lineup by a witness that jurors may be asked to evaluate. Jurors are also asked to make direct assessments of identity. A trend in recent years has been the introduction of closed-circuit television (CCTV) footage or security footage to juries, with jury members asked to compare the images to the defendant before them and use their impression of the similarity in appearance as the basis for determining identity (see *R v. Hien Puoc Tang*, 2006). Such procedures may significantly increase the possibility of wrongful conviction because of the degree of error associated with unfamiliar face matching. Davis and Valentine (2009) asked participants to match a previously unfamiliar person filmed on high-quality video with a single live "defendant." The video, which lasted 40 s, displayed views of each person's face and body from a number of different angles. In half of the trials the defendant was not the person in the video. The overall error rate was approximately 20% (22% target present, 17% target absent). That is, one in five participants was mistaken under ideal conditions when there was no requirement to remember the culprit's face and no time pressure. The video sequence could be played up to three times or until participants made their decision. Error rates varied considerably across different actors. Davies and Thasen (2000) have found similarly high error rates with false-alarm rates between 60% and 65%. These studies indicate the degree to which the courts can overestimate the abilities of jurors and the increase in risk of wrongful conviction presented by asking juries to attempt to evaluate whether an individual captured on CCTV is in fact the defendant.

Assessing Testimonial Accuracy

The criteria recommended by the courts for evaluating testimonial (as distinct from identification) accuracy are not clearly set out in court rulings, but they can be found by carefully reading the instructions that judges give to jurors at the conclusion of the presentation of evidence and closing statements. The criteria are also evident in some surveys of judges and jurors. Two criteria are most often relied on across jurisdictions: the consistency of the witness's statements and the degree of detail present in the witness's report. A second factor is corroboration (or agreement between witnesses). We treat this under the general heading of consistency. Finally, judges also comment on the certainty with which the testimony is offered by the witness, with warnings sometimes given against reliance on certainty.

In the United States, pattern instructions given to jurors indicate that they should pay attention to the consistency of the witnesses' statements. For example, standard federal jury instructions used in the United States direct jurors to pay attention to whether the witness testified inconsistently on the witness stand, if he or she said or did something, or failed to say or do something, at any other time that is inconsistent with what the witness said while testifying (Sixth Circuit Criminal Pattern Jury Instructions, No. 107, 2005, in Fisher, Brewer, & Mitchell, 2009). Such instructions indicate that the courts assume that inconsistencies are thought to reflect either a lack of memory for the events in question or a lack of honesty on behalf of the witness. Similarly, in Australian courts, judges follow "bench books" in their summing up, which reflect the belief that an inconsistency reflects poor memory on behalf of a neutral witness. A quote from a judge in the High Court of Australia illustrates the general view that inconsistencies in testimony are indicative of overall unreliability: "The whole purpose of contradicting the witness by proof of the inconsistent statement is to show that the witness is unreliable" (*Driscoll v. The Queen*, 1977). To illustrate further, consider the South Australian Uniform Evidence Act (1929) and the New South Wales Evidence Act (1995), where there are specific procedural requirements that must be followed by lawyers when establishing that a witness has made an inconsistent statement under cross-examination. That these procedures are set out in legislation indicates that the Australian criminal law sees the establishment of testimonial inconsistencies as a very powerful and consequential part of the presentation of evidence to a jury. Finally, surveys have shown that mock jurors believe that testimonial inconsistencies indicate that the rest of the testimony is likely to be inaccurate (Brewer, Potter, Fisher, Bond, & Luszcz, 1999). Another cue to the reliability of a witness's statement is considered to be the level of detail provided in the testimony. A highly detailed statement, which specifies a particular order of events consistent with the order presented by other witnesses or corroborated by physical evidence, is found to be much more compelling than one lacking in detail. Again, there is no single case that indicates the use of detail in assessing the accuracy of witness testimony. Rather, careful reading of judges' directions to juries suggests the strongly held assumption that a highly detailed account of an event is likely to indicate that the witness has a good memory. Further, surveys of U.S. and Norwegian judges indicate that a majority think that "a witness's ability to recall minor details about a crime is a good indicator of the accuracy of the witness's identification of the perpetrator of the crime" (Magnussen et al., 2008, p. 179). In addition, Benton et al.'s (2006) examination of the knowledge of eyewitness research among a juror pool from Tennessee indicated that the average juror in this jurisdiction held the assumption that detail is indicative of accuracy.

SCIENTIFIC METHODS USED IN THE RESEARCH
ON BELIEFS ABOUT EYEWITNESSES

In this section, we outline the methods used to study how jurors assess eyewitness testimony and evaluate the strengths and weaknesses of each method. Three broad categories of methodology are used to investigate jurors' beliefs in eyewitness testimony: (a) surveys of jurors (both actual and potential); (b) mock-witness or simulated trial methods; and (c) real witness methods. The survey research generally asks groups of researchers, police, lawyers, or jury-qualified individuals to (a) nominate the various factors they think affect eyewitness identification accuracy and (b) identify the behavioral indicators of accuracy. The majority of these surveys are aimed at understanding how well the empirical results of studies that look at the factors contributing to identification accuracy are known among people who make judgments about the probative value of such evidence in the legal system. Some surveys have also asked judges to estimate the levels of knowledge among other groups of individuals involved in the legal system (e.g., Stinson, Devenport, Cutler, & Kravitz, 1997). The studies suggest that laypeople and those with more expert legal knowledge (e.g., law students, lawyers, judges) believe that (a) confidence is a good indicator of accuracy, (b) consistency of the witness will predict the reliability of all of the witness's testimony, and (c) the level of detail provided in a witness's testimony is indicative of accuracy. They also show a general lack of knowledge among jurors and the jury-eligible population in regard to the effects of particular procedures and interviewing techniques on the accuracy and confidence of witnesses (Devenport, Penrod, & Cutler, 1997). Although these surveys are useful in defining the general levels of knowledge that legal decision makers have in regard to eyewitness testimony, they are limited in determining what real jurors actually do when working out whether or not an eyewitness is likely to be accurate. Much research (e.g., Cutler, Dexter, & Penrod, 1990; Leippe, Eisenstadt, Rauch, & Seib, 2004) has used mock-witness or mock-trial simulation methods in an attempt to understand how jurors evaluate testimonial accuracy. These methods vary considerably as to the degree to which they reflect actual trial procedures. On the low end of the verisimilitude continuum, studies present college student participants with written or audiotaped trial synopses or transcripts. The materials manipulate characteristics of the witness such as witnessing conditions (e.g., Bradfield & Wells, 2000), confidence (e.g., Bradfield & McQuiston, 2004), or inconsistency in report details (e.g., Brewer & Burke, 2002). Using this method, researchers can easily generate materials and manipulate variables precisely. For example, Cutler, Dexter, and Penrod (1990) presented undergraduate college students with a videotaped mock trial that involved an armed robbery of a liquor store; included were opening statements from the prosecution and defense, evidence from four to five witnesses, cross-examination and closing statements from both sides, and pattern jury instructions from the judge. Practicing attorneys played the roles of attorneys to increase the realism of the trial. Consequently, these studies have high internal validity, allowing clear causal conclusions to be drawn from experimental manipulations. An additional benefit of some of the videotaped trial studies is that they use jury-eligible adults (e.g., Cutler et al., 1990). A number of criticisms have been leveled at jury simulation studies (see Kerr & Bray, 2005, for an excellent discussion of relevant issues). One is that they include undergraduate students rather than jury-eligible adults. However, comparisons of college student participants versus jury-eligible participants have not revealed substantial differences between these populations (e.g., Cutler et al., 1990), suggesting that conclusions drawn from college student populations are often generalizable to members of a jury. A second is that the complexity and amount of information still pales in comparison with what real jurors would experience during a real trial. A third is that there is often no jury deliberation. Those that have included a deliberation phase (e.g., Maass, Brigham, & West, 1985) indicate that effects of eyewitness identification testimony are stronger after deliberation (i.e., belief polarization). These studies have also been criticized on the grounds that real lawyers would provide more effective cross-examination of witnesses. Fourth, mock-trial methodologies often suffer from a lack of stimulus variability (for a full discussion of this problem, see Wells & Windschitl, 1999). More specifically, mock trials often present testimony from a single witness with no other evidence in regard to the event details offered, and thus they may indicate performance levels and effects that are unique to the particular trial materials rather than representative of the processes and effects likely to operate in actual trials. To address this problem, Wells, Lindsay, and Ferguson (1979) developed the *three-phase paradigm*. Witnesses (typically undergraduate students) view a crime event (either video or staged), and they are then interviewed and attempt an identification with this procedure and the interview recorded (along with accuracy of the identification). A second sample of participants then view the recorded testimony and identification procedure, and they make a judgment about the accuracy of the witness. The advantage here is that there is an objective level of accuracy, so that the mock-juror responses can be classified in signal-detection terms (for a full discussion, see Martire & Kemp, 2009). However, in the few studies that have used this paradigm, not all witnesses are used in the second stage of the studies, with only those who are either most confident or least confident being used. There is a need for selecting the correct sample of witness testimony that is representative of the witnesses that jurors would see in the population to which generalization of the results is sought. Relying on a single sample of testimony imagined by the experimenter, as is the case in a mock-juror design, may be either underestimating or overestimating the ability of real jurors to assess eyewitness accuracy.

WHAT DO JURORS USE TO EVALUATE EYEWITNESS EVIDENCE, AND DO THEY GET IT RIGHT?

Jurors use commonsense evaluation to work out whether an eyewitness is accurate. A large body of empirical evidence indicates that this involves a reliance on many beliefs and cues that are not always predictive of accurate eyewitness reports. In this section, we evaluate the research that indicates when these cues are predictive of accuracy and when they are not, again focusing first on the evaluation of identification evidence and then on eyewitnesses' recall of event details.

When evaluating the accuracy of an eyewitness's identification, jurors tend to use eyewitnesses' courtroom expressions of confidence as a guide, even in the presence of other information that is more reliably correlated with accuracy. For example, people informed that a witness saw a culprit who was wearing a disguise believed a highly confident witness in spite of other factors present in the witnessing situation that should have suggested the likelihood of error. This pattern was observed in both college students and jury-eligible participants (Cutler et al., 1990). The tendency to use confidence as a guide to accuracy persists even in spite of strong exhortations that confidence should be used cautiously. In one study, participants heard an expert testify that "there is considerable research evidence showing that the confidence of an eyewitness may have little or no relationship to the accuracy of the eyewitness" and "it would not be uncommon for a highly confident witness to be wrong, to be entirely in error, even if he [was highly confident]" (Fox & Walters, 1986, p. 220). In spite of hearing this testimony, participants who received this warning still rated a highly confident witness as more likely to be accurate than a witness with low confidence.

Even though psycholegal researchers know that confidence and accuracy are not always strongly related (see Chapter 7, this volume), using confidence as a cue to accuracy is a sensible strategy for naïve jurors. However, triers of fact fail to adjust their evaluations appropriately in the presence of evidence that a witness's confidence may have grown over time or inflated in response to external variables. Confidence inflation is a common outcome of postidentification feedback (e.g., Chapter 7, this volume; Wells & Bradfield, 1998), information from cowitnesses (e.g., Luus & Wells, 1994), or repeated questioning of an eyewitness (e.g., Shaw & McClure, 1996). It is also a side effect of trial preparation procedures (Wells, Ferguson, & Lindsay, 1981). In these situations, witnesses' confidence increases even though the accuracy of their identification decision remains unchanged. The result can be highly confident—but inaccurate—witnesses. When discrepancies in confidence estimates provided over time suggest that confidence inflation has occurred, triers of fact should discount the witness's high confidence and evaluate the witness on the basis of the previous (lower) confidence report, if one is available.

In the first study to examine reactions to confidence inflation, Bradfield and McQuiston (2004) gave participants a trial transcript in which the presence of witness confidence inflation was manipulated. Participants received one of three versions of a trial transcript. In the first, the witness was highly confident at the time of her identification and similarly confident at the trial. In the second version, the *mere inflation* condition, the witness was minimally confident at the identification but highly confident at the trial. In the third version, the witness's confidence inflation was challenged by the defense attorney. Judgments of the defendant's guilt were affected only by the defense attorney challenge: Guilt ratings were equivalent in the control and mere inflation conditions.

In the second study on this issue, people ignored evidence of confidence inflation when the eyewitness explained it as an "epiphany," that is,

> I was nervous at the time of the identification and didn't really have a clear head. Now that I have calmed down, I am more certain of the details surrounding the robbery and am confident that I have chosen from the lineup the man who assaulted and robbed [the victim]. (Jones, Williams, & Brewer, 2008, p. 173)

In contrast, when witnesses claimed that they inflated their confidence so that they would be believed, mock jurors responded by reducing their belief in the defendant's guilt. A final study that examined the effect of confidence inflation on evaluations of witnesses demonstrates that these effects are robust. In this study (Douglass & Jones, 2011), some participants learned about the witness's confidence by watching a videotape of the identification procedure and then watching the same witness testify at trial. Even when the witness's confidence clearly increased from the identification procedure to the trial, evaluations of the defendant's guilt were the same as in a control (no inflation) condition. The same pattern occurred even when participants received instructions designed to increase their motivation to pay attention to trial materials. Taken together, these studies demonstrate the very important role of confidence in juror decisions and show that jurors are not always able to use confidence cues appropriately.

Bradfield and Wells (2000) also demonstrated some collateral effects of witness confidence and other criteria for assessing likely testimonial accuracy such as attention, view, distance, and time in view. For example, the amount of attention that a witness said that he or she paid led jurors to perceive that the witness reported a better view and gave a clearer description, even when the witness did not mention these criteria. The witness's higher confidence also led jurors to perceive that witnesses had paid more attention to the perpetrator. Such effects indicate that once a general impression of credibility is formed, all other aspects of the evidence may be distorted to match the general impression in the jurors' mind (see also Chapter 7, this volume). This study may not be representative of how real witnesses present on these criteria, given that a real witness is unlikely to say they are confident and that they paid little attention. But it does show that the interrelationships between such variables need to be explored to determine the process and time sequence in which jurors form an understanding of witness credibility.

Jurors are also required to evaluate testimony about the people and events that witnesses observed. Experimental studies have shown that mock jurors confronted with inconsistent testimony from a prosecution witness perceived the witness as less credible and the defendant as less likely to have committed the crime, and they were more likely to return a not-guilty verdict than when the testimony was consistent (Berman & Cutler, 1996; Brewer & Burke, 2002; Semmler & Brewer, 2002). In short, inconsistencies in testimony, including those that occur on the witness stand and as a result of pretrial testimony, have a powerful impact on juror judgment. An important yet underresearched aspect of testimonial inconsistencies is how they arise during a trial and whether this determines the impact they have on perceptions of eyewitness reliability (see Berman & Cutler, 1996). The majority of inconsistencies that occur during a real trial will be those that are highlighted by lawyers. However, there may be some that are deduced by jurors and only become apparent during deliberations. Do these inconsistencies have a greater impact on jurors than those adduced by the lawyers?

Another important question examined by Brewer and Burke (2002) is, What is the relative importance of inconsistencies in comparison to eyewitness confidence? They presented mock jurors in an armed robbery case with either highly consistent or inconsistent testimony, and crossed this manipulation with either a high or low level of confidence in the prosecution witnesses' testimony. They found that confidence, particularly in the identification of the defendant, had a larger impact on verdict and witness credibility ratings than did the consistency of the witnesses' testimony, perhaps reflecting an assumption among jurors that people sometimes misremember some details of an event, but a confident identification reflects that they would never forget the face of a person that robbed or assaulted them.

Is an inconsistency in an eyewitness's testimony an indication that all of the testimony is unreliable? A significant body of research suggests that inconsistencies are not related to the overall or global accuracy of the witness.

Fisher, Brewer, and Mitchell (2009) reported results from 19 experiments in which witnesses observed a crime event, were tested on their memory for the event details either in a face-to-face interview or a paper-and-pencil test, and were often reinterviewed after a delay (varying between 30 min and several weeks). Witnesses' statements were compared across interviews, and their responses were categorized as consistent, contradictory, reminiscent (the witness reports a new detail at the second or later interview), or forgotten (the witness fails to report a detail at the second interview that they did report at the first). Looking at the relationship between measures of overall accuracy and consistency, these studies showed that although two contradictory statements about some item of information indicate an inaccuracy at the item level, witnesses who produced more contradictions in their testimony were not less accurate overall than witnesses who made few contradictions. Similarly, the presence of reminiscent detail (i.e., reporting something in an interview that had never been reported in prior interviews) in the witnesses' testimony was not predictive of overall accuracy. Both of these findings fly in the face of the assumptions made by the courts and lawyers and used by jurors to evaluate the reliability and credibility of eyewitnesses.

Bell and Loftus (1989) examined the influence on juror assessments of another aspect of eyewitness testimony—its level of detail. Participants in one of their experiments read a variety of descriptions of a criminal trial. Within these descriptions the degree of detail provided by a prosecution witness varied from high to low, as did the degree of detail provided by a defense witness. Level of detail was manipulated by using witness statements that contained either the gist of the event or specific details about the event. When the prosecution eyewitness's testimonial detail level was high and the level of defense detail was also high, 32% of mock jurors voted to convict; in comparison, only 13% voted to convict when the level of prosecution detail was low and the level of defense detail was high. Whether or not the detail was related to the actions of the perpetrator did not influence verdicts.

Is detail a good indicator of the accuracy of eyewitness testimony? Weber and Brewer (2008) investigated the cognitive mechanisms that underlie the production of highly detailed (fine grained) and less detailed (coarse grained) responses among eyewitnesses. In general, the research has shown that eyewitnesses trade off the level of detail they provide in their answers against the accuracy of the information. Fine-grained answers may be more informative for the police (e.g., describing the perpetrator as wearing a dark blue fleece sweater with an Adidas logo on the front), but they are also more likely to be incorrect compared with a coarse-grained answer (e.g., a dark colored top). This trade-off is determined by factors such as (a) the report option that eyewitnesses have (i.e., whether they are free to withhold information they are unsure about or whether they must report it all), (b) the format of the questions (recall or recognition), and (c) the accuracy incentive that the witness has (e.g., whether they know that only their testimony will be used and that is the only information the police have to go on, or whether they are one of ten witnesses and the police have security footage). In short, jurors who rely on the simple short-cut inference that more detail is better may be less likely to form an impression of the witness that reflects their true memory accuracy. Jurors should pay very close attention to how the police interviewed the witness because this is likely to shape whether a fine-grained or highly detailed report is likely to be correct.

In summary, there are several facets to the errors of judgment that jurors may commit when evaluating eyewitness evidence. Errors may arise from the use of behavioral and testimonial cues to accuracy with low discriminant validity and from incorrect weighting and integration of these cues when making a judgment in regard to the accuracy of the witness's identification or account of events.

These studies highlight how factors that jurors may think are related to the accuracy of the eyewitness have an impact on their judgments of credibility. They do not, however, address the general question of whether jurors can distinguish a witness who has made a correct identification from a witness who is incorrect. This question is addressed by research that uses the real witness paradigm.

Wells et al. (1979) originally suggested that the jurors' task was essentially a problem of signal detection, that is, detecting a truly accurate or inaccurate witness from the "noise" provided by other testimony and the trial process. In signal-detection terms, a juror can correctly state that the identification was accurate when in fact it was (hit), correctly state that the identification was inaccurate when in fact it was (correct rejection), incorrectly state that the identification was accurate when it was not (false alarm), or incorrectly state that the identification was inaccurate when it was not (false rejection). The advantage of signal-detection measures is that they provide two measures: (a) the ability of the observer to discriminate the signal (in this case an accurate witness) from the noise (other evidence or misleading confidence levels) and (b) the degree of bias toward responding "yes" (the witness is correct) or "no" (the witness is incorrect). In signal-detection terms, these measures are referred to as sensitivity (or discriminability) and bias. Initial studies that look at the accuracy of mock jurors by using a selection of real witnesses indicated that the mock jurors believed incorrect witnesses as often as they did correct witnesses (Lindsay, Wells, & O'Connor, 1989). In the real witness study by Wells, Lindsay, and Ferguson (1979) mock jurors produced a negative measure of discriminative ability or sensitivity, indicating an inability to distinguish signal from noise. Confidence appeared to be the most important factor in determining mock-juror belief.

Lawyers criticized the approach used in this study because the interviewers were senior undergraduate and graduate students who followed a scripted set of questions (see Lindsay et al., 1989, p. 334). Later, the study was replicated with lawyers (both experienced and inexperienced) from Kingston, Ontario, Canada, acting as jurors (Lindsay et al., 1989). The findings were clear: Experienced lawyers were no better at picking inaccurate eyewitnesses than individuals with absolutely no experience, suggesting that the results of mock-juror studies do not overestimate the degree of error in juror judgments of eyewitness accuracy. Lindsay, Wells, and Rumpel (1981) also showed that jurors were insensitive to the influence of variables likely to undermine memory quality, failing to adjust their beliefs in the accuracy of the testimony to reflect the changes in identification accuracy that were the result of either poor, moderate, or good viewing conditions. Although these studies were conducted long ago, more recent studies (e.g., Martire & Kemp, 2009) also showed poor rates of accurate decisions on the behalf of mock jurors and have further refined signal-detection measures to aid understanding of mock-juror performance.

SCIENTIFIC PSYCHOLOGICAL FOUNDATIONS OF THE BELIEF OF EYEWITNESSES

Why do jurors tend to believe inaccurate witnesses? The answer to this question is likely to lie in the development and testing of a scientific theory of the psychological processes involved in assessing eyewitness testimonial accuracy.

The design and methodologies adopted in a research area are usually shaped by the theoretical frameworks that guide the research. However, the research that examined jurors' belief of eyewitnesses has not been guided by any dominant (and integrating) theoretical perspectives. Later, we discuss the potential applications of basic social and cognitive theories to understanding and improving jurors' judgments, thereby providing potential organizing frameworks for future research.

A comprehensive understanding of how jurors form impressions of the accuracy of eyewitness memory is likely to demand an integrated consideration of how memory works, how people form impressions of others, and intuitive beliefs about how our own memory operates. In recent years there has been a resurgence in interest in interpersonal metacognition (for a review, see Jost, Kruglanski, & Nelson, 1998). Although none of the studies discussed in our chapter drew directly on theories within this area of research, there is much to be gained by seeing the juror's task as a basic problem of interpersonal metacognition or, more plainly, of inferring the accuracy of another person's memory.

Jurors' inaccurate assessments of the accuracy of eyewitness memory stems from both a preexisting stereotype among jurors of memory credibility and the tendency for people to use their own behavior as a basis for inferring the causes of others' behavior (Leippe, 1995). When assessing the accuracy of a memory report provided by someone else, we rarely have the opportunity to verify their version of events against an objective record of what happened and, in general, social norms prevent us from questioning persons about what they recall. Thus, we have a tendency toward a truth bias in most interpersonal judgment situations (Vrij, 2000). A mock-trial study by Loftus (1974) found that the percentage of guilty verdicts increased from 18% to 72% when a single prosecution witness was added to a brief trial summary. A number of studies have followed up this result by having people read descriptions of staged-crime (or other event) studies and asking them to estimate the percentage of witnesses who made a correct identification in the package of trials. These studies consistently find that people overestimate the percentage of witnesses who made a correct identification of the culprit (Brigham & Bothwell, 1983; Kassin, 1979, reported in Wells, 1984). That these trials did not present real or even mock witnesses for evaluation suggests that generous judgments of eyewitness accuracy may be the result of a positive stereotype of eyewitness memory (Leippe, 1995). In addition to this starting point or positive bias toward acceptance of eyewitness memory reports, studies that look at how jurors integrate evidence have shown that an early leaning toward a particular verdict will distort subsequent evaluations of testimony (Carlson & Russo, 2001). Thus, early presentation of an eyewitness in a trial is likely to greatly benefit the side that their version of events supports. In summary, the research shows that in the absence of other information, jurors' baseline expectation is for eyewitness accuracy and not false memories or inaccurate identification decisions.

It is not just a trusting outlook that works against jurors' effective evaluation of eyewitness evidence. Jurors' assumption that unless the witness's memory has been proven to be flawed, the witness's testimony is a reflection of the witness's memory quality and not the way the witness was questioned, or if presented with a lineup, the witness is likely to be a major problem at the heart of jurors' mistaken trust in eyewitness reports. This assumption can be described as a specific instance of the fundamental attribution error: that is, the general tendency for people to assume that the causes of behavior are internal to the individual rather than the result of situational forces (Ross, 1977). People are thought to commit the fundamental attribution error because the person (versus the situation) is more salient in most judgment situations. Further, the automatic nature of attribution processes means that the attribution error will take conscious effort to reverse (Gilbert, 1989). This suggests that any successful intervention aimed at reducing this error will need to focus on effortful reversal of quickly made attributions and an increase in the salience of evidence in regard to the methods that police have used to collect the eyewitness evidence.

The consistent effect of eyewitness confidence on juror decision making is thought to be the result of jurors' using a confidence heuristic. Confidence is a fundamental mechanism by which people monitor and control the accuracy of their own memories (Koriat & Goldsmith, 1994) and a basic heuristic that people use to evaluate the accuracy of information provided by others (Price & Stone, 2004). Given these findings, the accuracy of a juror's judgment will be guided by any behavioral indicator of confidence (both overt statements such as "I'm sure that's the guy" and paravocal indicators of confidence such as speech rate, intonation, and pitch). Further, given the operation of the fundamental attribution error, this confidence is more likely to be attributed to memory accuracy than to any external social influence, such as confirming feedback from a cowitness. There is a substantial literature in the judgment and decision-making domain that has been aimed at improving the relationship between confidence and accuracy. Brewer, Keast, and Rishworth (2002) successfully applied these approaches to the relationship between confidence and accuracy of eyewitness identifications. One successful manipulation that helped to reduce overconfidence was *hypothesis disconfirmation*, which involves directing witnesses to think about reasons why their decision may have been incorrect. However, these approaches have yet to be explored in improving the relationship between jurors' confidence in their evaluations of eyewitness testimony and the accuracy of their decisions regarding the testimony. Can jurors be made to reduce their overconfidence in an eyewitness by generating reasons why the witness may be wrong? The real witness paradigm developed by Wells (1984), and refined by Martire and Kemp (2009), provides the groundwork necessary for exploring these possibilities.

RELEVANT RESEARCH ON BELIEFS OF EYEWITNESSES

In this section, we look at the research-evaluating approaches that have been adopted to improve the accuracy of the judgments made by jurors. The major focus has been the investigation of the effectiveness of expert psychological testimony in improving the accuracy of juror judgments. We begin our discussion with a review of expert evidence research, including the impact of the type and timing of expert testimony within a trial on mock-juror judgment. We also consider the effectiveness of traditional safeguards, including jury instructions and cross-examination. The voir dire process is covered within a review by Leippe (1995) and is not reviewed here.

Before reviewing the research on legal safeguards, it is worth considering the question of what we wish to improve. Is it that any intervention should be aimed at improving juror decision making? Or should the role of any intervention simply be one of education, with no attempt to change how jurors arrive at their verdict? The debate on the role of psychological science in the law is an ongoing one and is not canvassed here. We recommend the volume edited by Cutler (2009) to those interested in understanding the broader legal issues involved in the use of expert testimony and other interventions to improve juror decision making. Many have argued for interventions that improve the sensitivity of jurors to eyewitness evidence. As discussed previously, *sensitivity* refers to the ability of jurors to use the right or valid cues to infer witness accuracy. By increasing sensitivity, we would expect both fewer instances of conviction of the innocent and an increase in conviction of the guilty. In contrast, *skepticism* or *bias* is a tendency to raise the amount of certainty or evidence required before deciding that the witness is accurate (i.e., jurors may still use the wrong cues but require more certainty in their own beliefs to accept the testimony; Leippe, Eisenstadt, Rauch, & Seib, 2004; Martire & Kemp, 2009). Approaches that act only to increase skepticism are less efficient than approaches that encourage sensitivity because they do little to uphold the rate of conviction of the guilty.

There are several different types of expert testimony, including general instructions about witness reliability, general information about how human memory works, specific testimony about the factors likely to be at play in the case, quantitative testimony about the effects of different factors on memory accuracy, and opinion testimony. Expert testimony can also be in conflict both with evidence and with a prosecution witness. Cutler, Penrod, and Dexter (1989) proposed three possible effects of expert testimony on jurors. It may cause juror confusion, increase juror sensitivity, or increase juror skepticism. Some studies (e.g., Cutler, Penrod, & Dexter, 1989) have shown that the provision of expert testimony significantly improves jurors' ability to discriminate accurate witnesses from inaccurate ones, that is, improving sensitivity. However, others have shown that expert testimony has led jurors to become more skeptical of eyewitness testimony (Leippe et al., 2004; Wells, 1984), decreasing their belief in the eyewitness and delivering fewer guilty verdicts based on the testimony. In a review of the research, Leippe (1995) suggested that the majority of the impact of expert testimony is to produce juror skepticism.

The impact of expert testimony may depend in part on when the expert takes the stand. Expert testimony can be presented either before or after the eyewitness testimony (and other evidence) is presented, and in some instances in Australian and United Kingdom courts it is only heard during the voir dire or pretrial hearing. Leippe et al. (2004) examined the effects of preevidence eyewitness expert testimony in a "whole-trial" simulation and directly compared the effects of pre- and postevidence expert testimony within the same experiment. They also looked at the effects in strong versus weak prosecution cases. In most North American trials, eyewitness expert testimony is introduced toward the end of the trial, after the eyewitness has testified and after the prosecution has presented its case. This is because eyewitness experts most commonly are called by the defense, which presents its case after the prosecution has rested. Compared with an earlier preevidence presentation, this may have the advantage of recency. Coming late, the testimony may be more likely to be recalled than other evidence when jurors deliberate, particularly if the case is complex and tedious and jurors' comprehension suffers or they lapse into more heuristic (and less systematic) processing (Brewer & Hupfeld, 2004; Brewer & Williams, 2005). Alternatively, the typical postevidence testimony of an eyewitness expert might not be as be persuasive once jurors have already developed a story or theory of the crime at hand. Because eyewitnesses have already presented their testimony, jurors are not able to apply what they have learned about the cues they should be using to determine eyewitness accuracy when the eyewitnesses testify (Leippe, 1995). In summary, postevidence expert testimony would seem unlikely to heighten either skepticism or sensitivity to credibility-relevant aspects of the eyewitness testimony. In two studies that explored the impact of timing of expert testimony, Leippe et al. (2004) found that expert testimony induced skepticism when it followed the evidence and when jurors were reminded of it during the judge's summing up. Under the other conditions (preevidence), it had little or no impact on the judgments and decisions made by the jurors.

Expert testimony is far less common in Australian and United Kingdom courts. Jurors are much more likely to be exposed to the research regarding the scientific basis of eyewitness memory through judges' instructions. In both of these jurisdictions, judges sum up points of law but also discuss the evidence in the trial and how it is related to standards of proof and elements of each of the charges brought against the defendant. Relatively few studies have examined the impact of judges' instructions on jurors' decision making and judgments of eyewitness evidence. Martire and Kemp (2009) used a real witness paradigm and explored the impact of different types of expert testimony (congruent expert testimony or incongruent testimony or a no expert control) and judge's instructions (standard New South Wales instructions on identification evidence). In the congruent witness condition, the expert indicated that the confidence of the witness was a good indicator of accuracy. In the incongruent condition, they testified that confidence was not a good indication of the accuracy of the witnesses' memory report. This study also used signal-detection measures to evaluate the impact of the expert testimony and found little effect of the testimony on either sensitivity to the cues indicative of witness accuracy or on the bias or tendency to view the testimony as either incriminating or exonerating. More importantly, the methodology used in this study allowed examination of the question of whether knowledge of the confidence–accuracy relationship led to changes in the judgments made by mock jurors. The evidence suggested that knowledge did not improve judgment accuracy, nor did the presence of judicial instructions that warn jurors of the potential for mistaken identification.

In summary, most approaches have been relatively ineffective at producing a change in mock-juror performance (as defined by better discrimination of accurate eyewitness testimony). One of the major limitations of the expert testimony approach to limiting the possibility of wrongful convictions is that it rests on the assumption that knowledge alone is enough to improve decision making. There are several reasons why this may not be a safe assumption. First, aside from the mixed results in regard to the effectiveness of expert testimony in producing increased juror sensitivity (Leippe, 1995), empirical studies that examine the relationship between the accuracy of beliefs and willingness to convict on the basis of eyewitness testimony show small and nonsignificant relationships. For example, Magnussen, Melinder, Stridbeck, and Raja (2010) found that greater knowledge of general eyewitnesses factors was, in general, not associated with a more critical assessment of the value of eyewitness testimony. Second, the processes by which jurors evaluate eyewitness testimony are most likely the same that they use to estimate the accuracy of other people's memories on a daily basis. They are most likely automatic, highly practiced, and operating largely outside of the conscious awareness of the jurors. Changing these processes may be a much more difficult task than has been previously acknowledged and may be highly dependent on more theory-driven interventions.

APPLICATION OF RESEARCH ON BELIEFS OF EYEWITNESSES

Loftus and Ketchum (1991) documented how persistent the beliefs of eyewitnesses can be even in the face of contradictory evidence, citing a number of real cases of mistaken identification in which witnesses persist in believing their memories despite strong contrary evidence. As Goodman and Loftus (1992) indicated, these real cases "reveal the commitment and attachment of eyewitnesses to faulty memories even when faced with clear, incontrovertible evidence of their mistaken judgment" (p. 268).

At present, the problem of wrongful convictions is not adequately addressed by either the police, who often use procedures known to produce inaccurate identification decisions and false testimony (see Chapter 6, this volume), or jurors, who do not always respond to expert testimony that indicates how much weight they should place on testimony from eyewitnesses. Leippe (1994) argued that the increased skepticism produced by expert testimony is hardly surprising, given the design of most of the studies that look at the impact of expert testimony. However, he also argued that the best approach is to refocus jurors' attention on the factors that do indicate that the witness is accurate. The largest benefit to be gained in this approach is to recalibrate jurors' use of confidence related cues. The prevailing opinion in eyewitness memory research has been that confidence and accuracy are unrelated, but we now know the specific circumstances when confidence and accuracy are likely to be unrelated (i.e., when feedback has been given, the witness has been prepared for the trial, cross-examination has occurred, a witness has had contact with a cowitness, and when the lineup administrator has been aware of the position of the suspect in the lineup). When these factors are not present in the situation and the witness's original testimony (i.e., confidence assessment) has been preserved, jurors' focus on eyewitness confidence could be highly adaptive (cf. Brewer & Wells, 2006). Leippe (1994) also suggested that expert testimony, which focuses on what is not indicative of accuracy, is more likely to promote juror sensitivity to the right cues. Despite this assertion, little research has compared the impact of expert testimony, which focuses on what is diagnostic of accuracy and what is not. In sum, expert testimony needs to be offered to juries with knowledge of what sort of testimony will benefit the jurors. Moreover, we need to consider whether knowledge is enough or we need to look at specific training of jurors for the task of evaluating eyewitness testimony.

CONCLUSION

For many years now, psychologists have been illustrating and exploring problems associated with eyewitness evidence and making strong arguments for the inclusion of expert testimony in trials where there is a reliance on eyewitness memory. The research findings and field studies show that jurors do not possess the knowledge required to distinguish between accurate and inaccurate eyewitness testimony or identification decisions. They rely on cues such as confidence, detail, and consistency that, although intuitively appealing, are not always indicative of memory accuracy. Furthermore, they tend to be unaware of the power of the situation to shape eyewitnesses' reports. Legal safeguards against inaccurate eyewitness testimony do not provide much reassurance that wrongful convictions driven by eyewitness testimony will abate. Although there have been many advances made in better educating law enforcement in regard to the best techniques to obtain accurate reports from eyewitnesses (see Chapter 6, this volume), the same cannot be said of the education of jurors. Until this situation improves, it is likely that miscarriages of justice will continue to occur. More worrying is the emergence of new technologies such as "smart" CCTV and automated face-matching systems, which seem to provide stronger evidence of identification and are likely convincing for a jury but can still produce errors.

In conclusion, we know that jurors can make mistakes and the protections offered by the legal system are unlikely to dramatically improve the accuracy of jurors' decisions. We need theory-driven approaches to understanding when jurors are miscalibrated. Only when this occurs will we have the capacity to develop and test interventions that reduce the errors that are under the control of the legal system.

REFERENCES

Alexander v. The Queen, HCA 17; 145 CLR 395 (1981).

Bell, B. E., & Loftus, E. F. (1989). Trivial persuasion in the courtroom: The power of (a few) minor details. *Journal of Personality and Social Psychology, 56,* 669–679. doi:10.1037/0022-3514.56.5.669

Benton, T. R., Ross, D. F., Bradshaw, E., Thomas, W. N., & Bradshaw, G. S. (2006). Eyewitness memory is still not common sense: Comparing jurors, judges and law enforcement to eyewitness experts. *Applied Cognitive Psychology, 20,* 115–129. doi:10.1002/acp.1171

Berman, G. L., & Cutler, B. L. (1996). Effects of inconsistencies in eyewitness testimony on mock juror decision making. *Journal of Applied Psychology, 81,* 170–177. doi:10.1037/0021-9010.81.2.170

Bradfield, A., & McQuiston, D. E. (2004). When does evidence of eyewitness confidence inflation affect judgments in a criminal trial? *Law and Human Behavior, 28,* 369–387. doi:10.1023/B:LAHU.0000039331.54147.ff

Bradfield, A. L., & Wells, G. L. (2000). The perceived validity of eyewitness identification testimony: A test of the five Biggers criteria. *Law and Human Behavior, 24,* 581–594. doi:10.1023/A:1005523129437

Brewer, N., & Burke, A. (2002). Effects of testimonial inconsistencies and eyewitness confidence on mock-juror judgments. *Law and Human Behavior, 26,* 353–364. doi:10.1023/A:1015380522722

Brewer, N., & Hupfeld, R. M. (2004). Effects of testimonial inconsistencies and witness group identity on mock-juror judgments. *Journal of Applied Social Psychology, 34,* 493–513. doi:10.1111/j.1559-1816.2004.tb02558.x

Brewer, N., Keast, A., & Rishworth, A. (2002). The confidence–accuracy relationship in eyewitness identification: The effects of reflection and disconfirmation on correlation and calibration. *Journal of Experimental Psychology: Applied, 8,* 44–56. doi:10.1037/1076-898X.8.1.44

Brewer, N., & Palmer, M. (2010). Eyewitness identification tests. *Legal and Criminological Psychology, 15,* 77–96. doi:10.1348/135532509X414765

Brewer, N., Potter, R., Fisher, R. P., Bond, N., & Luszcz, M. (1999). Beliefs and data on the relationship between consistency and accuracy of eyewitness testimony. *Applied Cognitive Psychology, 13,* 297–313. doi:10.1002/(SICI)1099-0720 (199908)13:4<297::AID-ACP578>3.0.CO;2-S

Brewer, N., & Wells, G. L. (2006). The confidence-accuracy relationship in eyewitness identification: Effects of lineup instructions, foil similarity, and target-absent base rates. *Journal of Experimental Psychology: Applied, 12,* 11–30. doi: 10.1037/1076-898X.12.1.11

Brewer, N., & Williams, K. D. (2005). *Psychology and law: An empirical perspective.* New York, NY: Guilford Press.

Brigham, J. C., & Bothwell, R. K. (1983). The ability of prospective jurors to estimate the accuracy of eyewitness identifications. *Law and Human Behavior, 7,* 19–30. doi:10.1007/BF01045284

Carlson, K. A., & Russo, J. E. (2001). Biased interpretation of evidence by mock jurors. *Journal of Experimental Psychology: Applied, 7,* 91–103. doi:10.1037/1076-898X.7.2.91

Cutler, B. L. (2009). *Expert testimony on the psychology of eyewitness identification.* New York, NY: Oxford University Press.

Cutler, B. L., Dexter, H. R., & Penrod, S. D. (1989). Expert testimony and jury decision making: An empirical analysis. *Behavioral Sciences & the Law, 7,* 215–225. doi:10.1002/bsl.2370070206

Cutler, B. L., Dexter, H. R., & Penrod, S. D. (1990). Nonadversarial methods for sensitizing jurors to eyewitness evidence. *Journal of Applied Social Psychology, 20,* 1197–1207. doi:10.1111/j.1559-1816.1990.tb00400.x

Cutler, B. L., Penrod, S. D., & Dexter, H. R. (1989). The eyewitness, the expert psychologist, and the jury. *Law and Human Behavior, 13,* 311–332. doi:10.1007/ BF01067032

Davies, G., & Thasen, S. (2000). Closed-circuit television: How effective an identification aid? *The British Journal of Psychology, 91,* 411–426. doi:10.1348/ 000712600161907

Davis, J., & Valentine, T. (2009). CCTV on trial: Matching video images with the defendant in the doc. *Applied Cognitive Psychology, 23,* 482–505. doi:10.1002/ acp.1490

Devenport, J. L., Penrod, S. D., & Cutler, B. L. (1997). Eyewitness identification evidence: evaluating commonsense evaluations. *Psychology, Public Policy, and Law, 3,* 338–361. doi:10.1037/1076-8971.3.2-3.338

Devlin, L. (1976). *Report to the Secretary of State for the Home Department of the Departmental Committee on Evidence of Identification in Criminal Cases.* London, England: Her Majesty's Stationery Office.

Domican v. The Queen (1992) HCA 13; (1992) 173 CLR 555.

Douglass, A. B., Brewer, N., & Semmler, C. (2010). Moderators of post-identification feedback effects on eyewitnesses' memory reports. *Legal and Criminological Psychology, 15,* 279–292. doi:10.1348/135532509X446337

Douglass, A. B., & Jones, E. (2011). *Evaluations of confidence inflation in eyewitnesses: Does it matter how the original confidence statement is preserved?* Manuscript in preparation.

Driscoll v. The Queen HCA 43; 137 CLR 517 (1977).

Fisher, R., Brewer, N., & Mitchell, G. (2009). The relation between consistency and accuracy of witness testimony: Legal versus cognitive explanations. In R. Bull, T. Valentine, & T. Williamson (Eds.), *Handbook of psychology of investigative interviewing: Current developments and future directions* (pp. 121–136). Chichester, England: Wiley. doi:10.1002/9780470747599.ch8

Goodman, J., & Loftus, E. F. (1992). Judgment and memory: The role of expert psychological testimony on eyewitness accuracy. In P. Suedfeld & P. E. Tetlock (Eds.), *Psychology and social policy* (pp. 267–282). New York, NY: Hemisphere.

Jones, E. E., Williams, K. D., & Brewer, N. (2008). "I had a confidence epiphany!": Obstacles to combating post-identification confidence inflation. *Law and Human Behavior, 32,* 164–176. doi:10.1007/s10979-007-9101-0

Jost, J. T., Kruglanski, A. W., & Nelson, T. O. (1998). Social metacognition: An expansionist review. *Personality and Social Psychology Review, 2,* 137–154. doi:10.1207/s15327957pspr0202_6

Koriat, A., & Goldsmith, M. (1994). Memory in naturalistic and laboratory contexts: distinguishing the accuracy-oriented and quantity-oriented approaches to memory assessment. *Journal of Experimental Psychology: General, 123,* 297–315. doi:10.1037/0096-3445.123.3.297

Leippe, M. R. (1994). The appraisal of eyewitness testimony. In D. F. Ross, J. D. Read, & M. P. Toglia (Eds.), *Adult eyewitness testimony: Current trends and developments* (pp. 385–418). New York, NY: Cambridge University Press.

Leippe, M. R. (1995). The case for expert testimony about eyewitness memory. *Psychology, Public Policy, and Law, 1,* 909–959. doi:10.1037/1076-8971.1.4.909

Leippe, M. R., Eisenstadt, D., Rauch, S. M., & Seib, H. M. (2004). Timing of eyewitness expert testimony, jurors' need for cognition, and case strength as determinants of trial verdicts. *Journal of Applied Psychology, 89,* 524–541. doi:10.1037/0021-9010.89.3.524

Lindsay, R. C. L., Semmler, C., Weber, N., Brewer, N., & Lindsay, M. L. (2008). How variations in distance affect eyewitness reports and identification accuracy. *Law and Human Behavior, 32,* 526–535. doi:10.1007/s10979-008-9128-x

Lindsay, R. C. L., Wells, G., & O'Connor, F. (1989). Mock-juror belief of accurate and inaccurate witnesses. *Law and Human Behavior, 13,* 333–339. doi:10.1007/BF01067033

Lindsay, R. C. L., Wells, G. L., & Rumpel, C. (1981). Can people detect eyewitness identification accuracy within and across situations? *Journal of Applied Psychology, 66,* 79–89. doi:10.1037/0021-9010.66.1.79

Loftus, E. F. (1974). Reconstructing memory: The incredible witness. *Psychology Today, 8,* 116–119.

Luus, C. A. E., & Wells, G. L. (1994). The malleability of eyewitness confidence: Co-witness and perseverance effects. *Journal of Applied Psychology, 79,* 714–723. doi:10.1037/0021-9010.79.5.714

Maass, A., Brigham, J. C., & West, S. G. (1985). Testifying on eyewitness reliability: Expert advice is not always persuasive. *Journal of Applied Social Psychology, 15,* 207–229. doi:10.1111/j.1559-1816.1985.tb00897.x

Magnussen, S., Melinder, A., Stridbeck, U., & Raja, A. Q. (2010). Beliefs about factors affecting the reliability of eyewitness testimony: A comparison of judges, jurors and the general public. *Applied Cognitive Psychology, 24,* 122–133. doi:10.1002/acp.1550

Magnussen, S., Wise, R. A., Raja, A. Q., Safer, M. A., Pawlenko, N., & Stridbeck, U. (2008). What judges know about eyewitness testimony: A comparison of Norwegian and US judges. *Psychology, Crime & Law, 14,* 177–188. doi:10.1080/10683160701580099

Manson v. Braithwaite, 432 U.S. 98 (1977).

Martire, K. A., & Kemp, R. I. (2009). The impact of eyewitness expert evidence and judicial instruction on juror ability to evaluate eyewitness testimony. *Law and Human Behavior, 33,* 225–236. doi:10.1007/s10979-008-9134-z

Memon, A., Hope, L., & Bull, R. (2003). Exposure duration: Effects on eyewitness accuracy and confidence. *The British Journal of Psychology, 94,* 339–354. doi:10.1348/000712603767876262

New South Wales Evidence Act. (1995). Division 5, Section 43. Retrieved from http://portsea.austlii.edu.au/cgi-pit/maketoc.py?skel=/home/www/pit/xml/nsw/act/nswA1995-25_skel.xml&date=

Police and Criminal Evidence Act. (1984). Code D. Retrieved from http://police.homeoffice.gov.uk/publications/operational-policing/2008_PACE_Code_D_(final).html

Price, P. C., & Stone, E. R. (2004). Intuitive evaluation of likelihood judgment producers: Evidence for a confidence heuristic. *Journal of Behavioral Decision Making, 17,* 39–57. doi:10.1002/bdm.460

R v. Turnbull and Others, 3 All E.R. 549 (1976).

R v. Hien Puoc Tang, NSWCCA 167 (2006).

Sauer, J., Brewer, N., Zweck, T., & Weber, N. (2010). The effect of retention interval on the confidence-accuracy relationship for eyewitness identification. *Law and Human Behavior, 34,* 337–347. doi:10.1007/s10979-009-9192-x

Semmler, C., & Brewer, N. (2002). Effects of mood and emotion on juror processing and judgments. *Behavioral Sciences & the Law, 20,* 423–436. doi:10.1002/bsl.502

Semmler, C., Brewer, N., & Wells, G. L. (2004). Effects of postidentification feedback on eyewitness identification and nonidentification confidence. *Journal of Applied Psychology, 89,* 334–346. doi:10.1037/0021-9010.89.2.334

Shaw, J. S., III, & McClure, K. A. (1996). Repeated postevent questioning can lead to elevated levels of eyewitness confidence. *Law and Human Behavior, 20,* 629–653. doi:10.1007/BF01499235

South Australian Uniform Evidence Act. (1929). Part 2, Section 28. Retrieved from http://portsea.austlii.edu.au/cgi-pit/maketoc.py?skel=/home/www/pit/ xml/sa/act/saA1929-1907_skel.xml&date=

Stinson, V., Devenport, J. L., Cutler, B. L., & Kravitz, D. A. (1997). How effective is the motion-to-suppress-safeguard? Judges' perceptions of the suggestiveness and fairness of biased lineup procedures. *Journal of Applied Psychology, 82,* 211–220. doi:10.1037/0021-9010.82.2.211

Vrij, A. (2000). *Detecting lies and deceit.* West Sussex, England: Wiley.

Weber, N., & Brewer, N. (2008). Eyewitness recall: Regulation of grain size and the role of confidence. *Journal of Experimental Psychology: Applied, 14,* 50–60. doi: 10.1037/1076-898X.14.1.50

Wells, G. L. (1984). How adequate is human intuition for judging eyewitness testimony. In G. L. Wells & E. L. Loftus (Eds.), *Eyewitness testimony: Psychological perspectives* (pp. 256–272). New York, NY: Cambridge University Press.

Wells, G. L., & Bradfield, A. L. (1998). "Good you identified the suspect": Feedback to eyewitnesses distorts their reports of the witnessing experience. *Journal of Applied Psychology, 83,* 360–376. doi:10.1037/0021-9010.83.3.360

Wells, G. L., Ferguson, T. J., & Lindsay, R. C. L. (1981). The tractability of eyewitness confidence and its implications for triers of fact. *Journal of Applied Psychology, 66,* 688–696. doi:10.1037/0021-9010.66.6.688

Wells, G. L., Lindsay, R., & Ferguson, T. J. (1979). Accuracy, confidence, and juror perceptions in eyewitness identification. *Journal of Applied Psychology, 64,* 440–448. doi:10.1037/0021-9010.64.4.440

Wells, G. L., & Windschitl, P. D. (1999). Stimulus sampling and social psychological experimentation. *Personality and Social Psychology Bulletin, 25,* 1115–1125. doi:10.1177/01461672992512005

IV

THE TRIAL WITNESSES

10

UNRELIABLE INFORMANT TESTIMONY

JEFFREY S. NEUSCHATZ, NICHOLAOS JONES,
STACY A. WETMORE, AND JOY McCLUNG

The Prosecutors Committee Report (PCR) of the Working Group on the Prevention of Miscarriages of Justice (2009) defined a *jailhouse informant* as someone who, while in custody, allegedly receives one or more statements from an accused person, where the statements relate to some offense that occurred outside the custodial institution. The most familiar type of confession is a *primary confession*: a statement made by a person whereby he or she admits to committing a crime. The focus of this chapter, however, is on *secondary confessions* made by jailhouse informants. Unlike primary confessions, secondary confessions are not direct admissions of guilt; they are statements about another's admission of guilt. We define secondary confession as a report by a person to the effect that the person heard another person (the suspect) confess to a crime.

Consistent with experimental results in regard to the persuasiveness of primary confessions, Neuschatz, Lawson, Swanner, Meissner, and Neuschatz (2008) found secondary confessions to be extremely persuasive evidence. In fact, false testimony from jailhouse informants is the leading cause of wrongful convictions in capital cases (Warden, 2004). Even given the dangers associated with informant testimony, prosecutors routinely use jailhouse informants to obtain incriminating evidence in exchange for inducements.

The U.S. Supreme Court has indicated that bartered testimony from jailhouse informants is extremely unreliable and that inducements can motivate informants to fabricate evidence. They also argued, however, that existing safeguards sufficiently protect the accused (*Giglio v. United States*, 1972).

The goals of this chapter are fourfold. First, we outline the problems associated with jailhouse informant testimony by giving a brief history of the practice of using informants and reviewing the relevant data on wrongful convictions, major cases, and infamous informants. Second, we identify the foundational research that informs the research on informant testimony. Third, we review the current psychological research on informant testimony. Finally, we discuss suggested legal reforms pertaining to informant testimony and their likely efficacy in light of the psychological research.

RELEVANCE OF INFORMANT TESTIMONY TO CONVICTION OF THE INNOCENT

The use of informants dates to at least the 4th century BCE, when the Athenian government relied on informants to expose treasonous plots (see, e.g., Chapter 18 of Thucydides's *History of the Peloponnesian War*). The ancient Greek penal system punished treason with death, but it allowed those convicted of treason to receive a lesser penalty—banishment—in exchange for informing on other traitors. The medieval approver system had a similar structure (Bloom, 2002). Under the approver system (circa 1275), any person accused of a felony or treason could provide information on any other person. If the approver–informant was convicted of a felony—which, in all cases, was punishable by death—and the authorities accepted his or her testimony, the approver's record would be expunged and his or her sentence lessened from execution to exile. False information merited execution. As in ancient Greece, however, there was no penalty to becoming an approver for those already sentenced to death.

These ancient and medieval methods for handling informants were ineffective in preventing unreliable testimony. Those sentenced to death could only increase their chances of survival by providing information to the government, regardless of their information's veracity. This is a common theme throughout the history of informant testimony: The penalty for fabricating evidence is no worse than the informant's existing punishment, because the death sentence can be carried out only once. Thus, there is no risk and only potential reward for fabricating information.

Of course, informants are not the only source of unethical behavior in systems that use their testimony. In California, the same district attorney prosecuted both Thomas Thompson and David Leitch for the murder of Ginger

Fleischli (Call, 2001). In the Thompson case, the district attorney employed two jailhouse informants to substantiate his claim that Thompson had raped and killed Fleischli. Thompson was given the death penalty. In the Leitch trial, the same district attorney had four jailhouse informants testify that Leitch planned Fleischli's murder in an attempt to get at his ex-wife and that Thompson was an accomplice. Even though testimony from the two sets of jailhouse informants was contradictory, Thompson, never having been granted a new trial, was executed in July 1998.

In regard to the involvement and use of jailhouse informants in the contemporary criminal justice system, the Center for Wrongful Convictions reviewed the capital cases of 111 persons released from death row after their exonerations between 1973 and 2004. They found false testimony from informants in 45.9% of the cases. This makes false informant testimony a leading cause of wrongful convictions in U.S. capital cases (Warden, 2004).

According to the Innocence Project (2009), testimony from a jailhouse informant contributed to a wrongful sexual assault conviction in 16% of the 244 postconviction DNA exonerations in the United States. During cases that produce such convictions, the central convicting evidence is often a statement from an informant who has an incentive to testify. This incentive is often either money or a sentence reduction. Notably, in many cases the incentive remains undisclosed to the jury. Furthermore, DNA exonerations in cases that use informants show two important facts: first, that informants occasionally lie on the stand; second, that prosecutors continue to use informants in multiple ways, even though informants are sometimes known to lie. Innocent people have been wrongfully convicted in cases in which informants have been paid to testify, have testified in exchange for release from prison, or have testified in multiple cases that they have evidence of guilt in the form of an overheard confession or personal witnessing of the crime. Testifying falsely in exchange for an incentive is often the last resort for a desperate inmate. Providing informant testimony may be the only option for those who are not in prison but want to avoid being charged with a crime.

Statistics reported in relation to the prevalence of jailhouse informant testimony likely underestimate the prevalence of false informant testimony because they include only cases in which the defendant has been exonerated. For example, DNA testing might not have been available at the time of conviction, and DNA evidence often is not available for illuminating new facts in older cases. Thus, there is no way to know exactly how many people have been wrongfully convicted, and might even be on death row, due to false informant testimony. However, according to a study by Marshall, Warden, Geraghty, and Van Zandt (2005), there have been 51 people wrongfully convicted of a capital crime due, at least in part, to false informant testimony. This more than suffices to show that the scientific study of informant testimony is crucial for further understanding how to better regulate that testimony and prevent future wrongful convictions.

Cases and Informants

The first-known documented jailhouse informant case in America occurred in Manchester, Vermont, in 1819. Brothers Jesse and Stephen Boorn were accused of killing their brother-in-law, Russell Colvin. The Boorn brothers had made no secret of their distaste for Colvin, and when Colvin turned up missing, suspicion fell on the brothers. After the supposed murder, Jesse had the misfortune of sharing a cell with Silas Merill, a known and convicted forger. Merill testified that Jesse confessed to him. On the basis of Merill's testimony, Jesse and Stephen were sentenced to death. However, as the story goes, they were saved from the gallows when Colvin turned up alive in New Jersey.

Since the Boorn case, there have been numerous cases that involved unreliable informant testimony. Here we briefly discuss three. The case of Thomas Sophonow clearly demonstrates the dangers of using jailhouse informant testimony during trial. Sonya Singleton's case highlights some of the legal issues that have been debated in using informant testimony. Finally, Leslie Vernon White's story vividly conveys some of the ways in which currently existing safeguards against unreliable informant testimony are inadequate.

Thomas Sophonow

In December 1981, Barbara Stoppel, a waitress at the Ideal Donut shop in Winnipeg, Manitoba, Canada, was found strangled in the bathroom. Thomas Sophonow came up as a person of interest who might have been in the area at the time of the murder, and his appearance generally matched eyewitness descriptions of the suspect. Sophonow was charged and brought to trial for murdering Barbara Stoppel, the evidence of his guilt being multiple eyewitness identifications, Sophonow's demonstration to police of the twisting motion necessary to turn the lock on the donut shop, and, ultimately, informant testimony from three jailhouse informants. No physical evidence linked Sophonow to the crime.

The three jailhouse informants who provided evidence against Sophonow were Thomas Cheng, Adrian McQuade, and Douglas Martin. Thomas Cheng testified that Sophonow confessed to him and that he was not receiving an incentive in exchange for his testimony. The latter claim was proven false; he had other charges against him dropped in return for his testimony. Adrian McQuade and Douglas Martin also testified that Sophonow confessed. Unbeknownst to the defense attorney, Martin had been a jailhouse informant in the past and had a previous perjury conviction, and McQuade's testimony came about under great suspicion of unreliability. Sophonow was tried three times and spent nearly 4 years behind bars until the Manitoba Court of Appeals acquitted him in 1985. As a result of Sophonow's case and cases similar to it, the Manitoba government released a report in 2001, by retired Supreme Court judge Peter Cory, containing 43 recommendations in regard to the use of jailhouse informants.

Sonya Singleton

Sonya Singleton's case dramatically changed the management of informant testimony and incentive offers in the United States. Singleton was convicted of money laundering and conspiracy to distribute cocaine. An important piece of evidence against her was testimony from Napoleon Douglas. Douglas, who had been convicted as a coconspirator, was serving his sentence in Mississippi. In exchange for his testimony, the government attorneys promised that they would not prosecute him for other offenses and that they would notify the sentencing judge and the parole board. His sentence was reduced from 15 years to 5 years to be served concurrently with the time he had to serve in Mississippi. On appeal, Singleton's lawyer argued that Douglas's testimony should have been suppressed on the grounds that the presentation of incentives to Mr. Douglas violated Section 201(c)(2) of Title 18 of the United States Code, which prohibits presenting incentives in exchange for testimony. This motion against the admissibility of Douglas's testimony led to two court decisions in regard to the legality of presenting informants with incentives to testify (*United States v. Singleton*, 1998, 1999).

In summer 1998, a three-judge panel of the Tenth Circuit Court of Appeals ruled that testimony from a witness who had been offered a lower sentence in exchange for testimony against a codefendant violated the Federal Bribery statute and should not be admitted (*United States v. Singleton*, 1998). However, this decision was short-lived. In January 1999, the full Tenth Circuit Court of Appeals rejected the three-judge panel ruling with a nine to three vote. In its decision, the court said the earlier ruling was "patently absurd." As a result of *Singleton 2,* offering incentives to informants remains legal in the United States, despite widespread reservations that such incentives present inducements to lie.

Leslie Vernon White

Leslie Vernon White has lived the majority of his life in the criminal justice system. Beginning at age 8, he has been in and out of jail for a laundry list of crimes. Therefore, it is no surprise that White has become very well acquainted with the criminal justice system and has found ways to use the system to his advantage. White has been informing on his fellow inmates to secure his own early release from jail since the 1980s. In 1990, White appeared on *60 Minutes* and talked about the methods he used to secure a plausible secondary confession to barter for his freedom. He demonstrated the ease with which he is able to procure privileged information about crimes supposedly committed by fellow inmates. During the interview, White, posing as a Los Angeles police officer, phoned multiple state offices involved in the criminal justice process. Under this guise, he simply asked for information regarding a crime allegedly committed by a fellow inmate. After obtaining the information, White arranged to be in the same vicinity as the inmate, to create circumstances for receiving a plausible secondary confession. At trial, White would be able to demonstrate that he met the defendant in jail and that he had facts known only to those most intimately associated with the case (Bloom, 2002). Notably, the facts are true; what is not true is his testimony about how he obtained the facts.

As a result of White's *60 Minutes* interview and a multitude of articles published by the *Los Angeles Times*, a grand jury in Los Angeles County was convened to investigate White's influence in the criminal justice system and how other players—including prosecutors, defense attorneys, and prison officials—were involved in aiding informants. The grand jury found that corruption ran deep within the system and that the incentives given for testimony were heavily responsible for influencing informants to lie at trial (Los Angeles County Grand Jury, 1990). White, as a result of his cooperation in the grand jury investigation, is the first—and thus far only—informant to have been convicted of perjury for his involvement as a jailhouse informant. Furthermore, White has offered to come clean on all the cases—some of which are capital cases—in which he perjured himself, provided that the Los Angeles district attorney offers him immunity. At present, the district attorney's office has refused to do so.

Scientific Methods Used in Informant Research

Psychological research on informant testimony involves balancing experimental control against ecological validity. There is often a tradeoff between controlling experimental conditions and generating outcomes that reliably generalize to less controlled conditions: Strict experimental control of independent and extraneous variables inversely correlates with applicability of an experiment's results to more realistic circumstances. In this section, we discuss some of these tradeoffs in experiments designed to understand how jurors respond to witness testimony when that testimony is given under a variety of conditions. Although we give special attention to testimony from jailhouse informants, these tradeoffs are common to all research on jury decision making.

In a typical jury simulation procedure, participants watch or read portions of a trial. Then, either alone or through group deliberation, they judge whether the suspect in the trial is guilty or innocent. After reaching a decision, they answer questions about aspects of the trial. Bornstein (1999) examined a sample of 113 jury simulation studies. He found that 65% of these studies used university students as participants, 55% used written trials in either summary or transcript form, and participants more often were asked to reach decisions concerning guilt or innocence through individual rather than group deliberation.

There are tradeoffs with respect to several aspects of jury simulation methodology. One major concern is the format in which the trial is presented. Jury simulation research typically presents trials in either a videotape format (Hosch, Beck, & McIntyre, 1980; Miller, 1976; Williams et al., 1975) or a written format (Bermant, McGuire, McKinley, & Salo, 1974; Juhnke et al., 1979). The videotape format sometimes involves real actors who play the roles of lawyers, defendants, witnesses, and so on; more frequently, however, students play these roles. The written format is either a short summary of an actual trial or a longer transcript of such a trial.

Written transcripts are relatively easy and inexpensive to create and manipulate for the purposes of a study, and they are easy to create with limited resources (e.g., grant support). However, because jurors in real trials see and hear the events and people, written transcripts do not provide a realistic simulation for participants: They do not allow participants to experience the rich contextual and emotional cues associated with viewing a trial. This lack of realism can affect verdicts and generalizability (Bornstein, 1999). Accordingly, studies that use written trials control experimental conditions at some expense to the degree to which their results can be expected to apply to actual trials. In contrast to written transcripts, videotape trials more closely approximate actual trial events. Because the video format makes trials more realistic to participants, the results of experiments that use this format better generalize to actual trials. However, creating multiple videos for the purpose of simulating multiple experimental conditions can be expensive and time consuming (Bornstein, 1999).

Selecting participants for jury simulations introduces another tradeoff. Jury simulations, like most psychological studies, traditionally use university students as participants (Bornstein, 1999). Most research occurs in an academic setting, where university students are more easily accessible than community members. Students also are easier to compensate—they can be offered class credit rather than money—and they provide a relatively large sample in a short amount of time. However, although acquiring student samples is cost-effective, these samples differ from the population of jury-eligible people: Unlike student samples, juries typically involve people with diverse ages as well as educational and financial backgrounds. These differences sometimes significantly affect the external validity of studies that use students as participants. This issue is particularly important in jury simulation research because of the relative infrequency with which college students serve on actual juries (Bray & Kerr, 1982). A number of experimental studies (Berman & Cutler, 1996; Crowley, O'Callaghan, & Ball , 1994; Finkel & Duff, 1991; Fulero & Finkel, 1991; Neuschatz et al., 2008; Schuller & Hastings, 1996) have compared the verdicts of undergraduate mock jurors to those of a community sample. Although most studies revealed no difference in verdict decision based on participant type (Crowley et al., 1994; Finkel & Duff, 1991; Fulero & Finkel, 1991), some revealed that student jurors were more lenient than the community sample (Berman & Cutler, 1996; Bornstein, 1999; Schuller & Hastings, 1996). This is problematic when the defendant is guilty.

A third tradeoff concerns the process by which participants make their verdict decisions. Although student jurors traditionally make their verdict decisions individually, group deliberations are the norm in real trials (Bornstein, 1999). Individual decisions differ from group decisions in several ways. Literature from social psychology on social loafing shows that people exert less effort when performing a group activity than when working individually when their individual performance is not monitored (Jackson & Harkins, 1985). Moreover, although mock jurors who reach their verdicts individually are free from the pressure that they may experience in group deliberation, they also are more subject to their own biases, especially insofar as they find it difficult to imagine a different way of interpreting the same information. There is a good deal of evidence that, in the early phases of a trial, jurors organize the testimony they hear into a story. They then either assimilate additional information heard during the trial into their story or, if it contradicts their story, they explain it away (Ellsworth, 1989). Accordingly, although simulations that involve individual rather than group deliberation are easier to administer, they do not realistically simulate either the amount of effort that jurors exert in real trials or the feedback effects that real jurors experience when exposed to multiple perspectives in group deliberation. Research has shown that group deliberations result in greater leniency even when jurors have no clear verdict preference before deliberation (Davis, Kerr, Stasser, Meek, & Holt, 1977; Kerr, 1981, 1982; Kerr, Nerenz, & Herrick, 1979; MacCoun, 1984). Furthermore, leniency is observed during group deliberations even when jurors slightly favor conviction before deliberation (Tanford & Penrod, 1986).

Selecting participant samples, trial format, and deliberation procedure present only a few of the methodological tradeoffs in jury simulation research. Although jury decision-making research is a complex field, our discussion highlights that generating results with greater ecological validity requires greater investment of time and resources.

Scientific Psychological Foundations of Research on Informant Testimony

The research on jailhouse informants has its foundation in the social and cognitive areas of applied psychology. Research on the fundamental attribution error, lie detection, judgment, and jury-decision making has its roots in social and cognitive psychology. In this section, we outline this foundational research; in the next section, we discuss its relation to informant testimony.

Jury Decision Making

According to Hastie (1993), models of jury decision making fall into two categories: *mathematical models* and *explanation-based approaches*. Mathematical models conceptualize the juror's role as a series of mental calculations. The difficulty with such models, which limits their predictive scope, is that they tend to characterize the evidence in trials as discrete units (Hastie, 1993; Kerr, 1993). Explanation-based approaches focus on how jurors organize, understand, and make sense of trial evidence. The advantage of such approaches is their ability to account for how an individual juror's attitudes and beliefs can affect evidence processing and decision making (Hastie, 1993; Pennington & Hastie, 1986).

One of the most thorough explanation-based models of jury decision making is Pennington and Hastie's (1986) story model. This model divides decision making into three component tasks: constructing a story, representing the decision alternatives, and making a decision. The first task is to piece the evidence together into a story or otherwise create a story. According to Pennington and Hastie, a juror can use evidence from the trial, personal knowledge, and expectations to create a complete story about the event in question. The last two factors, personal knowledge and expectations, account for how individual jurors factor their unique experiences into the jury decision-making process, allowing individual jurors to have different interpretations of the evidence and to create different stories.

It is plausible that jurors can create many competing explanations of the events that transpired. Within the story model, jurors use three criteria in determining which explanation is most acceptable: *coverage, coherence*, and *uniqueness*. Coverage refers to how much evidence a story can accommodate. Coherence refers to the story's degree of plausibility, internal consistency (no contradiction among the pieces of the story), and completeness. If a juror's story covers all the evidence presented at trial and is coherent, the juror can have high confidence in the story. To the extent that that more than one story is coherent and covers all the facts, jurors will have less confidence in their decision making because their stories lack uniqueness: Because more than one interpretation can fit the fact pattern, it becomes difficult to know which explanation to accept.

After all the evidence is presented and the jurors have created their stories, they learn the different verdict definitions and decisions available to them. Then, according to the story model, each juror reaches a decision in light of the various available verdicts. According to Pennington and Hastie, each juror will choose the verdict that best matches his or her constructed story. Pennington and Hastie (1992) demonstrated that when the evidence is presented in a way that makes it easier for participants to create a story, the participants are more likely to vote in accordance with the preponderance of the evidence. Furthermore, the story model has been effective in describing jury decision making in a wide range of cases, including murder (Pennington & Hastie, 1992), rape (Olsen-Fulero & Fulero, 1997) and sexual harassment (Huntley & Costanzo, 2003).

Fundamental Attribution Error

According to the fundamental attribution error (L. Ross, 1977), a person's behavior can be explained through reference to either dispositional or situational factors (or a combination of both). Disposition-based explanations attribute a person's behavior to traits unique to his or her personality. Situation-based explanations, in contrast, attribute the behavior to the situation in which the person is involved. When judging the behavior of others, people tend to ignore situational constraints, attributing behavior entirely to the personality of the person in question. This is known as the fundamental attribution error or correspondence bias. Consider, for example, the experience of being stuck behind a really slow driver on the freeway. One might assume that the slow driver is incompetent and inconsiderate (why else would they drive so slow?), when in fact the person's speed might be due to some mechanical error with their car. The fundamental attribution error would be attributing the behavior (slow driving) to the person's personality (inconsiderate driver) as opposed to his or her situation (mechanical error).

Gilbert and Malone (1995) noted several reasons for why people can commit the fundamental attribution error: *wanting dispositions, misunderstanding the situation*, and *minimizing situational constraints*. Wanting dispositions are tendencies to commit the fundamental attribution error for the purpose of having a sense of control over life. These dispositions lead people to think that what happens to others is their own doing rather than a result of luck and thereby help them to deal with feelings of fear and gloom by thinking that bad outcomes are unlikely to happen to themselves in similar situations, because they have a better character and judgment. Another reason people commit the fundamental attribution error is that they underestimate the power of situations. People often do not realize there are situational constraints influencing behavior (such as a mechanical error in the car). Unlike people's personality traits, such constraints are much more difficult to identify (it would be impossible to know about the mechanical error unless the problem was observable). Moreover, if people do realize there is a situational constraint, they tend to underestimate the situation's power to influence behavior. Finally, people commit the fundamental attribution error by default and without conscience effort, because the error has become an automatic response (Gilbert & Malone, 1995).

Relevant Research on Informant Testimony

Because the research on informant testimony is in its infancy, there are few published psychological studies in this area. Extant research covers five topics: whether providing an incentive to cooperating witnesses motivates fabricated testimony; the extent to which jurors reliably detect such motivations and whether they reliably detect false testimony; whether guilty verdicts in cases that rely on cooperating witness testimony depend on knowledge of whether the witness is a jailhouse informant or an accomplice witness and whether the witness receives an incentive in exchange for the testimony; whether providing information about the testimony history of a jailhouse informant affects juror verdicts or changes juror perceptions of the informant's credibility; and whether expert testimony for the defense in regard to the unreliability of confessions from an informant or accomplice affects the likelihood of conviction.

Incentives as a Motivation to Lie

Informants who testify for the prosecution against a suspect might be rewarded with an incentive that provides a motive for giving a secondary confession. Such incentives usually come in the form of a reduced prison sentence or dropped charges. Bruggeman and Hart (1996) examined the incidence of lying for an incentive among a sample of high school students who attended either a religious or secular school. Bruggeman and Hart (1996) used the Defining Issues Test to measure the students' moral reasoning level and found that religious students did not differ from secular ones in their moral reasoning level. To assess whether incentives were a motivation to lie, Bruggeman and Hart used the circle test. For this test, comprising 10 circles filled with the numbers 1 through 10 in a random order, participants memorized the numbers after briefly viewing the circles. Immediately after the study phase, participants were given a blank set of circles identical to those they just saw but without the numbers. Each participant's task was to fill the correct numbers in the appropriate circles. As an incentive for the students, Bruggeman and Hart offered extra points on the semester grade of anyone who achieved a certain level of accuracy on the test. That level was set so high that it would be nearly impossible for students to obtain. Furthermore, they told participants that the circle test sheets would not be collected, so that students had to submit to the researchers only their overall number correct after 10 trials of the circle test. This way, the teacher would have no way of knowing whether the students were telling the truth.

Bruggeman and Hart (1996) defined a *liar* as anyone who achieved the accuracy level needed to get the extra credit. Both groups exhibited a high number of liars; 70% of the religious school students versus 79% of the secular school students lied on the measure. This shows that an incentive mixed with anonymity induces high school students to lie. That students in the Bruggeman and Hart (1996) study readily lied to gain a small amount of academic credit suggests that criminals will lie for a reduced or commuted jail sentence.

Swanner, Beike, and Cole (2010) tested whether incentives affect motivation for fabricating a secondary confession. They used a variation of the computer crash paradigm originally developed by Kassin and Kiechel (1996). Using that paradigm, Kassin and Kiechel demonstrated that under the right amount of social pressure, people will admit to acts they did not commit. In their study, individuals performed a typing task that required either a fast or a slow pace, and they were told to not hit the *Alt* key because that would result in the computer crashing and loss of all data. The computer was programmed to shut down automatically in the middle of the typing session. Participants were led to believe that this malfunction occurred due to their accidentally pushing the *Alt* key. Almost 70% of the participants in the study signed a confession admitting to pressing the *Alt* key. In addition, 28% of the participants claimed to remember pushing the *Alt* key, and 9% confabulated details.

Whereas Kassin and Kiechel (1996) designed their paradigm to investigate false primary confessions, Swanner et al. (2010) manipulated the paradigm to investigate false secondary confessions. They assigned participants to a role of either reader or typist. The reader read a string of numbers, while the typist entered the read data into a computer program. (For the purposes of this chapter, we focus on the reader, because the reader resembles informants.) Both the reader and the typist were cautioned that hitting the *Tab* key would crash the program. After 60 s, the computer crashed, and the experimenter separately interrogated each participant. Some of the readers were provided with false evidence that the typist had confessed to hitting the *Tab* key, and some were provided with an incentive (extra experimental credit) to give evidence against the typist.

Swanner et al. (2010) found that 79% of the readers were willing to sign a statement that indicated that the typist had admitted to hitting the forbidden key and had caused the program to crash. The admission rate was significantly higher for readers than for typists, of whom only 52% admitted to hitting the *Tab* key. Providing false evidence increased the signing rate for readers to nearly 100%. Thus, giving a reader minimal incentive to lie (not having to come back for the second session and still receiving full class credit) sufficed to motivate their falsely informing against the typist.

Confessions and Lie Detection

The psychological research on confessions provides a bleak view of mock jurors' abilities to evaluate adequately confession evidence. The research indicates that mock jurors are not only insensitive to the coercive nature of many forms of confession testimony but also give undue weight to that testimony when forming a verdict. Kassin and colleagues (see Kassin & Gudjonsson, 2004) have unequivocally demonstrated the persuasive effects of coerced confessions on judicial decision making. For example, Kassin and Sukel (1997) had participants evaluate trial transcripts that contained either a high-pressure confession (suspect was in pain and the officer was brandishing a gun), a low-pressure confession (suspect confessed during questioning while under mental and physical stress), or no confession. They found that when presented with a coerced confession, mock jurors were more likely to deliver guilty verdicts relative to no-confession control participants, regardless of the level of coercion under which the confession was obtained. Furthermore, participants in the high-pressure condition indicated that the confession was involuntary and that it did not affect their decision, even though they voted guilty more often than participants in the no-confession control group.

Jurors are often in the difficult position of trying to make a decision about the veracity of a witness' testimony without having all of the information about the witness' motivations. That jurors are insensitive to levels of coercion is disconcerting, especially if this generalizes to testimony obtained as secondary confessions from informants. If jurors cannot discount a confession when knowing that it was obtained under coercive conditions, it seems unlikely they will do so when the coercion (implied deal) remains concealed.

Kassin and Gudjonsson (2004) ascribed the uncritical examination of confession evidence by jurors to the fundamental attribution error. The same ascription can be used to predict jurors' acceptance of plea bargained or purchased testimonies. The fundamental attribution error, recall, is the tendency to attribute the behaviors of others to dispositional factors while diminishing situational contributions (Gilbert, Pelham, & Krull, 1988; Krull & Dill, 1996; L. Ross, 1977). For example, jurors might accept that accomplice witnesses and jailhouse informants are giving testimony as a way of repenting rather than as a way of receiving an incentive. This sort of attribution would allow jurors to accept the testimony at face value and discount the witness' true motives.

Jurors not only give unwarranted credit to false confessions but also poorly detect a confession's reliability and whether the confession is voluntary or coerced (Kassin & Gudjonsson, 2004). This is problematic, considering that once a confession is presented during a trial, it is the juror's responsibility to determine the confession's veracity and the witness's credibility. Lassiter, Clark, Daniels, and Soinski (2004) experimentally demonstrated these juror tendencies by conducting a modified version of the Kassin and Kiechel (1996) computer crash paradigm, videotaping the experiment and obtaining both true and false confessions. The videotapes were used as stimulus material in a second experiment, in which a different set of participants rated the veracity of confessions obtained from participants in the first experiment. The results indicated that participants were able to accurately classify these confessions only at chance levels. Participants made the fundamental attribution error, accepting the confession at face value without considering the situation (Kassin & Gudjonsson, 2004).

Effect of Revealing Testimony Source and Informant Incentive on Juror Decisions

To test the effect of revealing a testimony's source and the testifier's incentive on juror decisions, Neuschatz et al. (2008) manipulated the source of a secondary confession, which came from either a jailhouse informant, who was given the confession information while incarcerated with the defendant, or an accomplice witness, who had the information because of his involvement in the crime. They also manipulated whether the cooperating witness received an incentive (5-year jail-sentence reduction) for testifying. These conditions were compared with a no secondary confession, no incentive control condition. Overall, guilty verdicts did not differ as a function of whether an incentive was known to have been provided for the secondary confession testimony. Thus, participants did not see an incentive as a reason to doubt the validity of the secondary confession testimony, regardless of the testimony's source or the cooperating witness' potential motivation.

Neuschatz et al. (2008) used the fundamental attribution error to explain the null effect of incentive on jury decision making, hypothesizing that participants attributed noble reasons for testifying to the jailhouse informant, such as feeling bad after viewing the families of the victims on television and then feeling the need to come forward with the information overheard from the defendant. This would seem to discount the impact of personal incentives on the informant's decision to testify. Yet, as the literature shows, the incentive could have been an extremely motivating force that was among the informant's main reasons.

An alternative explanation for the results is that the testimony of the cooperating witness cohered with the story that the jurors created about the evidence in the case. Given that in Neuschatz et al. (2008) the witnesses testified about specific evidence, the story model predicts that to the extent that evidence from the witness is consistent with jurors' stories about the case the witness's credibility should not sway the jurors' verdict. A similar explanation for the null results is that the case in Neuschatz et al. focused on issues, and jurors are likely to not be influenced by witness credibility when the evidence is presented around issues rather than fit into a storyline of events Pennington and Hastie (1986).

Effect of Revealing Testimony History on Juror Decisions

Neuschatz and Wilkinson (2009) tested whether providing information about the testimony history of jailhouse informants—the number of times the witness had given testimony as an informant in other cases—affects juror verdicts or changes juror perceptions of a jailhouse informant's credibility. They had participants read a transcript of a murder trial in which a jailhouse informant, alleging that he heard the defendant confess, provided the main evidence. During cross-examination, the defense attorney asked the informant how many times the witness testified in previous trials, in exchange for an incentive, about a confession that he allegedly heard while in jail. The informant responded, depending on the condition, that he had given such testimony 0, 5, or 20 times in the past, each time for an incentive. Providing information about the testimony history of witnesses should have alerted jurors that the jailhouse informant had motives other than a desire to be truthful in providing testimony, and this should have raised doubts about the informant's credibility: The informant was testifying, not out of the goodness of his heart, but because he expected to be paid for the service. In general, witnesses perceived as having less credibility are less persuasive to jurors (Bell & Loftus, 1988: Tenney, MacCoun, Spellman, & Hastie, 2007). Thus, the information about testimony history was expected to provide jurors with a reason to doubt the informant's testimony, and this was expected to produce fewer guilty verdicts.

There were two important results. First and most surprising, guilty verdicts did not vary with testimony history. Participants voted guilty equally often, whether the informant had testified in 20 separate trials or had never testified. The only significant difference among experimental conditions was a decrease in guilty verdicts when there was no secondary confession. Second, testimony history did not significantly affect participants' ratings of the informant's credibility. Participants rated the informant as equally truthful and trustworthy regardless of the number of times he had testified in the past and regardless of whether he was receiving an incentive.

Effect of Expert Testimony on Juror Decisions

Neuschatz and Wilkinson (2009) examined the influence of having an expert testify for the defense about the unreliability of informant and accomplice confessions. Although there is no evidence about how expert testimony affects juror decision making in cases with informants, there is extensive research on expert testimony in other legal contexts. Several studies of criminal cases, using some version of a trial simulation procedure, have examined the effect of expert psychological testimony on jurors' evaluations of eyewitnesses by comparing conviction rates in conditions with expert testimony to those in conditions without such testimony. The general result of these studies is that expert testimony reduces guilty verdicts (Hosch, Beck, & McIntyre, 1980; Leippe, Eisenstadt, Rauch, & Sieb, 2004; Maass, Brigham, & West, 1985). Devenport and colleagues (Devenport & Cutler, 2004; Devenport, Stinson, Cutler, & Kravitz, 2002) found no evidence for experts causing a general increase in nonguilty verdicts. Instead, they found that, in certain situations related to eyewitness memory, an expert can increase jury sensitivity.

In view of the finding that giving jurors information about the unreliable nature of eyewitness memory can make them more sensitive to some factors leading to wrongful conviction, Neuschatz et al. (2008) hypothesized that having an expert testify about the unreliable nature of informant testimony would have the same effect. To test this, they manipulated the presence of expert testimony along with witness type (accomplice vs. jailhouse informant) on juror decision making. More specifically, in their study the expert is someone who is a former offender and has himself given testimony as an informant or accomplice many times in the past. The results of this study were that informing participants about the ease with which an informant can fabricate a confession did not affect participants' verdicts. That is, expert testimony to jurors in regard to the general unreliability of informant testimony had no influence on verdict decisions: Jurors voted guilty when the expert testified just as often as when there was no expert testimony.

Application of Research on Informant Testimony

The U.S. Supreme Court has recognized the biasing nature of incentives and their use as factors that motivate lying; however, they argued that current safeguards, based on the Sixth Amendment right to confrontation of witnesses, suffice to protect defendants. Despite the Supreme Court's confidence, these safeguards clearly do not effectively prevent wrongful convictions.

Given the persuasiveness of any confession evidence, the failure, in practice, of the safeguards endorsed by the Supreme Court to protect accused persons from the false testimony of informants and that capital cases frequently rely on jailhouse informants (Rappold, 2005), it is not surprising that legal scholars recommend reforming extant practices in regard to informant testimony (California Commission for Fair Administration of Justice, 2007; The Justice Project, 2007; Kaufman, 1998; Sherrin, 1998). Scant as it is, existing psychological research on cooperating witnesses suggests that several of these recommendations are likely to be ineffective.

Information Acquisition

Several authors have offered recommendations designed to discourage jailhouse informants from providing unreliable information to authorities. To decrease jailhouse informants' motivation to provide unreliable testimony, some authors have recommended closer supervision of informant handlers, including oversight of handler-informant interactions and guidelines about rewarding informants for information (California Commission, 2007; Joy, 2007; M. S. Ross, 2002; Sherrin, 1998; Zimmerman, 1994). Sherrin (1998) also recommended providing stronger disincentives to jailhouse informants for knowingly giving unreliable information, such as instituting an active policy to prosecute for any perjury or provision of fabricated evidence. While results from Swanner et al. (2010) suggest that giving informants even minimal incentives will produce fabricated secondary confessions, they are inconclusive regarding the likely effectiveness of these recommendations, because Swanner et al.'s study does not consider the effect of either providing informants with disincentives for lying or giving handlers instructions designed to preclude their receiving false information.

Information Disclosure

Several authors have recommended (Bloom, 2002; Sherrin, 1998; Zimmerman, 1994) that the prosecution be mandated to disclose to defense counsel all potentially exculpatory information relating to a jailhouse informant and his testimony. This requires expanding the scope of information prosecutors must disclose to defense counsel to include (a) the prosecution's intention to use jailhouse informant testimony; (b) the informant's criminal record and testimony history; (c) records of all meetings with the informant, all evidence provided by the informant, the informant's actions while in custody, the circumstances under which the informant obtained his information, and all benefits given or inducements offered (explicitly or implicitly) to the informant; and (d) the results of any lie detector tests (e.g., polygraphs or brain scans) given to the informant (Cassidy, 2004; Clemens, 2004; Dodds, 2008; Joy, 2007; Justice Project, 2007; Mazur, 2002; Sherrin, 1998).

Expanding information disclosed is designed to provide defense counsel with the means to zealously and meaningfully cross-examine jailhouse informants through scrutinizing the informant's likely reliability, motivation, and biases. However, results from Neuschatz et al. (2008) showed that when issuing verdicts, jurors are generally insensitive to an informant's potential motivation and biases; and results from Neuschatz and Wilkinson (2009) indicated that when making verdicts, jurors do not take into account the informant's testimony even when that history is revealed during the trial.

Expert Testimony and Jury Instructions

To allow jurors to appraise meaningfully the reliability of a jailhouse informant's testimony, Gershman (2002) recommended allowing experts from cognitive psychology to testify in regard to the ways in which an informant's testimony might be influenced improperly by suggestive or coercive interaction with handlers. Several authors have recommended mandatory cautionary instructions from the trial judge to the trial jury pertaining specifically to jailhouse informant testimony (California Commission, 2007; Elliott, 2003; Justice Project, 2007; Mazur, 2002; Sherrin, 1998). Sherrin (1998), for example, recommended cautioning jurors not only that jailhouse informant testimony tends to be untrustworthy even if it is not bartered for formally arranged benefits but also that there are various dangers with relying on uncorroborated evidence. The goal of using expert testimony and cautionary jury instruction is to minimize the chance that perjured or fabricated testimony harms the defendant, by bringing to jurors' attention factors that tend to make that testimony unreliable.

However, results from Neuschatz and Wilkinson (2009) suggested that expert testimony to jurors regarding the general unreliability of informant testimony likely will not influence jurors' verdicts. Moreover, other research suggests that judicial instruction is unlikely to educate jurors about the unreliable nature of jailhouse informants. It has been unequivocally demonstrated in the literature that cautionary instructions generally have little effect on jury decision making. For example, in a recent meta-analysis on inadmissible evidence, Steblay, Hosch, Culhane, and McWethy (2006) examined the impact on juror verdicts of judicial instructions to disregard inadmissible evidence. They found that juror verdicts did not vary with cautionary instructions: The instructions were ineffective. However, Steblay et al. suggested that having judges provide a rationale for their ruling might increase jury compliance. There is no reason to assume that cautionary instructions would be more effective when they pertain to the reliability of jailhouse informant testimony.

Furthermore, for jurors to effectively use judicial instructions, they must first understand them. Without a thorough understanding, jurors cannot correctly apply the instructions. Unfortunately, the psychological literature suggests that jurors have difficulty understanding and accurately applying judicial instructions (Ogloff & Rose, 2005; Reifman, Gusick, & Ellsworth, 1992). For example, Ogloff (1998) examined the comprehension of judicial instructions with more than 500 jury-eligible participants. In this study, mock jurors watched a 2.5-hr simulated video trial and then deliberated in groups. The videotaped trial included lengthy judicial instructions similar to those typically used in real trials. Thus, Ogloff went to great lengths to ensure that the experiment simulated real-life conditions in actual jury trials so the results would be generalizable to actual judicial settings. The results revealed that mock jurors had very little comprehension of the judicial instructions. For example, when jurors were asked how sure one must be of the accused's guilt under the reasonable doubt standard, the majority of people responded as 100% sure. This is an unreasonably high standard given the legal definition of reasonable doubt, according to which doubt that the accused committed the crime can remain provided it does not exceed a reasonable person's opinion that the defendant is guilty. Clearly this standard does not require 100% certainty of guilt, contrary to what the mock jurors indicated. Furthermore, not only do jurors have trouble understanding the judicial instructions but also the remedies that have been devised to increase juror understanding—such as note taking and giving jurors written copies of the instructions—do not improve juror comprehension or application of the instructions (see Ogloff & Rose, 2005).

However, some innovations, such as the use of flow charts, have led to improved jury comprehension. The flow charts contain the legal decision that need to be addressed and the order in which they can be handled. Using a mock-jury paradigm, Semmler and Brewer (2002) found that allowing jury members to refer to flow charts increases comprehension and application of judicial instructions relative to participants who were not exposed to flow chart. However, results about the use of flow charts are not always positive. For instance, Ogloff (1998) did not find that flow chart use increased juror comprehension of judicial instructions. Ogloff suggested that participants may not have referred to the flow chart often enough, so that his null result could be due to the ineffective use of the flow chart as opposed to flow chart itself.

CONCLUSION

Although the obvious way to avoid problems that accompany jailhouse informant testimony is to eliminate its use during trials, there is a widespread consensus that the benefits of retaining informant testimony, including increased chances of convicting more dangerous criminals and deterring other criminals, override better safeguarding the innocent from wrongful conviction and deterring informants from committing perjury (see Martinez, 1999). Existing measures, endorsed by the U. S. Supreme Court, to protect the innocent against false informant testimony are inadequate in practice. Existing psychological research further suggests that several recommendations for modifying those measures or introducing new safeguards, although prima facie reasonable, are unlikely to be effective. However, this research is predominantly from one laboratory by using one set of stimuli. Future research can increase the accuracy and reliability of this research by, for example, using different stimuli (e.g., a live courtroom rather than a reading of trial transcripts) and testing for the effect of more variables (e.g., disincentives for lying).

There are, moreover, many recommendations for which no extant psychological research on informant testimony is pertinent. These include (a) giving trial judges discretion to exclude unreliable informant testimony through a pretrial motion (Sherrin, 1998; Uviller, 2002); (b) instituting pretrial "taint" hearings that determine whether an informant's testimony is probably true and whether handlers in any way coerced, manufactured, or otherwise influenced the informant's testimony (Call, 2001; Gershman, 2002; Joy, 2007); (c) obtaining corroboration for the informant's testimony, restricting the use of uncorroborated testimony, or both (American Bar Association, 2005; California Commission, 2007; Elliott, 2003; Joy, 2007, Justice Project, 2007; Sherrin, 1998; Zimmerman, 1994); (d) expanding the kinds of information authorities acquire and maintain about jailhouse informants, to include more kinds of information that is potentially exculpatory (California Commission, 2007; Cassidy, 2004; Gershman, 2002; Joy, 2007; Mazur, 2002; Roberts, 2005; Zimmerman, 1994); (e) maintaining a database of jailhouse informants, including information about their past and present service, to "avoid informants who use more than one handler [and] allow a handler to cross-check an informant's effectiveness, reliability, and veracity" (Zimmerman, 1994, p. 140); (f) limiting the pool of eligible informants to those who have more to lose than gain by testifying or those who previously have testified fewer than some given number of times (Sherrin, 1998); (g) only allowing information to flow from informant to handler (Zimmerman, 1994); (h) treating jailhouse informants as state actors or as acting under color of law, to minimize the opportunities informants have to fabricate information by subjecting them to the same rules and restrictions as, say, undercover officers (Sherrin, 1998; Zimmerman, 1994); (i) training prosecutors in lie detecting and improving pay, hiring standards, and training for police officers (California Commission, 2007; Clemens, 2004; Elliott, 2003; Joy, 2007; Kassin, 2002); and (j) imposing stricter penalties on police officers or prosecutors who knowingly fail to avoid miscreant informers and unreliable information (Clemens, 2004; Elliott, 2003; M. S. Ross, 2002). Investigating these topics is one way to augment psychological research on informant testimony.

There are ways to make psychological studies of informant testimony more sophisticated and definitive beyond designing experiments that test particular policy recommendations. These include repeating experiments with different stimuli and developing theories on why people accept confessions as reliable despite their unreliable sources. Having a database of information about the frequency with which false secondary confessions occur, similar to the Innocence Project's database in regard to the frequency with which eyewitness memory is unreliable, would also provide a rich resource on which to base future theoretical and experimental work.

REFERENCES

American Bar Association. (2005, February 14). Resolution 108B. Adopted by the House of Delegates. Retrieved from http://www.abanet.org/leadership/2005/midyear/daily/108B.doc

Bell, B. E., & Loftus, E. L. (1988). Degree of detail of eyewitness testimony of mock juror judgments. *Journal of Applied Social Psychology, 18*, 1171–1192. doi:10.1111/j.1559-1816.1988.tb01200.x

Berman, G. L., & Cutler, B. L. (1996). Effects of inconsistencies in eyewitness testimony on mock-juror decision making. *Journal of Applied Psychology, 81*, 170–177. doi:10.1037/0021-9010.81.2.170

Bermant, G., McGuire, M., McKinley, W., & Salo, C. (1974). The logic of simulation in jury research. *Criminal Justice and Behavior, 1*, 224–233. doi:10.1177/009385487400100302

Bloom, R. M. (2002). *Ratting: The use and abuse of informants in the American justice system.* Westport, CT: Praeger.

Bornstein, B. H. (1999). The ecological validity of jury simulations: Is the jury still out? *Law and Human Behavior, 23*, 75–91. doi:10.1023/A:1022326807441

Bray, R. M., & Kerr, N. L. (1982). Methodological considerations in the study of the psychology of the courtroom. In N. L. Kerr & R. M. Brady (Eds.), *The psychology of the courtroom* (pp. 287–323). New York, NY: Academic Press.

Bruggeman, E. L., & Hart, K. J. (1996). Cheating, lying and moral reasoning by religious and secular high school students. *The Journal of Educational Research, 89*, 340–344. doi:10.1080/00220671.1996.9941337

California Commission on the Fair Administration of Justice. (2006 November 20). *Official recommendations on the use of jailhouse informants.* Retrieved from http://www.ccfaj.org/rr-use-official.html

Call, J. (2001). Legal notes. *The Justice System Journal, 22*, 73–83.

Cassidy, R. M. (2004). "Soft words of hope": *Giglio*, accomplice witnesses, and the problem of implied inducements. *Northwestern University Law Review, 98*, 1129–1177.

Clemens, A. M. (2004). Removing the market for lying snitches: Reforms to prevent unjust convictions. *Quinnipiac Law Review, 23*, 151–245.

Crowley, M. J., O'Callaghan, M. G., & Ball, P. J. (1994). The judicial impact of psychological expert testimony in a simulated child sexual abuse trial. *Law and Human Behavior, 18*, 89–105.

Davis, J. H., Kerr, N. L., Stasser, G., Meek, D., & Holt, R. (1977). Victim consequences, sentence severity, and decision processes in mock juries. *Organizational Behavior and Group Performance, 18*, 346–365. doi:10.1016/0030-5073(77) 90035-6

Devenport, J. L., & Cutler, B. L. (2004). Impact of defense-only and opposing eyewitness experts on juror judgments. *Law and Human Behavior, 28*, 569–576. doi:10.1023/B:LAHU.0000046434.39181.07

Devenport, J. L., Stinson, V., Cutler, B. L., & Kravitz, D. A. (2002). How effective are the cross-examination and expert testimony safeguards? Jurors' perceptions of the suggestiveness and fairness of biased lineup procedures. *Journal of Applied Psychology, 87*, 1042–1054. doi:10.1037/0021-9010.87.6.1042

Diamond, S. S. (1997). Illuminations and shadows from jury simulations. *Law and Human Behavior, 21*, 561–571. doi:10.1023/A:1024831908377

Dodds, E. J. (2008). I'll make you a deal: How repeat informants are corrupting the criminal justice system and what to do about it. *William and Mary Law Review, 50*, 1063–1104.

Elliott, C. E. (2003). Life's uncertainties: How to deal with cooperating witnesses and jailhouse snitches. *Capital Defense Journal, 16*, 1–17.

Ellsworth, P. C. (1989). Are twelve heads better than one? *Law and Contemporary Problems, 52*, 205–224. doi:10.2307/1191911

Finkel, N. J., & Duff, K. B. (1991). Felony-murder and community sentiment: Testing the Supreme Court's assertions. *Law and Human Behavior, 15*, 405–429. doi:10.1007/BF02074079

Fulero, S. M., & Finkel, N. J. (1991). Barring ultimate issue testimony: An "insane" rule? *Law and Human Behavior, 15*, 495–507. doi:10.1007/BF01650291

Gershman, B. L. (2002). Symposium: Effective screening for truth telling: Is it possible? Witness coaching by prosecutors. *Cardozo Law Review, 23*, 829–863.

Giglio v. United States, 405 U.S. 150 (1972).

Gilbert, D. T., & Malone, P. S. (1995). The correspondence bias. *Psychological Bulletin, 117*, 21–38.

Gilbert, D. T., Pelham, B. W., & Krull, D. S. (1988). On cognitive busyness: When person perceivers meet person perceived. *Journal of Personality and Social Psychology, 54*, 733–740. doi:10.1037/0022-3514.54.5.733

Hastie, R. (1993). Algebraic models of juror decision processes. In R. Hastie (Ed.), *Inside the juror: The psychology of juror decision making* (pp. 84–115). New York, NY: Cambridge University Press. doi:10.1017/CBO9780511752896.006

Hosch, H. M., Beck, E. L., & McIntyre, P. (1980). Influence of expert testimony regarding eyewitness accuracy on jury decisions. *Law and Human Behavior, 4,* 287–296. doi:10.1007/BF01040620

Huntley, J. E., & Costanzo, M. (2003). Sexual harassment stories: Testing a story-mediated model of juror decision-making in civil litigation. *Law and Human Behavior, 27,* 29–51. doi:10.1023/A:1021674811225

Innocence Project. (2009). *Understand the causes: Eyewitness misidentification.* Retrieved from http://www.innocenceproject.org/understand/Eyewitness-Misidentification.php

Jackson, J. M., & Harkins, S. G. (1985). Equity in effort: An explanation of the social loafing effect. *Journal of Personality and Social Psychology, 49,* 1199–1206. doi:10.1037/0022-3514.49.5.1199

Joy, P. A. (2007). Brady and jailhouse informants: Responding to injustice. *Case Western Reserve Law Review, 57,* 619–650.

Juhnke, R., Vought, C., Pyszczynski, T. A., Dane, F. C., Losure, B. D., & Wrightsman, L. S. (1979). Effects of presentation mode upon mock jurors' reactions to a trial. *Personality and Social Psychology Bulletin, 5,* 36–39. doi:10.1177/014616727900500107

The Justice Project. (2010, April 5). *In-custody informant testimony: A policy review.* Retrieved from http://www.thejusticeproject.org/wp-content/uploads/pr-in-custody-informant-testimony.pdf

Kassin, S. M. (2002). Human judges of truth, deception, and credibility: Confident but erroneous. *Cardozo Law Review, 23,* 809–816.

Kassin, S. M., & Gudjonsson, G. H. (2004). The psychology of confessions: A review of the literature and issues. *Psychological Science in the Public Interest, 5,* 33–67. doi:10.1111/j.1529-1006.2004.00016.x

Kassin, S. M., & Kiechel, K. L. (1996). The social psychology of false confessions: Compliance, internalization, and confabulation. *Psychological Science, 7,* 125–128. doi:10.1111/j.1467-9280.1996.tb00344.x

Kassin, S. M., & Sukel, H. (1997). Coerced confessions and the jury: An experimental test of the "harmless error" rule. *Law and Human Behavior, 21,* 27–46. doi:10.1023/A:1024814009769

Kaufman, F. (1998). *Report of the commission of proceedings involving Guy Paul Morin.* Ontario, Canada: Ontario Royal Commission.

Kerr, N. L. (1981). Social transition schemes: charting the group's road to agreement. *Journal of Personality and Social Psychology, 41,* 684–702. doi:10.1037/0022-3514.41.4.684

Kerr, N. L. (1982). Social transition schemes: Model, method, and application. In H. Brandstatter, J. H. Davis, & G. Stocker-Kreichgauer (Eds.), *Group decision making* (pp. 59–80). London, England: Academic Press.

Kerr, N. L. (1993). Stochastic models of juror decision making. In R. Hastie (Ed.), *Inside the juror: The psychology of juror decision making* (pp. 116–135). New York, NY: Cambridge University Press.

Kerr, N. L., Nerenz, D. R., & Herrick, D. (1979). Role playing and the study of jury behavior. *Sociological Methods & Research, 7,* 337–355. doi:10.1177/004912417900700305

Krull, D. S., & Dill, J. C. (1996). On thinking first and responding fast: Flexibility in social inference processes. *Personality and Social Psychology Bulletin, 22,* 949–959. doi:10.1177/0146167296229008

Lassiter, G. D., Clark, J. K., Daniels, L. E., & Soinski, M. (2004, March). Can we recognize false confessions and does the presentation format make a difference? Paper presented at the annual meeting of the American Psychology-Law Society, Scottsdale, AZ.

Leippe, M. R., Eisenstadt, D., Rauch, S. M., & Seib, H. M. (2004). Timing of eyewitness expert testimony, Jurors' need for cognition, and case strength as determinants of trial verdicts. *Journal of Applied Psychology, 89,* 524–541. doi:10.1037/0021-9010.89.3.524

Los Angeles County Grand Jury (1990). *Report of the 1989–90 Los Angeles County Grand jury: Investigation of the involvement of jailhouse informants in the criminal justice system in Los Angeles County.*

Maass, A., Brigham, J. C., & West, S. G. (1985). Testifying on eyewitness reliability: Expert advice is not always persuasive. *Journal of Applied Social Psychology, 15,* 207–229. doi:10.1111/j.1559-1816.1985.tb00897

MacCoun, R. J. (1984). Modeling the impact of extralegal bias and defined standards of proof on the decisions of mock jurors and juries. *Dissertation Abstracts International, 46,* 700B.

Marshall, L. C., Warden, R., Geraghty, T. F., & Van Zandt, D. E. (2005). *The snitch system: How snitch testimony sent Randy Steidl and other innocent Americans to death row.* Chicago, IL: Center on Wrongful Convictions.

Martinez, S. (1999). Bargaining for testimony: Bias of witnesses who testify in exchange for leniency. *Cleveland State Law Review, 47,* 141–160.

Mazur, E. P. (2002). Rational expectations of leniency: Implicit plea agreements and the prosecutor's role as a minister of justice. *Duke Law Journal, 51,* 1333–1365. doi:10.2307/1373121

Miller, G. R. (1976). The effects of videotaped trial materials on juror response. In G. Bermant, C. Nemeth, & N. Vidmar (Eds.), *Psychology and the law* (pp. 185–208). Lexington, MA: Heath.

Neuschatz, J. S., Lawson, D. S., Swanner, J. K., Meissner, C. A., & Neuschatz, J. S. (2008). The effects of accomplice witnesses and jailhouse informants on jury decision making. *Law and Human Behavior, 32,* 137–149. doi:10.1007/s10979-007-9100-1

Neuschatz, J. S., & Wilkinson, M. L. (2009, March). Jailhouse informant testimony: How much is too much? Plenary Panel presentation at the annual American Psychology and Law Society conference, San Antonio, TX.

Ogloff, J. R. P. (1998). *Judicial instructions and the jury: A comparison of alternative strategies. Final Report*. Vancouver, British Columbia, Canada: British Columbia Law Foundation.

Ogloff, J. R. P., & Rose, G. V. (2005). The comprehension of judicial instructions. In N. Brewer & K. D. Kipling (Eds.), *Psychology and law: An empirical perspective* (pp. 407–444). New York, NY: Guilford Press.

Olsen-Fulero, L., & Fulero, S. M. (1997). Commonsense rape judgments: An empathy–complexity theory of rape juror story making. *Psychology, Public Policy, and Law, 3*, 402–427. doi:10.1037/1076-8971.3.2-3.402

Pennington, N., & Hastie, R. (1986). Evidence evaluation in complex decision making. *Journal of Personality and Social Psychology, 51*, 242–258. doi:10.1037/0022-3514.51.2.242

Pennington, N., & Hastie, R. (1992). Explaining the evidence: Tests of the story model for juror decision making. *Journal of Personality and Social Psychology, 62*, 189–206. doi:10.1037/0022-3514.62.2.189

Rappold, S. (2005, November 20). Jailhouse informers: A risky bet. *The Gazette*.

Reifman, A., Gusick, S. M., & Ellsworth, P. C. (1992). Real jurors' understanding of the law in real cases. *Law and Human Behavior, 16*, 539–554. doi:10.1007/BF01044622

Roberts, S. (2005). Should prosecutors be required to record their pretrial interviews with accomplices and snitches? *Fordham Law Review, 74*, 257–302.

Ross, L. (1977). The intuitive psychologist and his shortcomings: Distortions in the attribution process. In L. Berkowitz (Ed.), *Advances in experimental social psychology* (Vol. 10, pp. 173–220). New York, NY: Academic Press.

Ross, M. S. (2002). Thinking Outside the Box: How the Enforcement of Ethical Rules can Minimize the Dangers of Prosecutorial Leniency and Immunity Deals. *Cardozo Law Review, 23*, 875–892.

Schuller, R. A., & Hastings, P. A. (1996). Trials of battered women who kill: The impact of alternative forms of expert evidence. *Law and Human Behavior, 20*, 167–187. doi:10.1007/BF01499353

Semmler, C., & Brewer, N. (2002). The effect of mood and emotion on juror processing and judgments. *Behavioral Sciences and the Law, 20*, 423–436. doi:10.1002/bsl.502

Sherrin, C. (1998). Jailhouse informants in the Canadian Criminal Justice System, Part II: Options for reform. *Criminal Law Quarterly, 40*, 157–187.

Steblay, N., Hosch, H. M., Culhane, S. E., & McWethy, A. (2006). The impact on juror verdicts of judicial instruction to disregard inadmissible evidence: A meta-analysis. *Law and Human Behavior, 30*, 469–492. doi:10.1007/s10979-006-9039-7

Swanner, J. K., Beike, D. R., & Cole, A. T. (2010). Snitching, lies, and computer crashes: An experimental investigation of secondary confessions. *Law and Human Behavior, 34*, 53–65. doi:10.1007/s10979-008-9173-5

Tanford, S., & Penrod, S. (1986). Jury deliberations: Discussion content and influence processes in jury decision making. *Journal of Applied Social Psychology, 16*, 322–347. doi:10.1111/j.1559-1816.1986.tb01144.x

Tenney, E. R., MacCoun, R. J., Spellman, B. A., & Hastie, R. (2007). Calibration trumps confidence as a basis for witness credibility. *Psychological Science, 18*, 46–50. doi:10.1111/j.1467-9280.2007.01847.x

United States v. Singleton, 144 F.3d 1343 (10th Cir. 1998).

United States v. Singleton, 165 F.3d 1297 (1999).

Uviller, H. R. (2002). No sauce for the gander: Valuable consideration for helpful testimony from tainted witnesses in criminal cases. *Cardozo Law Review, 23*, 771–794.

Warden, R. (2004). The snitch system: How incentivized witnesses put 38 innocent Americans on death row. *Northwestern University School of Law, Center on Wrongful Convictions*, 1–16.

Williams, G. R., Farmer, L. C., Lee, R. E., Cundick, B. P., Howell, R. J., & Rooker, C. K. (1975). Juror perceptions of trial testimony as a function of the method of presentation. *Brigham Young University Law Review, 2*, 375–421.

Working Group on the Prevention of Miscarriages of Justice. (2009). *Prosecutors committee report.* Available from http://www.justice.gc.ca/eng/dept-min/pub/pmj-pej/toc-tdm.html

Zimmerman, C. S. (1994). Toward a new vision of informants: A history of abuses and suggestions for reform. *Hastings Constitutional Law Quarterly, 22*, 81–178.

11

ALIBI WITNESSES

TARA M. BURKE AND STÉPHANIE B. MARION

The stories of the wrongly convicted are often heartbreaking. Walter Swift was exonerated in May 2008, twenty-six years after he was first sent to prison for rape. His conviction was particularly puzzling given the presence of a strong alibi witness who corroborated his alibi. At the time of the rape, Swift was dating a woman who told police he was with her at the time the crime was committed, and she even produced shopping receipts to support this claim. Although her relationship with Swift ended, she continued to maintain his innocence during the intervening years, years in which she herself became a police officer. This alibi witness was not believed despite supporting physical evidence until new DNA evidence helped to convince the courts that the conviction was in error.

An examination of the first 40 DNA exoneration cases determined that for 11 of those individuals, their "weak" or "absent" alibi contributed to their wrongful conviction (Connors, Lundregan, Miller, & McEwen, 1996; Wells et al., 1998). In many instances, it appears that exonerees face conviction despite providing alibis during the trial, perhaps due to the presence of compelling eyewitness evidence. Such findings allow us to see the ultimate paradox in these cases. The alibi, deemed weak by those in a position to judge, was presumably correct but rejected, whereas the eyewitness evidence, presumably false, was accepted, eventually leading to a wrongful conviction. The mystery, then, is how one reliably differentiates a weak alibi from a strong one, or one that could carry as much weight as eyewitness evidence. A review of a sample of court cases from Canada and the United States that included an alibi defense may provide a clue. Results of this review indicated that in the vast majority of the cases—up to 86%—the defendant also had an alibi witness to support his or her claim of being elsewhere at the time the crime was committed. In contrast, relatively few (14%) had any physical evidence to support their alibi (Turtle & Burke, 2003). In all but two of the cases in which an alibi witness was present, this witness was a friend or family member of the defendant. Although these were not known-innocent cases, they do establish that the most common type of alibi corroboration is in the form of an alibi witness and that these witnesses are typically not strangers to the suspect. These findings are similar to those found in a survey by Culhane, Hosch, and Kehn (2008), who asked participants the likelihood of their being able to provide an alibi witness or exonerating physical evidence if they ever found themselves suspected of a crime. Most (88%) believed they could find an alibi witness, but only 29% believed they would be able to provide physical evidence of their innocence. When asked to indicate who they assumed would provide their alibi corroboration, 84% indicated this would probably be someone they knew—a *motivated witness*. As Gooderson (1977) pointed out, the problem with an alibi defense in general is that it is perceived as being easy to fabricate, and this may appear to be of greater concern if the defendant and the witness know each other well. Thus, it appears that police, judges, and juries view an alibi as weak when it is corroborated by a witness who also knows the suspect, because this individual may be motivated to lie on behalf of the defendant. Lessons from the Innocence Project files (http://www.innocenceproject.org) suggest that even testimony from multiple alibi witnesses is not always enough to keep an innocent person out of prison. Edward Honaker, who spent 9.5 years in prison, had three alibi witnesses, including his brother, sister-in-law, and mother's housemate. Jerry Watkins, who spent 13.5 years in prison, was supported by his wife's alibi; she stated that she had picked him up from work on the day in question so that they could attend a church meeting together. They spent the rest of the evening with relatives. Kenneth Waters, who spent 18 years in prison, told police he had been at work at the time of the crime; his alibi witnesses included a colleague who drove him home from work and his lawyer, with whom he attended court on an unrelated charge.

Although the use and misuse of alibi evidence do seem to play a role in wrongful conviction cases, there is currently no official category for this (as there is for eyewitness evidence or false confessions) in U.S. or Canadian databases. Although alibi errors could presumably fall under several different existing categories, such as tunnel vision or ineffective defense council, they most typically are found under the broader heading of *police misconduct* as they may demonstrate a failure to investigate this particular evidence on the part of the police or prosecutors. Leo (2005) described police and prosecutorial misconduct as often taking the form of "the withholding of exculpatory information and the knowledgeable or willful mischaracterization of case facts at pretrial proceedings and at trial" (p. 207). If the prosecution, or "crown," is aware that the police have potential alibi witnesses, for example, but do not follow up on this evidence nor disclose it to the defense, this would constitute misconduct (Greenspon, 2002, as cited in Denov & Campbell, 2005).

Although numerous case studies provide important anecdotal evidence of the role of alibis in wrongful convictions, Leo's (2005) contention that it is essential to move beyond this narrative approach forms the basis for the remainder of this chapter. The research, largely social psychological in nature, that is most relevant to the use of alibi evidence is explored, with the goal of both synthesizing the current state of the literature, and where possible, making recommendations regarding the use of alibi evidence in the justice system.

SCIENTIFIC PSYCHOLOGICAL FOUNDATIONS OF ALIBI WITNESSES

Understanding the mechanisms by which judgments are made by those involved in wrongful conviction cases (or criminal trials in general, for that matter), either as witnesses or decision makers, is essential to understanding why alibis are, or are not, believed. As is discussed in Chapters 5 through 9 of this volume, a great deal of research has explored the role that memory plays in the accuracy of eyewitness evidence (e.g., see also Loftus, 1991; Wells, 1984). If one considers an alibi witness to be analogous to an eyewitness to a crime, then it seems reasonable to assume that many of the same variables and underlying processes are at play. An eyewitness who is making an identification is offering inculpatory evidence, whereas an alibi witness is offering exculpatory information, but both are still simply "witnesses" (Burke, Turtle, & Olson, 2007).

The Role of Memory

D. S. Lindsay (2007) described the process by which we try to recall events from our own past: If I am a witness to a crime, I must try to recall information I actually witnessed without integrating information that seems like it should have been there but that I did not in fact see. If I am the suspect in a crime, I must recall where I was at the time the crime was committed, particularly if I am innocent. Autobiographical memory therefore plays a role in both the suspect's ability to recall his or her whereabouts and offer an alibi, and also the alibi witness's ability to correctly recall what he or she saw, and when. Lindsay described a source-monitoring framework whereby information about one event or one person blurs with another event or person, depending on the circumstances present when we try to recall these memories. As is explored in other chapters in this volume, eyewitnesses can make errors in a variety of situations and circumstances (e.g., see R. C. L. Lindsay, Ross, Read, & Toglia, 2006), and therefore it is reasonable to assume that many of the errors that can affect an eyewitness could also influence an alibi witness. Similarly, if there is reason to believe that eyewitness identifications are generally accurate, it seems reasonable to assume that the same is true of alibi witness testimony. We should therefore believe both eyewitnesses and alibi witnesses equally. As already noted, however, this does not seem to be the case.

Biased Information Processing

To understand why we are less likely to believe alibi witnesses than we are to believe witnesses making eyewitness identifications, we might consider the way we process information that is available to us. Petty and Cacioppo's (1984) elaboration likelihood model argues that when we are the targets of a persuasion attempt, we process the information presented either centrally—thinking carefully and logically about the strength of the arguments before making a decision—or peripherally—using cognitive shortcuts, such as the attractiveness or celebrity of the speaker, when responding to a persuasion attempt. As decision makers, we often fall short when it comes to thinking carefully and deeply about the issues and thoroughly considering the evidence. We often take cognitive shortcuts to help us reach decisions quickly, even when an accurate outcome is imperative (Chaiken & Maheswaran, 1994; Petty & Cacioppo, 1984). J. M. Olson, Roese, and Zanna (1996) extensively discussed the role of expectations in how we process information and how such expectations can lead to affective behavioral and cognitive consequences for both the observer and the observed. For example, according to Heath (2009), police and jurors may infer guilt in a suspect or defendant whom they feel does not display an appropriate emotional reaction in response to the situation. There is nothing in the literature to suggest such emotional reactions on the part of a suspect are at all correlated to actual guilt or innocence, but still such beliefs persist.

Not only might our preexisting views of others cloud our perceptions of them but we also may unknowingly change our own behavior to fit this view without even being aware we are doing so through a process known as *behav-*

ioral confirmation. Kassin, Goldstein, and Savitsky (2003) demonstrated behavioral confirmation in a clever study in which they randomly assigned participants to be either suspects or interrogators. If they led interrogators to believe there was a high likelihood that the suspect they were interacting with was guilty, interrogators asked more questions suggestive of guilt and exerted more pressure on the suspects to confess than did those who were led to believe that their suspects were likely innocent. In the second phase of the study, independent observers who were blind to condition listened to audiotapes of the suspect–interrogator dyad and, in the guilt-presumptive condition, also rated the suspect as more likely to be guilty. Expectations of guilt or innocence can therefore influence an individual's decisions in regard to which evidence trail to follow and the credibility of a suspect or alibi witness.

Stereotypes

There is little doubt that stereotypes can play a role in determining guilt or innocence. If one holds a particular schema for what a typical criminal should look like, then this stereotype may lead to a filtering of evidence to continue to support this particular belief. Therefore, if a suspect matches a schema for criminal, then a witness is more likely to factor in information that points to guilt while overlooking or ignoring information, suggesting innocence. We know, for example, that attractive defendants tend to get lighter sentences, presumably based on the "what is beautiful is good" stereotype (e.g., Castellow, Wuensch, & Moore, 1990). There is also ample evidence that minorities are overrepresented in the justice system, and indeed the Innocence Project statistics substantiate this claim; close to 70% of the exonerees are non-Caucasian persons (Innocence Project in Print, 2009; Parker, Dewees, & Radelet, 2001). Although the role that race and prejudice may play in wrongful convictions is discussed elsewhere in this text (see Chapter 13, this volume) it is important to note that stereotypes and prejudice about particular suspects or witnesses can have a detrimental impact on how decision makers view their testimony.

Thus, several basic social psychological processes may be behind the judgments and attributions made about suspect statements and alibi witness credibility. Researchers have begun to explore some of these more specifically (e.g., Allison, 2006; Sargent & Bradfield, 2004). Although it is often the case with applied research that more of the focus centers on outcomes than on underlying processes, it is important to keep these mechanisms and processes in mind, particularly when trying to remedy the problems that contribute to wrongful convictions. Such an understanding is starting to be reflected in the emerging alibi literature; two recent doctoral-level dissertations have explored issues that relate to the psychology of alibis (i.e., Allison, 2006; Jolly, 2008).

SCIENTIFIC METHODS USED IN THE
RESEARCH ON ALIBI WITNESSES

The genesis of much of the alibi research today began with a small notation in Connors et al.'s (1996) report that indicated that some of the first exonerees had weak alibis. This mention led to the interest in the field that we see today. Archival research and experimental paradigms are the primary methods used in alibi research.

Archival Analysis

Connors et al. (1996) gathered the data for their report by combing through the case files of the first 28 DNA exoneration cases. Wells et al. (1998) expanded the analysis to 40 cases. Gathering the materials to study was not an easy task:

> Once initially identified as likely candidates for the study, cases were verified and assessed through interviews with the involved defense counsel, prosecutors, and forensic laboratory staff; through reviews of court opinions; and, in some instances, through examinations of case files. (Connors et al., 1996, p. 3)

More recently, Garrett (2008) sought to update the statistics associated with wrongful convictions in DNA exoneration cases. Gathering information from several sources, including case files and media reports, he created his own database to better tabulate the common factors associated with wrongful convictions and found, among other things, that eyewitness error is still the number one factor that leads to erroneous convictions. He did not specifically code for alibi data, however. Although the Innocence Project case files are a treasure trove of information, an ongoing review of original documents from the Innocence Project case files (Burke & El-Sibaey, 2009) has revealed that much of the existing coding attached to these case files is not always consistent or systematic. Unless each case file is read in detail (and some of these files are several thousand pages long), it is not possible to know what is behind the statistics. For example, case files may indicate that several eyewitnesses offered statements, but how those statements were collected, whether biased interviewing techniques were used, or whether witnesses had contact with one another are not indicated in the case summary. Instead, the summary indicates only the presence or absence of a witness. Similarly, that alibi witnesses were available in some of the cases is often missing from the summary coding sheets used by the attorneys involved in the cases, thus leaving the erroneous impression that there was no alibi information present (Burke & El-Sibaey, 2008). A more in-depth reading of the files shows multiple examples of defendants who offered alibis and witnesses to support their alibis, but the witnesses were not interviewed, or even if they were, their statements were ultimately not considered credible.

Several U.S. states are now involved in the process of conducting post-mortems on the wrongful conviction cases in their jurisdictions (e.g., the Pennsylvania Joint State Government Commission Committee on Wrongful Convictions). The results of the latest archival research suggest that the outcome of such endeavors may be in jeopardy if the information necessary to determine what led to the wrongful convictions is not readily accessible (or is listed inaccurately) in the case files themselves. Thus, access to the files is useful from a real-world perspective, but there are limitations in regard to the amount and accuracy of the information available. As Leo (2005) pointed out, relying on the case-study narrative allows for some important first steps in uncovering the causes of wrongful convictions, but without empirical research, including the use of random samples and control groups, the use of such data to determine causality is limited.

Experimental Procedures

Empirical research that examines the use of alibi evidence has grown over the past few years and continues to expand to encompass many different points along the investigative time line. Although some research examines how alibi evidence is judged in the initial investigator stage (e.g., Dahl, Brimacombe, & Lindsay, 2009), the majority of the research has focused on the trial or jury phase, with most researchers measuring alibi credibility by manipulating the relationship between the suspect and the alibi witness (see Burke & Turtle, 2003; Culhane & Hosch, 2004; E. A. Olson & Wells, 2004). One study by Sommers and Douglass (2007) compared the use of alibi evidence in both stages—investigation versus trial. What follows is a more thorough discussion of the experimental research that surrounds alibi witnesses.

RELEVANT RESEARCH ON ALIBI WITNESSES

E. A. Olson (2002) was the first to describe a model for understanding the evaluation of an alibi as it progresses through the justice system. In the generation domain, the alibi providers come up with their story (story phase) and then try to validate this story (validation phase) by using person or physical evidence. The alibi providers or others (e.g., police investigators) can validate the alibi. It is the validation stage, according to Olson, that is essential to understanding the perception of alibi evidence. It is during this stage that the strength of the alibi is determined. The evaluation of alibi strength depends in large part on what suspects believe they will be able to produce to help corroborate the alibi. Both person evidence and physical evidence can be quite difficult to come by. The evaluation of the alibi for truthfulness (believability domain) occurs in the third stage with a final overall evaluation occurring in the fourth stage.

One may take several avenues when exploring issues relating to alibi research. As the focus of this chapter is on alibi witnesses in particular, we begin with a discussion of research that relates to the perception of alibi witnesses in the early stages of an investigation followed by the impact of alibi witnesses on juries.

Alibi Witnesses and the Investigation Phase

E. A. Olson and Wells (2004) were the first to try to experimentally manipulate some alibi-related variables to validate a taxonomy based on the type of evidence used to support an alibi. They hypothesized that decision makers would consider alibi evidence that they perceive to be suspicious or easy to fabricate (i.e., relatives and friends who offer supporting testimony, and physical evidence that one can easily alter or obtain) as less credible. In addition, E. A. Olson and Wells suggested that different alibi witnesses would be more or less credible, depending on how close their relationships were with the suspect. In particular, they hypothesized that a "nonmotivated familiar other" (i.e., someone who has a passing acquaintance with the suspect) who offered corroborating testimony would be more believable than a complete stranger ("nonmotivated stranger"), given that the former would be less likely mistaken in his or her identification of the suspect, but that a "motivated other" (i.e., someone well-known to the suspect and perhaps inclined to lie for the suspect) would not be considered credible. They asked mock investigators to evaluate three different alibis and measured the perceived credibility of each alibi, the likelihood that the suspect was guilty, and various personality traits of the alibi providers. They found that person evidence (i.e., the presence of an alibi witnesses) only had an effect on alibi believability when there was no physical evidence available to support the alibi. Within this no physical evidence condition, alibis in the nonmotivated stranger condition were considered more believable than were alibis that were not supported by witnesses or were supported only by motivated witnesses (i.e., someone well-known to the suspect). In a similar way, the type of person evidence influenced likelihood of guilt ratings only in the no physical evidence condition: Mock investigators rated suspects in the nonmotivated stranger condition as less likely to be the culprit than they rated suspects in the no-person evidence condition. Thus, alibi witnesses seemed to play a greater role in cases in which there was little if any physical evidence. The relationship of the witness to the suspect appeared to influence both the credibility of the alibi offered and the perceived guilt of the suspect.

Similarly, Dahl et al. (2009) asked participants to take on a mock-investigator role while evaluating different types of evidence derived from the work of E. A. Olson and Wells (2004). They predicted that the order of evidence presentation could have an impact on the evaluation phase. Eyewitness evidence typically comes last in mock-investigator research paradigms and therefore may be having a larger-than-expected impact on decision of guilt due to a recency effect. In the second of two experiments, they asked participant investigators to read descriptions of a crime and then to view videos of an alibi witness and an eyewitness being questioned about the suspect. They manipulated the strength of the alibi by varying whether the alibi witness was a good friend of the accused who had no supporting physical evidence to substantiate the accused's story (weak alibi) or a work colleague who also had hotel receipts to support the claim (strong alibi). They also varied which type of evidence came first—alibi or eyewitness. Although they had expected that alibi evidence in general would be less influential than eyewitness evidence, they found that this was not always the case. If a strong alibi was presented after eyewitness evidence, then guilt ratings were lower. Similarly, if a positive identification came after the presentation of alibi evidence, guilt ratings were higher. Overall, there was a significant three-way interaction: A strong alibi and a positive identification led to lower guilt ratings only if the strong alibi was presented second. Their findings appear to support the idea of a recency effect as well but only when the different types of evidence presented were contradictory (i.e., positive eyewitness identification followed by strong alibi corroboration). A strong alibi presented last receives higher credibility ratings. As Dahl et al. (2009) noted, the research provides evidence that prior beliefs and expectations influence subsequent decisions of guilt or innocence. Thus, research on the investigative phase supports the idea that nonevidentiary factors can also influence decisions made early, perhaps because of cognitive shortcuts rather than fact finding.

Alibi Witnesses and the Jury

Understanding how jurors process and evaluate alibi witness evidence is also central to understanding the role of alibis in wrongful convictions. To explore these issues, several investigators have asked participants to take on the role of mock jurors. For example, Golding, Stewart, Yozwiak, Djadali, and Sanchez (2000), in the second of two studies, examined the impact of DNA evidence when offered with or without the testimony from an alibi witness in a child sexual assault trial. Having established in their first study that DNA evidence enhanced the credibility of a child's accusatory statements, the second study explored whether an alibi witness could reduce this impact of DNA evidence. Participants read a fictional scenario that involved the sexual assault of a child. The child claimed that the defendant offered to drive her home in his car but instead took her to an isolated wooded area and assaulted her. In the alibi condition, a store clerk corroborated the defendant's alibi that he was in the store and nowhere near the vicinity of the woods when the crime occurred. Similar to Dahl et al.'s (2009) finding that a strong alibi witness could reduce the impact of a strong eyewitness identification, Golding et al. (2000) found that the inclusion of an alibi witness lowered guilt ratings for the suspect as compared with a DNA-evidence only condition; however, the ratings were not as low as in the child-testimony-only condition, in which guilt ratings for the suspect were lowest. They concluded that DNA evidence does not completely sway jurors and that the testimony of an alibi witness can help to mitigate the potential damage that DNA evidence can do. The alibi witness in this study, however, was a stranger; therefore, it is difficult to know whether evidence from a motivated corroborator—someone known to the defendant—would have a similar impact on juror's decisions or might rather be considered weak.

R. C. L. Lindsay, Lim, Marando, and Cully (1986), in the second of four studies, compared the impact of testimony of an alibi witness to eyewitness testimony to determine the relative influence of the two types of evidence. In their trial video, the victim testified that the defendant was the culprit. In some conditions, an additional witness testified: another prosecution witness who identified the accused as the perpetrator, a defense witness who testified that the man he saw commit the crime was not the accused, a family member of the accused who corroborated his alibi, or a stranger who corroborated his alibi. If two eyewitnesses were present to implicate the suspect, there was no significant increase in guilty verdicts as compared with when only one eyewitness was present (80% vs. 60%, respectively). However, if a defense eyewitness offered conflicting identification testimony (i.e., claimed the defendant was not the culprit) or if the witness who corroborated the alibi was a stranger to the suspect, then guilty verdicts significantly decreased to a rather remarkable 27%. When it was a relative who provided the corroborating statement, on the other hand, the number of guilty verdicts (57%) was similar to the numbers found in the condition where one eyewitness implicated the suspect, and no other testimony was provided. R. C. L. Lindsay et al. (1986) concluded that the inclusion of the witness for the defense introduced the possibility of memory error: Two eyewitnesses who recalled the same event differently led to reasonable doubt. Given that the alibi corroborated by a stranger reduced guilty verdicts to the same level as the contradictory eyewitness condition, it appears that the only alibi that was deemed less credible was the one offered by a relative of the suspect.

McAllister and Bregman (1989) also directly compared eyewitnesses with alibi witnesses and manipulated the confidence of those witnesses. In addition, they specifically tested the disconfirmation evidence explanation: that the weight given to specific evidence depends on the initial hypothesis held by the jurors. Using an elaborate 3 (strength of early evidence) × 3 (crime eyewitness) × 3 (alibi eyewitness) design, mock jurors read a case summary that described an armed robbery in which the victim was unable to make a positive identification and to determine guilt or innocence of the accused. The relevant alibi condition described a defendant who claimed he was playing poker until the police picked him up for questioning. The alibi witness, a fellow poker player, later either confirmed the alibi (he saw the suspect at the poker table), discredited the alibi (claimed that the suspect was not at the poker table), or offered ambiguous testimony (he could not be sure whether the suspect was at the table). They expected that if a juror had already decided that the suspect was guilty (based on an eyewitness identification which always came first), subsequent information that contradicted this information would be underutilized by the jurors. Results indicated that guilty ratings were highest when an eyewitness identified the accused and the alibi witnesses stated that the suspect was not at the poker table. However, the alibi identification condition (where the witness stated that the suspect was indeed at the table with him) did not significantly decrease guilty ratings as compared to the condition in which the alibi witness was unsure whether the suspect was at the table. An opposite pattern of results emerged when the eyewitness claimed that the suspect was not the perpetrator or when he claimed that he was unsure whether he saw him that night; in these cases, the alibi nonidentification (stating the suspect was not at the table) did not lead to a significant increase in guilty ratings as compared to the condition where he was unsure whether the suspect was at the table or not. A clear statement that the suspect was at the poker table (alibi identification), however, led to significantly decreased guilty ratings when the eyewitness did not make a positive identification. Results supported the idea that a noncorroboration (or what they termed a nonidentification) by an alibi witness has a significant impact on ratings of guilt but only when an eyewitness identified a suspect. However, eyewitness testimony always preceded the alibi testimony, and this could have served to manipulate the strength of early evidence, as the above interaction suggests.

Culhane and Hosch (2004) looked more specifically at whether an alibi witness who has a personal relationship with the defendant but is not a family member (e.g., girlfriend) is met with the same skepticism by mock jurors as an alibi witness who is a relative of the defendant. In their fictional crime scenario, they varied the confidence of an eyewitness and the relationship of the alibi witness to the defendant. They found that although the corroboration of an alibi resulted in lower ratings of the suspect's guilt overall, if the girlfriend was the corroborator, the guilt ratings were still higher than if the witness was a neighbor. They also found an interesting interaction between corroboration and witness: The neighbor's noncorroboration of an alibi resulted in more guilty verdicts than did his corroboration of an alibi, whereas the girlfriend's noncorroboration did not result in more guilty verdicts than did her corroboration. Presumably, the testimony of the neighbor is more credible because he has no personal stake in the outcome for the defendant.

In an extension of this previous work, Hosch, Culhane, Jolly, Chavez, and Shaw (2010) examined the perception of alibi witness credibility from a kinship theory perspective. In the first of two experiments, they asked participants to indicate who would be most credible in corroborating an alibi. They varied whether the relationship between the suspect and the alibi witness was biological, affinal (i.e., in-laws), or social, as well as the degree of relatedness (e.g., sibling vs. cousin, wife vs. sister-in-law). They found that alibis corroborated by biologically related witnesses were less credible than those provided by affinally related witnesses, who in turn were viewed as less credible than those provided by witnesses unrelated to the defendant (or who share only a social relationship). It is interesting to note that participants indicated that they themselves would be most willing to lie (i.e., corroborate what they knew to be a false alibi) for biologically related defendants, followed by affinally related then socially related defendants. Given these results, it is not surprising that mock jurors in their second study, who viewed case summaries that involved different types of alibi witnesses, believed that biologically related alibi witnesses were more likely to lie than were socially related witnesses.

Although it is evident that the bulk of the research at press focuses heavily on the relationship of the alibi witness to the suspect, Sargent and Bradfield (2004) are among the few to look more specifically at the cognitive biases that may be involved in the evaluation of alibi evidence. They investigated whether a defendant's race can affect how jurors process legally relevant information, namely, the strength of the defendant's alibi (Study 1) and the effectiveness of prosecutor's cross-examination (Study 2), using Petty and Cacioppo's (1984) elaboration likelihood model of persuasion as the backdrop to their research. Sargent and Bradfield (2004) explored how the race of a defendant (Black or White) would influence the evaluation of his alibi (strong or weak) in an armed robbery case and whether this effect would depend on the extent to which participants were motivated to make an accurate judgment. The suspect maintained that he was eating in a restaurant nowhere near where the crime took place. The alibi manipulation was a blend of person and physical evidence: A strong alibi was one corroborated by a security camera (physical evidence placing him at the restaurant), whereas the weak alibi condition noted that the waitress whom he claimed served him that night could not be found and no security cameras were used. Sargent and

Bradfield found an expected main effect of alibi strength (strong alibis being rated as more credible than weak alibis), but they also found a three-way interaction. When participants were motivated to make an accurate judgment in regard to the accused, guilt ratings were higher when the alibi was strong than when it was weak (regardless of the defendant's race). However, when motivation was low and the defendant was of Black race, guilt ratings were higher when the alibi was weak than when the alibi was strong. When motivation was low and the defendant was of White race, guilt ratings were equal, regardless of alibi strength. Thus, it appears that race became a factor in the decision-making process only when the alibi evidence presented was weak. In the case of strong alibi corroboration, the treatment of Black and White defendants was the same. The researchers concluded that White participants are more likely to carefully scrutinize the evidence in a case involving a Black than a White defendant, perhaps due to heightened sensitivity to race issues in a courtroom setting. They argued that it may not be a simple race bias that influences the processing of information; instead, White jurors may work harder to overcome biases in a courtroom to avoid even the possibility of being judged as biased, and thus it may be a matter of cognitive engagement (or central processing) that drives some of these effects rather than issues of racism or prejudice. The issue of race in wrongful conviction cases is explored further in Chapter 13 (this volume).

Finally, Sommers and Douglass (2007) examined how the presence of an alibi witness (a family member) affected the perception of the alibi evidence at both the investigative and trial stages. They were particularly interested in the differential treatment of alibi evidence at various points along the investigative time line. In Sommers and Douglass's first study, participants who acted as either police investigators or mock jurors judged the same alibi. In their second study, they introduced an alibi witness in the form of a family member of the accused. As they expected, they found a main effect of context whereby those in the police investigation condition rated the alibis as stronger than did those in the trial condition. They also found a main effect of corroboration as those who heard a corroborated alibi rated it as stronger than did those in the uncorroborated condition. However, the presence of an alibi witnesses only influenced ratings of alibi credibility for those in the police investigator condition; they rated the corroborated alibi as stronger than did mock jurors, who appeared to be unaffected by the introduction of an alibi witness who offered supporting testimony. The results suggested an awareness on the part of the decision makers that because a case makes it to trial, the alibi is presumably weaker or the case would not have made it that far in the first place.

Sommers and Douglass's (2007) findings may explain in part why inculpatory eyewitness evidence is also given more weight by jurors than is sometimes warranted: If the presumption is that the suspect is likely guilty by virtue of being a defendant, then—as schema theory would suggest—information that supports this view is more likely to be filtered in while information that refutes this view is more likely to be ignored. One might therefore expect to find systematic differences in the alibi literature according to whether or not the decision makers are being asked to form an opinion during the investigation stage (when all evidence is perhaps more likely to be considered in a more equitable fashion) or to render a verdict as a member of a jury (when jurors may assume a guilty defendant is more likely to be on trial than an innocent one). Thus, manipulations of alibi witness and corroboration variables might have a larger effect during the investigation phase than during the trial phase. These findings highlight the importance of context when trying to determine the role of alibis in wrongful conviction cases. As we have discussed throughout this chapter, few researchers travel down the same path and measure alibis the same way or at the same point in the timeline. Many researchers continue to explore the archival data that surrounds innocence cases (e.g., Burke & El-Sibaey, 2008), whereas other researchers, using primarily experimental methods, examine issues of relatedness in suspect–alibi provider dyads (e.g., Culhane et al., 2008; Hosch et al., 2010). Others focus on ways in which jurors process the alibi evidence and include such factors as the perspective of the decision maker (e.g., Dahl et al., 2009; Sommers & Douglass, 2007) or the race of the defendant (e.g., Sargent & Bradfield, 2004) in their experimental paradigms. Although this is still a young field, the variety of research methods and variables of interest suggests that it is one that will only continue to grow.

APPLICATION OF RESEARCH ON ALIBI WITNESSES

To reduce the frequency or likelihood of a wrongful conviction, policies and procedures are needed to reduce potential biases and errors that lead to these outcomes. Although such policies and procedures are now well documented within the eyewitness identification (see Chapter 6, this volume) and interrogations literatures (see Chapter 3, this volume), it is more difficult to make such recommendations at this relatively early stage in the emerging field of alibi research. As Sommers and Douglass (2007) pointed out, "studying police and juror perceptions of alibis are qualitatively different pursuits, and researchers would be wise to treat them as such" (p. 52). It may come to pass that concrete recommendations can be made to improve the justice system itself. Until then, consistency in research methodology and careful isolation and manipulation of related variables (e.g., clearly separating out person evidence from physical evidence) may allow alibi researchers to understand better the mechanisms involved in the interpretation of alibi-witness evidence. Using experimental methods to more clearly understand the role of alibis in wrongful convictions is essential for isolating and understanding causes. However such methods make it difficult to take into account the myriad of factors—and interactions of these factors—that ultimately lead to wrongful convictions in specific cases. Exploring the role of alibi witnesses in wrongful conviction cases must be an iterative and dynamic process: The case files provide an important narrative from which we may then find clues as to which factors are the most influential, and from there we can design better laboratory studies. As there is now strong evidence that the relationship of the alibi witness to the defendant can play an important role in the perceived credibility of the alibi, future research might examine two important and related issues. First, assumptions aside, it is important to determine the extent to which—or under what circumstances—people close to us are in fact willing to lie for us in the context of a criminal investigation. Second, given the number of wrongly convicted individuals who did present truthful alibis that were not believed (often due to the relatedness of their alibi witnesses), it is essential to explore ways to reduce the implicit negative assumptions associated with these witnesses and assist the decision makers in focusing instead on the factual evidence before them.

CONCLUSION

Although alibi research is still in its infancy, it appears to be a rapidly growing area. What we know is that errors in the evaluation of alibis occur at every stage of the game and that the ultimate goal is to implement systematic changes that can reduce the likelihood of wrongful convictions. No matter the context, it appears that relatives who act as alibi witnesses are viewed as less credible, which is problematic when we consider that the most common type of alibi corroboration comes from just such a witnesses. We surely cannot recommend that potential suspects surround themselves with unmotivated witnesses, as this does not mirror real life. We presumably spend most of our time with friends, not strangers. As policy and procedural recommendations may be premature, our best recommendation is to continue research on the various facets of alibi witnesses in order to improve our understanding of the strengths and limitations.

REFERENCES

Allison, M. L. J. (2006). *Biased perceptions of alibis and suspects: An elaboration likelihood model perspective on alibi believability* (University of Victoria, Doctoral dissertation). Available from ProQuest Dissertations and Theses database. (NR 18663)

Burke, T. M., & El-Sibaey, S. (2008, March). *The use and misuse of alibi information in wrongful convictions: A review of case files from the Innocence Project.* Paper presented at the Annual Conference of the American Psychology-Law Society, Jacksonville, Florida.

Burke, T. M., & El-Sibaey, S. (2009, March). *When (truthful) alibi evidence is overlooked in favour of (false) eyewitness evidence: Findings from the Innocence Project Case Files.* Paper presented at the annual meeting of the American Psychology-Law Society, San Antonio, Texas.

Burke, T. M., & Turtle, J. W. (2003). Alibi evidence in criminal investigations and trials: Psychological and legal factors. *The Canadian Journal of Police and Security Services, 1,* 193–200.

Burke, T. M., Turtle, J. W., & Olson, E. (2007). A psychological approach to the study of alibis. In M. Toglia, J. D. Read, D. Ross, & R. C. L. Lindsay (Eds.), *The handbook of eyewitness psychology* (pp. 157–174). Mahwah, NJ: Erlbaum.

Castellow, W. A., Wuensch, K. L., & Moore, C. H. (1990). Effects of physical attractiveness of the plaintiff and defendant in sexual harassment judgments. *Journal of Social Behavior and Personality, 5,* 547–562.

Chaiken, S., & Maheswaran, D. (1994). Heuristic processing can bias systematic processing: Effects of source credibility, argument ambiguity, and task importance on attitude judgment. *Journal of Personality and Social Psychology, 66,* 460–473 doi: 10.1037/0022-3514 .66.3.460

Culhane, S. E. & Hosch, H. M. (2004). An alibi witness's influence on jurors' verdicts. *Journal of Applied Social Psychology, 34.* doi: 1604-1616 10.1111/j.1559-1816 .2004.tb02789.x

Culhane, S. E., Hosch, H. M., & Kehn, A. (2008). Alibi generation: Data from U.S. Hispanics and U.S. non-Hispanic Whites. *Journal of Ethnicity in Criminal Justice, 6,* 177–199. doi:10.1080/15377930802243395

Connors, E. T., Lundregan, T., Miller, N., & McEwen, T. (1996). *Convicted by juries, exonerated by science: Case studies in the use of DNA evidence to establish innocence after trial* (Publication No. NCJ 161258). Washington, DC: U.S. Department of Justice, National Institute of Justice.

Dahl, L. C., Brimacombe, C. A. E., & Lindsay, D. S. (2009). Investigating investigators: How presentation order influences participant–investigators' interpretations of eyewitness identification and alibi evidence. *Law and Human Behavior, 33,* 368–380. doi:10.1007/s10979-008-9151-y

Denov, M. S., & Campbell, K. M. (2005). Criminal injustice. Understanding the causes, effects, and responses to wrongful conviction in Canada. *Journal of Contemporary Criminal Justice, 21,* 224–249. doi:10.1177/1043986205278627

Garrett, B. L. (2008). Judging innocence. *Columbia Law Review, 108,* 55–142. Available at SSRN: http://ssrn.com/abstract=999984

Golding, J. M., Stewart, T. L., Yozwiak, J. A., Djadali, Y., & Sanchez, R. P. (2000). The impact of DNA evidence in a child sexual assault trial. *Child Maltreatment, 5,* 373–383. doi:10.1177/1077559500005004009

Gooderson, R. N. (1977). *Alibi*. London, England: Heinemann Educational.

Heath, W. (2009). Arresting and convicting the innocent: The potential role of an "inappropriate" emotional display in the accused. *Behavioral Sciences & the Law, 27,* 313–332. doi:10.1002/bsl.864

Hosch, H. M., Culhane, S. E., Jolly, K. W., Chavez, R. M., & Shaw, L. H. (2010). Effects of an alibi witness's relationship to the defendant on mock jurors' judgments. *Law and Human Behavior.* Advance online publication.

The Innocence Project in Print (2009). In Their Own Words: Christina Swarns, Director of the criminal justice project, NAACP Legal Defense and Educational Fund. Benjamin N. Cardozo School of Law, Yeshiva University. Retrieved from http://www.innocenceproject.org/Images/2140/ip_summer2009.pdf

Jolly, K. W. (2008). *I'd be helping is we weren't so committed: The application of the investment model to the study of alibis* (Master's thesis). Available from ProQuest Dissertations & Theses database. (UMI No. 1453832)

Kassin, S. M., Goldstein, C. C. & Savitsky, K. (2003). Behavioral confirmation in the interrogation room: On the dangers of presuming guilt. *Law and Human Behavior, 27,* doi: 187-203 10.1023/A:1022599230598

Leo, R. A. (2005). Rethinking the study of miscarriages of justice: Developing a criminology of wrongful conviction. *Journal of Contemporary Criminal Justice, 21,* 201–223. doi:10.1177/1043986205277477

Lindsay, D. S. (2007). Autobiographical memory, eyewitness reports, and public policy. *Canadian Psychology, 48,* 57–66. doi:10.1037/cp2007007

Lindsay, R. C. L., Lim, R., Marando, L., & Cully, D. (1986). Mock-juror evaluations of eyewitness testimony: A test of metamemory hypotheses. *Journal of Applied Social Psychology, 16,* 447–459. doi:10.1111/j.1559-1816.1986.tb01151.x

Lindsay, R. C. L., Ross, D. F., Read, J. D., & Toglia, M. P. (Eds.). (2006). *Handbook of eyewitness memory: Vol. 2. Memory for people.* Mahwah, NJ: Erlbaum.

Loftus, E. F. (1991). Made in memory: Distortions in recollection after misleading information. In G. H. Bower (Ed.), *The psychology of learning and motivation* (pp. 187–215). New York, NY: Academic Press.

McAllister, H., & Bregman, N. J. (1989). Juror underutilization of eyewitness nonidentifications: A test of the disconfirmed expectancy explanation. *Journal of Applied Social Psychology, 19,* 20–29. doi:10.1111/j.1559-1816.1989.tb01218.x

Olson, E. A. (2002). *Where were you last night? Alibi believability and corroborating evidence: A new direction in psychology and law* (Unpublished master's thesis). Iowa State University, Ames, Iowa.

Olson, E. A., & Wells, G.L. (2004). What makes a good alibi? A proposed taxonomy. *Law and Human Behavior, 28,* 157–176. doi: 10.1023/B:LAHU .0000022320. 47112 .d3

Olson, J. M., Roese, N. J., & Zanna, M. P. (1996). Expectancies. In E. T. Higgins & A. W. Kruglanski (Eds.), *Social psychology: Handbook of basic principles* (pp. 211–238). New York, NY: Guilford Press.

Parker, K., Dewees, M., & Radelet, M. (2001). Racial bias and the conviction of the innocent. In S. Westervelt & J. Humphrey (Eds.), *Wrongly convicted: Perspectives on failed justice* (pp. 114–131). New Brunswick, NJ: Rutgers University Press.

Petty, R. E., & Cacioppo, J. T. (1984). The effects of involvement on responses to argument quantity and quality: Central and peripheral routes to persuasion. *Journal of Personality and Social Psychology, 46,* 69–81. doi: 10.1037/0022-3514 .46.1.69

Sargent, M. J., & Bradfield, A. L. (2004). Race and information processing in criminal trials: Does the defendant's race affect how the facts are evaluated? *Personality and Social Psychology Bulletin, 30,* 995–1008. doi:10.1177/0146167204265741

Sommers, S. R., & Douglass, A. B. (2007). Context matters: Alibi strength varies according to evaluator perspective. *Legal and Criminological Psychology, 12,* 41–54. doi: 10.1348 /135532506X114301

Turtle, J. W., & Burke, T. M. (2003, July). *Alibi evidence in criminal investigations and trials: An archival analysis of Canadian and U.S. cases.* Paper presented at the International Psychology-Law Conference, Edinburgh, Scotland.

Wells, G. L. (1984). How adequate is human intuition for judging eyewitness testimony? In G. L. Wells & E. F. Loftus (Eds.), *Eyewitness testimony: Psychological perspectives* (pp. 256–272). New York, NY: Cambridge University Press.

Wells, G. L., Small, M., Penrod, S., Malpass, R. S., Fulero, S. M., & Brimacombe, C. A. E. (1998). Eyewitness identification procedures: Recommendations for lineups and photospreads. *Law and Human Behavior, 22,* 603–647. doi:10.1023/ A:1025750605807

12

PSYCHOLOGICAL PERSPECTIVES ON PROBLEMS WITH FORENSIC SCIENCE EVIDENCE

ITIEL E. DROR AND REBECCA BUCHT

Psychology has, for the most part, been deemed as irrelevant to the work of forensic science, resulting in the neglect of the crucial and central role of the human examiner. Conceptualized as objective and as an exact science, infallible with zero error rates (e.g., Ashbaugh, 1994; Cole, 2005; Evett, 1996; Federal Bureau of Investigation [FBI], 1985), forensic science has failed to properly acknowledge that in many forensic disciplines the human examiner is the instrument of analysis (see Figure 12.1). In such disciplines (e.g., fingerprints, shoe and tire marks, blood stains, ear prints, handwriting, firearms, hair, bite marks), it is up to the human examiner to make judgments and interpretations of visual patterns. The determinations in such disciplines often lack measurements (Dror, 2009a) and are based on a subjective assessment by the human examiner (e.g., "sufficient similarity" between two patterns, usually one collected from the crime scene and the other from a suspect). They pertain even to examinations where part of the analysis is done by instruments, as is

Correspondence concerning this chapter should be addressed to Itiel E. Dror, Institute of Cognitive Neuroscience, Department of Psychology, University College London, London, United Kingdom. E-mail: i.dror@ucl.ac.uk. More information is available at http://www.cci-hq.com

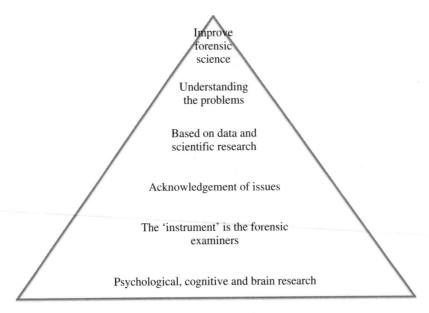

Figure 12.1. The role of psychology in forensic science.

the case with mixed profile, degraded or low copy number DNA analysis, each of which involves subjective judgments that are susceptible to bias.

In this chapter, we examine and evaluate forensic science from psychological perspectives. We show how psychology not only provides important insights into a variety of problems in forensic science but also how psychological issues underpin them. Psychology even offers solutions to many of these problems.

RELEVANCE OF FORENSIC SCIENCE TO CONVICTION OF THE INNOCENT

Forensic science is one of the most powerful and compelling sources of evidence for both conviction and exculpation. Eyewitness testimony and lineup identifications have implicated innocent people, but this type of evidence has been repeatedly exposed as questionable (Loftus, 1975, 1997; see Chapters 5 and 6, this volume). Even confessions have recently been shown to be less reliable than previously assumed (Hasel & Kassin, 2009; see Chapters 1 and 3, this volume). As a result, the role of forensic science evidence has become more important and powerful. It has been endorsed and accepted as unquestionably reliable by the general public, the media (both serious journalism as well as fictional Hollywood crime scene investigation [CSI]), juries, lawyers (for the prosecution and for the defense), and the judges themselves.

Given the incriminating power of forensic science evidence, it is disconcerting that forensic science evidence may have contributed to the conviction of innocent people (Garrett, 2008). Mnookin (2008) suggested that "one of the most significant contributing factors to those wrongful convictions that we know about has been the problematic use of forensic science evidence" (p. 1009). Because ground truth is often unknown, we cannot always be certain that a convicted person is not innocent (or, conversely, that an exonerated person is indeed innocent). At best, we can speculate and estimate the prevalence of wrongful convictions.

Furthermore, exonerations almost always concern serious crimes for which people are sentenced for long periods of time, whereas the vast majority of lesser crimes are rarely subjected to such scrutiny. It may be that these lesser crimes have higher rates of conviction of innocent people because these cases are not put through the same processes and safeguards as the more serious crimes. In the more serious crimes, physical evidence (if it has been collected in the first instance) may have been destroyed or lost, making exonerations practically impossible. When biological material is available, many convicted felons who protest and maintain their innocence lack resources and opportunities to have their cases reexamined. Jurisdictions vary in laws that relate to access to postconviction DNA testing, and even where laws do exist they tend to be very restrictive.

Exoneration data, therefore, are very limited, and the cases available for examination are not a random or representative sample of the falsely convicted. The Innocence Project, which focuses on cases in which biological evidence suitable for DNA analysis is available, estimates that "unvalidated or improper forensic science" played a role in approximately 50% of their exoneration cases (Innocence Project, 2010a). However, even this estimate is problematic, as it is hard to validate (Collins & Jarvis, 2009) and may be only the tip of the iceberg (for reasons specified earlier).

The most problematic and disturbing instances of conviction of the innocent occur in death penalty cases. In the Willingham case, a person who was most probably innocent was convicted of arson and executed. The potentially false conviction of Willingham was largely a result of faulty forensic science and psychological issues that followed from the forensic error (Grann, 2009). A fire at Willingham's home killed his three baby daughters. Fire examiners concluded that the fire was not accidental, based on theories that have since been scientifically disproven. Once forensic evidence "revealed" that arson was involved, the authorities were determined to build a case against Willingham. Although there was no evidence that he abused his children, and his wife told police he would never harm the children, authorities nevertheless claimed that he set fire to the house to cover up his abuse of the children. After concluding that he was most likely guilty according to the faulty forensic science evidence and the motive, witnesses' initial statements were revised and reinterpreted (see Loftus, 1975, for issues that pertain to witness revising and reinterpreting their testimony). For example, an initial statement from an eyewitness that Willingham was devastated, as would be expected in such a situation, was revised to suggest that he was too emotional and behaved like he had something to do with the setting of the fire. This influence and psychological contamination of evidence to conform to supposedly objective and infallible forensic science evidence, along with an inadequate defense at trial, led to his conviction and execution. We will never know with certainty whether Willingham was guilty or innocent, but the case raises questions, concerns, and serious doubts, particularly surrounding the use or misuse of forensic science. The Willingham case is not an isolated incident of concern—more than 130 people on death row have been exonerated in the United States.

In other cases, such as the Drew Whitley case (Innocence Project, 2010b), the problem seems to have been misunderstanding and inappropriate weight being assigned to the forensic evidence. In this case, the victim was shot in a parking lot. The police retrieved from the crime scene a trench coat, hat, and a 12-in. long nylon stocking that the shooter used as a mask. At trial, a crime laboratory technician testified that tiny hairs in the mask were similar to Whitley's hairs but that he could not be certain they were his. The technician also testified that saliva from the mask did not match Whitley's. The prosecutor, however, argued in his closing arguments that the hairs were positively Whitley's. Police also collected Whitley's tennis shoes, which had a drop of blood on them. Whitley told police that his son had bled on his shoes the day before. When serology testing was performed, the blood was found to be type A. Both the victim and Whitley's son had the same type A blood. On the basis of this evidence as well as eyewitness testimony, Whitley was convicted of second degree murder and sentenced to life in prison. Whitley was later exonerated after DNA tests on the hairs excluded him. However, some of the forensic evidence presented in court to which his initial conviction was attributed was in fact more in favor of the defense than the prosecution. In this case, the wrongful conviction relates more to the misinterpretation of forensic evidence in court.

Other cases of wrongful conviction, however, are a direct result of erroneous forensic science, due largely to psychological issues. Take, for example, the case of Cowans. He was wrongfully convicted for shooting a police officer in Massachusetts largely on the basis of an erroneous fingerprint identification, which was later characterized as "an honest mistake" (Saltzman & Daniel, 2004). In another case of erroneous fingerprint identification, the Mayfield case, the error was attributed, at least in part, to confirmation bias (Fine, 2006; Stacey, 2004). The Cowans and Mayfield cases are especially interesting because they involve a widely used and accepted type of forensic evidence: fingerprints. Furthermore, these errors were not detected during verification by another forensic examiner in the laboratory or by forensic experts used by the defense. They all unanimously, but erroneously, concluded identification with absolute certainty. Forensic science errors have therefore not only occurred in the less established forensic disciplines but also they are apparent across forensic domains (Dror & Cole, 2010), including DNA (Thompson, 2006, 2009a, 2009b).

Clearly, there have been numerous cases in which forensic science evidence has led to wrongful convictions; however, there is a limited number of anecdotal cases in which incidental circumstances have allowed for exoneration and for postexoneration assessment of forensic science's role in false convictions. Nevertheless, examining the role of the human examiners in forensic processes can show where such mistakes might originate and reveal the psychological issues involved.

SCIENTIFIC PSYCHOLOGICAL FOUNDATIONS OF FORENSIC SCIENCE EXAMINATIONS

Forensic science is based on facts, on objective physical evidence left at the crime scene. However, the practice of forensic science draws on traditional areas of psychological inquiry, such as perception, cognition, social psychology, personality, decision making, and expertise. When the forensic artifacts interact with the human examiners, who often lack objective measurements, then psychological issues intervene. These issues are relatively prevalent and strong because the forensic community has not sufficiently acknowledged the relevance of psychology and has not taken sufficient steps to address these issues. For example, self-fulfilling prophecies illustrate how what we want, or what we think will happen, influences what we actually perceive and how we interpret information. If we are thirsty, we are more likely to perceive images as containing characteristics of water; thus, our states of thirst modulate our perception (Changizi & Hall, 2001). Our emotional state and mood likewise influence how we interpret information (Byrne & Eysenck, 1993; Halberstadt, Niedenthal, & Kushner, 1995; Niedenthal, Halberstadt, Margolin, & Innes-Ker, 2000).

Bottom-up and top-down processes (e.g., Humphreys, Riddoch, & Price, 1997) are relevant to forensic science testing. Bottom-up processing is data driven. The incoming information from the external environment guides the processing mechanisms and the interpretation of information. These types of processes are relatively passive and are dependent on the input itself. In contrast, top-down processing depends more on the human processor (forensic examiners in this case) and less on the data being processed: The processor's state of mind and the information already contained in the system drive the processes. Every cognitive process, such as learning, thinking, identifying, comparing, matching, decision making, and problem solving, involves some level of top-down processing. It is not a matter of choice or even a conscious process, but it is the nature of human cognition.

The dynamic nature of cognition and how the mind works is a clear characteristic of adaptive and intelligent systems. In fact, as we get more experienced and become real experts, top-down processes play a greater role in how we process information (Dror, 2011). Top-down processing plays a significant role in forensic work; the forensic evidence is factual, but it is up to the human forensic examiners to make sense of it and that is where psychology is critical:

> Wherever he steps, whatever he touches, whatever he leaves, even unconsciously, will serve as silent evidence against him. Not only his fingerprints or his footprints, but his hair, the fibers from his clothes, the glass he breaks, the tool mark he leaves, the paint he scratches, the blood or semen he deposits or collects—all these and more bear mute witness against him. This is evidence that does not forget. It is not confused by the excitement of the moment. It is not absent because human witnesses are. It is factual evidence. Physical evidence cannot be wrong; it cannot perjure itself; it cannot be wholly absent. *Only its interpretation can err. Only human failure to find it, study and understand it, can diminish its value* [emphasis added]. (Kirk, 1953, p. 4)

SCIENTIFIC METHODS USED IN PSYCHOLOGICAL RESEARCH ON FORENSIC SCIENCE EVALUATIONS

Forensic science lends itself well to well-established and classical scientific methods used in psychological research. Experimental studies and research designs that examine performance under different conditions are very applicable to forensic science. These methods can be used to compare the performance between different examiners, but they also permit a more robust within-subject experimental design where performance of the same persons may be compared to themselves under different conditions. In such an experimental design the participants act as their own control.

For example, in two separate studies (Dror & Charlton, 2006; Dror, Charlton, & Péron, 2006), forensic fingerprint examiners were to take part in a study while conducting ordinary criminal case work. The examiners were given fingerprints that they themselves examined years ago in real criminal cases; however, this time the fingerprints were now re-presented to the examiners within a different extraneous context. Many examiners changed their decisions; when the same forensic evidence was presented within different contextual information, they reached opposite conclusions (see Dror & Rosenthal, 2008; Dror & Cole, 2010, for a review and summary).

With these scientific methods, long and extensively used in psychology, researchers can examine how different top-down information may influence how forensic examiners perceive and interpret forensic evidence. Behavioral data from experimental studies can then be complemented by other research tools and methodologies, such as eye tracking.

RELEVANT PSYCHOLOGICAL RESEARCH ON FORENSIC SCIENCE EVALUATIONS

The forensic science process can often be characterized as occurring in three phases. First, there is the identification and collection of evidence from the crime scene, and then decisions are made concerning which items to submit for further examination. During this first phase, a great deal of screening occurs, and only a very small fraction of the available information ever gets to the next phase. Crime scenes and circumstances vary greatly, and the processes and actions by the crime scene investigator (CSI) rely heavily on the subjective judgments, training, experience, and personal abilities of the specific CSI at the crime scene.

Many forensic errors may occur at this initial stage, for example, losing evidence, accidentally contaminating or destroying evidence, failing to collect and preserve evidence properly, and incorrectly judging evidence as unsuitable for further examination. When such errors occur, crucial exonerating evidence may never be used in an investigation, and this can lead to conviction of the innocent. This can occur directly when a piece of evidence that excludes a suspect is absent, or it can occur indirectly when this piece of evidence incriminates the real perpetrator. This critical initial phase of forensic work has been the subject of very little research.

The second phase of forensic work is the examination of the evidence in the laboratory. The role of technology and instrumentation in this part of the process depends on the type of evidence being examined and the questions that the examination seeks to answer. The forensic examiner must make decisions that concern the methods to be used and the sequence in which the methods are to be used. Even with routine examinations that are highly standardized, someone still has to evaluate the case and ascertain the suitability for conducting such routine examination. Many forensic domains, even the most widely used and reliable (e.g., DNA, fingerprinting), require the human examiner to play critical roles. For example, mixture DNA requires the analyst to make judgments that concern whether certain parts in the electropherogram are signals or just noise. Latent fingerprinting often requires the examiner to identify and designate minutia for the Automated Fingerprint Identification System (AFIS), and then AFIS only provides suggested matches for the human examiner to consider (Dror & Mnookin, 2010).

The third and final part of the process is the interpretation of the results of the forensic examination and the contextualization of those results to the case in question. In this phase, not only does the forensic expert have to evaluate and interpret the result of the examination but also the result needs to be communicated to the end user and understood in the context of the specific case at hand. The potential impact of forensic evidence on the investigative process, its influence on (and perhaps contamination of) other evidence, and its effect on pretrial negotiations should not be underestimated.

The involvement of forensic experts in these three phases varies by jurisdiction. The backgrounds and training of those who process crime scenes vary, as does their involvement in the decision of which items should be sent for examination. There are also differences in the degree to which forensic examiners themselves are involved in the contextualization of the forensic evidence in the investigative process, in the pretrial preparation, and in the presentation of the evidence in court. In current research and much of this chapter the focus is on the second phase, the laboratory examination; however, this laboratory work is no more important than the other two phases. For example, the examination of evidence and interpretation of results are wholly dependent on what items are made available for analysis. Even the most careful examination and interpretation cannot make up for evidence not having been identified, correctly collected, and submitted, and the best laboratory results are useless unless they can be properly communicated to the end user.

Forensic Science Sources of Errors

Forensic science–related errors (leading to wrongful conviction or not) can originate from different sources and can be attributed to different causes and factors. In this section, we specify some of these sources.

Bogus Forensic Experts

There have been a number of cases in which people intentionally and fraudulently presented themselves as forensic experts. These people had no background, training, qualification, or education in forensic science, but nevertheless they appeared in court under the false pretense of being forensic experts. Such fraudulent behavior has resulted in erroneous forensic evidence presented in court and wrongful conviction. Take, for example, a man in the United Kingdom, Gene Morrison, who appeared as a qualified forensic expert in hundreds of cases over 20 years. His alleged qualifications included a bachelor of science degree in forensic science, a master's degree in forensic investigation, and a doctorate in criminology, all from a U.S. university. However, these degrees were obtained over the Internet from a fictitious university (Bradshaw, 2008). He was convicted on various counts of deception, perjury, and perverting the course of justice, and he was sentenced to 5 years in prison.

Unqualified Forensic Examiners

Genuine forensic examiners may lack appropriate training and qualification to carry out certain forensic work. When forensic evidence is provided by examiners who lack the needed expertise, errors may be introduced and lead to wrongful convictions. Forensic examiners in most countries (including the United States and the United Kingdom) are not even licensed. In the United States, as in many countries, there is no accepted standard for training or for continuing education, there is no mandatory testing, and there are neither robust performance standards nor effective oversight (National Academy of Sciences, 2009).

Corruption and Fraud

Genuine and qualified forensic examiners may intentionally sabotage the forensic science process by compromising or contaminating the crime scene, by falsifying or fabricating forensic evidence or examination results, and by misrepresenting their findings. Most such cases arise either from being sure the suspect is guilty but lacking evidence to prove it or from personal motivation to enhance their own reputation and advance their careers (Wertheim, 2008).

The contribution of such factors to wrongful conviction is clear, but how prevalent are such cases? And more important to ask, what percentage of forensic-based wrongful convictions can be attributed to such factors? Wrongful convictions due to malicious, incompetent, and careless forensic work do occur but more important and interesting from a psychological perspective are systemic failures in forensic science evidence that can lead to wrongful convictions, beyond the "bad apples" (Thompson, 2009b).

Exaggerated and Unsupported Statements

Forensic science evidence is often misperceived as being more powerful and valuable than it really is (McQuiston-Surrett & Saks, 2009). This misperception distorts forensic science evidence in the courtroom and can cause the evidence to be more convincing than it ought to be and thus sway the verdict. The misperception is a result of the providers and of the receivers of forensic evidence. The providers, the forensic examiners themselves, often appear in court overstating their conclusions and sometimes making unsupported statements. For example, fingerprint examiners may state that they can confidently "individualize," that is, attribute the latent fingerprint mark from a crime scene to a particular individual, to the exclusion of all others in the world (Barnes, in press). Such claims, however, are exaggerated, overstated, and not supported by research data (NAS, 2009). One study revealed that 60% of the cases of wrongful conviction of people in the Innocence Project included forensic expert testimony with conclusions that mischaracterized empirical data, sometimes even wholly unsupported by the empirical data (Garrett & Neufeld, 2009). Mischaracterizations of forensic science evidence can also occur during pretrial negotiations, where there are even fewer checks and balances because there is no judge or jury involved (and the vast majority of cases are settled in such plea bargain negotiations).

The receivers of forensic evidence in the court—whether they are juries, lawyers, or the judges—also contribute to the exaggeration of forensic evidence. Forensic science has been unrealistically portrayed by Hollywood depictions of CSI. This has caused many to misconceptualize and misunderstand the true powers and limitation of forensic evidence—a phenomenon that has been termed the "CSI effect" (Houck, 2006; Schweitzer & Saks, 2007). Furthermore, jurors considered experts' willingness to draw firm conclusions and their abilities to convey technical information nontechnically as more important in determining the experts' credibility than the experts' actual qualifications (Shuman, Whitaker, & Champagne, 1994).

Often, defense lawyers accept the overstated claims made by forensic examiners, without proper cross-examinations or questioning of their forensic conclusions. Opposing counsel scrutiny of forensic experts centers on their qualifications but too often neglects to examine whether they applied science correctly, the results are properly contextualized, and potentially biasing extraneous information and influences were present during the forensic examination. Even judges assume that "forensic disciplines are well grounded in scientific methodology and that crime laboratories and forensic practitioners follow proven practices that ensure the validity and reliability of forensic evidence offered in the court" (Edwards, 2010, p. 2). This assumption, however, is mistaken.

Error

Beyond bad apples and misperceived exaggerated forensic evidence, there are forensic errors that are perhaps the most culpable for wrongful convictions of innocent people. The Cowans case (Saltzman & Daniel, 2004), described earlier in the chapter, is an example of such forensic error. The psychological issues and reasons for such errors are discussed later in this chapter, but here we ask, what are the forensic science sources that can contribute to such errors?

Lack of standards, procedures, and agreed terminology clearly contribute to error (Dror, 2009a), as do lack of mandatory training and testing of individuals (NAS, 2009) and regulation of crime laboratories (Giannelli, 2007).

Cross-Contamination of Evidence

Once incriminating evidence such as forensic science evidence is presented, pressure and contamination affect other lines of evidence to conform. This presentation violates evidentiary independence and can cause wrongful convictions. We have described such an effect in the Willingham case (Grann, 2009). Such evidentiary cross-contaminations can also occur when powerful forensic science evidence leads to false confessions (Hasel & Kassin, 2009).

Judicial System

The structure and funding of many judicial systems can contribute to forensic-based wrongful convictions. For example, the adversarial system hinges on comparable resources available to both sides; however, the defense often does not have the same access to funding and forensic expertise as does the prosecution (American Bar Association [ABA], 2004). Forensic evidence, therefore, is hard to challenge. Furthermore, most criminal cases end in plea bargaining (Pastore & Maguire, 2004, see Table 5.17.2004), thereby preventing close examination and scrutiny of the forensic evidence in the court. Finally, defense lawyers as well as judges lack education as to the weakness and limitations of forensic science. This is further exacerbated by the lack of minimal standards of reporting forensic evidence to the court (NAS, 2009). Such standards would "facilitate the ability of lawyers, judges, and jurors to better comprehend the limits of forensic evidence that is offered in a case. Obviously, this is crucially important" (Edwards, 2010, p. 11).

Psychological Issues and Sources of Errors

There are many psychological issues that underpin the problems in forensic science evidence. These issues provide insight into the problems and to their solutions. However, for the most part, the forensic community has neglected to take these psychological issues in hand. Indeed, the National Academy of Sciences (NAS, 2009) report stated that "the extent to which a practitioner in a particular forensic discipline rely on human interpretation that could be tainted by error, [or] the threat of bias . . . [is] significant." (p. 9), and the report further stated that "unfortunately, at least to date, there is no good evidence to indicate that the forensic science community has made a sufficient effort to address the bias issue" (p. 8).

An example that illustrates some of the forensic community's responses to psychological issues is a letter to the editor published by the chair of the International Fingerprint Society (Leadbetter, 2008). It stated that any fingerprint examiner who is susceptible to bias and psychological issues is "an incompetent idiot" (p. 20). In another letter to the editor, the chair of the International Fingerprint Society stated that any examiner who is susceptible to contextual bias or confirmation bias should not be a fingerprint examiner and needs to "seek employment in Disneyland" (Leadbetter, 2007, p. 231).

Social and Motivation

Forensic examiners often work with other examiners, within law enforcement agencies and the adversarial judicial system. This introduces a whole set of psychological issues. NAS recognized these problems and has even recommended "removing all public forensic laboratories and facilities from the administrative control of law enforcement or prosecutors' offices" so as "to improve the scientific bases of forensic science examinations and to maximize independence" (NAS, 2009, p. 24). Indeed, motivation to solve crime related to catching criminals, especially in high profile, serious, or long-running cases, is characteristic of forensic examiners (Charlton, Fraser-Mackenzie, & Dror, 2010). However, separation of forensic scientists from the investigation is not a simple matter (see, Dror, 2009a).

Perception, Judgment, and Decision Making

Many years of psychological research have provided ample evidence and insights into a variety of errors in perception, judgment, and decision making. Hundreds of articles and dozens of books have been written on issues such as *belief perseverance* (Nisbett & Ross, 1980), *confirmation bias* (Nickerson, 1998), *cognitive dissonance* (Festinger, 1957), and *escalation of commitment* (Staw, 1976).

What underpins many of the errors in perception, judgment, and decision making is that the *human mind is not a camera*. It is not passively data driven; it actively and dynamically processes information. By doing so it filters out and ignores much of the information, and it imposes order and certain interpretations. These are guided by the active nature of cognition and not by the information itself that is provided by the real world. As noted earlier in this chapter, psychologists often distinguish between bottom-up and top-down processing; these relate to whether processes are governed by the data itself (i.e., bottom-up) or by the person (i.e., top-down). Human perception, judgment, and decision making are very much top-down oriented. Top-down processing is the foundation of intelligence and enables us to make sense of complex environments, but it can also lead to error. This is especially pronounced in expert domains (Dror, 2011).

The areas of perception, judgment, and decision making in forensic science have only started to receive attention in the past few years. A theoretical review of the issues is available in Risinger, Saks, Thompson, and Rosenthal (2002) and in Dror (2009a); a review of the empirical research is available in Dror and Cole (2010). Although there are conflicting findings, research shows that bias exists in forensic science, even though it does not necessarily have the power to determine the final decision outcome.

Research using within-subject experimental design is most telling because it compares the judgments of the same experts on the same information at two different times. Indeed, research has presented fingerprints to forensic experts within extraneous contextual information that was intended to see if this would bias their decisions. Most important is that unknowing to the examiners, they were actually presented with prints they have judged previously in real criminal cases. Furthermore, the study was covert, taking place under the pretense of normal everyday casework. As noted earlier in this chapter, two such studies demonstrated that the extraneous contextual information biased the forensic experts and affected their decision outcomes. Many of them reach different and conflicting decisions to those they themselves reached in the past based on the same identical fingerprints (see the summary and meta-analysis of these studies in Dror & Rosenthal, 2008).

Other studies showed effects on bias but not on decision outcomes. These studies, however, were not under the disguise of routine casework, and for contextual information to have full impact participants must truly believe it (see Dror & Cole, 2010). When participants know they are taking part in a study, the contrived set up and artificial context diminish the biasing effects (see, e.g., the studies by Hall & Player, 2008; Kerstholt et al., 2010; Kerstholt, Paashuis, & Sjerps, 2007; Langenburg, Champod, & Wertheim, 2009; Schiffer & Champod, 2007; Wertheim, Langenburg, & Moenssens, 2006). Furthermore, much of the research in this area is not carried out by psychologists but by forensically trained examiners, working in forensic laboratories, studying themselves. This leads to major concerns about the integrity of the research (Risinger & Saks, 2003), as well as issues that pertain to proper experimental design and analysis (see, e.g., the Hall & Player, 2008, study, which contains numerous faults; Dror, 2009b; Saks, 2009).

The forensic science community has been resistant to acknowledging that psychological influences affect their work and may cause error. This is due, in part, to the long held belief that forensics is an exact science, infallible, with zero error rates (e.g., Ashbaugh, 1994; Cole, 2005; Evett, 1996; FBI, 1985). Furthermore, scientific and research environments are in contrast to the forensic science working environment within the adversarial judicial system. The resistance within the forensic science community and the contrasting non-scientific environments in which forensic examiners work have served as obstacles to conducting proper scientific studies into the psychology of forensic examination. This resistance, however, is beginning to change. High profile and public erroneous forensic identifications by the best laboratories (e.g., the FBI) in highly established and widely used forensic disciplines (e.g., fingerprinting), combined with the NAS (2009) report on forensic science, have opened up this area for research. With the growing psychological led research in this area, we can start to develop remedies to some of the biases that affect forensic science judgment.

APPLICATION OF PSYCHOLOGICAL RESEARCH ON FORENSIC SCIENCE

Problems in forensic science can be addressed in a number of ways. Remedies must be based on proper research and data with a clear understanding of psychology and cognition, while taking into account the pragmatics and realities of forensic laboratories. In this section, we illustrate some potential psychologically based remedies to judgment bias.

Cognitive Profiles

> Different professions require different abilities. This is obvious when one considers what distinguishes accountants from interior decorators, but the observation applies to all specialized professions . . . special abilities enable people to excel in occupations that depend critically on specific mental processes. (Dror, Kosslyn, & Waag, 1993, p. 763)

Surely, different forensic disciplines rely on specific cognitive abilities. Examining and characterizing the cognitive profiles of different forensic expertise will facilitate selection of the right people to these professions, allowing the profession to achieve the highest levels of performance. At press time, there is no scientific understanding or characterization of these abilities, and selection during recruitment is far from optimal.

Training

Training and education on psychological issues, and specifically about bias, are not widely available. The few that are available are offered predominantly by forensic examiners who have little to no understanding of the human cognitive system. Training in these areas must be properly developed and delivered by people with the relevant expertise.

Best Practices

Certain procedures can help control a variety of psychologically based problems. For example, sequential unmasking (Krane et al., 2008, 2009a, 2009b) of information minimizes contextual influences (Dror, 2009a) and follows the principles of "keep the processes of data collection and analysis as blind as possible for as long as possible" (Rosenthal, 1978, p. 1007).

Verification can also be an important tool in minimizing errors. However, forensic errors, such as the errors discovered in the Cowans and Mayfield cases, have not been detected by verification, the quality control measure in which another examiner checks the work of the initial examiner so as to capture errors. A reason for this failure may be the way verifications are carried out, specifically in regard to the failure to conduct them blindly. Psychologists have a long understanding and experience in how to conduct blind examinations and can suggest ways to implement them in forensic science (Dror, 2009a).

Technology

The growing use of technology in forensic science opens new opportunities, both in terms of efficiency and quality of work. However, forensic technology has its limits (don't be fooled by the unrealistic Hollywood depictions) and can introduce new problems, some of which may lead to erroneous identification and wrongful convictions (Dror & Mnookin, 2010). For example, the use of automated fingerprint identification systems (AFIS) that searches huge databases of fingerprints is likely to provide look-alike nonmatch prints that are more susceptible to error. Another example is that the format in which AFIS provides information may bias the cognitive process of the human examiner (Dror & Mnookin, 2010). This has now been empirically demonstrated in a data collection of 55,200 forensic decisions that showed how the human fingerprint examiners are affected and biased from this technology (Dror, Wertheim, Fraser-Mackenzie, & Walajtys, in press). How to best distribute cognition between the human examiners and technology is a key to fruitful collaboration (Dror & Harnad, 2008).

CONCLUSION

The role of forensic science evidence in wrongful conviction raises pertinent and difficult questions about some of the most powerful incriminating and exculpatory evidence in the judicial system. The issues are complex, but it is clear that psychology is an integral part of forensic science work. This pertains to how forensic evidence is selected at the crime scene; how it is perceived and evaluated; the processes and biases that may affect how decisions are reached, as well as how forensic evidence is presented in court; and how it is perceived by the lawyers, juries, and judges.

With a greater psychological understanding of the issues involved in the different aspects of forensic science, research and data-based remedies can be developed to minimize errors in forensic decision making and use forensic evidence in the most proper and efficient manner. We hope to see and anticipate such developments in the coming years.

REFERENCES

American Bar Association. (2004). *Gideon's broken promise: America's continuing quest for equal justice. A report on the American Bar Association's hearings on the Right to Counsel in Criminal Proceedings*. Washington, DC: American Bar Association Press. Retrieved from http://www.abanet.org/legalservices/sclaid/defender/brokenpromise/fullreport.pdf

Ashbaugh, D. R. (1994). The premise of friction ridge identification, clarity, and the identification process. *Journal of Forensic Identification, 44*, 499–516.

Barnes, J. G. (in press). History. In *The fingerprint sourcebook*. Washington, DC: NIJ Press.

Bradshaw, S. (2008, February 3). How to fake a living. *The Sunday Times*. Retrieved from http://www.timesonline.co.uk/tol/news/uk/crime/article3277057.ece

Byrne, A., & Eysenck, M. W. (1993). Individual differences in positive and negative interpretive biases. *Personality and Individual Differences, 14*, 849–851. doi:10.1016/0191-8869(93)90100-H

Changizi, M. A., & Hall, W. G. (2001). Thirst modulates a perception. *Perception, 30*, 1489–1497. doi:10.1068/p3266

Charlton, D., Fraser-Mackenzie, P., & Dror, I. E. (2010). Emotional experiences and motivating factors associated with fingerprint analysis. *Journal of Forensic Sciences, 55*, 385–393. doi:10.1111/j.1556-4029.2009.01295.x

Cole, S. A. (2005). More than zero: Accounting for error in latent fingerprint identification. *The Journal of Criminal Law & Criminology, 95*, 985–1078.

Collins, J. M., & Jarvis, J. (2009). The wrongful conviction of forensic science. *Forensic Science Policy & Management, 1*, 17–31. doi:10.1080/19409040802624067

Dror, I. E. (2011). The paradox of human expertise: Why experts can get it wrong. In N. Kapur, A. Pascual-Leone, T. Manly, & J. Cole (Eds.), *The paradoxical brain* (pp. 177–188). Cambridge, England: Cambridge University Press.

Dror, I. E. (2009a). How can Francis Bacon help forensic science? The four idols of human biases. *Jurimetrics: The Journal of Law, Science, and Technology, 50*, 93–110.

Dror, I. E. (2009b). On proper research and understanding of the interplay between bias and decision outcomes. *Forensic Science International, 191*, e17–e18. doi:10.1016/j.forsciint.2009.03.012251658240

Dror, I. E., & Charlton, D. (2006). Why experts make errors. *Journal of Forensic Identification, 56,* 600–616.

Dror, I. E., Charlton, D., & Péron, A. E. (2006). Contextual information renders experts vulnerable to make erroneous identifications. *Forensic Science International, 156,* 74–78. doi:10.1016/j.forsciint.2005.10.017

Dror, I. E., & Cole, S. (2010). The vision in "blind" justice: Expert perception, judgment, and visual cognition in forensic pattern recognition. *Psychonomic Bulletin & Review, 17,* 161–167. doi:10.3758/PBR.17.2.161

Dror, I. E., & Harnad, S. (2008). Offloading cognition onto cognitive technology. In I. E. Dror & S. Harnad (Eds.), *Cognition distributed: How cognitive technology extends our minds* (pp. 1–23). Amsterdam, the Netherlands: John Benjamins.

Dror, I. E., Kosslyn, S. M., & Waag, W. (1993). Visual-spatial abilities of pilots. *Journal of Applied Psychology, 78,* 763–773. doi:10.1037/0021-9010.78.5.763

Dror, I. E., & Mnookin, J. L. (2010). The use of technology in human expert domains: Challenges and risks arising from the use of automated fingerprint identification systems in forensics. *Law Probability and Risk, 9,* 47–67. doi:10.1093/lpr/mgp031

Dror, I. E., & Rosenthal, R. (2008). Meta-analytically quantifying the reliability and biasability of fingerprint experts' decision making. *Journal of Forensic Sciences, 53,* 900–903. doi:10.1111/j.1556-4029.2008.00762.x

Dror, I. E., Wertheim, K., Fraser-Mackenzie, P., & Walajtys, J. (in press). The impact of human-technology cooperation and distributed cognition in forensic science: Biasing effects of AFIS contextual information on human experts. *Journal of Forensic Sciences.*

Edwards, H. T. (2010, May 6). *The National Academy of Sciences report on forensic sciences: What it means for the bench and bar.* Presentation at the Conference on the Role of the Court in an Age of Developing Science and Technology, Washington, DC. Retrieved from http://www.cadc.uscourts.gov/internet/home.nsf/content/VL+-+Judge+-+HTE

Evett, I. W. (1996). Expert evidence and forensic misconceptions of the nature of exact science. *Science & Justice, 36,* 118–122. doi:10.1016/S1355-0306(96)72576-5251658240

Federal Bureau of Investigation. (1985). *The science of fingerprints: Classification and uses.* Washington, DC: U.S. Government Printing Office.

Festinger, L. (1957). *A theory of cognitive dissonance.* Stanford, CA: Stanford University Press.

Fine, G. A. (2006). *A Review of the FBI's handling of the Brandon Mayfield Case.* Washington, DC: U.S. Department of Justice Office of the Inspector General.

Garrett, B. L. (2008). Judging innocence. *Columbia Law Review, 108,* 55–142.

Garrett, B. L., & Neufeld, P. J. (2009). Invalid forensic science testimony and wrongful convictions. *Virginia Law Review, 95,* 1–97.

Giannelli, P. C. (2007). Wrongful convictions and forensic science: The need to regulate crime labs. *North Carolina Law Review, 86,* 163–236.

Grann, D. (2009, September 7). Trial by fire: Did Texas execute an innocent man? *The New Yorker, 7*, 1–17.

Halberstadt, J. B., Niedenthal, P. M., & Kushner, J. (1995). Resolution of lexical ambiguity by emotional state. *Psychological Science, 6*, 278–282. doi:10.1111/j.1467-9280.1995.tb00511.x

Hall, L. J., & Player, E. (2008). Will the instruction of an emotional context affect fingerprint analysis and decision making? *Forensic Science International, 181*, 36–39. doi:10.1016/j.forsciint.2008.08.008251658240

Hasel, L. E., & Kassin, S. M. (2009). On the presumption of evidentiary independence. *Psychological Science, 20*, 122–126. doi:10.1111/j.1467-9280.2008.02262.x

Houck, M. M. (2006). CSI: The reality. *Scientific American, 295*, 84–99. doi:10.1038/scientificamerican0706-84

Humphreys, G. W., Riddoch, M. J., & Price, C. J. (1997). Top-down processes in object identification: Evidence from experimental psychology, neuropsychology, and functional anatomy. *Philosophical Transactions of the Royal Society of London, 352*, 1275–1282. doi:10.1098/rstb.1997.0110

Innocence Project. (2010a). *Facts on post-conviction DNA exonerations.* Retrieved from http://www.innocenceproject.org/Content/Facts_on_PostConviction_DNA_Exonerations.php

Innocence Project. (2010b). *Drew Whitley.* Retrieved from http://www.innocenceproject.org/Content/292.php

Kerstholt, J., Eikelboom, A., Dijkman, T., Stoel, R., Hermsen, R., & Leuven, B. (2010). Does suggestive information cause a confirmation bias in bullet comparisons? *Forensic Science International, 198*, 138–142. doi:10.1016/j.forsciint.2010.02.007251658240

Kerstholt, J., Paashuis, R., & Sjerps, M. (2007). Shoe print examinations: Effects of expectation, complexity and experience. *Forensic Science International, 165*, 30–34. doi:10.1016/j.forsciint.2006.02.039251658240

Kirk, P. (1953). *Crime investigation.* Ontario, Canada: John Wiley & Sons Canada.

Krane, D., Ford, S., Gilder, J., Inman, J., Jamieson, A., Koppl, R., . . . Thompson, J. D. (2008). Sequential unmasking: A means of minimizing observer effects in forensic DNA interpretation. *Journal of Forensic Sciences, 53*, 1006–1007. doi:10.1111/j.1556-4029.2008.00787.x

Krane, D., Ford, S., Gilder, J., Inman, J., Jamieson, A., Koppl, R., . . . Thompson, J. D. (2009a). Authors' response. *Journal of Forensic Sciences, 54*, 501. doi:10.1111/j.1556-4029.2009.00990.x

Krane, D., Ford, S., Gilder, J., Inman, J., Jamieson, A., Koppl, R., . . . Taylor, B. S. (2009b). Authors' response. *Journal of Forensic Sciences, 54*, 1500–1501. doi:10.1111/j.1556-4029.2009.01192.x

Langenburg, G., Champod, C., & Wertheim, P. (2009). Testing for potential contextual bias effects during the verification stage of the ace-v methodology when conducting fingerprint comparisons. *Journal of Forensic Sciences, 54*, 571–582. doi:10.1111/j.1556-4029.2009.01025.x

Leadbetter, M. (2007). [Letter to the editor]. *Fingerprint Whorld, 33*, 231.

Leadbetter, M. (2008, June 13). Two fingers to research [Letter to the editor]. *Police Review, 20*.

Loftus, E. F. (1975). Leading questions and the eyewitness report. *Cognitive Psychology, 7*, 560–572. doi:10.1016/0010-0285(75)90023-7

Loftus, E. F. (1997). Creating false memories. *Scientific American, 277*, 70–75. doi:10.1038/scientificamerican0997-70

McQuiston-Surrett, D., & Saks, M. J. (2009). The testimony of forensic identification science: What expert witnesses say and what factfinders hear. *Law and Human Behavior, 33*, 436–453. doi:10.1007/s10979-008-9169-1

Mnookin, J. (2008). Experts and forensic evidence. *Southwestern University Law Review, 37*, 1009–1025.

National Academy of Sciences. (2009). *Strengthening forensic science in the United States: A path forward*. Washington, DC: Author.

Nickerson, R. S. (1998). Confirmation bias: A ubiquitous phenomenon in many guises. *Review of General Psychology, 2*, 175–220. doi:10.1037/1089-2680.2.2.175

Niedenthal, P. M., Halberstadt, J. B., Margolin, J., & Innes-Ker, A. H. (2000). Emotional state and the detection of change in facial expression of emotion. *European Journal of Social Psychology, 30*, 211–222. doi:10.1002/(SICI)1099-0992 (200003/04)30:2<211::AID-EJSP988>3.0.CO;2-3

Nisbett, R. E., & Ross, L. D. (1980). *Human inference: Strategies and shortcomings of social judgment*. Englewood Cliffs, NJ: Prentice-Hall.

Pastore, A. L., & Maguire, K. (2004). Utilization of criminal justice statistics project, sourcebook of *Criminal Justice Statistics Online*. Retrieved from http://www.albany.edu/sourcebook/; see Table 5.17.2004, retrieved from http://www.albany.edu/sourcebook/pdf/t5172004.pdf

Risinger, D. M., & Saks, M. J. (2003). Rationality, research and leviathan: law enforcement-sponsored research and the criminal process. *Michigan State Law Review, 4*, 1023–1050.

Risinger, D. M., Saks, M. J., Thompson, W. C., & Rosenthal, R. (2002). The *Daubert/Kumho* implications of observer effects in forensic science: Hidden problems of expectation and suggestion. *California Law Review, 90*, 1–56. doi:10.2307/3481305

Rosenthal, R. (1978). How often are our numbers wrong? *American Psychologist, 33*, 1005–1008. doi:10.1037/0003-066X.33.11.1005

Saks, M. (2009). Concerning L.J. Hall, E. Player, "Will the introduction of an emotional context affect fingerprint analysis and decision-making?" *Forensic Science International, 191*, e19. doi:10.1016/j.forsciint.2009.06.011

Saltzman, J., & Daniel, M. (2004, January 24). Man freed in 1997 shooting of officer: Judge gives ruling after fingerprint revelation. *Boston Globe*. Retrieved from http://www.boston.com/news/local/articles/2004/01/24/man_freed_in_1997_shooting_of_officer/

Schiffer, B., & Champod, C. (2007). The potential (negative) influence of observational biases at the analysis stage of fingermark individualisation. *Forensic Science International, 167,* 116–120. doi:10.1016/j.forsciint.2006.06.036251658240

Schweitzer, N. J., & Saks, M. J. (2007). The CSI Effect: Popular fiction about forensic science affects public expectations about real forensic science. *Jurimetrics: The Journal of Law, Science, and Technology, 47,* 357–364.

Shuman, D., Whitaker, E., & Champagne, A. (1994). An empirical examination of the use of expert witnesses in the courts–Part ii: A three city study. *Jurimetrics: The Journal of Law, Science, and Technology, 34,* 193–201.

Stacey, R. B. (2004). Report on the erroneous fingerprint individualization bombing case. *Journal of Forensic Identification, 54,* 706–718.

Staw, B. M. (1976). Knee-deep in the big muddy: A study of escalating commitment to a chosen course of action. *Organizational Behavior and Human Performance, 16,* 27–44. doi:10.1016/0030-5073(76)90005-2

Thompson, W. C. (2006). Tarnish on the "gold standard:" Understanding recent problems in forensic DNA testing. *The Champion, 30*(1), 10–16.

Thompson, W. C. (2009a). Beyond bad apples: Analyzing the role of forensic science in wrongful convictions. *Southwestern Law Review, 37,* 1027–1050.

Thompson, W. C. (2009b). Painting the target around the matching profile: The Texas sharpshooter fallacy in forensic DNA interpretation. *Law Probability and Risk, 8,* 257–276. doi:10.1093/lpr/mgp013

Wertheim, K., Langenburg, G., & Moenssens, A. (2006). A report of latent print examiner accuracy during comparison training exercises. *Journal of Forensic Identification, 56,* 55–93.

Wertheim, P. A. (2008). Latent fingerprint evidence: Fabrication, not error. *The Champion, 32,* 16.

V

PERVASIVE ISSUES

13

RACE AND RACISM

ELLEN S. COHN, DONALD BUCOLO, AND SAMUEL R. SOMMERS

Korey Wise was a New York teenager in 1989, the year of the brutal attack of an anonymous woman who would come to be known as the Central Park Jogger. The victim in this crime had been injured so badly that she was left with no memory of the assault. No physical evidence linked Wise to the scene. But investigators almost immediately focused their efforts on five African American youths, including Wise, who were already in police custody for another altercation in the park that night. All five eventually confessed during video-recorded interrogations. All five were convicted. Wise served 11.5 years in prison until DNA evidence and the confession of the actual attacker finally exonerated him.

In fall 1996, Santa Monica, California police ordered Darryl Hicks and George Washington, also both African Americans, out of their car at gunpoint as they pulled into the parking garage of a hotel. They were handcuffed and placed in separate police cars while their vehicle was searched. Police claimed the men were detained because they fit the description of suspects wanted in a string of 19 armed robberies and because one of the men appeared to be "nervous." Washington and Hicks would later sue the police department for false arrest and civil rights violations. In ruling for the two men, the court determined that the armed robberies had not even occurred in Santa Monica and that neither of them even fit the descriptions of the robbers to begin with.

However, for the media attention garnered by the Central Park attack, neither of these miscarriages of justice stand out as particularly remarkable. In both cases—one of false conviction and the other of false arrest—innocent individuals were targeted by investigators for crimes they did not commit. As the various chapters in this book attest, a wide range of factors contribute to such outcomes, including problematic police practices, fallible eyewitnesses, and the misuse of forensic evidence. Although it is possible and even plausible that some of these factors were at play in the two cases just described, the unambiguous common denominator of these incidents is that they both involved Black men. Indeed, analysis of postconviction DNA exonerations indicates that these two cases are more rule than exception: As of 2010, 60% of the wrongful convictions identified by the Innocence Project have involved a Black defendant. As such, the focus of this chapter is to explore the role played by race in the arrest, conviction, and sentencing of individuals charged with criminal offenses and by association to consider the role played by race in the conviction of the innocent.

Race can impact the investigation and prosecution of crimes in many different ways. As just one example, the robust *cross-race bias* (or *other-race effect*) in eyewitness identification indicates the potential for race to contribute to wrongful conviction. This mismatch between the race of a witness and culprit is one way in which race can facilitate wrongful conviction even absent racial animus or prejudice on the part of the individuals involved. Of course, simply because race is implicated in a process that makes conviction of the innocent more likely does not necessarily implicate racism in said process. That said, racism, particularly against Black suspects and defendants, has a long and pervasive history in the United States legal system. In this chapter, we trace the prevalence of racism in the legal arena and assess the circumstances under which such racism is most likely to occur. By doing so, we do not mean to imply that all racial disparities in the system—including those related to wrongful conviction—are attributable to racism. However, given that other chapters in this volume touch on race as it relates to other issues, such as eyewitnesses and at-risk populations, we focus our present analyses on the matter of racism.

Much of this analysis will focus on differences in how the system treats White and Black individuals, as this racial dichotomy has influenced decades of research in the social sciences (Hagan, 1987). At the same time, more recently researchers have argued that the analysis of racism and discrimination in the legal system must be expanded to include members of other minorities, such as Hispanics and Asian Americans (e.g., B. D. Johnson & Betsinger, 2009). Less data exist on this question of other racial and ethnic groups outside of White and Black groups, but when possible, we explore this literature as well (e.g., Reitzel, Rice, & Piquero, 2004).

We examine current theoretical explanations for racial bias and prejudice (e.g., Dovidio & Gaertner, 2004) and examine psychological mechanisms and social conditions that contribute to racism in various legal contexts. We focus on attitudes toward the legal system, issues of racial policing, juror decision making, and racial bias experienced by legal actors (attorneys, court employees, court users). We then review psychological research that demonstrates how racism can be reduced and offer examples of how this research can be applied to the legal system. Finally, we offer conclusions that draw explicit links between the present analysis of racism and this volume's more specific focus on wrongful conviction.

PSYCHOLOGICAL FOUNDATIONS OF RACISM

Researchers who study racism have approached the topic from various theoretical viewpoints. Early research, conducted during the first part of the 20th century, focused on describing racism and measuring its prevalence in society (e.g., Katz & Braly, 1933). During this period, racism and prejudice were thought to be forms of psychopathology by the expression of some abnormal behavior (Dovidio, 2001). Considering racism to be abnormal, researchers investigated root causes for the behavior and focused on individual factors that may contribute to it. Racists were conceived to be a particular subset of society, and researchers presumed that if they could identify these individuals, racism could be rooted out by helping those people with biased beliefs (Dovidio, 2001).

This model of racism changed in the face of the rise of Nazi Germany and the Holocaust. By mid-century, it had become clear that prejudice toward outgroups could be developed and expressed by ordinary citizens. Classic social psychological research studies conducted at this time also revealed how easily individuals altered their behavior when social norms, authorities, or both pressured them to do so. With regard to prejudice, in particular, research indicated that societal hierarchies and competition quickly led to the development of bias, retaliatory behavior, and hatred between two competing groups (Sherif, White, & Harvey, 1955). It was during this time that researchers began to approach the study of prejudice and racism from a different vantage point, suggesting that development and maintenance of prejudice occurred naturally through social and cognitive processes.

In Allport's (1954) seminal text, *The Nature of Prejudice*, he argued that human beings have a natural tendency to form groups, favor members of groups to which they belong (i.e., ingroups), and dislike and compete against individuals from other groups (i.e., outgroups). Such divisions had serious consequences—individuals' attitudes, beliefs, and interactions with members of outgroups ("them") were reported to be considerably less positive than with ingroup members ("us"). Given that race is one of the first features individuals notice when perceiving other people (see Ito & Urland, 2003), it follows that prejudice toward members of another race—or racism—can result from normal cognitive processing. Allport (1954) also argued that racism was maintained and encouraged through societal structure, such as segregation in the American South, which separated the races and encouraged detrimental treatment of the outgroup, as less contact between the races led to misunderstandings of traditions, cultural values, and beliefs. These observations had a great impact on the study of prejudice, and Allport's research is considered the foundation of modern day approaches to understanding and reducing prejudice.

In more recent times, researchers have built on Allport's work by acknowledging the effects that societal norms and socialization have on racism, but they have also found that racism can take different forms and be expressed in different ways in different circumstances (e.g., Dovidio, Kawakami, & Beach, 2002). Modern day racism theories have grown out of the changing racial landscape of the United States (and, to a lesser extent, other societies). Following the Civil Rights Movement and into today, blatant racism is no longer socially acceptable in most circles. Whites report more positive attitudes in regard to Blacks, view racial integration more favorably, and report fewer negative stereotypes in regard to Blacks than they used to. However, even in the 21st century, Black individuals continue to suffer disadvantages in health care, employment, and other domains that can be linked to processes of racism (Pearson, Dovidio, & Gaertner, 2009). Contemporary theorists suggest that many individuals hold two separate but influential forms of prejudice: *implicit prejudice* (i.e., an unconscious, automatic reaction to outgroup members) and *explicit prejudice* (i.e., a cognizant, openly reported prejudiced toward outgroup members; e.g., Dovidio, Kawakami, Johnson, Johnson, & Howard, 1997; Lepore & Brown, 1997).

To explain how these forms of prejudice affect Whites' reactions to Blacks, Dovidio and Gaertner (2004) proposed a theory of *aversive racism*. According to the theory, White individuals are socialized to believe that racism and discrimination are wrong, so they openly report explicit attitudes congruent with this racial egalitarianism. However, society still reinforces and maintains negative stereotypes regarding Black individuals (Devine & Elliot, 1995). Although Whites who report they are not prejudiced reject blatant racist ideology, they still typically have knowledge of negative stereotypes in regard to Blacks, which fosters a feeling of uneasiness and discomfort toward Black persons (Dovidio & Gaertner, 2008).

Thus, White aversive racists do not openly endorse negative stereotypes about Black people, but they do report implicit attitudes congruent with these stereotypes, which can unknowingly affect their behavior (for a review, see Dovidio, Kawakami, & Beach, 2002). For instance, Dovidio et al. (1997) conducted a study in which respondents had to report both their explicit racism by using self-report surveys, as well as implicit racism by using a reaction-time task. Although self-report measures of racism predicted White individuals' observable behavior in an interracial interaction, implicit attitudes predicted their nonverbal behavior toward a Black confederate. White people with more negative implicit attitudes toward Black people appeared more uncomfortable, made less eye contact, and were rated as being less friendly overall by an independent observer.

Although White aversive racists are prepared to react in socially desirable ways to situations in which their actions could be construed as prejudiced, they often defer to stereotypical beliefs expressed in subtle and discreet ways in situations where their actions will not seem influenced by race (Dovidio & Gaertner, 2004). White aversive racists are also more likely to express biased beliefs about Black persons when social norms in regard to the task are ambiguous. For instance, Dovidio and Gaertner (2000) reported that prejudice toward a Black candidate was only expressed by White individuals when the candidate's qualifications for the position were not clear. When both a White and Black candidate had strong (or weak) qualifications for a job, racism was not expressed. Racism toward Blacks is also more likely to be exhibited in situations where Whites' behavior can be rationalized, with Whites claiming their racist decisions were based on other factors and not race (Hodson, Hooper, Dovidio, & Gaertner, 2005).

Aversive racism theory suggests that racism toward Black individuals in the modern legal system should take different forms depending on the specific context. Thus, implicit racism toward Black individuals may occur in situations in which actors in the legal system must make quick decisions, and therefore may be forced to rely on their knowledge of negative stereotypes about Blacks, causing them to react in a racist manner. Because individuals who are prejudiced understand that blatant expressions of racism are not socially appropriate, overt displays of racism toward Blacks should be most likely in situations in which there are no social norms in the environment or in which factors besides race can be used to justify an action or decision.

SCIENTIFIC METHODS USED IN RACISM RESEARCH

A number of methodologies have been used to study racism in the legal system. In this section, we discuss and give examples of these methodologies, including archival analyses of justice data, public opinion polls, experiments using mock jurors, and self-report data in regard to legal experiences and perceptions. As with any type of research, each of the methods reviewed here has limitations. Researchers and research programs therefore benefit from striving to converge empirical conclusions arrived at through studies using a range of methodologies.

Secondary Analyses

These studies reexamine existing data sets to investigate whether race makes a difference in such areas as police profiling, sentencing, and the death penalty. These studies take one of two approaches. Either they reanalyze an existing data set or data from an existing study or they conduct a meta-analysis that combines data across several existing studies. For example, Baldus, Pulaski, and Woodworth (1983) examined 2,000 murder cases in Georgia over the span of 5 years and found that Black individuals were disproportionately sentenced to death when the victim was White, controlling for 230 race-neutral variables such as prior convictions. Their analysis found that among defendants who killed a White victim, Black defendants were 4.2 times more likely than White defendants to be sentenced to death. Regardless of race of the victim, Black defendants in were 1.1 times more likely than White defendants to be sentenced to death. Similar analyses of death penalty cases from other states have found that in controlling for other characteristics, Black defendants (compared with White defendants) who kill White victims are disproportionately likely to be sentenced to death (e.g., Bowers, 1984).

The major limitation of any kind of reanalysis of existing data is that the current researchers have no control over methodological issues, including the selection of participants, measures, manipulations (if relevant), and dependent measures. For example, two studies described in more detail later in this chapter (Bucolo, 2007; Singer, 2004) were reanalyses of data collected by the first circuit federal court. A major limitation of the findings has to do with sample selection. Each of the three samples of participants (attorneys, court employees, and court users) was selected differently. The attorney sample included all female attorneys in the First Circuit and a subset of male attorneys because only 20% of the attorneys were female. The employee sample included the whole population of court employees. The court users were a nonrandom sample of people coming out of the federal courthouses in the first circuit. This means that the sample included couriers who were just in the courthouse to deliver packages as well as witnesses in cases. Further, trying to make causal statements regarding preexisting data sets can also be difficult. Numerous potential confounds can affect the results of any case, and even controlling for multiple covariates cannot eliminate the possibility that there are other factors besides race that can account for racial differences found in these archival analyses.

Public Opinion Polls

A variety of public opinion polls have examined racial and ethnic differences in attitudes about justice issues, including racial profiling. These public opinion polls are often national polls. As one example, the Gallup Poll (Gallup & Newport, 2004) conducted a telephone survey of a randomly selected national sample of 2,250 adults, ages 18 years and older on the topic of racial profiling. The survey explored whether people thought racial profiling was widespread and justified in the domains of highway driving, airport checkpoints, and theft prevention in shopping malls or stores. Although a majority of Black and Hispanic respondents thought that racial profiling was widespread when it came to motorist stops and shopping mall questions, only half of White respondents thought racial profiling was widespread. Hispanic respondents were more likely than Black respondents (who were more likely than White respondents) to think racial profiling was widespread in airports.

The major disadvantage to surveys such as this one has to do with the limitations of self-report data. Respondents may not know the answers to the questions they are asked, or they may know their true beliefs but be unwilling to share them. Poll respondents may vary in how much they have thought about these issues. In addition, on the sampling front with the availability of caller ID and cell phones, fewer people are willing to participate in national polls, and the attitudes of some groups (e.g., young adults who only have a cell phone) may be underrepresented.

Lab-Based Experiments Using Mock Jurors

The majority of psychologists who study racism in the courts have used mock juror research designs. Some of these experiments have used college student participants (Bucolo & Cohn, in press; Cohn, Bucolo, Pride, & Sommers, 2009), whereas others have made a concerted effort to obtain more representative samples (Sommers, 2006). These experiments have manipulated different aspects of court proceedings in examining the impact of race. Some have manipulated the opening and closing statements (Bucolo & Cohn, in press). Others have manipulated the testimony of the defendant during the court proceedings (Cohn et al., 2009). Still others have manipulated the simplicity of jury instruction and diversity of the jury in the penalty phase of capital trials (Shaked-Schroer, Costanzo, & Marcus-Newhall, 2008).

An example of one of these studies is Cohn et al. (2009), in which college student participants were shown one of two videotapes of an actual case that involved a Black defendant and a White victim. In the study, mock jurors always knew the race of the defendant and victim. But the testimony was manipulated such that in one condition the incident in question was depicted as a racially charged dispute (race salient) and in the other condition the altercation was described in race-neutral terms (race not salient). When race was a salient trial issue, White mock jurors were significantly less likely to convict the Black defendant than when race was not a salient issue at trial. In addition, in the race-not-salient condition, racial attitudes were related to verdict decision: the higher the participants' racism scores, the more likely they were to convict the Black defendant.

Self-Report Perception and Behavior Studies

Yet another means of studying racism in the courts is to ask participants in the legal system about their perceptions and experiences of racial bias (Bucolo, 2007; Singer, 2004). Each of the circuits of the federal court and several of the state courts has commissioned studies of gender and racial–ethnic bias within their respective court systems. In the first circuit of the federal court, for example, surveys were sent to male and female White and minority court employees, attorneys, and court users about their perceptions of and experiences with racial and ethnic bias in the court (Bucolo, 2007; Singer, 2004).

Singer (2004) studied perceptions and experiences of racial bias by judges and attorneys of the first circuit court. Among court employees, 50.9% of minority employees believed that there was race bias in the court, compared to 36.3% of White employees. Among minority attorneys, 52.6% believed there was race bias in the court, compared with 31.1% of White attorneys. Respondents who perceived racial bias were also asked whether the race, ethnic, or both biases were widespread or limited. Among employees, 51.7% of non-White employees and 30.5% of White employees thought that racial bias was widespread. Among attorneys, 30.6% of non-White attorneys and 25.4% of White attorneys thought that racial bias was widespread. This means that although minority employees and attorneys are equally likely to believe there is race bias in the court, minority employees are more likely to perceive it as widespread. When it comes to believing that the managers of the court are trying to eradicate racial bias, the discrepancy is between employees and attorneys, regardless of race. Among employees, 22.7% of minority employees and 32% of White employees believed the managers were trying to eradicate racial bias. In contrast, 66.7% of minority attorneys and 86.2% of White attorneys believe that managers are trying to eradicate racial bias.

Attorneys and employees in this study were asked about experiences with race, ethnic, or both types of bias with regard to the following five behaviors: (a) did not take my opinions seriously, (b) was unwilling to accommodate my schedule or time requirements, (c) made inaccurate assumptions regarding my professional status, (d) made demeaning or derogatory comments to me, and (e) made inappropriate comments about my physical appearance or clothing.

Singer (2004) found that minority employees were more likely than White employees to report that their views were not taken seriously, that comments were made about their physical appearance, or that they were targeted by demeaning or derogatory comments. Interestingly, minority and White attorneys did not differ in these experiences.

RELEVANT RESEARCH ON RACISM IN JUDICIAL DECISION MAKING

The relevant research on racism in judicial decision making focuses on the following three areas: secondary analysis of arrests and sentencing, racism in decisions made by mock jurors, and racial profiling and treatment by police. The secondary analyses section focuses on both juveniles and adults. The racism in mock juror decisions argues that the nature of racism has changed. The racial profiling and treatment by police section differentiates between objective and subjective perception and between citizen and police perception.

Secondary Analysis of Arrests and Sentencing

By accessing existing databases, researchers have been able to demonstrate that an individual's race affects how he or she is treated within the legal system; unfortunately, these analyses typically find that racism toward Black individuals exists at many points in the system (e.g., Hagan, 1987). Analyses have consistently found that Black individuals are more likely than their White counterparts to be arrested by police, to be referred to the criminal justice system to be processed, and to be placed in prison when found guilty of committing a crime (e.g., Keen & Jacobs, 2009).

Although some attempts have been made to explain these racial discrepancies by examining other factors associated with contact with the criminal legal system, these analyses often reveal that racism accounts for some of the differences found between Blacks' and Whites' interactions in the legal system. Aversive racism provides a useful theoretical perspective for examining these disparities. For instance, Fite, Wynn, and Pardini (2009) examined the racial discrepancies among White and Black juveniles arrested for three types of crime: property crime, violent crime, and drug offenses. Although Black individuals were more likely than White individuals to be arrested for all three types of crimes, analyses indicated that childhood risk factors (e.g., living in a disadvantaged neighborhood) accounted for some of the differences found among White and Black juveniles arrested for violent crimes and property crimes. However, these factors could not explain differences in arrest for drug crimes. One possibility is, therefore, that race has a direct effect on police enforcement priorities when it comes to the stereotypic crime of drug use.

Similar secondary analyses that investigate prison sentences have sought to explain differences found in the length of prison sentences given to Black and White defendants. Researchers have analyzed prison data from many states over different time periods and found that Blacks receive significantly longer prison sentences than do Whites who commit the same crimes (e.g., Hagan, 1987; S. L. Johnson, 1985). However, it should be noted that these racial discrepancies appear to exist only for comparisons of Black and White men, with Black women being sentenced to the same prison terms as White women (Steffensmeier & Stephen, 2006). Furthermore, although sentencing guidelines were enacted during the late 1980s and early 1990s to reduce the effects of extralegal factors on sentencing decisions, research assessing racial disparities following the establishment of these guidelines still finds that Blacks receive longer sentences than Whites, usually because judges have departed from the guidelines (B. D. Johnson, 2003).

Mitchell, Haw, Pfeifer, and Meissner (2005) analyzed 70 archival studies of racial bias in sentencing to identify 116 separate effects of race on prison sentences. Overall, they found that there was a small, yet significant, racial disparity with Black individuals receiving longer prison sentences than White individuals. This disparity persisted even when researchers controlled for prior record and crime severity. This effect was substantially weaker, but still significant, in studies in which other societal factors were included in the prediction models, such as socioeconomic status, presence of an attorney for the defendant, and other legal factors.

Although the results of Mitchell et al.'s (2005) meta-analysis were not interpreted using an aversive racism framework (Dovidio & Gaertner, 2004), some of the effect-size moderator analyses revealed that racism toward Blacks was expressed in unique patterns across situations. For example, racism experienced by Blacks did not occur for all crime types. The effects of race on prison sentences were the strongest (i.e., the greatest discrepancies existed between sentences for Blacks and Whites) when researchers compared prison sentences given to White and Black individuals convicted of nonfederal drug crimes; however, there were no significant differences in prison sentences given to Whites and Blacks convicted of nonfederal property crimes. Furthermore, the strength of the race effect was found to decrease over time, with the largest disparities evident in studies conducted prior to 1970 and the smallest racial disparities evident in studies conducted after 1990. These results suggest that even though Blacks still experience racism in the sentencing decisions, it is not as widespread or as pervasive as it was only a few decades ago.

Even more sobering are analyses indicating that Blacks are more likely than Whites to receive the death penalty in capital cases. Although approximately 12.3% of the U.S. population is Black, 42% of inmates on death row are Black (NAACP Legal Defense and Educational Fund, 2006). Although early comparisons of this racial disparity were very basic and did not consider other potential factors that could account for it, more rigorous reviews have concluded that such disparities can be attributed, at least in part, to racial bias (e.g., Baldus, Woodworth, Zuckerman, Weiner, & Broffitt, 1998). In particular, victim race is a significant variable that affects decisions in capital cases: Defendants who victimize Whites are more likely than those who victimize Blacks to be charged with a capital crime, to be convicted, and to be sentenced to death (U.S. General Accounting Office, 1990).

Research has found that Blacks who murder Whites are more likely than Whites who murder Whites to be sentenced to death row in various states, including Maryland, Georgia, Missouri, Ohio, Florida, and Texas (Baldus et al., 1983; Bowers, 1984). An aversive racism theoretical approach (Dovidio & Gaertner, 2004) might explain that such crimes elicit negative stereotypes and beliefs about Black individuals of which Whites are aware but often do not utilize when interacting with Blacks (Devine & Elliot, 1995).

In short, race has the clear potential to influence police enforcement priorities, arrest decisions, and judicial and capital sentencing. Moreover, experimental research not reviewed in this section also indicates the impact of suspect race on crime-related perceptions and split-second judgments (see Eberhardt, Goff, Purdie, & Davies, 2004). The conclusion that individuals of particular races are more likely to be targeted by law enforcement, perceived as dangerous, arrested, and sentenced harshly raises a variety of serious concerns in regard to equity in the legal system, not the least of which is the increased risk factor for wrongful arrest and conviction among members of certain racial groups. This is a sobering conclusion that transcends mere speculation: As just one quite serious example, quantitative analysis has identified defendant (and victim) race as a statistically significant risk factor for erroneous conviction in capital cases (e.g., Harmon, 2004).

Racism in Decisions Made by Mock Jurors

Although it is difficult to ascertain the precise extent to which aversive racism (Dovidio & Gaertner, 2004) affects issues such as arrests and sentencing, experimental studies that use mock jurors provide researchers with the opportunity to directly test hypotheses derived from the theory. Early studies of mock juror decisions tended to find that Black defendants were more likely than White defendants to be found guilty, sentenced to longer prison sentences for various crimes, or both, including burglary (Gordon, Bindrim, McNicholas, & Walden, 1988), manslaughter (Gray & Ashmore, 1976), and rape (Klein & Creech, 1982).

Despite these findings, Sommers's (2007) review pointed out that the effect of defendant race in mock-juror research has not always been consistent. Although some researchers find that White jurors treated Black defendants more harshly than they treated White defendants, other researchers find that race has no effects on guilt and sentencing decisions. Still other researchers report that White jurors treat members of their own race more harshly than they treat Black defendants. Meta-analyses that assess the effect of defendant race and juror decisions have also been difficult to interpret with some finding no effect (Mazzella & Feingold, 1994), whereas others find that both White and Black jurors are more likely to find minority (as compared with White) defendants guilty and sentence them to longer prison sentences (Mitchell et al., 2005). Furthermore, the effect of defendants' race on jurors' decisions is minimized in experiments that include more formal legal procedures, such as judge's instructions.

The result of Mitchell et al.'s (2005) recent meta-analysis also supports contentions by Sommers and his colleagues (Sommers, 2007; Sommers & Ellsworth, 2001, 2009) that the nature of racism toward Black defendants in the modern legal system has changed. Their observations are consistent with the aversive racism approach (Dovidio & Gaertner, 2004) by suggesting that many jurors are aware that blatant prejudice toward Black defendants is no longer acceptable. However, White jurors are still aware of negative stereotypes of Black persons and may hold implicit attitudes about Black persons that are negative and therefore may still use these stereotypes under certain occasions. Consistent with this hypothesis, researchers who examine what have been termed *stereotypic crimes* (i.e., crimes perceived as being performed exclusively by members of a particular race) find that when Black persons commit such crimes, they are more likely than White persons to be found guilty and receive longer prison terms (Gordon et al., 1988). As noted earlier, secondary analyses of sentencing also find that Black persons are sentenced to longer prison terms than are Whites for particular crimes (Mitchell et al., 2005), suggesting that these stereotypes are pervasive within society and the legal system.

According to the aversive racism framework (Dovidio & Gaertner, 2004), White aversive racists are more likely to refrain from engaging in behavior when they are reminded that their actions could appear prejudiced. Similarly, White jurors are more likely to find Black defendants guilty when they are not reminded that such decisions could appear prejudiced. For example, Pfeifer and Ogloff (1991) found that judges' instructions that included a specific charge stating that jurors could not rely on any prejudices or biases when reaching a verdict eliminated White juror racial bias toward a Black defendant. Such a charge most likely reminded jurors that their decision could appear racist, so when jurors heard the instructions, they were more sensitive to race and less likely to find a Black defendant guilty. Aversive racism theory suggests that White jurors are also more likely to find Black defendants guilty of a crime when they are able to rely on other nonracial factors to make their decisions. For example, Hodson et al. (2005) found that White jurors expressed racial bias toward Black defendants (and not White defendants) when they were made aware of inadmissible evidence pointing to the defendant's guilt. Using this additional evidence, White jurors could rationalize a guilty decision against a Black defendant by feeling that they do not want a guilty person going free.

Sommers and Ellsworth (2001, 2009) have demonstrated that bringing up racial issues can attenuate White juror bias in interracial trials. In their studies, when a trial did not include racially charged witness testimony highlighting racial conflict between a Black defendant and White victim, White jurors were more likely to find a Black defendant (as compared with a White defendant) guilty. When the same incident was depicted as the result of a racially charged altercation, White jurors were not more likely to treat a Black defendant more severely than they were to treat a White defendant. A similar result was reported by Thomas and Balmer (2007), who found that White juror racial bias toward a Black defendant only existed in a case in which issues in regard to the interracial nature of the crime were not emphasized. When mock jurors were not made aware of racial motivations for the crime, they were more likely to find a Black defendant than a White defendant guilty.

More recent research by Cohn et al. (2009) indicated that making racial issues salient at a simulated trial reduced White juror racial bias of both prejudiced and nonprejudiced participants. In their study, self-reported levels of racism were found to predict White juror verdicts only in conditions in which racial salient issues were not brought up during a trial. When racially salient issues were included in witness testimony in a trial, respondents with both high and low racist beliefs were less likely to find a Black defendant than a White defendant guilty. The robustness of these manipulations has been found in other studies that reported that making racial issues salient during voir dire (Sommers, 2006) and during a defense attorney's opening and closing statements (Bucolo & Cohn, in press) also reduces White juror bias by making jurors cognizant of racial issues. Not only do these converging findings that race has the potential to influence jurors' decision making suggest one additional way in which racism can contribute to wrongful conviction but they also identify some of the specific circumstances and case types that are particularly susceptible to such problematic outcomes.

Racial Profiling and Treatment by Police

Another area of psycholegal inquiry that has implications for the consideration of wrongful conviction is that of racial profiling. To the extent that police profile and target members of some racial groups more than others, the potential for overzealous investigation and prosecution of individuals increases with membership in such a social category. Therefore, understanding the causes, effects, and perceptions of racial profiling are research goals that also have relevance to the effort to examine and prevent wrongful conviction.

Researchers who study racial profiling have focused on the issue from both an objective behavioral perspective and a more subjective perceptual perspective. From an objective perspective, researchers have tried to determine whether minority drivers, particularly Black persons, are disproportionately stopped by police on highways (Lamberth, 1998). The subjective researchers are more interested in perceptions that citizens and police have about racial profiling and the factors that increase the likelihood of perceiving racial profiling (Tyler & Wakslak, 2004).

Objective Behavioral Perspective

Researchers who conduct the objective studies (e.g., Lamberth, 1998) recorded the race of drivers on different sections of highways and then recorded the race of drivers stopped on the same area of the highway. They then compared the percentage of minority drivers on the highway with the percentage of minority drivers stopped by police. This has been referred to as *baseline/benchmark research* (Walker, 2001). Lamberth (1998), who was among the first to conduct such studies, measured disproportionate minority traffic stops on both New Jersey and Maryland highways. He found that Black drivers were disproportionately likely to be pulled over on the highway given the number of Black drivers who use the highway.

Subjective Perception

The majority of researchers have focused on racial profiling from the perspective of citizens. This is referred to as *public perception research* (Tyler & Wakslak, 2004). With a few exceptions (Glover, 2007), researchers have neglected the perspective of police officers in regard to racial profiling.

Citizens' Perspective

Most of the research on racial profiling has focused on national or local public opinion polls to determine citizen perceptions of and experiences with racial profiling (Tyler & Wakslak, 2004). Typically, these polls focus on three questions: whether racial profiling is widespread, whether the practice is justified or approved, and whether respondents feel they have been stopped by police due to their race or ethnic background (e.g., Weitzer & Tuch, 2005). With the exception of studies by Piquero and colleagues (e.g., Piquero, 2008; Reitzel et al., 2004), most researchers have focused almost exclusively on differences between Blacks and Whites and have ignored the citizens' perspective.

There is a great deal of consistency in the findings on Black versus White differences (Weitzer & Tuch, 2005). Black persons are significantly more likely than White persons to feel that racial profiling is widespread and that police have stopped them because of their race or ethnic backgrounds. Black persons are significantly less likely than White persons to approve of racial profiling and to feel it is justified.

There seems to be some inconsistency in studies that compare Hispanic with non-Hispanic persons (Reitzel et al., 2004; Weitzer & Tuch, 2005). Blacks are more likely than Hispanics to believe racial profiling is widespread, whereas Hispanics are more likely than Blacks to believe racial profiling is justified. In contrast, Reitzel et al. (2004) found that both Black and Hispanic respondents were more likely than non-Black and non-Hispanic respondents to believe that profiling was widespread. There was no difference between Hispanic and non-Hispanic individuals on whether profiling was justified. Blacks and Hispanics were more likely than Whites to believe they had been profiled.

Some researchers have gone beyond demographic differences and have looked at the factors that predict the belief that racial profiling is widespread and unjustified. In a theoretically sophisticated analysis, Tyler and Wakslak (2004) applied procedural justice principles to predict profiling. Both White and Black individuals see racial profiling as negative, but Whites tend to see it as the result of crime, whereas non-Whites are more likely to see racial profiling as resulting from prejudice. People are more likely to infer that racial profiling occurs when they have not experienced fair treatment from the police or the police have not been fair in dealing with their community. People are more likely to infer that they have been profiled when they are not treated with politeness and respect by the police.

Police Officers' Perspective

The only research on police perspectives on racial profiling (Glover, 2007) is a very preliminary study. Glover conducted in-depth interviews with 11 police officers from a small Texas town with a racially diverse population. In addition, 16 police officers completed surveys. Glover found that the police officers acknowledged the racial profiling but rationalized the use of racial profiling. Police used the expression, "White boy in a no White boy zone" (Glover, 2007, p. 239) and explained racial profiling by using the image of a White person in a predominantly minority neighborhood to justify racial profiling. Of course, in practice, racial profiling is often used when a minority individual is in a predominantly White area. Clearly, the police officers have recognized that it is more politically correct to give as the exemplar image the profiling of a White person rather than a Black person.

APPLICATION OF THE RESEARCH ON RACISM

Although the research mentioned earlier finds that racism toward Black persons occurs in many different aspects of the legal system, racial bias in the system has changed over time from blatant expressions of bias to more subtle and complex associations. Contemporary research indicates that successful attempts to remove such bias from the legal system require multiple approaches specifically designed to curtail the different racial biases that exist. As Piquero (2008) argued, remedies for reducing legal system racial bias toward Black persons needs to be grounded in sound research. On the basis of solid theory and research data, such reforms can specifically target the inequities found in particular areas of the criminal legal system (e.g., policing, the courts). Both national programs and local communities need to draw from this research literature and establish policies aimed at eliminating the racial discrepancies in the system and reduce the disadvantages that minority members experience when they come into contact with the legal system. In addition, of course, efforts to combat racism more generally in the legal system may also have the advantageous effect of reducing racial disparities in wrongful conviction.

In their review of legal remedies to reduce discrimination, Crosby and Dovidio (2008) argued that findings that have originated from the aversive racism framework (Dovidio & Gaertner, 2004) provide a starting point for how such reforms may be structured. Effective policy changes to reduce racism in the legal system should not be hostile and aimed at punishing previous behavior but rather should be proactive and based on social psychological findings regarding human behavior. Such initiatives would focus on factors associated with racism, noting that it is often done implicitly and that discrepancies and small imbalances can account for greater racial disparities.

The theory of aversive racism points to the importance of accountability (Dovidio & Gaertner, 2004). Individuals are not likely to act in a prejudicial manner when there are strong norms that indicate such behavior is not appropriate. For example, racial bias in police work is often attributable to a small number of officers who have significant contact with minorities (Ridgeway & MacDonald, 2009). The prospects of future sanctions against such officers may make all officers more accountable for prejudicial behavior and would most likely reduce discrimination against minorities. On a larger scale, a legal culture in which racism is clearly not tolerated and accepted should reduce racism, primarily by changing the norms of those who work and interact in this system (Crosby & Dovidio, 2008; Piquero, 2008).

Gaertner and Dovidio's (2000) common in-group identity model provides examples of how certain reforms and initiatives could reduce racial bias in the legal system. This model is based on other similar approaches to reducing prejudice among competing groups, such as increased positive interaction among members of different groups (Allport, 1954) and reducing outgroup bias through cooperation and working toward unifying goals (Sherif et al., 1955). Gaertner and Dovidio's (2000) model aims at reducing bias through group recategorization. Through recategorization of group membership, individuals from competing groups are more likely to build favorable attitudes, cognitions, and emotions in regard to former out-group members. This does not necessarily mean that original group membership no longer exists; rather, through contact or working toward shared goals and objectives, group members realize that once competing members do share membership in some "superordinate identity" (Gaertner & Dovidio, 2000). Experimental analyses have revealed that superordinate identities lead White individuals to behave more favorably toward Black individuals in different situations. It is important to note that the subgroup identities (e.g., White, Black) are maintained to increase the potential that positive attributes that become associated with other subgroup members could generalize to other groups who become part of the superordinate identity.

The common ingroup identity model (Gaertner & Dovidio, 2000) suggests that positive contact between outgroup members reduces bias. Researchers have documented that increased racial diversity in settings such as schools leads to more positive attitudes, cognitions, better interactions, and increased acceptance of minorities by White persons (Denson, 2009). However, for such diversity programs to be effective, they must be purposeful with the intention to reduce bias toward minorities. Further, programs that are more successful at reducing bias are not only informative but also provide positive interactions among minority members and White individuals.

Although researchers have not examined how racial diversity programs affect police officers and court officials directly, such programs combined with interactions with minorities may reduce biased behavior by these legal officials. Positive contact and interactions with police are vital not only to reduce racism among police and other legal actors but also to strengthen relationships between Blacks and the police. Many Black individuals report negative experiences when interacting with police officers (e.g., Brunson, 2007), and such contact is often associated with negative attitudes and beliefs about the police, indicating that many Blacks feel the police are prejudiced toward them (Gabbidon & Higgins, 2008). Community programs that increase positive police presence and beneficial interactions between Black persons and the police would benefit both police and community members. Such diversity programs should be rooted in the elimination of negative stereotypes about minorities. By interacting with the police, an "us" versus "them" culture that currently exists could be eliminated, as individuals work together to recategorize themselves into the superordinate identity of "community members."

No research has as yet assessed whether such programs reduce racism in the legal system, but anecdotal evidence suggests that a greater presence of Black persons in a majority-White community is associated with smaller racial discrepancies in arrests between White and Black persons (Keen & Jacobs, 2009). Thus, it possible that more positive interactions between police and Black individuals would eliminate some of the racial bias exhibited by police.

Increasing contact and interactions among Whites and Blacks has also been found to eliminate racial bias exhibited in trial simulation research. For instance, Sommers (2006) found that racial bias toward a Black defendant was reduced when White jurors deliberated in interracial juries rather than in all-White juries. This decreased racial bias was related to improved cognitive processing, as White persons who deliberated in the interracial juries—compared with White individuals who deliberated in homogenous juries—remembered more details and facts about the case and made fewer factual errors in discussing it. In short, one way to combat racial bias at the trial level seems to be to take steps to facilitate the selection of racially representative juries.

Some have also posited that the increased presence of minority members who enter the justice professions would help shape the culture and norms and thereby decrease racism. So far, empirical evidence for this prediction is lacking. Steffensmeier and Britt (2001) actually found that compared with White judges, Black judges gave both White and Black defendants significantly longer prison terms. These researchers explain this finding by suggesting that Black judges recognize that their decisions may be scrutinized more than those of White judges and give harsher sentences to demonstrate that they are "tough on crime." Further empirical assessment of the effects of the demographics of justice professionals on legal outcomes is clearly needed.

CONCLUSION

Most of this chapter has not focused on the specific question of race and wrongful conviction per se. This is because little research has directly examined the link between race, racism, and such miscarriages of justice, with the exception of some quantitative and qualitative analysis of race and capital cases (e.g., Harmon, 2004). Instead, this chapter has addressed current theoretical explanations for racial bias and prejudice, particularly aversive racism theory, as well as the psychological mechanisms and social conditions that can exaggerate and attenuate racism in settings legal and otherwise.

The relationship between race and wrongful conviction is underresearched and complex. It is unambiguous that wrongful conviction is a miscarriage of justice suffered by Black individuals at a rate disproportionate to their representation in the population at large. What is less clear is whether this disparity reflects the same disproportionality observed for arrest rates or whether Black individuals are at an even greater risk of wrongful conviction than their already higher rate of arrest and incarceration would predict. In other words, do the high rates of mistaken conviction of Black individuals simply reflect the higher arrest rates for Blacks? Or are there additional factors and processes that lead Black individuals to be overrepresented among the wrongfully convicted, even controlling for baseline racial disparities in arrests? These are important questions that deserve empirical answers.

But either way, it remains the case that by examining the scope, implications, and causes of racism in the legal system more generally, we learn about the potential links between race, racism, and wrongful conviction. When police departments rely on racial profiling, members of particular racial groups become more likely to experience unwarranted police attention or overzealous investigation, rendering arrest of the innocent more likely. To the extent that a suspect's race influences prosecutors' determinations of whether to press forward with charges (or their decisions regarding which charges to seek), weak cases become more likely to go to trial for suspects of some racial groups than others, increasing the risk of wrongful conviction for these groups. The presence of racial bias in jury decision making is yet another potential risk factor increases the odds of mistaken conviction for minority individuals.

Accordingly, it seems appropriate to add wrongful conviction to the litany of the potential and documented problems caused by racism in the legal arena. We propose that direct investigation of the link between race and such miscarriages of justice is called for, to more precisely quantify this relationship and to begin to generate concrete strategies for rectifying this important problem. Moreover, we also suggest that a wide range of future directions in the more general investigation of racism in the legal system will also have implications for the examination of wrongful conviction. In short, any study with the objective of better understanding the processes by which race impacts perception and judgment in legal domains may also shed light on the documented yet underresearched link between race and conviction of the innocent.

REFERENCES

Allport, G. W. (1954). *The nature of prejudice*. Cambridge, MA: Addison-Wesley.

Baldus, D. C. Pulaski, C., & Woodworth, G. (1983). Comparative review of death sentences: An empirical study of the Georgia experience. *Journal of Criminal Law and Criminology, 74*, 661–701. doi: 0091-4169/83/7403-661

Baldus, D. C., Woodworth, G., Zuckerman, D., Weiner, N. A., & Broffitt, B. (1998). Racial discrimination and the death penalty in the post-Furman era: An empirical and legal overview, with recent findings from Philadelphia. *Cornell Law Review*, *83*, 1638–1770.

Bowers, W. C. (1984). *Legal homicide: Death as punishment in America, 1864-1982.* Boston, MA: Northeastern University Press.

Brunson, R. K. (2007). "Police don't like Black people": African-American young men's accumulated police experiences. *Criminology & Public Policy, 6*, 71–102. doi:10.1111/j.1745-9133.2007.00423.x

Bucolo, D. O. (2007). *Experiences of bias and court users' satisfaction with outcomes in the justice system.* Unpublished manuscript, University of New Hampshire.

Bucolo, D. O., & Cohn, E. S. (in press). Playing the race card: Making race salient in defense opening and closing statements. *Legal and Criminological Psychology.*

Cohn, E. S., Bucolo, D., Pride, M., & Sommers, S. R. (2009). Racial salience and racial bias in the courts: Do racial attitudes make a difference? *Journal of Applied Social Psychology, 39*, 1953–1973. doi:10.1111/j.1559-1816.2009.00511.x

Crosby, F. J., & Dovidio, J. F. (2008). Discrimination in America and legal strategies for reducing it. In E. Borgida & S. T. Fiske (Eds.), *Beyond common sense: Psychological science in the courtroom: Beyond common knowledge* (pp. 23–43). Mahwah, NJ: Erlbaum.

Denson, N. (2009). Do curricular and cocurricular diversity activities influence racial bias? A meta-analysis. *Review of Educational Research, 79*, 805–838. doi:10.3102/0034654309331551

Devine, P. G., & Elliot, A. (1995). Are racial stereotypes really fading? The Princeton trilogy revisited. *Personality and Social Psychology Bulletin, 22*, 22–37. doi:10.1177/01461672952111002

Dovidio, J. F. (2001). On the nature of contemporary prejudice: The third wave. *Journal of Social Issues, 57*, 829–849. doi:10.1111/0022-4537.00244

Dovidio, J. F., & Gaertner, S. L. (2000). Aversive racism and selection decisions: 1989 and 1999. *Psychological Science, 11*, 315–319. doi:10.1111/1467-9280.00262

Dovidio, J. F., & Gaertner, S. L. (2004). Aversive racism. In M. P. Zanna (Ed.), *Advances in experimental social psychology* (Vol. 36, pp. 1–51). San Diego, CA: Academic Press.

Dovidio, J. F., & Gaertner, S. L. (2008). New directions in aversive racism research: Persistence and pervasiveness. In C. Willis-Esqueda (Ed.), *Motivational aspects of prejudice and racism* (pp. 43–67). New York, NY: Springer Science and Business Media.

Dovidio, J. F., Kawakami, K., & Beach, K. R. (2002). Implicit and explicit attitudes: Examinations of the relationship between measures of intergroup bias. In R. Brown & S. Gaertner (Eds.), *Blackwell handbook of social psychology: Intergroup processes* (pp. 175–197). Malden, MA: Blackwell.

Dovidio, J. F., Kawakami, K., Johnson, C., Johnson, B., & Howard, A. (1997). On the nature of prejudice: Automatic and controlled processes. *Journal of Experimental Social Psychology, 33*, 510–540. doi:10.1006/jesp.1997.1331

Eberhardt, J. L., Goff, P. A., Purdie, V. J., & Davies, P. G. (2004). Seeing Black: Race, crime, and visual processing. *Journal of Personality and Social Psychology, 87,* 876–893. doi:10.1037/0022-3514.87.6.876

Fite, P. J., Wynn, P., & Pardini, D. A. (2009). Explaining discrepancies in arrest rates between Black and White male juveniles. *Journal of Consulting and Clinical Psychology, 77,* 916–927. doi:10.1037/a0016626

Gabbidon, S. L., & Higgins, G. E. (2008). The role of race/ethnicity and race relations on public opinion related to the treatment of Blacks by the police. *Police Quarterly, 12,* 102–115. doi:10.1177/1098611108329692

Gaertner, S. L., & Dovidio, J. F. (2000). *Reducing intergroup bias: The common ingroup identity model.* Philadelphia, PA: The Psychology Press.

Gallup, A. M., & Newport, F. (2004). *The Gallup poll: Public opinion 2004.* Lanham, MD: Rowman and Littlefield.

Glover, K. S. (2007). Police discourse on racial profiling. *Journal of Contemporary Criminal Justice, 23,* 239–247. doi:10.1177/1043986207306866

Gordon, R. A., Bindrim, T. A., McNicholas, M. L., & Walden, T. L. (1988). Perceptions of blue-collar and white-collar crime: The effect of defendant race on simulated juror decisions. *The Journal of Social Psychology, 128,* 191–197. doi:10.1080/00224545.1988.9711362

Gray, D. B., & Ashmore, R. D. (1976). Biasing influence of defendant characteristics on simulated sentencing. *Psychological Reports, 38,* 727–738.

Hagan, J. (1987). Review essay: A great truth in the study of crime. *Criminology, 25,* 421–428. doi:10.1111/j.1745-9125.1987.tb00804.x

Harmon, T. R. (2004). Race for your life: An analysis of the role of race in erroneous capital convictions. *Criminal Justice Review, 29,* 76–96. doi:10.1177/073401680402900106

Hodson, G., Hooper, H., Dovidio, J. F., & Gaertner, S. L. (2005). Aversive racism in Britain: The use of inadmissible evidence in legal decisions. *European Journal of Social Psychology, 35,* 437–448. doi:10.1002/ejsp.261

Ito, T. A., & Urland, G. R. (2003). Race and gender on the brain: Electrocortical measures of attention to the race and gender of multiply categorizable individuals. *Journal of Personality and Social Psychology, 85,* 616–626. doi:10.1037/0022-3514.85.4.616

Johnson, B. D. (2003). Racial and ethnic disparities in sentencing departures across modes of conviction. *Criminology, 41,* 449–490. doi:10.1111/j.1745-9125.2003.tb00994.x

Johnson, B. D., & Betsinger, S. (2009). Punishing the "model minority": Asian-American criminal sentencing outcomes in federal district courts. *Criminology, 47,* 1045–1090.

Johnson, S. L. (1985). Black innocence and the white jury. *Michigan Law Review, 83,* 1611–1708. doi:10.2307/1288969

Katz, D., & Braly, K. (1933). Racial attitudes in one hundred college students. *Journal of Abnormal and Social Psychology, 28,* 280–290. doi:10.1037/h0074049

Keen, B., & Jacobs, D. (2009). Racial threat, partisan politics, and racial disparities in prison admissions: A panel analysis. *Criminology, 47,* 209–238. doi:10.1111/j.1745-9125.2009.00143.x

Klein, K., & Creech, B. (1982). Race, rape, and bias: Distortion of prior odds and meaning changes. *Basic and Applied Social Psychology, 3,* 21–33. doi:10.1207/s15324834basp0301_2

Lamberth, J. (1998, August 16). Driving while black: A statistician proves that prejudice still rules the road. *The Washington Post,* C1.

Lepore, L., & Brown, R. (1997). Category and stereotype activation. Is prejudice inevitable? *Journal of Personality and Social Psychology, 72,* 275–287. doi:10.1037/0022-3514.72.2.275

Mazzella, R., & Feingold, A. (1994). The effects of physical attractiveness, race, socioeconomic status, and gender of defendants and victims on judgments of mock jurors: A meta-analysis. *Journal of Applied Social Psychology, 24,* 1315–1338 doi:10.1111/j.1559-1816.1994.tb01552.x

Mitchell, T. L., Haw, R. M., Pfeifer, J. E., & Meissner, C. A. (2005). Racial bias in mock juror decision-making: A meta-analytic review of defendant treatment. *Law and Human Behavior, 29,* 621–637. doi:10.1007/s10979-005-8122-9

NAACP Legal Defense and Educational Fund. (2006, Winter). *Death row U.S.A.* New York, NY: NAACP Legal Defense and Educational Fund.

Pearson, A. R., Dovidio, J. F., & Gaertner, S. L. (2009). The nature of contemporary prejudice: Insights from aversive racism. *Social and Personality Psychology Compass, 3,* 314–338. doi:10.1111/j.1751-9004.2009.00183.x

Pfeifer, J. E., & Ogloff, J. R. (1991). Ambiguity and guilt terminations: A modern racism perspective. *Journal of Applied Social Psychology, 21,* 1713–1725. doi:10.1111/j.1559-1816.1991.tb00500.x

Piquero, A. (2008). Disproportionate minority contact. *The Future of Children, 18,* 59–79. doi:10.1353/foc.0.0013

Reitzel, J. D., Rice, S. K., & Piquero, A. R. (2004). Lines and shadows: Perceptions of racial profiling and the Hispanic experience. *Journal of Criminal Justice, 32,* 607–616.

Ridgeway, G., & MacDonald, J. M. (2009). Doubly robust internal benchmarking and false discovery rates for detecting racial bias. *Journal of the American Statistical Association, 104,* 661–668. doi:10.1198/jasa.2009.0034

Shaked-Schroer, N., Costanzo, M., & Marcus-Newhall, A. (2008). Reducing racial bias in the penalty phase of capital trials. *Behavioral Sciences & the Law, 26,* 603–617. doi:10.1002/bsl.829

Sherif, M., White, B. J., & Harvey, O. J. (1955). Status in experimentally produced groups. *American Journal of Sociology, 60,* S370–S379. doi:10.1086/221569

Singer, J. (2004). *Race and ethnic bias in the courts: Perceptions of attorneys and court employees.* Unpublished honors thesis, University of New Hampshire.

Sommers, S. R. (2006). On racial diversity and group decision-making: Identifying multiple effects of racial composition on jury deliberations. *Journal of Personality and Social Psychology, 90,* 597–612. doi:10.1037/0022-3514.90.4.597

Sommers, S. R. (2007). Race and the decision-making of juries. *Legal and Criminological Psychology, 12,* 171–187. doi:10.1348/135532507X189687

Sommers, S. R., & Ellsworth, P. C. (2001). White juror bias: An investigation of racial prejudice against Black defendants in the American courtroom. *Psychology, Public Policy, and Law, 7,* 201 229. doi:10.1037/1076-8971.7.1.201

Sommers, S. R., & Ellsworth, P. C. (2009). "Race salience" in juror decision-making: Misconceptions, clarifications, and unanswered questions. *Behavioral Sciences & the Law, 27,* 599–609. doi:10.1002/bsl.877

Steffensmeier, D., & Britt, C. L. (2001). Judges' race and judicial decision making: Do Black judges sentence differently? *Social Science Quarterly, 82,* 749–764. doi:10.1111/0038-4941.00057

Steffensmeier, D., & Stephen, D. (2006). Does gender modify the effects of race-ethnicity on criminal sanctioning? Sentences for male and female White, Black, and Hispanic defendants. *Journal of Quantitative Criminology, 22,* 241–261. doi:10.1007/s10940-006-9010-2

Thomas, C., & Balmer, N. (2007). Diversity and fairness in the jury system. *Ministry of Justice Research Series.* Retrieved from http://www.justice.gov.uk/docs/Pages fromJuries-report2-07C1.pdf

Tyler, T. R., & Wakslak, C. J. (2004). Profiling and police legitimacy: Procedural justice, attributions of motive, and acceptance of police authority. *Criminology, 42,* 253–282. doi:10.1111/j.1745-9125.2004.tb00520.x

U.S. General Accounting Office. (1990). Death penalty sentencing: Research indicates pattern of racial disparities. *Report to the Senate and House Committees on the Judiciary* (GGD-90-57). Washington, DC: Author.

Walker, S. (2001). Searching for the denominator: Problems with police traffic stop data and an early warning system solution. *Justice Research and Policy, 3,* 63–96. doi:10.3818/JRP.3.1.2001.63

Weitzer, R., & Tuch, S. A. (2005). Racially biased policing: Determinants of citizen perceptions. *Social Forces, 83,* 1009–1030. doi:10.1353/sof.2005.0050

14

TUNNEL VISION

KEITH A. FINDLEY

The study of wrongful convictions has increased our understanding of the recurrent causes of error in the criminal justice system—some of which are examined in other chapters of this book—including eyewitness error, false confessions, jailhouse informant testimony, police and prosecutorial misconduct, forensic science error or fraud, and inadequate defense counsel (Scheck, Neufeld, & Dwyer, 2000). In recent years, growing attention has been focused on an additional and pervasive contributor of wrongful convictions, present in almost every wrongful conviction along with each of these specific causes— the problem of *tunnel vision* (Bibas, 2004; Findley & Scott, 2006; Martin, 2002; Rossmo, 2009).

Tunnel vision is a natural human tendency that has particularly pernicious effects in the criminal justice system. Tunnel vision in this context is generally understood to mean that "compendium of common heuristics and logical fallacies," to which we are all susceptible, that lead actors in the criminal justice system to "focus on a suspect, select and filter the evidence that

This chapter was adapted and developed from an article by the author and Michael Scott that first appeared in the *Wisconsin Law Review* in 2006.

will 'build a case' for conviction, while ignoring or suppressing evidence that points away from guilt" (Martin, 2002, p. 848). This process leads investigators, prosecutors, judges, and defense lawyers alike to focus on a particular conclusion and then filter all evidence in a case through the lens provided by that conclusion. Through that filter, all information that supports the adopted conclusion is elevated in significance, viewed as consistent with the other evidence, and deemed relevant and probative. Evidence inconsistent with the chosen theory is easily overlooked or dismissed as irrelevant, incredible, or unreliable. Properly understood, tunnel vision is more often the product of the human condition, as well as institutional and cultural pressures, than of maliciousness or indifference.

Tunnel vision both affects and is affected by other flawed procedures in the criminal justice system. For example, mistaken eyewitness identifications—the most frequent single cause of wrongful convictions (Gross, Jacoby, Matheson, Montgomery, & Patil, 2005; Scheck, Neufeld, & Dwyer, 2000)—can convince investigators early in a case that a particular individual is the perpetrator. Convinced of guilt, investigators might then set out to obtain a confession from that suspect, producing apparently inculpatory reactions or statements from the suspect, leading investigators to interpret the suspect's innocent responses as inculpatory, or even producing a false confession from an innocent person (see Chapter 3, this volume). Police and prosecutors convinced of guilt might recruit or encourage testimony from unreliable jailhouse snitches, who fabricate stories that the defendant confessed to them, in hopes that they will benefit in their own cases from cooperation with authorities (see Chapter 10, this volume; Martin, 2002). Forensic scientists, aware of the desired result of their analyses, might be influenced—even unwittingly—to interpret ambiguous data or fabricate results to support the police theory (see Chapter 12, this volume; Dror, Charlton, & Péron, 2006; Risinger, Saks, Thompson, & Rosenthal, 2002). All of this additional evidence then enters a feedback loop that bolsters the witnesses' confidence in the reliability and accuracy of their incriminating testimony (see Chapter 7, this volume) and reinforces the original assessment of guilt.

The wrongful conviction of Marvin Anderson illustrates how tunnel vision can corrupt the truth-finding functions of the criminal process. In 1982, Anderson was convicted of robbery, forcible sodomy, abduction, and rape of a 24-year-old woman in Hanover, Virginia (Joannou & Winstead, 2006). Police focused on Anderson because the rapist, who was African American, had mentioned to the victim that he had a White girlfriend, and Anderson was the only Black man police knew of who was living with a White woman.

However, Anderson did not fit the victim's description of her attacker in several respects. Anderson was taller than the man the victim described, and unlike the attacker, Anderson had a dark complexion, no mustache, and no scratches on his face. Nonetheless, the victim selected Anderson's photo from a photo array—an array in which Anderson's photo was the only one in color and the only one with his Social Security number printed on it. Thirty minutes later, police presented Anderson again in a live-person lineup, and the victim again picked him. Many of the procedures used in Anderson's identification process are now widely recognized as suggestive or flawed in ways that can lead an eyewitness to mistakenly identify an innocent person (see Chapter 6, this volume).

There were other reasons to doubt the identification. A forensic scientist testified that she had performed blood typing on swabs from both Anderson and the victim and was unable to identify Anderson as the source of semen samples collected in the rape kit. In addition, Anderson presented four alibi witnesses who all testified that they saw him outside his mother's house washing his car at the time of the attack (see Chapter 11, this volume, for a discussion of the effectiveness of alibi witnesses). None of this evidence, however, was enough to overcome the eyewitness identification.

Tunnel vision infected Anderson's case from the beginning, leading police, prosecutors, defense counsel, and eventually the jury and reviewing courts to minimize and discredit the alibi evidence, the mismatch between the victim's description of the perpetrator and Anderson's appearance, and the absence of physical evidence. Even more significantly, the premature focus on Anderson meant that no one pursued evidence that was available before trial that pointed toward the true perpetrator (Joannou & Winstead, 2006).

In 2002, 20 years after Anderson's conviction, DNA testing proved that he did not commit the crime. The DNA testing also identified the true perpetrator—a man named Otis "Pop" Lincoln. The match to Lincoln should not have come as a surprise. Two friends of the Anderson family said before the trial that just before the rape they had seen Lincoln riding a bicycle toward the shopping center where the attack had occurred—a significant fact because the attacker rode a bicycle. Moreover, these witnesses heard Lincoln make sexually suggestive comments to two young girls and then boast that he would force himself onto a woman if she refused his advances, as he rode past. The owner of the bicycle that was used by the assailant said that Lincoln had stolen it from him approximately 30 min before the rape. After Anderson was arrested, others in the community reported that Lincoln drove by Anderson's house because he wanted to see "the young boy who was taking his rap" (Joannou & Winstead, 2006, p. 12). Moreover, unlike Anderson, Lincoln had a criminal record for sexual assault and was awaiting trial for another sexual attack at the time. Despite all this, no one had investigated Lincoln.

Eventually, 6 years later, at proceedings on Anderson's application for habeas corpus, Lincoln confessed fully to the crime in court under oath and provided details of the attack. Nevertheless, the same judge who presided over Anderson's original trial refused to credit Lincoln's confession. The governor subsequently refused to intervene and denied clemency. Anderson remained in prison, and then on parole, for several more years until DNA testing confirmed that Lincoln, not Anderson, was the attacker.

Other aspects of the case also reveal just how sticky erroneous beliefs in guilt can be. Despite the weakness of the case against Anderson and the abundance of evidence that should have alerted authorities to investigate Lincoln, the original prosecutor in the case claimed that until the exoneration he thought the Anderson case was "the clearest case he had ever had" (Joannou & Winstead, 2006, p. 18). And although Anderson's trial lawyer made numerous egregious errors, including failing to disclose a conflict of interest and failing to introduce known evidence against Lincoln, the trial court was unwilling to grant a new trial on a claim of ineffective assistance of counsel.

In short, from start to finish, actors at every stage of the process focused entirely on Anderson and refused to consider the possibility that other compelling evidence pointed toward another person. The system clung to the early belief in Anderson's guilt until DNA testing conclusively and irrefutably proved the error and forced the system to look outside the tunnel.

As Anderson's case illustrates, tunnel vision is a serious problem in police investigations, but it also infects all other phases of the criminal process. The rest of this chapter explores the ways in which tunnel vision infects all phases of criminal proceedings, beginning with the investigation of cases and then proceeding through the prosecution, trial or plea bargaining, appeal, and postconviction stages. This chapter examines the roots of the problem in cognitive biases that are reinforced by institutional pressures and deliberate policies reflected in rules and training throughout the system.

SCIENTIFIC PSYCHOLOGICAL FOUNDATIONS OF TUNNEL VISION

The tendency toward tunnel vision is partly innate; it is part of our psychological makeup (Findley & Scott, 2006). Tunnel vision is the product of a variety of cognitive distortions, such as confirmation bias, hindsight bias, and outcome bias, which can impede accuracy in what we perceive and in how we interpret what we perceive. These cognitive biases help explain how and why tunnel vision is so ubiquitous, even among well-meaning actors in the criminal justice system.

CONFIRMATION BIAS

Confirmation bias connotes the tendency to seek or interpret evidence in ways that support existing beliefs, expectations, or hypotheses (Nickerson, 1998; Nisbett & Ross, 1980; Trope & Liberman, 1996). The concept of confirmation bias has a well-established foundation in social science research, although most of it is outside the context of the criminal justice system.

Confirmation bias has several expressions. In part, confirmation bias reflects that when testing a hypothesis or conclusion people tend to seek information that confirms their hypotheses and to avoid information that would disconfirm their hypotheses (Gilovich, 1991; Nickerson, 1998; Wason, 1959, 1966, 1968).

For example, in a study that has been repeated numerous times in different ways, subjects were asked to interview a target person to determine whether that person was an introvert or an extrovert (Snyder & Swann, 1978a, 1978b). In one study, the interviewers were given a list of questions from which they could select whichever questions they wished to probe the target's personality (Bassok & Trope, 1984). Half of the interviewers were told to choose questions that would test whether the person was an extrovert, and the other half were told to choose questions that would test whether the person was an introvert. Consistently, interviewers chose questions that would prove, but never disprove, their implicit hypotheses. Hence, subjects told to ask questions to test for extroversion chose questions like, "What would you do if you wanted to liven things up at a party?" while subjects who tested for introversion asked questions like, "What is it about large groups that make you feel uncomfortable?" (Burke, 2006, p. 9).

Numerous studies have repeatedly shown this confirmation bias and have found that people seek information in ways that increase their confidence in prior beliefs or hypotheses and disfavor choices that would disprove their hypotheses. Ironically, this confirmation preference not only inhibits discovering the incorrectness of a particular hypothesis but also "this strategy would not yield as strongly confirmatory evidence, logically, as would that of deliberately selecting tests that would show the hypothesis to be wrong, if it is wrong, and failing in the attempt" (Nickerson, 1998, p. 179). Although such confirmation-biased information is often less probative than disconfirming information might be, people fail to recognize the weakness of the confirming feedback they receive or recall. In this sense, the data "suggest that feedback that is typically interpreted by participants to be strongly confirmatory often is not logically confirmatory, or at least not strongly so. The 'confirmation' the participant receives in this situation is, to some degree, illusory" (Nickerson, 1998, p. 179).

Empirical research also demonstrates that people not only seek confirming information but also tend to recall information in a biased manner. Experiments show that when recollecting information previously obtained, people search their memories in biased ways, preferring information that tends to confirm a presented hypothesis or belief. For example, in one study, participants were read a story about a woman who behaved in a number of both introverted and extroverted ways (Gilovich, 1991). Two days later, half of the participants were asked to assess the woman's suitability for a job that obviously required extroversion; the other half were asked to assess the woman's suitability for a job that would presumably demand introversion. Those asked to assess the woman's suitability for the extroverted job recalled more examples of the woman's extroversion, and those asked to assess her suitability for the intro-verted job recalled more instances of her introversion. The hypothesis at issue—the woman's suitability for the particular job—biased the way partic-ipants searched their memories for confirming evidence.

In addition to seeking and recalling confirming information, people also tend to give greater weight to information that supports existing beliefs than to information that runs counter to them; that is to say, people tend to inter-pret data in ways that support their prior beliefs. Empirical research demon-strates that people are "incapable of evaluating the strength of evidence independently of their prior beliefs" (Burke, 2006, p. 10). That is, the research shows a general tendency to "overweight positive confirmatory evidence" and "underweight negative disconfirmatory evidence" (Nickerson, 1998, p. 180). In other words, "people generally require less hypothesis-consistent evidence to accept a hypothesis than hypothesis-inconsistent evidence to reject a hypothesis" (Nickerson 1998, p. 180).

In some circumstances, people do not respond to information at vari-ance with their beliefs by simply ignoring it but rather by working hard to examine it critically so as to undermine it. "The end product of this intense scrutiny is that the contradictory information is either considered too flawed to be relevant, or is redefined into a less damaging category" (Gilovich, 1991, pp. 55–56). Moreover, people tend to use different criteria when they evalu-ate data or conclusions that they desire than when they evaluate conclusions they disfavor. For preferred conclusions, "we ask only that the evidence not force us to believe otherwise"; for disfavored conclusions, however, "we ask whether the evidence *compels* such a distasteful conclusion—a much more difficult standard to achieve" (Gilovich, 1991, p. 84). Thus, for "desired con-clusions . . . it is as if we ask, '*Can* I believe this?' but for unpalatable conclu-sions we ask, '*Must* I believe this?'" (Gilovich, 1991, p. 84).

Accordingly, when considering data, people sometimes see patterns they are looking for, even when those patterns are not really there. On a social level, numerous studies have shown that descriptions provided in advance (expectations) about a person's qualities affect how others assess that person. For example, observers who were told in advance that a person had particular personality characteristics tended to see those qualities in that person, whether or not those characteristics were objectively present (Kelley, 1950; Snyder, 1981; Snyder & Campbell, 1980; Snyder & Gangestad, 1981; Snyder & Swann, 1978a, 1978b). This phenomenon can be particularly significant in criminal cases, where an individual is being judged—by police, prosecutors, defense lawyers, judges, and jurors—and where the initial working hypothesis presented to each actor in the system is that the defendant is guilty (despite the theoretical presumption of innocence).

BELIEF PERSEVERANCE

Although biases thus affect the acquisition and interpretation of information, and thereby impede rational or logical adjustment of hypotheses or conclusions to reflect new information, natural tendencies also make people resistant to change even in the face of new evidence that wholly undermines their initial hypotheses. This phenomenon, known as *belief perseverance* or *belief persistence,* can render a belief or opinion intractable (Burke, 2006; Lieberman & Arndt, 2000). People are naturally disinclined to relinquish initial conclusions or beliefs, even when the bases for those initial beliefs are undermined. Thus, people are more likely to question information that conflicts with preexisting beliefs and are more likely to interpret ambiguous information as supporting rather than disconfirming their original beliefs. People "can be quite facile at explaining away events that are inconsistent with their established beliefs" (Nickerson, 1998, p. 187).

For example, research has shown that people find it quite easy to form beliefs that generally explain an individual's behavior and to persevere with those beliefs even after the premise for the initial belief is shown to be fictitious (Ross, Lepper, & Hubbard, 1975; Ross, Lepper, Strack, & Steinmetz, 1977). In a well-known study, subjects were asked to distinguish between authentic and fake suicide notes (Ross, Lepper, & Hubbard, 1975). At various points, subjects were given feedback about how they were performing. The feedback was in fact independent of the choices they made: Researchers randomly informed the participants that they were performing far above average or far below average. Researchers then debriefed the participants, explicitly revealing to them that the feedback had been false, predetermined, and independent of their choices. Yet, when later asked to rate their ability to make such judgments, those who had received positive feedback rated their ability much higher than those who had received negative feedback, even though they had all been told that their feedback was arbitrary.

The belief perseverance phenomenon is apparent in many wrongful conviction cases. For example, even when presented with DNA evidence that proves that semen taken from a sexual assault victim could not have come from the defendant, prosecutors sometimes persist in their guilt judgments and resist relief for the defendant (Medwed, 2004). As Liebman (2002) observed, "prosecutors have become . . . sophisticated about hypothesizing the existence of 'unindicted co-ejaculators' (to borrow Peter Neufeld's phrase) to explain how the defendant can still be guilty, though another man's semen is found on the rape-murder victim" (p. 243).

Thus, these cognitive biases help explain what went wrong in many wrongful conviction cases, including Marvin Anderson's. Convinced by an early—although flawed—eyewitness identification, police and prosecutors sought evidence that would confirm guilt, not disconfirm it. They searched for incriminating evidence against Anderson but never looked at viable alternative perpetrators. When confronted with ambiguous or inherently weak evidence, police and prosecutors interpreted it as powerfully incriminating. When confronted with contrary evidence—such as the alibi witnesses and the perpetrator's confession—they sought to discredit or minimize that evidence. The stubborn assessment of guilt persisted on appeal and through postconviction proceedings, tainting perspectives on the relative strength of the state's and defendant's cases and even leading authorities to reject a full confession by the true perpetrator.

Hindsight Bias

Significant among other biases that contribute to tunnel vision is *hindsight bias*, or the "knew-it-all-along effect." Cognitive research has repeatedly shown that, in hindsight, people tend to think that an eventual outcome was inevitable, or more likely or predictable, than originally expected (Harley, Carlsen, & Loftus, 2004; Hawkins & Hastie, 1990). Hindsight bias essentially operates as a means through which people project new knowledge— outcomes—into the past, without any awareness that the perception of the past has been tainted by the subsequent information.

Hindsight bias is a product of the fact that memory is a dynamic process of reconstruction (Weinstein, 2003). Memories are not drawn from our brains fully formed; rather, they are assembled from little bits and pieces of information as we recall an event. Those little pieces of information about an event or situation are constantly being updated and replaced in our brains by new information. The updated information is then used each time we reconstruct a relevant memory, making the ultimate conclusion appear preordained or more likely than we could have known at the outset. Understood another way, the process is one in which an individual reanalyzes an event so that the early stages of the process connect causally to the end.

During this process, evidence consistent with the reported outcome is elaborated, and evidence inconsistent with the outcome is minimized or discounted. The result of this rejudgment process is that the given outcome seems inevitable or, at least, more plausible than alternative outcomes. (Harley et al., 2004, p. 960)

Hindsight bias can reinforce premature or unwarranted focus on an innocent suspect in several ways (Findley & Scott, 2006). First, once a suspect becomes the focus of an investigation or prosecution—that is, once police or prosecutors arrive at an outcome in their own quests to determine who they believe is guilty—hindsight bias would suggest that, on reflection, the suspect would appear to have been the inevitable and likely suspect from the beginning. Moreover, events that support a given outcome are typically better remembered than events that do not support that outcome. Hence, once police and prosecutors conclude that a particular person is guilty, not only might they overestimate the degree to which that suspect appeared guilty from the beginning but also they will likely best remember those facts that are incriminating (thereby reinforcing their commitment to focus on that person as the culprit).

Second, hindsight bias has implications for the quality of the evidence used to convict. For example, hindsight bias helps explain one way that eyewitness identification errors can contribute to tunnel vision and ultimately to conviction of the innocent. It is well-known that eyewitness confidence is highly malleable. Confirming feedback offered after an eyewitness identification can dramatically inflate not only the witness's confidence in the ultimate identification but also the witness's assessment of the conditions surrounding the identification (Bradfield, Wells, & Olson, 2002; Wells & Bradfield, 1998; see also Chapter 7, this volume). If, for example, an eyewitness had a poor view of a perpetrator or paid little attention to the incident at the time, the witness likely had a poor memory of the perpetrator. However, if the witness nonetheless were to attempt an identification by examining a clear picture of a suspect in a photo spread, or a good view of the suspect in a live lineup, the witness would likely replace the original, low-quality memory of the suspect with a clearer image from the identification procedure. Given that the witness really had a very poor memory of the perpetrator, the witness very well could be mistaken in the identification. But, especially if given confirming feedback, the witness might draw on the cleaned-up memory of the perpetrator together with the confirming feedback to overstate both the quality of the original viewing conditions and the confidence—the inevitability—of the ultimate identification. In hindsight, the identification will appear as if it was always inevitable and was based on clear memories and an excellent opportunity to view the suspect (see Chapter 7, this volume; Harley et al., 2004).

Third, a *reiteration effect* is also linked to hindsight bias. Studies have established that confidence in the truth of an assertion naturally increases if the assertion is repeated (Hertwig, Gigerenzer, & Hoffrage, 1997). This increase in confidence from repetition is independent of the truth or falsity of the assertion. Accordingly, the longer that police and prosecutors (and witnesses) live with a conclusion of guilt, repeating the conclusion and its bases, the more entrenched their conclusion is likely to become and the more obvious it will appear to them that all evidence pointed to that conclusion from the very beginning. As a result, the reiteration effect makes it increasingly difficult for police and prosecutors to consider alternative perpetrators or theories of a crime (Findley & Scott, 2006).

Outcome Bias

Closely related to hindsight bias is *outcome bias*. Like hindsight bias, outcome bias involves a process in which people project new knowledge—outcomes—into the past without any awareness that the outcome information has influenced their perception of the past (Baron & Hershey, 1988). Outcome bias differs from hindsight bias in that outcome bias does not refer to the effect of outcome information on the judged probability of an outcome but to its effect on the evaluations of *decision quality*. In other words, outcome bias does not reflect hindsight judgments about how likely an event appears to have been but rather hindsight judgments about whether a decision was a good or bad one. For example, in a medical context, subjects are more likely to judge the decision to perform surgery as a bad decision when they are told that the patient died during surgery than when told that the same patient survived the surgery. Although this might seem intuitively reasonable, decision analysts teach that, rationally,

> information that is available only after a decision is made is irrelevant to the quality of the decision. Such information plays no direct role in the advice we may give decision makers ex ante or in the lessons they may learn. The outcome of a decision, by itself, cannot be used to improve a decision unless the decision maker is clairvoyant. (Baron & Hershey, 1988, p. 569)

Other Cognitive Biases

Tunnel vision is reinforced by a host of other cognitive distortions as well, including, among others, *anchoring effects* (referring to the fact that estimates people make of points along a continuum are influenced by preexisting or predetermined but task-irrelevant data); *role effects* (referring to the fact that asking people to adopt a particular function or perspective affects the way they seek and perceive information); *conformity effects* (reflecting that people tend to conform to the perceptions, beliefs, and behavior of others); and *experimenter effects* (referring to the tendency of subjects in an experiment to alter their behavior in response to an experimenter's behavior; Risinger, Saks, Thompson, & Rosenthal, 2002).

Other Facilitators of Tunnel Vision

Both institutional pressures inherent in the adversary system and explicit policy choices in many ways reinforce the natural tendencies toward tunnel vision in the criminal justice system. The adversary system—the hallmark of our criminal process—has many virtues. But one by-product of an adversary model is that it polarizes the participants, imposing pressures on them to dogmatically pursue their own perceived interests or their own assessments of the proper outcomes of their cases. The adversary system thereby produces biasing pressures that exacerbate natural cognitive biases.

Tunnel vision is thus not just a product of psychological tendencies but also of multiple external forces imposed by the adversary system at various stages of the process. These forces include institutional pressures on police (particularly with respect to highly publicized crimes), the standards of performance by which police investigators are measured (i.e., clearance rates), police culture and training, institutional pressures on prosecutors, the selective funneling of information to prosecutors, lack of diagnostic feedback about the accuracy of prosecutions, institutional pressures on defense lawyers, rules of law that limit inquiry, and some features of the trial and appeals experience (e.g., rules that limit the admissibility of exculpatory evidence, restriction of appeals process to procedural rather than factual errors). For a more thorough discussion of the factors that facilitate tunnel vision, see Findley and Scott (2006).

SCIENTIFIC METHODS IN TUNNEL VISION RESEARCH

Although there is a wealth of research on cognitive heuristics and biases that underlie tunnel vision in the social psychological literature, only a small portion of that research focuses on tunnel vision in criminal cases (Snook & Cullen, 2008). Dror's research (e.g., see Chapter 12, this volume; Dror et al., 2006) simulated investigation procedures by providing forensic evidence and other case information to forensic scientists and obtaining their evaluations of the forensic evidence. O'Brien (2009) simulated investigators' evaluations of evidence by varying the instructions at the outset and examining whether the context provided to the investigators influenced their evaluations of case evidence. The relevant studies reviewed are drawn from a variety of investigative areas and use traditional social psychological research methods. The relevant research on interrogations procedures, for example, draws on simulated crimes and interrogations (see Chapter 3, this volume).

The research methods used in this nascent literature, therefore, possess the typical benefits and drawbacks of social psychological research methods. With respect to benefits, the reliance on simulations of investigations enables the researcher to manipulate certain variables of interest while controlling other relevant variables, to use random assignment to conditions in order to rule out differences among participants that can affect judgments, and ultimately to draw causal conclusions about the factors that influence participants' judgments. With respect to drawbacks, the reliance on simulation methods removes some potentially important features of investigations, such as consequences that are important to individual suspects and accountability of decisions. The extent to which the absence of these features influences the generalizability of simulation studies remains an open question. The use of practicing investigators (e.g., forensic scientists in Dror and colleagues' research and experienced police investigators in Ask & Granhag's, 2007, research) enhances the likelihood that the research generalizes to actual investigations.

RESEARCH ON TUNNEL VISION AND CONVICTION OF THE INNOCENT

Most of the research that establishes the effects of confirmation bias and other cognitive distortions involves lay subjects and is not conducted specifically in the arena of criminal investigations (O'Brien, 2009). Consequently, Snook and Cullen (2008) argued that there is no empirical research on tunnel vision in criminal cases and that without it we cannot assume that the heuristics and cognitive biases that produce tunnel vision are detrimental; to the contrary, they argued that heuristics and biases might be efficient reflections of the exercise of bounded rationality. But there is, in fact, good reason to believe that the psychological findings are fully applicable to investigators in criminal cases—some of it involves trained professionals—as well as good evidence that although these heuristics can sometimes lead to efficiencies, they also can have disastrous effects when left completely unchecked.

To begin, research has established that professionals in other fields are not immune. Schulz-Hardt, Frey, Lüthgens, and Moscovici (2000) found that bank and industry managers exhibit confirmation bias in financial decision making. LeBlanc, Brooks, and Norman (2002) found biased decision making among doctors when diagnosing patients (see also Elstein, Shulman, & Sprafka, 1978). It thus appears that expertise does not eliminate confirmation bias. And, as mentioned above, other pressures on police, prosecutors, and judges, likely enhance the natural tendencies toward confirmation bias among professionals in the criminal justice system.

Moreover, recent research has confirmed that investigators in criminal cases are indeed susceptible to the cognitive distortions that underlie tunnel vision (see Chapters 3 and 12, this volume). Dror et al. (2006) found that fingerprint experts were influenced to interpret fingerprints consistently with other information provided to them prior to their forensic analysis. Kassin, Goldstein, and Savitsky (2003) found that people assigned to interview suspects used more aggressive and guilt-presuming interrogation tactics, and they interpreted responses as more inculpatory when they began the task with a belief that the subject of their interrogation was guilty. Similarly, Meissner and Kassin (2002) found that police officers who are convinced that a suspect is lying are very resistant to changing their minds. In addition, recent research has shown that both experienced police investigators and police trainees rate disconfirming or exonerating evidence as less reliable or credible than guilt-confirming evidence that supports their initial hypotheses (Ask & Granhag, 2007; Ask, Rebelius, & Granhag, 2008). Similarly, O'Brien (2009) found that people who were given a police investigative scenario showed marked confirmation bias when they were asked to form a hypothesis of guilt early in the evaluation of the evidence, as compared to subjects who were not asked for a hypothesis until the end of the review of all evidence. Compared with those who waited to form a hypothesis until the end of the investigation, early hypothesizers (a) showed better memory for facts consistent (as opposed to inconsistent) with the theory that their suspect was guilty; (b) interpreted more ambiguous information as consistent with their suspect's guilt; (c) remembered as true more evidence that implicates their suspect and more evidence as false if it tended to exculpate him; (d) chose more lines of investigation that focused on their suspect and fewer investigative steps directed toward a leading alternative suspect; and (e) changed their attitudes about the usefulness and reliability of certain kinds of evidence (e.g., eyewitness evidence), depending on whether such evidence supported or undermined their hypotheses of guilt. Research therefore suggests that, as expected, cognitive biases are likely quite active in the process of investigating crimes just as they are in other human endeavors and that they can indeed produce investigative errors.

IMPLICATIONS OF TUNNEL VISION FOR THE CRIMINAL JUSTICE SYSTEM

To suggest that tunnel vision infects police investigations, prosecutions, and judicial proceedings is not necessarily to make a value judgment about the nature or qualities of police, prosecutors, and judges, but to some degree at least merely to acknowledge the natural tendencies that can and do influ-ence anyone's access to and interpretation of data. In this sense, police, pros-ecutors, and judges are not bad people because they are affected by tunnel vision; they are merely human. However, benign intent does not negate the harmful effects of tunnel vision in the criminal justice system.

As discussed, cognitive biases can skew the investigation into crimes and the consideration of evidence before and at trial. But these biases do not stop there. Hindsight bias and outcome bias have particularly serious impli-cations for appellate and postconviction review by judges, especially in the application of harmless error (*Chapman v. California*, 1967) and related doc-trines such as the prejudice prong of the ineffective assistance of counsel analysis and the materiality prong of *Brady v. Maryland* (1963). Under inef-fective assistance of counsel analysis, to obtain relief the defendant must prove not only that her counsel made serious errors in representing her, but also that the errors were prejudicial, meaning there is a reasonable probabil-ity that, absent the errors, the outcome of the proceeding would have been different (*Strickland v. Washington*, 1984). Under *Brady v. Maryland,* to show that a prosecutor violated his duty to disclose exculpatory evidence, the defendant must show that the withheld evidence was material—again, that there is a reasonable probability of a different outcome if the evidence had been disclosed. Hindsight bias and outcome bias, together, can be expected to have an affirmance-biasing effect in postconviction and appellate review because the outcome of the case—conviction—tends to appear, in hindsight, to have been both inevitable and a "good" decision.[1]

Empirical data support this conclusion, as reversals in criminal cases are quite rare (Findley, in press; Garrett, 2008). Even where courts find error, they frequently forgive the error as harmless, which typically involves an assess-ment of likely guilt. Indeed, Garrett's (2008) analysis of the first 200 DNA exonerations—that is, cases in which DNA evidence conclusively estab-lished that the defendants were actually innocent—shows that reviewing courts failed to recognize innocence in almost all of the cases. Courts affirmed 84% of these wrongful convictions of actually innocent defendants. In nearly one third of those cases (32%), courts found error but affirmed nonetheless because the error was deemed harmless (Garrett, 2008). Moreover, fully half of the courts referred to the likely guilt of the defendant, and 10% described the evidence of guilt against the actually innocent defendant in the case as "overwhelming" (Garrett, 2008, p. 108). These data are at least consistent

---

[1]This discussion assumes that the convicted defendant is the one appealing, because in criminal cases, except in limited circumstances and involving a limited range of issues, the prosecution is generally barred by the Double Jeopardy Clause from appealing, at least after an acquittal (*United States v. Sanges*, 1892).

with the hypothesis that with hindsight knowledge that a jury found the defendant guilty beyond a reasonable doubt, judges are likely to be predisposed to view the conviction as both inevitable and a sound decision, despite a procedural or constitutional error in the proceedings. Such reluctance to see innocence and to assess errors as harmful might well be, in part, due to hindsight bias and outcome bias working in tandem with other values, such as a desire to respect finality and avoid wasteful retrials of obviously guilty defendants. Understood in this way, it is not at all surprising that the courts denied ineffective assistance of counsel claims in cases like Marvin Anderson's.

The presence and persistence of tunnel vision in all of its manifestations is deeply problematic for a criminal justice system that is dedicated to fairness and guarding against wrongful conviction of the innocent. Tunnel vision is problematic not only because it harms the wrongly accused but also because it threatens the system's ability to identify and convict the guilty. When law enforcement focuses on the wrong person and fails to look outside the tunnel to find the true perpetrator, that guilty person remains free and unrestrained.

Solutions to the problem of tunnel vision, however, are complex and uncertain. A variety of reforms have been suggested (Findley & Scott, 2006). Legal principles and rules of procedure can be modified to reduce obstacles that currently make it difficult for innocent people to be vindicated in judicial proceedings. Police training and standards can be modified to minimize policies and practices, such as guilt-presuming interrogation practices, that foster tunnel vision. Incentives for police and prosecutors can be modified, to reward not just clearance and conviction rates but also to reward efforts to "do justice," to vindicate the wrongly accused, and to pursue all investigative leads, including those that lead away from the primary suspect (see also Medwed, 2004).

Most difficult among the challenges for overcoming tunnel vision is devising ways to reduce the cognitive biases that can produce tunnel vision. Education—for police, prosecutors, defense attorneys, and judges—would seem to be an obvious measure for reducing misguided conclusions created by cognitive biases. Unfortunately, research suggests that education is only of limited value. Merely informing people about a cognitive bias and urging them not to use that bias is not particularly effective. Research shows, for example, that people are incapable of overcoming hindsight bias even when advised about it and instructed to try to ignore outcomes when assessing probabilities or strategies (Hawkins & Hastie, 1990).

But there is empirical evidence that supports other techniques for managing cognitive biases. Research shows that asking individuals to consider the opposite of their position and to articulate the reasons why the results at issue could have been different, has some effect on hindsight bias (Hawkins & Hastie, 1990). Likewise, forcing people to articulate reasons that counter their own position can minimize the "illusion of validity" that produces confirmation bias (Nickerson, 1998, p. 188).

O'Brien's (2009) recent research provided further empirical support for the idea that requiring people to consider and articulate counter arguments can be somewhat effective. O'Brien found that people asked to discuss the evidence both for and against their hypotheses showed less bias than those asked to discuss only the evidence supporting their hypotheses of guilt; indeed, people who expressly considered counterevidence showed no more bias than people who had stated no hypothesis at all.

Empirical evidence, therefore, supports recommendations for institutionalizing counterarguing within police departments and prosecutors' offices. Institutionalizing this process can occur by, as a matter of protocol, requiring investigators and prosecutors to explicitly identify contrary evidence and arguments. Similarly, creating "devil's advocates" within police or prosecutor's offices on select cases—that is, individuals whose role it is to envision different outcomes or contrary evidence—might serve this purpose (Findley & Scott, 2006).

However, O'Brien's research also cautions that the solutions are not as simple or direct as they might seem. O'Brien (2009) found that whereas requiring investigators to actively consider evidence that points away from their suspect can reduce bias, requiring them to consider several possible alternative suspects did not help. In fact, it is surprising that requiring police to consider alternate suspects actually made them just as biased as people who considered only evidence that favored one suspect and no contrary evidence. There are hypotheses about why this happens, but these counterintuitive results nonetheless caution against jumping too quickly to commonsense conclusions about what correctives might work to neutralize cognitive biases.

In the end, no countermeasures will be fully effective against cognitive biases. Given that police and prosecutors, because they are human, cannot be expected to recognize and correct for all of their natural biases, the system must find a way to give sufficient case information to those who have different incentives and different natural biases. In the end, greater transparence at all stages of the criminal process might be the most powerful way to counter tunnel vision.

In criminal cases, greater transparence requires providing the fullest possible investigative information to the defendant—that is, expanded discovery. Traditionally, discovery is very limited in criminal cases—as opposed to civil cases, in which expansive discovery is the rule (Prosser, 2006). Armed with full investigative information, the defense might at least have a chance to push back against the bias-enhanced police hypotheses—to identify alternative suspects, credible evidence undermining the hypothesis of the defendant's guilt, or the absence of significant evidence against the defendant.

Transparency helps to counter tunnel vision in another important way as well. In addition to sharing the information with actors who have an incentive to look outside the tunnel, transparency also helps to modify the effects of biases on decision makers. Research shows that when people know that their actions are being observed and they will be held publicly accountable, they tend to exhibit less bias in their hypothesis testing strategies (Leo, 2004). Thus, theoretically at least, the more that police investigations are conducted and prosecutors' decisions are made in open and observable ways, the more likely they will be to resist biasing pressures and tendencies.

CONCLUSION

Tunnel vision is the product of cognitive biases, institutional pressures, and normative features of the criminal justice system. Tunnel vision permeates all levels of the criminal justice system and intensifies in response to these three dimensions as criminal cases pass through each stage of the system—from police investigation, to prosecution and trial, and to appeal and postconviction review. Although tunnel vision can be harmless—or even helpful—when the system focuses on the right person, it can have devastating effects when it focuses suspicion relentlessly on an innocent person.

An important body of scholarship about the causes and implications of tunnel vision, as well as its remedies, is emerging and providing guidance to policymakers and criminal justice practitioners. Although much is understood, more research is needed to help the system cope appropriately with tunnel vision in all of its manifestations. Research on the kinds of cognitive biases that can contribute to tunnel vision is well established, but more research is needed on how those biases operate in actual criminal investigations and what consequences they produce. Perhaps it is most important to note that more research is needed on identifying the measures that might be useful in effectively countering the biases that can lead investigators, prosecutors, defense lawyers, and judges to err. Armed with this information, the criminal justice system can do a better job of both convicting the guilty and protecting the innocent from wrongful conviction.

REFERENCES

Ask, K., & Granhag, P. A. (2007). Motivational bias in criminal investigators' judgments of witness reliability. *Journal of Applied Social Psychology, 37*, 561–591. doi:10.1111/j.1559-1816.2007.00175.x

Ask, K., Rebelius, A., & Granhag, P. A. (2008). The "elasticity" of criminal evidence: A moderator of investigator bias. *Applied Cognitive Psychology, 22*, 1245–1259. doi:10.1002/acp.1432.

Baron, J., & Hershey, J. C. (1988). Outcome bias in decision evaluation. *Journal of Personality and Social Psychology, 54,* 569–579. doi:10.1037/0022-3514.54.4.569

Bassok, M. & Trope, Y. (1984). People's strategies for testing hypotheses about another's personality: Confirmatory or diagnostic? *Social Cognition, 2,* 199–216.

Bibas, S. (2004). The psychology of hindsight and after-the-fact review of ineffective assistance of counsel. *Utah Law Review, 2004,* 1–11.

Bradfield, A. L., Wells, G. L., & Olson, E. A. (2002). The damaging effect of confirming feedback on the relation between eyewitness certainty and identification accuracy. *Journal of Applied Psychology, 87,* 112–120. doi:10.1037/0021-9010.87.1.112

Brady v. Maryland, 373 U.S. 83 (1963).

Burke, A. (2006). Improving prosecutorial decision making: Some lessons of cognitive science. *William and Mary Law Review, 47,* 1587–1633.

Chapman v. California, 386 U.S. 18 (1967).

Dror, I. E., Charlton, D., & Péron, A. E. (2006). Contextual information renders experts vulnerable to making erroneous identifications. *Forensic Science International, 156,* 74–78. doi:10.1016/j.forsciint.2005.10.017

Elstein, A. S., Shulman, L. S., & Sprafka, S. A. (1978). *Medical problem solving: An analysis of clinical reasoning.* Cambridge, MA: Harvard University Press.

Findley, K. A. (in press). Innocence protection in the appellate process. *Marquette Law Review.*

Findley, K. A., & Scott, M. S. (2006). The multiple dimensions of tunnel vision in criminal cases. *Wisconsin Law Review, 2006,* 291–397.

Garrett, B. L. (2008). Judging innocence. *Columbia Law Review, 108,* 55–142.

Gilovich, T. (1991). *How we know what isn't so: The fallibility of human reason in everyday life.* New York, NY: Free Press.

Gross, S. R., Jacoby, K., Matheson, D. J., Montgomery, N., & Patil, S. (2005). Exonerations in the United States 1989 through 2003. *The Journal of Criminal Law & Criminology, 95,* 523–553.

Harley, E. M., Carlsen, K. A., & Loftus, G. R. (2004). The "saw-it-all-along" effect: Demonstrations of visual hindsight bias. *Journal of Experimental Psychology: Learning, Memory, and Cognition, 30,* 960–968. doi:10.1037/0278-7393.30.5.960

Hawkins, S. A., & Hastie, R. (1990). Hindsight: Biased judgments of past events after the outcomes are known. *Psychological Bulletin, 107,* 311–327. doi:10.1037/0033-2909.107.3.311

Hertwig, R., Gigerenzer, G., & Hoffrage, U. (1997). The reiteration effect in hindsight bias. *Psychological Review, 104,* 194–202. doi:10.1037/0033-295X.104.1.194

Joannou, D. D., & Winstead, W. H. (2006). *A report on the case of Marvin Anderson.* Unpublished report prepared for the Innocence Commission of Virginia, on file with author.

Kassin, S. M., Goldstein, C. C., & Savitsky, K. (2003). Behavioral confirmation in the interrogation room: On the dangers of presuming guilt. *Law and Human Behavior, 27*, 187–203. doi:10.1023/A:1022599230598

Kassin, S. M., Meissner, C. A., & Norwick, R. J. (2005). "I'd know a false confession if I saw one": A comparative study of college students and police investigators. *Law and Human Behavior, 29*, 211–227. doi:10.1007/s10979-005-2416-9.

Kelley, H. H. (1950). The warm-cold variable in first impressions of persons. *Journal of Personality, 18*, 431–439. doi:10.1111/j.1467-6494.1950.tb01260.x

LeBlanc, V. R., Brooks, L. R., & Norman, G. R. (2002). Believing is seeing: The influence of diagnostic hypothesis on the interpretation of clinical features. *Academic Medicine, 77*, S67–S69. doi:10.1097/00001888-200210001-00022

Leo, R. (2004). The third degree and the origins of psychological interrogation in the United States. In G. D. Lassiter (Ed.), *Interrogations, confessions and entrapment* (pp. 37–84). New York, NY: Kluwer Academic.

Lieberman, J. D., & Arndt, J. (2000). Understanding the limits of limiting instructions: Social psychological explanations for the failures of instructions to disregard pretrial publicity and other inadmissible evidence. *Psychology, Public Policy, and Law, 6*, 677–711. doi:10.1037/1076-8971.6.3.677

Liebman, J. (2002). The new death penalty debate: What's DNA got to do with it? *Columbia Human Rights Law Review, 33*, 527–554.

Martin, D. L. (2002). Lessons about justice from the "laboratory" of wrongful convictions: Tunnel vision, the construction of guilt and informer evidence. *University of Missouri-Kansas City Law Review, 70*, 847–864.

Medwed, D. S. (2004). The zeal deal: Prosecutorial resistance to post-conviction claims of innocence. *Boston University Law Review. Boston University. School of Law, 84*, 125–183.

Meissner, C. A., & Kassin, S. M. (2002). "He's guilty!": Investigator bias in judgments of truth and deception. *Law and Human Behavior, 26*, 469–480. doi: 10.1023/A:1020278620751

Nickerson, R. S. (1998). Confirmation bias: A ubiquitous phenomenon in many guises. *Review of General Psychology, 2*, 175–220. doi:10.1037/1089-2680.2.2.175

Nisbett, R., & Ross, L. (1980). *Human inference: Strategies and shortcomings of social judgment.* Englewood Cliffs, NJ: Prentice Hall.

O'Brien, B. (2009). Prime suspect: An examination of factors that aggravate and counteract confirmation bias in criminal investigations. *Psychology, Public Policy, and Law, 15*, 315–334.

Prosser, M. (2006). Reforming criminal discovery: Why old objections must yield to new realities. *Wisconsin Law Review, 2006*, 541–614.

Risinger, D. M., Saks, M. J., Thompson, W. C., & Rosenthal, R. (2002). The *Daubert/Kumho* implications of observer effects in forensic science: Hidden problems of expectation and suggestion. *California Law Review, 90,* 1–56. doi:10.2307/3481305

Ross, L., Lepper, M. R., & Hubbard, M. (1975). Perseverance in self-perception and social perception: Biased attributional processes in the debriefing paradigm. *Journal of Personality and Social Psychology, 32,* 880–892. doi:10.1037/0022-3514.32.5.880

Ross, L., Lepper, M. R., Strack, F., & Steinmetz, J. L. (1977). Social explanation and social expectation: The effects of real and hypothetical explanations upon subjective likelihood. *Journal of Personality and Social Psychology, 35,* 817–829. doi:10.1037/0022-3514.35.11.817

Rossmo, D. K. (2009). *Criminal Investigative Failures.* Boca Raton, FL: Taylor & Francis.

Scheck, B., Neufeld, P., & Dwyer, J. (2000). *Actual innocence: Five days to execution and other dispatches from the wrongly convicted.* New York, NY: Doubleday.

Schulz-Hardt, S., Frey, D., Lüthgens, C., & Moscovici, S. (2000). Biased information search in group decision making. *Journal of Personality & Social Psychology, 78,* 655-669. doi: 10.1037OTO22-3514.78.4.655

Snook, B., & Cullen, R. M. (2008). Bounded rationality and criminal investigations: Has tunnel vision been wrongfully convicted? In K. D. Rossmo (Ed.), *Criminal investigative failures* (pp. 69–96). Oxford, England: Taylor & Francis.

Snyder, M. (1981). Seek and ye shall find: Testing hypotheses about other people. In E. G. Higgins, C. P. Heiman, & M. P. Zanna (Eds.), *Social cognition: The Ontario symposium on personality and social psychology* (pp. 277–303). Hillsdale, NJ: Erlbaum.

Snyder, M., & Campbell, B. H. (1980). Testing hypotheses about other people: The role of the hypothesis. *Personality and Social Psychology Bulletin, 6,* 421–426. doi:10.1177/014616728063015

Snyder, M., & Gangestad, S. (1981). Hypotheses-testing processes. In J. H. Harvey, W. J. Ickes, & R. F. Kidd (Eds.), *New directions in attribution research* (Vol. 3, pp. 171–196). Hillsdale, NJ: Erlbaum.

Snyder, M., & Swann, W. B. (1978a). Behavioral confirmation in social interaction: From social perception to social reality. *Journal of Experimental Social Psychology, 14,* 148–162. doi:10.1016/0022-1031(78)90021-5

Snyder, M., & Swann, W. B. (1978b). Hypothesis-testing processes in social interaction. *Journal of Personality and Social Psychology, 36,* 1202–1212. doi:10.1037/0022-3514.36.11.1202

Strickland v. Washington, 466 U.S. 668 (1984).

Trope, Y., & Liberman, A. (1996). Social hypothesis testing: Cognitive and motivational mechanisms. In E. T. Higgens & A. W. Kruglanski (Eds.), *Social psychology: Handbook of basic principles* (pp. 239–270). New York, NY: Guilford Press.

United States v. Sanges, 144 U.S. 310 (1892).

Wason, P. C. (1959). On the failure to eliminate hypotheses in a conceptual task. *The Quarterly Journal of Experimental Psychology, 11,* 92–107. doi:10.1080/17470215908416296

Wason, P. C. (1966). Reasoning. In B. M. Foss (Ed.), *New horizons in psychology* (pp. 135-151). Harmondsworth, Middlesex, England: Penguin.

Wason, P. C. (1968). Reasoning about a rule. *The Quarterly Journal of Experimental Psychology, 20,* 273–281. doi:10.1080/14640746808400161

Weinstein, I. (2003). Don't believe everything you think: Cognitive bias in legal decision making. *Clinical Law Review, 9,* 783–834.

Wells, G. L., & Bradfield, A. L. (1998). "Good, you identified the suspect": Feedback to eyewitnesses distorts their reports of the witnessing experience. *Journal of Applied Psychology, 83,* 360–376. doi:10.1037/0021-9010.83.3.360

VI

THE EXONERATED

15

LIFE AFTER WRONGFUL CONVICTION

KIMBERLEY A. CLOW, AMY-MAY LEACH,
AND ROSEMARY RICCIARDELLI

Comparatively little research has examined the lives of exonerees post-conviction. What research has been done in this area generally offers a clinical or criminological perspective on the tremendous consequences for the innocent (e.g., Campbell & Denov, 2004; Grounds, 2004; Westervelt & Cook, 2009). This chapter reviews the literature on the consequences of wrongful conviction, highlights current psychological research on the topic, offers suggestions for future research, and explores the impact research may have on policy and practice. Although some of the topics discussed may affect both offenders and wrongly convicted persons, the consequences of these factors may be particularly damaging for the innocent.

CONSEQUENCES OF CONVICTION FOR THE INNOCENT

One of the most dramatic consequences of wrongful conviction is incarceration. Imagine being strip searched, forced to relinquish your personal belongings, and processed. Then you are sent to prison—a culture and place very different from the life you have known—where your activities are monitored and regimented. William (Bill) Mullins-Johnson was wrongly convicted of murdering his young niece (who, in fact, died of unknown natural causes). His first night in prison, inmates pounded on his cell walls as they yelled threats and insults (Bayliss, 2006). He was immediately labeled a pedophile, even though he was innocent of any wrongdoing and had not been convicted of sexual assault. In fact, Mullins-Johnson found that the only inmates who would associate with him during the 12 years that he spent in prison were inmates convicted of sexual crimes (B. Mullins-Johnson, personal communication, March 23, 2006). Unfortunately, his experiences are not unique. Other individuals who have been wrongly convicted have endured similar isolation and threats (e.g., Campbell & Denov, 2004; Westervelt & Cook, 2007).

Although prison violence is not unique to wrongful conviction, it is a consequence that innocent individuals endure. Violence, and the fear of violence, is a theme that emerges in the lives of individuals who have been wrongly imprisoned (e.g., Badkhen, 2005; Campbell & Denov, 2004; Grounds, 2004). One man described how he coped with the fear of prison violence after his wrongful conviction by creating an improvised puncture-proof vest that consisted of duct taping National Geographic magazines around his chest (Campbell & Denov, 2004). He wore this makeshift vest underneath his clothing whenever he was required to leave his cell. Michael Williams, who was wrongly incarcerated in Angola Prison for 24 years, bears a scar on his left elbow from being stabbed with an ice pick by another inmate (Badkhen, 2005).

One of the unique difficulties that wrongly convicted individuals face in prison is that it is difficult for them to gain privileges or parole unless they lie and take ownership for a crime that they did not commit (e.g., Campbell & Denov, 2004; Weisman, 2004). For many people—including personnel working in the criminal justice system—admitting to a crime is the first step in demonstrating remorse (e.g., Weisman, 2004). Research suggests that remorse is an important variable that influences decision making throughout the criminal justice system, including conviction, sentencing, and parole (e.g., Campbell & Denov, 2004; Grounds, 2004; Weisman, 2004). In addition, lack of remorse is implicated in the diagnosis of psychopathy and antisocial personality disorder (e.g., Bishop & Hare, 2008; Weisman, 2004). For example, one wrongly convicted individual was told that

> the parole board takes this [protesting your innocence] as if you're denying the crime . . . that you're not healed . . . you're not fixed . . . You have to admit to the crime in order to fix your problems. (Campbell & Denov, 2004, p. 152)

However, confessing to a crime, even once, can make it very difficult for an individual to later convince people that he or she is innocent (e.g., Kassin & Gudjonsson, 2004). Thus, wrongly convicted individuals are caught in a no-win situation: If they maintain their innocence, then they are punished more severely; if they confess to crimes that they did not commit, they irrevocably damage their ability to convince others that they are innocent.

When actual offenders are released from prison, they are often offered services and programs, such as job placement, drug rehabilitation, and temporary housing, to assist with their transition to life outside prison walls. Paradoxically, when people who have been wrongly convicted of crimes are released from prison, they receive less assistance than actual offenders (e.g., Burnett, 2005; Grounds, 2004; Innocence Project, 2009; Roberts & Stanton, 2007; Westervelt & Cook, 2009). Furthermore, exonerees often discover that they are being released from prison mere hours before it occurs, without the time or assistance to arrange housing or even transportation to leave the prison grounds. For example, Shabaka Brown, who was wrongly convicted of raping and murdering a Florida shop owner on the basis of the perjured evidence of a jailhouse informant (Center on Wrongful Convictions, 2010), needed to live with his postconviction defense lawyer for 6 months after his release (Westervelt & Cook, 2009). Earl Truvia and Gregory Bright were released after spending 27 years in prison for a murder they did not commit (convicted on the testimony of an individual with paranoid schizophrenia who testified under a false name to conceal her own criminal record—information that was not disclosed to the defense or jury). They were given a $10 check from the state of Louisiana and left prison with a garbage bag full of legal documents (Innocence Project New Orleans, 2010). David Shephard, who was wrongly convicted of sexual assault as a result of mistaken cross-race eyewitness identification, contacted four agencies that provide services to ex-offenders but was denied assistance because he had not actually committed a crime (Buck, 2004; Innocence Project, 2009). Thus, individuals who have been wrongly convicted might suffer more severe consequences postincarceration than actual offenders because policies and resources do not seem to target the reintegration of innocent persons.

A recent Innocence Project (2009) report indicated that nearly half of U.S. states (n = 23) did not offer any compensation for exonerees. Even among the 27 states that did have compensation law, exonerees had to wait, on average, 3 years before receiving funds. Of the Innocence Project's DNA exonerations, only 60% of exonerees received any sort of assistance, and that assistance was generally small and financial. In addition, some states (e.g., Nebraska) would not provide compensation to individuals who pled guilty or falsely confessed, as this was seen as contributing to their own wrongful conviction. Florida would not compensate individuals with a prior felony conviction. The provision of social assistance or social services, in particular, was rare. Overall, exonerees leave prison with next to nothing, which further impedes their ability to secure transportation, employment, and housing.

Individuals who have been wrongly convicted are likely to have been changed by their experiences. One mother, when describing her son, said, "He always used to be affectionate. Now he can't express emotion, he can't sit and talk. He jumps about, he is unsettled. Prison has changed him. His personality has changed" (Grounds, 2004, p. 168). David Shephard, after 12 years of wrongful imprisonment, was plagued by fears that it would happen all over again (Buck, 2004). After he was released, he would collect physical evidence (e.g., bus ticket stubs) to corroborate his activities. Kirk Bloodsworth, after 8 years in prison, ensures that someone knows where he is at all times (Westervelt & Cook, 2008). Exonerees mourn a number of different losses (Westervelt & Cook, 2009), ranging from the time they have lost while in prison to the loved ones they may have lost due to death. Many exonerees lose their personal feelings of security and often their sense of self or identity. Personality change, anxiety disorders, depression and suicide ideation, anger, and grief seem to be common consequences of wrongful conviction (Campbell & Denov, 2004; Grounds, 2004; Innocence Project, 2009; Westervelt & Cook, 2009).

Finally, as exonerees struggle to cope with these issues, they also need to adjust to changes that have occurred while they were incarcerated. Neighborhoods will have changed, possibly looking nothing like the communities that were left behind. Friends and family will have aged and may seem like entirely different people. In particular, a number of individuals who have been wrongly convicted have reported inexperience and anxiety associated with technological advances (e.g., Badkhen, 2005; Grounds, 2004; Innocence Project, 2009; Westervelt & Cook, 2009). Exonerees may not have previously encountered what is now rather mundane technology, such as computers, cell phones, answering machines, ATMs, and the Internet. Adjusting to all these changes all at once can be very overwhelming.

The wrongly convicted have their rights and freedoms taken away, they are imprisoned, they suffer from violence and fear for their safety, they are often punished more severely than actual offenders because they maintain that they are innocent, they need to adapt to a world that has changed while they were in prison, and they are not provided with services or assistance to readjust to society. In addition, they must cope with the fact that many people believe they are guilty—that they are thieves, murderers, or rapists—despite what they say themselves or what the evidence demonstrates. Thus, the consequences of wrongful conviction do not end when the innocent are released from prison; the consequences for the innocent are lifelong.

SCIENTIFIC PSYCHOLOGICAL FOUNDATIONS OF RESEARCH ON LIFE AFTER WRONGFUL CONVICTION

Individuals who have been wrongly convicted are often stigmatized. Although wrongful conviction is not a visible identifier per se, someone who is wrongly convicted may feel exposed or visible because of the publicity surrounding his or her case. Individuals who have been wrongly convicted may, at times, have control over whether they reveal that they have been wrongly convicted (e.g., in social settings); at other times, however, their status as an exoneree might be revealed without their permission or control (e.g., media attention). For example, Kirk Bloodsworth, the first man exonerated from death row due to postconviction DNA testing (Innocence Project, 2010), found "child killer" written in the dirt on his truck after his exoneration (Westervelt & Cook, 2009). Ken Wyniemko, who had managed a bowling alley before his wrongful conviction, applied to more than 100 jobs after his release and was not able to find employment. He described wrongful conviction as "walking around with a scarlet letter" (Roberts & Stanton, 2007, p. 2).

Goffman (1963) defined *stigma* as a discrediting attribute that reduces the stigmatized individual to someone tainted and discounted from society. He described stigma as a "spoiled identity." Moreover, he suggested that there are important differences between being discreditable (i.e., having control over revealing a disadvantaged social group membership) and discredited (i.e., others already knowing that one belongs to a disadvantaged social group). Individuals who have been wrongly convicted may vacillate between being discreditable and discredited and may not know, in any given situation, whether or not others know that they have been wrongly convicted.

Although, on the surface, stigmatization may not seem to be as severe an issue as a lack of finances or housing, stigmatization can lead to—or exacerbate—other situations and variables, which can have far-reaching negative consequences for exonerees. For example, after his release from prison, Robert Baltovich, who was wrongly convicted of second degree murder in 1992, was able to find gainful employment. When a fellow employee recognized him, he suddenly had to defend himself—and his job—to a panel of senior employees (R. Baltovich, personal communication, April 2009). Sabrina Butler, wrongly convicted at age 19 for child abuse, was filling out the paperwork to begin employment at a grocery store only to have her employment terminated when an assistant manager walked by and recognized her (Westervelt & Cook, 2009). After serving 5 years in prison—and 2 of those years on death row—she is now trying to deal with the death of her child and being stigmatized by her community. She was even rejected by her church (Westervelt & Cook, 2009). Darryl Hunt, who was wrongly imprisoned for 19 years, 4 of which he spent in solitary confinement, told students at Colgate University that "even though I've been exonerated, there's still a stigma associated with my past" (Adornato, 2009). Steven Truscott was convicted of murdering a 12-year-old friend in 1959 and was eventually acquitted in 2007 and compensated by the Ontario government in 2008. In a written statement, the Truscotts claimed that although they were grateful for the financial compensation,

> we are also painfully aware that no amount of money could ever truly compensate Steven for the terror of being sentenced to hang at the age of 14, the loss of his youth or the stigma of living for almost 50 years as a convicted murderer. (CBC News, 2008)

Thus, the remainder of this chapter focuses on two pervasive social psychological factors that potentially affect individuals who have been wrongly convicted for the rest of their lives: attitudes and stigma.

Attitudes are believed to have three conceptually distinct, yet interrelated, components: an affective component, consisting of emotions and evaluations; a cognitive component, encompassing beliefs and thoughts; and a behavioral component, involving behavior and behavioral intentions. Relating this model to wrongful conviction, the attitudes that people hold about wrongful conviction and individuals who have been wrongly convicted involve emotions, thoughts, and beliefs, as well as behaviors and behavioral intentions.

When the three-component attitude model is applied to intergroup research, the affective component is called *prejudice*, the cognitive component is called *stereotyping*, and the behavioral component is called *discrimination*. Thus, prejudice is our emotional reactions to an individual due to his or her group membership, stereotypes are our thoughts about an individual on the basis of his or her group membership, and discrimination is our behavior and behavioral intentions toward that individual because of his or her group membership. As these thoughts, emotions, and behaviors are based on an individual's group membership, if the group membership is perceived to be negative, the group membership itself can be viewed as a stigma.

Overall, stigmatized groups are negatively stereotyped, responded to with negative emotions, and generally avoided by others (e.g., Crocker & Major, 1989; Crocker, Major, & Steele, 1998; Pryor, Reeder, Yeadon, & Hesson-McInnis, 2004). Efforts to conceal a stigma may have the adverse effect of increasing an individual's preoccupation with stigma-related thoughts (e.g., Smart & Wegner, 1999). Being a member of a stigmatized group can lead to *stigma consciousness* (Pinel, 1999), that is, the expectation of being stereotyped due to the stigma. In addition, stigmas may function to alter self-esteem and mood under various circumstances (e.g., Crocker, Cornwell, & Major, 1993; Crocker & Major, 1989; Crocker, Voelkl, Testa, & Major, 1991).

Research has yet to establish the exact nature of the stigma wrongful conviction imparts or the factors that might assist exonerees in managing or escaping the consequences of society's stereotypes, prejudice, and discrimination.

SCIENTIFIC METHODS OF RESEARCH ON LIFE AFTER WRONGFUL CONVICTION

At press time, there are no unique methodologies or paradigms to examine the consequences of wrongful conviction. The few published studies on the topic have used surveys, interviews, or descriptive methods.

Surveys

The Angus Reid Group (1995) seems to have been the first to empirically investigate attitudes toward wrongful conviction. They polled 7,000 participants across Canada to ask them about their attitudes on a diverse array of topics, ranging from job anxiety and spending to the Canada–Europe fishing dispute. Within their public opinion survey were two forced-choice questions related to attitudes in regard to wrongful conviction: (a) whether the government should increase its efforts in dealing with wrongful conviction or whether wrongful convictions were so rare that no government changes were necessary and (b) whether or not the government should be responsible for compensating individuals who had been wrongly convicted. Their results indicated that 65% of respondents felt that the government should "increase its efforts to deal with people who claim they have been wrongly convicted" (Angus Reid Group, 1995, p. 76) and that approximately 90% of respondents felt that it was the government's responsibility to compensate individuals who had been wrongly convicted. Although these findings may seem to indicate positive attitudes toward victims of wrongful conviction, that might not actually be the case. Both items focused on the role of government in wrongful conviction rather than on attitudes toward wrongly convicted persons.

It is unfortunate that there were only these two items related to wrongful conviction, and both items involved forced-choice answer options, providing very limited data on two very specific issues. In addition, the first question was double barreled, such that the second answer option involved both the idea that (a) wrongful convictions were rare and that (b) the government did not need to change. Nonetheless, the Angus Reid Group (1995) appears to have been the first to investigate public attitudes regarding wrongful conviction.

More recent survey research has used a large variety of questions to assess attitudes toward wrongful conviction (e.g., Bell & Clow, 2007; Bell, Clow, & Ricciardelli, 2008; Ricciardelli, Bell, & Clow, 2009). These questions probed participants' knowledge of the factors that underlie wrongful conviction (Bell et al., 2008), their attitudes toward the postconviction review process (Bell & Clow, 2007), and their attitudes in regard to wrongful conviction more generally (Ricciardelli et al., 2009). Participants did report that they felt wrongful conviction was a problem in the criminal justice system (Bell & Clow, 2007). Although participants were aware of some factors that contribute to wrongful conviction (e.g., mistaken eyewitnesses, false confessions), they did not generally believe that the behavior of lawyers or police officers greatly contributed to miscarriages of justice (Bell et al., 2008). In addition, participants' choice of university major and their year of study impacted their knowledge about wrongful conviction. Bell and Clow (2007) found that participants supported the idea of an independent nongovernment party being responsible for reviewing cases of wrongful conviction and that individuals applying for their cases to be reviewed as possible incidences of wrongful conviction should have lawyers appointed to assist them—neither of which actually occurs. When asked to indicate what they believed to be an acceptable ratio of wrongful to correct convictions, the majority of participants desired the ideal system that does not result in any wrongful convictions (Bell & Clow, 2007).

Although this research examined issues related to attitudes toward wrongful conviction, the focus was more on process than on specific attitudes toward wrongly convicted individuals. To date, we are unaware of any published survey research in regard to attitudes toward individuals who have been wrongly convicted. This is an area that future research may wish to address.

Interviews

Campbell and Denov (2004) interviewed five men who had been wrongly convicted in Canada. Their research outlined the various mechanisms these individuals used to cope with innocence while incarcerated, such as withdrawal, preoccupation with exoneration, assisting other inmates, and psychologically distancing themselves from the label of "criminal." Westervelt and Cook (2007, 2008, 2009) interviewed 18 death row exonerees in the United States. They compared the exonerees' experiences to survivor guilt, commenting on hyperarousal, intrusive thoughts, feelings of hopelessness, difficulties emotionally connecting to others, and troubles envisioning the future (Westervelt & Cook, 2008, 2009). In terms of coping strategies, exonerees tended to use *incorporation strategies* (i.e., strategies that tried to put a positive spin on the experiences, such as becoming an advocate for others who are wrongly convicted or embracing greater spirituality) or *rejection strategies* (i.e., strategies that tended to contribute to further isolation and, occasionally, self-destructive behaviors; Westervelt & Cook, 2008).

By using face-to-face interviews, these researchers were able to establish rapport with their participants, making them more comfortable talking about very personal and disturbing experiences, such as suicide ideation, the death of loved ones, and fear of prison violence (Campbell & Denov, 2004; Westervelt & Cook, 2007, 2008, 2009). The personal accounts described in interview research provide readers a glimpse of the realities of wrongful conviction and give interviewees a chance to express themselves in their own words. The experiences described and themes uncovered would be very difficult to obtain using other methodologies. As the sample sizes in this research are very small, a major limitation is whether or not the findings are generalizable to the population from which the samples are drawn or whether the findings pertain only to the specific participants.

Descriptive Research

Many influential books on wrongful conviction—what Leo (2005) called "the Big Picture" books—are detailed descriptions of different collections of cases (e.g., Anderson & Anderson, 1998; Borchard, 1932; Frank & Frank, 1957; Scheck, Neufeld, & Dwyer, 2000). These collections, along with true-crime novels (e.g., Grisham, 2006), have captured the interest of the public and focused attention onto the issue of wrongful conviction. From an academic perspective, these collections allow researchers to compare cases and identify common variables. For example, examining a collection of 36 cases, Frank and Frank (1957) identified a number of similarities in the underlying factors that seemed to contribute to wrongful convictions (e.g., eyewitness misidentification). In addition, they suggested that prosecutorial behavior, such as approaching cases with a "win" mentality, was also an important factor. These collections help to demonstrate that there are particular variables that lead to the wrongful conviction of a number of different individuals across a number of different situations and locations. This has assisted in the identification of a variety of common factors that contribute to wrongful conviction, many of which are discussed in earlier chapters in this volume.

Whereas the Big Picture books focus on the events leading up to wrongful convictions, Grounds (2004) analyzed the psychiatric assessments of 18 wrongly convicted men in the United Kingdom to determine their mental states after they were released from prison. He found that 12 of the 18 wrongly convicted individuals in his sample met the criteria for posttraumatic stress disorder and most also suffered from mood or anxiety disorders. In addition, these men had difficulties socially adjusting, which Grounds compared to the difficulties experienced by some war veterans when they try to readjust to society.

Descriptive research is a great tool for describing the experiences of exonerees and going into detail on a number of different cases. As this descriptive research often combines interviews with archival research or other techniques, it has many of the same strengths as were described for interviews. Similar to interviews, these descriptive studies portray the experiences of the wrongly convicted and allow their stories to be told. Whereas the rich descriptions and details are strengths of this research design, the limitations tend to be in theory, prediction, and generalizability.

CURRENT RESEARCH ON LIFE AFTER WRONGFUL CONVICTION

Research on the consequences of wrongful conviction is in its infancy. Newer experimental research has specifically begun to investigate attitudes and stigma toward individuals who have been wrongly convicted. For example, participants who were randomly assigned to read an article about an individual who had been wrongfully convicted of murder due to a false confession (vs. mistaken eyewitness identification vs. jailhouse snitch vs. no reason given) were most likely to stigmatize him (Clow & Leach, 2009). Participants in the false-confession condition were more likely than participants in the other conditions to rate the wrongly convicted person low in competence and warmth and to avoid the most intimate social situations with him (e.g., dating, marriage). In a second study, perceptions of the wrongly convicted were compared with perceptions of actual offenders and noncriminal citizens. Results indicated that the wrongly convicted were stigmatized similar to offenders in many respects, although stereotypes of offenders were generally more negative. These findings suggest that participants may be reporting positive attitudes toward policies regarding wrongful conviction in surveys (e.g., Angus Reid Group, 1995; Bell & Clow, 2007; Bell, Clow, & Ricciardelli, 2008; Ricciardelli et al., 2009) but that participants nonetheless stigmatize wrongly convicted persons.

APPLICATION OF RESEARCH ON LIFE AFTER WRONGFUL CONVICTION

Research on the consequences of wrongful conviction does not appear to have currently influenced practice or policy. That is unsurprising because this research literature is sparse, and further replication and generalization is warranted. However, as research grows in this area, it is expected that findings will become incorporated into practice and policy.

For example, research may assist in improving the conditions under which exonerees are released from prison and the assistance—both social services and financial compensation—that they are entitled to receive. If research continues to find public support for government compensation for individuals who have been wrongly convicted (e.g., Angus Reid Group, 1995), then there may be increased pressure to create systems where government financial compensation for wrongful conviction is mandatory. In addition, if participants hold more positive attitudes toward individuals who have been wrongly convicted when they are compensated than when they are not compensated, then this information may assist lawyers and advocates for the wrongly convicted as they fight for compensation after exoneration.

Current experimental research tentatively suggests a possible way to improve attitudes toward individuals who have been wrongly convicted: exposure. Ricciardelli and Clow (in press) tested the impact of an exoneree's guest lecture on participants' attitudes in regard to wrongful conviction and wrongly convicted persons. Attitudes were assessed before and after attending a guest lecture on wrongful conviction or another social issue. Participants were not aware of the topic of the guest lecture prior to attending. In general, participants who attended the wrongful conviction guest lecture reported more positive attitude change toward wrongly convicted individuals than did participants who attended the other guest lecture.

McWade, Leach, and Clow (2009) randomly assigned pairs of participants to one of three conditions: wrongful conviction, conviction, or control. In the convicted condition, one of the participants in the pair was led to believe that he or she was interacting with an individual who had been convicted of armed robbery; in the wrongful conviction condition, participants were led to believe that their partners had been wrongly convicted of armed robbery; in the control condition, participants were led to believe that their partners had no prior criminal record. In reality, none of the participants had prior criminal records (as determined through prescreening). The researchers examined participants' impressions of their interaction partner in the three different conditions. Preliminary analyses revealed that condition affected participants' impressions of their partners prior to engaging in a conversation with them, such that convicted and wrongly convicted partners were perceived more negatively than no conviction control partners. After conversing with their partners, however, impressions improved. For example, by the end of the study, most participants were willing to provide their contact information (e.g., e-mail address, phone number) to their partner, and this behavior did not differ by condition. It is possible that these preliminary analyses revealed a contact hypothesis effect, such that positive contact with an individual believed to be wrongly convicted improved attitudes toward that individual by the end of the study. This interpretation is tentative, as the study was not designed to test for the contact hypothesis and did not investigate whether attitudes toward wrongful conviction more generally were affected, but it is an idea for future research to explore.

It is difficult to combat bias without first empirically demonstrating that it exists. More generally, amassing research on attitudes and stigma toward wrongful conviction may make the public more aware of their own biases and draw more attention to the plight of exonerees. In addition, if systematic bias can be empirically demonstrated, such research could be of use to lawyers and advocates for the wrongly convicted as they argue for more resources and better accommodation for their clients. Thus, there appears to be great potential for research in this area to contribute to policy and practice.

CONCLUSION

The consequences of wrongful conviction are in need of further research. Although it is important to try to identify the factors that lead to wrongful conviction in order to reduce such instances, it is also critical to research the implications and impact of wrongful conviction on the individuals themselves. The consequences of wrongful imprisonment do not end with exoneration: The effects of having been wrongly convicted can last a lifetime. Although self-report attitude research seems to suggest public support for policies that would assist individuals who have been wrongly convicted, the findings from current research using experimental designs suggest that people actually stigmatize individuals who have been wrongly convicted. Further research on how we can better assist these victims of the criminal justice system and improve their lives postincarceration is needed.

REFERENCES

Adornato, A. (2009, April 23). *Memories of wrongful imprisonment haunt speakers.* Retrieved from http://blogs.colgate.edu/anthony-adornato/2009/04

Anderson, B., & Anderson, D. (1998). *Manufacturing guilt: Wrongful convictions in Canada.* Halifax, Nova Scotia, Canada: Fernwood Books.

Angus Reid Group. (1995). Public perspectives on wrongful conviction. Justice and Public Safety Issues. *The Angus Reid Report, 10,* 75–77.

Badkhen, A. (2005, May 9). Rough landing for exonerated inmate: He's one of 159 who have been freed after DNA testing. *San Francisco Chronicle.* Retrieved from http://articles.sfgate.com/2005-05-09/news/17373296_1_wrongful-convictions-wrong-man-post-conviction-dna-testing

Bayliss, D. (2006). The Mullins-Johnson case: The murder that wasn't. *The AIDWYC Journal, 6,* 1–4.

Bell, J. G., & Clow, K. A. (2007). Student attitudes toward the post-conviction review process in Canada. *Journal of the Institute of Justice & International Studies, 7*, 90–103.

Bell, J. G., Clow, K. A., & Ricciardelli, R. (2008). Causes of wrongful conviction: Looking at student knowledge. *Journal of Criminal Justice Education, 19*, 75–96. doi:10.1080/10511250801892979

Bishop, D., & Hare, R. D. (2008). A multidimensional scaling analysis of the Hare PCL-R: Unfolding the structure of psychopathy. *Psychology, Crime & Law, 14*, 117–132. doi:10.1080/10683160701483484

Borchard, E. M. (1932). *Convicting the innocent: Sixty-five actual errors of criminal justice.* New York, NY: Garden City.

Buck, G. (2004). They took my life: His wrongful arrest led to 12 years in jail. David Shephard can't make up for the lost time—but he's determined to try. *Reader's Digest.* Retrieved from http://www.rd.com/content/printContent.do?contentId=28504&KeepThis=true&TB_iframe=true&height=500&width=790&modal=true

Burnett, C. (2005). Restorative justice and wrongful capital convictions: A simple proposal. *Journal of Contemporary Criminal Justice, 21*, 272–289. doi:10.1177/1043986205278630

Campbell, K., & Denov, M. (2004). The burden of innocence: Coping with a wrongful imprisonment. *Canadian Journal of Criminology and Criminal Justice, 46*, 139–163.

CBC News. (2008, July 7). *Steven Truscott to get $6.5M for wrongful conviction: Sentenced to hang at age of 144 for murdering classmate.* Retrieved from http://www.cbc.ca/canada/story/2008/07/07/truscott-bentley.html

Center on Wrongful Convictions. Northwestern University School of Law. Bluhm Legal Clinic. (2010). Retrieved from http://www.law.northwestern.edu/wrongfulconvictions/

Clow, K. A., & Leach, A.-M. (2009, March). After innocence: Perceptions of the wrongfully convicted. In B. L. Cutler (Chair), *Conviction of the innocent: Psychology perspectives and research.* Symposium conducted at the meeting of the American Psychology-Law Society, San Antonio, TX.

Crocker, J., Cornwell, B., & Major, B. M. (1993). The stigma of overweight: Affective consequences of attributional ambiguity. *Journal of Personality and Social Psychology, 64*, 60–70. doi:10.1037/0022-3514.64.1.60

Crocker, J., & Major, B. (1989). Social stigma and self-esteem: The self-protective properties of stigma. *Psychological Review, 96*, 608–630. doi:10.1037/0033-295X.96.4.608

Crocker, J., Major, B., & Steele, C. (1998). Social stigma. In D. T. Gilbert, S. T. Fiske, & G. Lindzey (Eds.), *The handbook of social psychology* (4th ed., Vol. 2, pp. 504–553). Boston, MA: McGraw-Hill.

Crocker, J., Voelkl, K., Testa, M., & Major, B. (1991). Social stigma: The affective consequences of attributional ambiguity. *Journal of Personality and Social Psychology, 60*, 218–228. doi:10.1037/0022-3514.60.2.218

Frank, J., & Frank, B. (1957). *Not guilty*. New York, NY: Doubleday.

Goffman, E. (1963). *Stigma: Notes on the management of spoiled identity*. Upper Saddle River, NJ: Prentice-Hall.

Grisham, J. (2006). *The innocent man: Murder and injustice in a small town*. New York, NY: Doubleday.

Grounds, A. (2004). Psychological consequences of wrongful conviction and imprisonment. *Canadian Journal of Criminology and Criminal Justice, 46*, 165–182.

Innocence Project. (2009). *Making up for lost time: What the wrongfully convicted endure and how to provide fair compensation*. Report for the Innocence Project. Benjamin N. Cardozo School of Law, Yeshiva University.

Innocence Project. (2010). *Know the cases: Kirk Bloodsworth*. Retrieved from http://www.innocenceproject.org/Content/54.php

Innocence Project New Orleans. (2010). *Two innocent men go home after 27 years in prison, the charges against them dismissed: Gregory Bright and Earl Truvia released after over 27 years in prison*. Retrieved from http://truthinjustice.org/bright-truvia.htm

Kassin, S. M., & Gudjonsson, G. H. (2004). The psychology of confessions: A review of the literature and issues. *Psychological Science in the Public Interest, 5*(2), 33–67. doi:10.1111/j.1529-1006.2004.00016.x

Leo, R. A. (2005). Rethinking the study of miscarriages of justice: Developing a criminology of wrongful conviction. *Journal of Contemporary Criminal Justice, 21*, 201–223. doi:10.1177/1043986205277477

McWade, M., Leach, A.-M., & Clow, K. A. (2009). *Public perceptions and stereotypes of the wrongly convicted*. Unpublished honors thesis, University of Ontario Institute of Technology, Oshawa, Canada.

Pinel, E. C. (1999). Stigma consciousness: The psychological legacy of social stereotypes. *Journal of Personality and Social Psychology, 76*, 114–128. doi:10.1037/0022-3514.76.1.114

Pryor, J. B., Reeder, G. D., Yeadon, C., & Hesson-McInnis, M. (2004). A dual-process model of reactions to perceived stigma. *Journal of Personality and Social Psychology, 87*, 436–452. doi:10.1037/0022-3514.87.4.436

Ricciardelli, R., Bell, J. G., & Clow, K. A. (2009). Student attitudes toward wrongful conviction. *Canadian Journal of Criminology and Criminal Justice, 51*, 411–427. doi:10.3138/cjccj.51.3.411

Ricciardelli, R., & Clow, K. A. (in press). The impact of an exoneree's guest lecture on students' attitudes toward wrongly convicted persons. *Journal of Criminal Justice Education*.

Roberts, J., & Stanton, E. (2007, November 25). Free and uneasy: A long road back after exoneration, and justice is slow to make amends. *The New York*

Times. Retrieved from http://www.nytimes.com/2007/11/25/us/25dna.html?ex=1353646800&en=4ce9ccb7633c3cc5&ei=5088

Scheck, B., Neufeld, P., & Dwyer, J. (2000). *Actual innocence: Five days to execution and other dispatches from the wrongly convicted*. New York, NY: Doubleday.

Smart, L., & Wegner, D. M. (1999). Covering up what can't be seen: Concealable stigma and mental control. *Journal of Personality and Social Psychology, 77*, 474–486. doi:10.1037/0022-3514.77.3.474

Weisman, R. (2004). Showing remorse: Reflections on the gap between expression and attribution in cases of wrongful conviction. *Canadian Journal of Criminology and Criminal Justice, 46*, 121–138.

Westervelt, S. D., & Cook, K. J. (2007). Feminist research methods in theory and action: Learning from death row exonerees. In S. Miller (Ed.), *Criminal justice research and practice: Diverse voices from the field* (pp. 21–38). Boston, MA: University Press of New England.

Westervelt, S. D., & Cook, K. J. (2008). Coping with innocence after death row. *Contexts, 7*, 32–37. doi:10.1525/ctx.2008.7.4.32

Westervelt, S. D., & Cook, K. J. (2009). Framing innocents: The wrongly convicted as victims of state harm. *Crime, Law, and Social Change, 53*, 259–275. doi:10.1007/s10611-009-9231-z

VII

CONCLUSION

CONCLUSION

BRIAN L. CUTLER

I set forth three goals for this volume in the Introduction: advance the literature on conviction of the innocent; integrate the research; and encourage research. I am confident that we have achieved each of these goals.

As noted in the Introduction, this volume may be situated within a larger literature on miscarriages of justice as an example of a "specialized literature"— an approach that shows great promise to enhance our understanding of this pressing social phenomenon (Leo, 2005). Although there are numerous articles, chapters, authored books, and edited books on most of the individual topics covered in our chapters, this volume contributes uniquely to the literature by drawing the diverse topics together under a larger umbrella that may be labeled *conviction of the innocent research*.

The drawing together of research on these seemingly independent topics provides the opportunity to examine my second goal, which was to achieve some level of integration of this research. In the Introduction, I asked: Are there common social and cognitive psychological phenomena that underlay the seemingly independent causes of wrongful conviction? How similar are the research methods used to study the independent causes? Are there parallels in the reforms that emerge from this research? These are just a few of the integrative questions that can be asked of this literature.

The chapter authors have drawn on a wide variety of theories and bodies of research in social and cognitive psychology. The more common areas include basic research on human memory, metacognition, social influence, social cognition, attitudes and persuasion, heuristics, biases, and decision making. Every chapter draws from one or more of these basic research areas. Some of the chapters draw from more specialized literatures, for example, procedural justice theories (Chapter 4); intergroup processing, stigma theories, and aversive racism theories (Chapters 13 and 15); and intelligence systems (Chapter 12). In addition, several chapters draw from areas of psychology other than social and cognitive. Chapter 1 draws on developmental and clinical psychological research on cognitive impairments, developmental disabilities, and psychosocial skills. Chapter 12 draws on human factors research on intelligence systems. In sum, psychology, particularly—though not exclusively—social and cognitive psychology, has a great deal to contribute to our understanding of conviction of the innocent.

Given that most of the contributors to this volume are social and cognitive psychologists, it is not surprising that the methodologies used in research on the varied topics of these chapters share some characteristics. There is a heavy reliance on carefully controlled laboratory research with a high priority given to internal validity. There is also a healthy and growing body of field research that gives a high priority to both internal and external validity. Chapter 1 also draws on research methods of clinical psychology, particularly with respect to forensic assessment with vulnerable populations. Chapter 12 draws on research from human factors, such as the research on expert decision making. Some chapters (e.g., Chapters 13, 15) also draw on research from other disciplines.

The chapter sections that address the implications of the research on policy and practice revealed some common types of recommendations. For example, nearly all authors called for increased transparency in all procedures that lead up to trial. Toward this end, the video recording of interrogations, confessions, and eyewitness identification procedures, eyewitness confidence assessments, and enhancing disclosure of pretrial investigation and discovery (including incentives used to encourage informant testimony) all serve to make the evidence and evidence-gathering techniques more transparent. Increased transparency should encourage all parties to more carefully assess the quality of evidence and the potential influence of evidence-gathering techniques on the quality of evidence and should reduce ambiguity about the interpretation of evidence. Some of these reforms (e.g., video recording of interrogations and confessions) are beginning to be implemented (Chapter 3). Others deserve serious consideration.

The call for procedural reforms represents another common theme among the recommendations. Some such recommendations are closer to being implemented than others. For example, the authors of several chapters recommend the elimination of suggestive photo array and lineup procedures and replacing them with better practices that have emerged from the scientific literature. The immediate assessment of eyewitness confidence and the recording of these assessments—the topic of Chapters 7 and 8—are eyewitness reforms that have already been implemented in some states and police departments (Chapter 6). For example, both the U.S. Department of Justice and the New Jersey guidelines have sections devoted to recording identification results. Both state that the lineup administrator or investigator should record both the witness's identification or nonidentification together with his or her level of certainty in his or her own words. Some authors discuss reforms that have not been implemented but are clearly deserving of more consideration. These include protections for vulnerable populations during interrogation (Chapters 1 and 3), innovative approaches to improving lie detection (Chapter 2), the use of less confrontative interrogation procedures (Chapters 1, 2, and 3), changes to suppression hearings for suggestive eyewitness identifications (Chapter 8), changes to incentives associated with informant testimony (Chapter 10), and changes in the methods we used to select and train forensic scientists (Chapter 12).

Another set of proposed reforms can generally be referred to as education, training, and consciousness raising. Many of the proposed reforms center on making actors in the criminal justice and legal systems more knowledgeable about the psychological research relevant to the evidence and testimony, as well as the psychological factors that can influence their own behavior and judgment. Some authors herein call for the routine education of police, attorneys, and judges about psychological issues that affect investigations and trials. Such education topics would include factors that affect eyewitness identification (e.g., Chapter 5, 7, and 8) and the possibility of unjust outcomes that arise from coercive interrogation procedures (Chapter 4). As another example, Chapter 12 calls for better educating forensic scientists about the factors that can bias their decisions. With respect to the trial context, some authors call for greater education of judges and juries through the use of expert psychological testimony (e.g., Chapters 5, 7, 8, 9, and 10) and judges' instructions that include (accurate) psychological content (e.g., Chapters 1 and 9). Some of the recommendations associated with racism and stigmatization (Chapters 13 and 15) and other forms of debiasing (Chapter 14) are innovative and deserve further attention as well.

My third goal was to encourage future research. I have no doubt that research on the various topics covered in the chapters will continue, as the chapters described vibrant and productive areas of research. Some of these areas of research are well established (e.g., eyewitness memory, detection of deception, racial biases). Others are becoming well established (e.g., confessions, interrogation). Still others are relatively new (e.g., forensic science, informant testimony, consequences of conviction of the innocent) but will undoubtedly attract more research attention. It is my hope that the research will continue to inform the more general literature on conviction of the innocent and miscarriages of justice and that the research will lead to important reforms that reduce the risk of conviction of the innocent. Finally, I hope that these exciting areas of research will provide fulfilling research careers for new scholars.

REFERENCE

Leo, R. A. (2005). Rethinking the study of miscarriages of justice: Developing a criminology of wrongful conviction. *Journal of Contemporary Criminal Justice, 21,* 201–223. doi:10.1177/1043986205277477.

INDEX

Brigham, J. C., 112, 117, 119
Brimacombe, C. A. E., 156
Briscoe, John, 182
Britt, C. L., 296
Brockner, J., 87
Brooks, L. R., 314
Brown, Shabaka, 329
Bruggeman, E. L., 223–224
Brunsman, B., 154
Bull, R., 114
Burke, A., 195
Butler, Sabrina, 331

Cacioppo, J. T., 242, 250
Camera angles, 68
Campbell, K., 328, 334
Canada, 4
Capabilities, 21–26
Case study method, 58, 107–108
Causal conclusions, 85, 110–111
CBCA (criteria-based content analysis), 41–42
CBC News, 332
CCTV (closed-circuit television), 189, 205
Center for Wrongful Convictions, 215
Central Park Jogger case, 54, 55, 94, 279
Certainty, 159, 170, 178–180
Change of appearance instruction, 131–132
Charles, Earl, 150
Charlton, D., 67
Charman, S. D., 116
Chavez, R. M., 250
Chen, R., 21
Cheng, Thomas, 216
Childhood risk factors, 287
Children, 18
Citizen perception, 292–293
Civil Rights Movement, 282
Clare, I. C. H., 21
Clark, J. K., 226
Clark, S. E., 131
Clearly, H. M. D., 21
Closed-circuit television (CCTV), 189, 205
Clow, K. A., 334, 337
Coercive techniques, 27–28. *See also*
    Suggestive eyewitness procedures

Cognition
    bottom-up processes in, 261–262
    and deception, 37–38
    in three-component attitude model, 332
    top-down processes in, 261–262
Cognitive bias
    in alibi witness credibility, 250–251
    in appellate and postconviction reviews, 316–317
    solutions for, 317–319
    in tunnel vision, 306–313
Cognitive disabilities, 13, 24–25
Cognitive dissonance, 38, 268
Cognitive distortions, 306, 312, 314, 315
Cognitive load, 37–38, 46, 47
Cognitive processes, 153, 281–282
Cognitive profiles, 270
Cognitive psychology, 6, 346
Cognitive shortcuts, 242
Coherence, 221
Cohn, E. S., 285–286, 291
Cole, A. T., 224
Cole, S., 269
College students, 219–220
Colorado Supreme Court, 27
Colorado v. Connelly, 27–28
Colvin, Russell, 216
Common ingroup identity model, 294–295
Common sense, 106, 107, 169, 193
Compensation, 329–330, 336–337
Competence, 15, 24–25. *See also*
    Adjudicative competence
Compliance, 62
Compliant false confessions, 54
Computer crash paradigm, 224
Conditioning, operant, 56
Confession(s). *See also* False
    confessions
    corruption of evidence by, 67
    fundamental attribution errors in, 225–226
    incentives for suspect to make, 16
    by innocent suspects, 53–55
    involuntary, 65
    mock-jury studies on, 15, 225
    primary, 213
    in prosecution phase, 53
    secondary, 213–214, 224–225

ABOUT THE EDITOR

Brian L. Cutler, PhD, received his doctorate in social psychology in 1987 from the University of Wisconsin–Madison. He is a professor in the Faculty of Social Science and Humanities at the University of Ontario Institute of Technology (UOIT), Oshawa, Ontario, Canada. Prior to joining UOIT's faculty, Dr. Cutler served on the psychology faculties at Florida International University and the University of North Carolina at Charlotte.

Dr. Cutler has been conducting research on the psychology of eyewitness identification and its role in conviction of the innocent for more than 25 years. His research has been funded by the National Science Foundation. In addition to this volume, he has authored and edited three books and more than 60 book chapters and research articles about the psychology of eyewitness identification. His research has been cited in court cases, the media, other research, and psychology textbooks. In addition, Dr. Cutler has served as editor of the journal *Law and Human Behavior*, and he is currently president of the American Psychology-Law Society (Division 41, American Psychological Association).

In collaboration with his students and other eyewitness scientists, Dr. Cutler continues to maintain an active research program, focusing on eyewitness identification. He teaches undergraduate and graduate courses in various aspects of psychology, criminology, research methods, and writing for the social sciences.